MW00638623

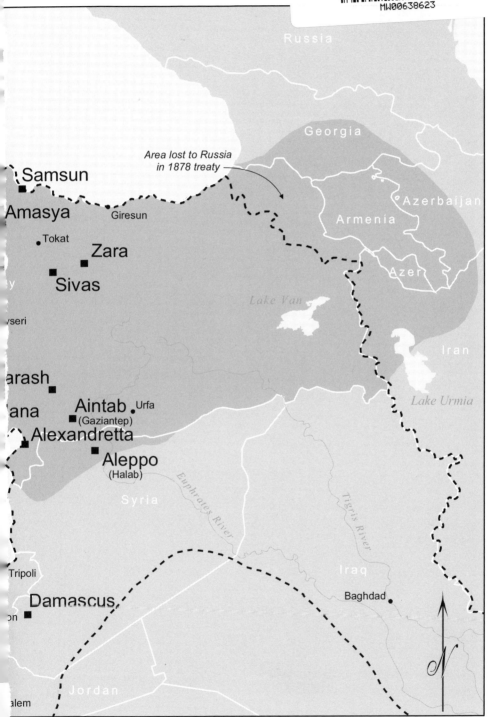

Russia

Georgia

Area lost to Russia
in 1878 treaty

Azerbaijan

Armenia

Samsun

Amasya   Giresun

Azer

Tokat

Zara

Sivas

Lake Van

Iran

yseri

Lake Urmia

arash

ana   Aintab. Urfa
      (Gaziantep)

Alexandretta

Aleppo
(Halab)

Syria

Euphrates River

Tigris River

Tripoli

Iraq

Baghdad

Damascus

on

N

Jordan

alem

HOLY

A HISTORY OF THE LATTER-DAY SAINTS IN THE NEAR EAST

LANDS

HOLY

A HISTORY OF THE LATTER-DAY SAINTS IN THE NEAR EAST

LANDS

LaMar C. Berrett

Blair G. Van Dyke

Covenant Communications, Inc.

Cover map by Cartesia © Photodisc Green/Getty Images.
Cover design copyrighted 2005 by Covenant Communications, Inc.

Published by Covenant Communications, Inc.
American Fork, Utah

Printed in Canada
First Printing: April 2005

11 10 09 08 07 06 05   10 9 8 7 6 5 4 3 2 1

ISBN 1-59156-660-6

This book is dedicated to the memory of

Orson Hyde

Jacob Spori

Ferdinand F. Hintze

Joseph W. Booth

Badwagan Piranian

Harold B. Lee

Robert C. Taylor

and

Howard W. Hunter

*—each of whose undying commitment
to the gospel of Jesus Christ took them to the
unfamiliar lands of the Near East.*

We honor them and the pioneering spirit reflected in their lives.

FOREWORD

It is time the experiences of our own nineteenth- and early-twentieth-century pioneers in the Near East came to the attention of the Latter-day Saints generally. As students and authors of Near Eastern history, especially as it relates to The Church of Jesus Christ of Latter-day Saints, we feel that this work is the most comprehensive and definitive treatment ever written on this subject. LaMar Berrett and Blair Van Dyke have painstakingly sought out original and primary sources and have penned a fascinating, revealing account of the Church's early proselytizing activities in the Near East, involving Turkey, Armenia, Syria, Lebanon, and Palestine, as well as the establishment of Brigham Young University's Jerusalem Center in modern-day Israel.

The authors have succeeded in capturing an important, but largely neglected, part of Church history. Their portrayal of the prevailing political and social conditions and of their impact on missionary work makes the book readable and enjoyable even to those not familiar with that part of the world. Above and beyond the political and social backgrounds are stirring, testimony-building accounts of trials, hardships, persecutions, and also accomplishments and success stories of missionaries and members alike in that faraway corner of the Lord's vineyard.

This book belongs in the library of every member who has an interest in the great worldwide missionary effort of the Church. It fills a long-standing void in the spiritual history of a region that we Latter-day Saints consider historically sacred and prophetically captivating.

DAVID B. GALBRAITH

D. KELLY OGDEN

ACKNOWLEDGMENTS

We are acutely aware that publishing a history such as this requires a meeting of minds and a synthesis of talents that significantly exceeds the abilities of those listed as its authors. In this light, we are indebted to many friends and colleagues who, over the course of many years, offered support and encouragement to see this research through to publication.

We are thankful for the contributions of Lucille Hurst Anderson, Michelle Ludlow Judd, and Mary Dyer, whose secretarial skills and research abilities proved to be invaluable. We are particularly grateful to D. Kelly Ogden, Kent P. Jackson, David B. Galbraith, Daniel H. Ludlow, Dann W. Hone, David C. Montgomery, Haws Marble, S. Kent Brown, and Dilworth Parkinson, who read all or part of the manuscript. Taken together, their recommendations and suggestions brought greater balance, comprehensiveness, and accuracy to our work.

Additionally, we recognize the contributions of Rao H. Lindsay, Robert C. Taylor, Steven W. Baldridge and Marilyn M. Rona, Nephi Kezarian, David B. Galbraith, Dale T. Tingey, James A. Toronto, and others, whose writings frequently served as a foundation upon which we could build. We also express our gratitude to Bill Slaughter at the LDS Church Archives, D. Kelly Ogden, Leo C. Wilcox, James McFarlane, Howard Daniels, Albert P. Ostraff, Mark Wilcox, Dilworth Parkinson, Ghassan Bikhazi, Kathleen Rasmussen, Joel Judd, Orin Parker, Kent P. Jackson, and Dennis A. Wright, who generously assisted in our efforts to compile a collection of rich photographic images with which to illustrate and enhance this history. We thanks Brandon Plewe, David Nixon, and Sterling Quinn, who created a helpful and reader-friendly map.

Furthermore, we applaud the efforts of Shauna Humphreys, managing editor of Covenant Communications, whose appreciation and enthusiasm for this history has never waned. We also thank her team of editors, artistic directors, and designers, whose labors have made it possible for our work to be considered by a broader reading audience than we ever could have reached ourselves. Individuals of particular note in this regard are editors Peter Jasinski and Emily Halverson, art director Margaret Weber, and lead designer Jessica Warner.

Finally, and most important, we thank our wives, Darlene Berrett and Katie Van Dyke, whose tireless support of our work over the years has allowed us to maintain a focus on this project that was necessary to bring it to publication. Time and again, Darlene and Katie shouldered enormous workloads, enabling us to freely pour ourselves into this historical undertaking. Their work has, without question, been monumental, and we honor them.

The above-mentioned individuals have in every way strengthened our work. We alone take responsibility for any errors or inaccuracies herein.

CONTENTS

Unveiling a Rich History

Nishan Sherinian was twenty-eight years old and operated a small merchandise store in the Turkish city Zara. An Armenian Christian in the predominantly Muslim Ottoman Empire, Nishan was a staunch member of the Baptist Church who oversaw the financing and construction of the soon-to-be-dedicated Baptist meetinghouse in the city. He was not searching for a new faith when Latter-day Saint missionary Ferdinand Hintze arrived in Zara in 1888.

Hintze preached a peculiar message about the restoration of Christ's ancient Church, which included prophets, apostles, priesthood authority, revelation, and additional scripture. The message aroused a great deal of interest in Zara, and Nishan's father-in-law, Nigogos Sherinian, welcomed the foreign missionary into his home and introduced him to the extended family, including Nishan. Nishan, however, was not interested and stayed away from his father-in-law's home, encouraging others to do the same. Nevertheless, reports of meetings held in the Sherinian home circulated through the city like a flood. Nishan felt a deep curiosity arise within him and wondered if he was doing the right thing by avoiding the message conveyed by this stranger from Salt Lake City. The thought even crossed his mind that it might all be true.

To satisfy his curiosity, Nishan attended an evening meeting on October 4, 1888. Hintze preached a sermon in broken Turkish, and afterward Nishan asked him some questions, which the missionary answered to his satisfaction. Nishan returned the next night and asked more questions, which in turn were answered completely. Then Hintze challenged Nishan to pray to God that he might know if this Latter-day Saint message was from God or man.

It was late in the night when Nishan finally arrived at his home. Everyone had gone to bed. He knelt down and prayed more fervently than he ever had before. He genuinely desired to know if Hintze's message was true. That night he dreamed that he was in a small room with his father-in-law, Nigogos Sherinian, and two other elderly Sherinians, discussing a variety of religious subjects that they had heard the night before during Hintze's sermon. Though unable to come to an agreement on several points, they continued until a strange person walked into the room and stood in front of them. The man was holding an open book. He read several passages from the book, and as he read, Nigogos Sherinian rose to his feet, walked across the room, and stood by the stranger. From this vantage point, Nigogos pointed at Nishan and said, "Nishan, only me and you will accept this man's message, not these others," and gestured toward the other Sherinians in the room. The dream ended.

The next morning, Nishan went to work in his store but could not get the dream out of his mind. Already in the habit of reading daily from the Bible, he stopped his work and began reading in hopes of finding some relief. As he read, Ferdinand Hintze approached the shop and leaned against the open doorway without disturbing Nishan's deep contemplations. After a few moments, Nishan discovered Hintze at the door and invited him in. Hintze sensed that his friend was unsettled, and he asked Nishan what was troubling him. After some hesitation, Nishan related the dream.

Upon hearing the details of the dream, Hintze looked at Nishan for a long time and then said, "Your dream is perfect. Your father-in-law Nigogos told you in your dream, 'Nishan, me and you will accept the

Gospel.' He was baptized yesterday, according to your dream. It's your turn now." Nishan was surprised at this news but quickly told Hintze, "In that case there is nothing to hold me back, for I feel in my soul the message you brought to us is the true Gospel of Jesus Christ. I am ready for baptism." Nishan closed his store, and the two walked to the nearby Red River, where Ferdinand Hintze baptized Nishan Sherinian. It was noon on October 6, 1888, just two days after their first meeting.[1]

This remarkable story raises an important question: How was it that, only fifty-eight years after the founding of the Church in upstate New York, a Latter-day Saint missionary found himself actively proselytizing not only in the Near East but in the heart of the predominantly Islamic Ottoman Empire? The answer to this question is essential to understanding the history of The Church of Jesus Christ of Latter-day Saints in the Near East. One must begin with the story of the young Prophet Joseph Smith to see that from its inception, the Church has had a deep interest in the Near East.

In 1823, seventeen-year-old Joseph Smith lived in upstate New York with his parents, five brothers, and three sisters in a log home typical of the day. Three years had passed since his extraordinary vision of the Father and the Son in a grove of trees near his home, and he was anxious to receive additional understanding through a manifestation from heaven. On the night of September 21, 1823, he prayed to be forgiven and to know his standing before the Lord. While he prayed, a bright light filled the room,

Joseph Smith Jr., first prophet and President of The Church of Jesus Christ of Latter-day Saints.

and a heavenly messenger appeared at his bedside. The appearance of the angel initially shocked Joseph, but he was soon filled with feelings of calm and joy. Joseph described the being as a little above the common stature of men in his day. He was dressed in a garment that was perfectly white. His countenance was like lightning, and he was glorious beyond description. The personage called Joseph by name and explained that he was a messenger sent from God and that his name was Moroni. He told Joseph about an ancient book that was written on gold plates and hidden in a hill not far from his home. He said the book contained an account of ancient inhabitants of the Americas and that it contained the fullness of the everlasting gospel. Furthermore, Moroni told Joseph that buried with the plates were two stones in silver bows fastened to a breastplate, which constituted the Urim and Thummim. God had prepared the Urim and Thummim for the purpose of translating the book.[2]

Four years later, Moroni delivered the gold plates to Joseph Smith, who translated the ancient record—the Book of Mormon—by the gift and power of God. As he translated, Joseph also learned that some ancient inhabitants of America had actually come from Jerusalem and that many prophecies in the Book of Mormon concern the Jews and their return to the land of Jerusalem. The most significant of these prophecies was uttered by the Savior Himself, who visited the inhabitants of America shortly after His resurrection at Jerusalem:

> And I will remember the covenant which I have made with my people; and I have covenanted with them that I would gather them together in mine own due time, that I would give unto them again the land of their fathers for their inheritance, which is the land of Jerusalem, which is the promised land unto them forever, saith the Father. And it shall come to pass that the time cometh, when the fulness of my gospel shall be preached unto them; and they shall believe in me, that I am Jesus Christ, the Son of God, and shall pray unto the Father in my name. . . . Then will the Father gather them together again, and give unto them Jerusalem for the land of their inheritance. (3 Ne. 20:29–31, 33)

Additional revelations found in the Doctrine and Covenants further establish the importance of the Near East in Latter-day Saint theology. For example, in conjunction with the first Latter-day Saint temple, built in Kirtland, Ohio, the Lord revealed that Joseph should request in his prayer:

> But thou knowest that thou hast a great love for the children of Jacob, who have been scattered upon the mountains for a long time. . . . We therefore ask thee to have mercy upon the children of

Jacob, *that Jerusalem, from this hour, may begin to be redeemed;* and the yoke of bondage may begin to be broken off from the house of David; and the children of Judah may begin to return to the lands which thou didst give to Abraham, their father. (D&C 109:61–64; italics added)

The Prophet Joseph Smith further explained that the gathering of all the scattered tribes of Israel and the subsequent conversion and gathering of Judah to their promised land

is a principle I esteem to be of the greatest importance to those who are looking for salvation in this generation, or in these, that may be called "the latter times." All that the prophets have written, from the days of righteous Abel, down to the last man that has left any testimony on record for our consideration, in speaking of the salvation of Israel in the last days, goes directly to show that it consists in the work of the gathering.[3]

The Kirtland Temple

While The Church of Jesus Christ of Latter-day Saints has many friends among the Jewish people, to date, latter-day prophets have not directed any broad or far-reaching attempts to gather Judah through proselytizing. Although latter-day prophets have always been and are very mindful of the Jews, most proselytizing efforts have focused more on other scattered remnants of the house of Israel, such as Ephraim, Manasseh, and so on. In this light, it should come as no surprise that most of the rich Latter-day Saint history in the Near East has relatively little to do with Jewish people and more to do with the European, Armenian, and occasionally Arab Christians living in the Near East.

As will be seen, many Latter-day Saint pioneers stand out on this stage of history. Ferdinand Hintze's missionary experiences in central Anatolia and the conversions of Dekran Shahabian and the Sherinian family serve as just one instance of the remarkable stories of faith in these lands. Orson Hyde, George A. Smith, Lorenzo Snow, and Albert Carrington, for example, each undertook dedicatory missions to Palestine. The first proselytizing missionary in the Near East, Jacob Spori, was invited to travel to Constantinople at the request of an Armenian Christian in 1884. Johann Georg Grau, a German Christian in Palestine, followed the instructions of a heavenly dream and became the first Latter-day Saint convert in the Holy Land in 1886. Joseph W. Booth served tirelessly as a missionary in the Near East for almost two decades and died in Syria in 1928. Carlos E. Asay utilized his all-star basketball skills as a young missionary to win the trust and admiration of the Syrian and Lebanese people when proselytizing in public places was almost impossible. In the 1960s, Daniel H. Ludlow developed travel-study workshops for Brigham Young University faculty members and forged significant friendships with leaders of the fledgling nation of Israel. Additionally, without President Harold B. Lee's prophetic vision and foresight in the early 1970s, the Church's physical presence in Jerusalem may never have become a reality. Finally, Howard W. Hunter, James E. Faust, Jeffrey R. Holland, Daniel Ludlow, Robert C. Taylor, David B. Galbraith, Robert J. Smith, and many others helped see Brigham Young University's Jerusalem Center for Near Eastern Studies erected on the Mount of Olives in Jerusalem in the 1980s. Each of these pioneers has contributed in singular ways to the Church's heritage in the Near East. In many instances, their stories are virtually unknown. The intent of this book is to help unveil that rich history of The Church of Jesus Christ of Latter-day Saints in the Near East.

Notes to Introduction

1.   See Arick S. Kezerian, "Personal Record and Autobiography of Arick Sheranian Kezerian," 1963, L. Tom Perry Special Collections, Harold B. Lee Library, Brigham Young University, Provo, UT. Arick Kezerian is the daughter of Nishan Sherinian. As is evident in this citation, the spelling of the name

Sherinian is sometimes rendered *Sheranian*. See also Nephi K. Kezerian, *Ektee! Ektee! The Life of Armenag Khachig Kezerian* (Provo, UT: Utah Valley Associates, 1982), 45–52.

2. See Joseph Smith—History 1:30–35, 42, 51.

3. Joseph Smith, *Teachings of the Prophet Joseph Smith,* sel. Joseph Fielding Smith (Salt Lake City: Deseret Book, 1976), 83.

CHAPTER ONE

Orson Hyde and the First Dedicatory Missions to the Holy Land

1840–1842 AND 1873

Orson Hyde pronounced the first dedication of the Holy Land for the gathering of the Jews in the latter days. It was an undertaking of compelling import in the history of the Church, and Latter-day Saints believe that it continues to hold sway in the spiritual and secular events of the Near East to this day. Some thirty years after Elder Hyde's journey, another dedicatory mission, headed by President George A. Smith, was sent to Palestine to dedicate the land again. These significant undertakings were undergirded by a doctrinal heritage concerning the gathering of scattered Israel. In order to more fully understand these dedicatory missions, a brief overview of the scattering of Israel and the subsequent efforts to gather it will be considered.

DEFINITION OF ISRAEL

The word *Israel* is a transliteration from Hebrew. Although the exact meaning of the word is not clear, *Israel* is commonly interpreted to mean "God will prevail or overcome."[1] Jacob (Isaac's son and Abraham's grandson) had his name changed by Jehovah to *Israel*.

Israel's sons constitute the tribal heads of his descendants. Over time the significance of the word *Israel* has expanded in meaning. In Latter-day Saint theology, the term *Israel* is generally associated with one of three applications: *blood, land,* or *covenant.*

A *blood Israelite* is any bloodline descendant of Jacob. Over the centuries, blood Israelites have been scattered throughout the earth. Today, Jews throughout the world are probably the most prominent and recognized population of blood Israelites. A *land Israelite* is someone who lives in and has a strong attachment to the land that constitutes the modern state of Israel. Citizens of this modern nation are referred to as *Israelis.* Finally, a *covenant Israelite* is anyone who accepts the restored gospel of Jesus Christ and is baptized into The Church of Jesus Christ of Latter-day Saints. These individuals set themselves apart from the rest of the world by covenanting to live a godlike life. They are Christians who yearn to serve their fellow beings and help others draw closer to God. They do not consider themselves better than anyone else; rather, their covenants move them to make every effort to lift, bolster, and edify the human family.[2]

Obviously, these three applications are not mutually exclusive. For example, a Jew who lives in the modern Israeli city of Tel Aviv but is not a member of The Church of Jesus Christ of Latter-day Saints is a land Israelite and a blood Israelite, but not a covenant Israelite. The essence of Orson Hyde's and other dedicatory prayers pertains to becoming a covenant Israelite and to both the physical and spiritual aspects of gathering Israel.

THE SCATTERING AND GATHERING OF ISRAEL

Throughout its history, Israel has been scattered from time to time. In some instances, scattering occurred because of the wickedness of the Israelites. In other instances, scattering occurred to ensure that the influence of covenant Israelites would be felt throughout the world (see Jacob 5).

In 721 B.C., Assyrian armies swept through the land of Israel, killing thousands and taking captive the vast majority of the remaining members of the northern ten tribes of Israel. That scattering was so complete that from that time until now, those ten tribes were lost to the world. Subsequent events such as the destruction of

Jerusalem by the Babylonians in 586 B.C., the hellenization of Judea beginning in 333 B.C., and the Roman destruction of Jerusalem led by Titus in A.D. 70 culminated in the general scattering of the remaining Israelites in the region. Through all these events, Israelite prophets foretold a future gathering of the lost and scattered tribes of Israel and explained that while the gathering was an ongoing work, the greatest gathering of Israel would take place in the last days. This latter-day gathering would bring God's covenant people together in close proximity and give them an understanding of holy temples and their binding influence. The need to gather scattered Israel is so significant to Latter-day Saints that Joseph Smith included it in the Church's thirteen Articles of Faith, of which the tenth states: "We believe in the literal gathering of Israel and in the restoration of the Ten Tribes."

While many aspects of the latter-day gathering have yet to be revealed, there are at least three that may be stated with confidence: (1) the gathering has two parts—a spiritual gathering and a physical gathering; (2) the results of the gathering will be astonishing in their scope and accomplished through miraculous means; and (3) the gathering has commenced and continues due to influence stemming from Melchizedek Priesthood keys. These three aspects provide the context to more fully appreciate the significance of the dedication of the Holy Land.

As a general pattern, God's faithful followers receive spiritual blessings for their obedience before they receive physical blessings. This principle seems firmly fixed to the gathering of scattered Israel. Prophecies associated with the gathering of Israel in the last days bear this pattern out (see Deut. 30:1–10); the gathering of Israel will first be a great spiritual gathering because of genuine conversion to the gospel of Jesus Christ (see 2 Nephi 6:11).[3] That is to say, Israel must accept and live according to *covenants* made at conversion. Gathering to a particular physical location will then follow. For this reason, we discourage the direct correlation between doctrines and prophecies found in scripture regarding the gathering of Israel to the Holy Land and the secular and political philosophies driving movements such as Zionism. They are not necessarily one and the same. When modern Israel progresses as a nation but generally rejects God's covenant laws in order to further its political power or embrace secular ideologies and lifestyles, it is not fulfilling prophecies that describe God's faithful Israelites. Ultimately, the people of Israel must be faithful to spiritual laws in order to enjoy the temporal blessings of covenants as described by the prophets.

The gathering of scattered Israel will be miraculous. Exact details regarding this spiritual and physical gathering are generally unknown. It is clear, however, that remnants of the tribes of Ephraim and Manasseh will play a key role. Moses prophesied that in the last days ten thousands of Ephraim and thousands of Manasseh would gather scattered Israel from the farthest reaches of the earth. These two tribes were likened to a large and powerful horned ox, and they will use their strength and power to convert and gather the children of Israel in the last days (see Deut. 33:16–17). The miraculous results of their labors were prophetically described by Jeremiah, who wrote that "the days come, saith the Lord, that it shall no more be said, The Lord liveth that brought up the children of Israel out of the land of Egypt; but The Lord liveth, that brought up the children of Israel from the land of the north, and from all the lands whither he had driven them: and I will bring them again into their land that I gave unto their fathers" (Jer. 16:14–15).

This gathering cannot take place without priesthood keys. These keys are held by Apostles, who are authorized to act in the interests of God's earthly kingdom. Priesthood keys make it possible to activate or deactivate, open or close, seal or loose the powers of God in the lives of the peoples of the earth. The keys of the gathering of Israel were restored by Moses to Joseph Smith and Oliver Cowdery on April 3, 1836 (see D&C 110). Joseph Smith then bestowed these keys upon the entire Quorum of the Twelve Apostles.

The nature of the keys of gathering Israel further shore up the doctrine that there must be two gatherings in the last days: spiritual and then temporal. President Joseph Fielding Smith explained the role of the restoration of keys in this twofold gathering of early members of the latter-day Church.

> Moses was sent to restore the keys of the gathering, not the preaching of the gospel. It was after people were converted that the spirit of gathering entered their souls, and it was due to the

influence of the Spirit of the Lord, based upon the restoration of the keys given to Moses, that the members of the Church, when they were brought into the Church, obtained the desire to gather to the body of the Church.[4]

Through priesthood keys, the dedication of the Holy Land activated forces on the earth that would draw the children of Israel back to their promised lands in the Near East. But they would not merely be gathered to a land; they would also be gathered back to a covenant people and a covenant-centered lifestyle. As an Apostle, Orson Hyde held the keys and was given the calling to dedicate the Holy Land. The story of his conversion to Mormonism, call to the Quorum of the Twelve Apostles, and mission to the Holy Land constitute the beginning of Latter-day Saint history in the Near East.

THE MISSION OF ORSON HYDE

Orson Hyde was a man of unusual character and ability. He was a strong individual who submitted his will to God's, making him an effective instrument in the hands of the Lord. Orson was born at Oxford, Connecticut, January 8, 1805, to Nathan and Sally Hyde. After the death of both parents, the eleven children were raised in foster homes. When he was eighteen years old, Orson decided to strike out for himself in 1823. He converted to the Methodist Church in 1827 but soon joined the Reformed Baptist, or Campbellite, movement as preached by Sidney Rigdon of Mentor, Ohio. He acquired enough education to teach at Florence, Ohio, and by 1830 he was a Campbellite pastor over two congregations. Orson was introduced to The Church of Jesus Christ of Latter-day Saints through the preaching of Parley P. Pratt, and he eventually sought baptism.[5]

From his first day as a Latter-day Saint, Orson Hyde knew he would perform an

Orson Hyde of the Quorum of the Twelve was commissioned by Joseph Smith to dedicate the Holy Land.

important work relating to the gathering of Israel. He was baptized October 30, 1831, and was told by Joseph Smith following his confirmation that soon he would "go to Jerusalem, the land of thy fathers, and be a watchman unto the house of Israel; and by thy hands shall the Most High do a great work, which shall prepare the way and greatly facilitate the gathering together of that people."[6]

In 1835, Orson was chosen to be a member of the first latter-day Quorum of the Twelve Apostles. As the time for leaving on his destined mission to the Holy Land drew near, Orson Hyde was granted a lengthy vision as a sign to succor his faith. The year was 1840, and a mission to Jerusalem had occupied his thoughts and prayers for some nine years. Hyde recalled the vision as follows:

> In the early part of March last (1840), I retired to my bed one evening as usual, and while contemplating and enquiring out, in my own mind, the field of my ministerial for the then coming season, the vision of the Lord, like clouds of light, burst upon my view. The cities of London, Amsterdam, Constantinople, and Jerusalem all appeared in succession before me; and the Spirit said unto me, "Here are many of the children of Abraham whom I will gather to the land that I gave to their fathers, and here also is the field of your labours."[7]

Just one month following this vision, on April 6, 1840, Orson Hyde was called by Joseph Smith to travel to the Holy Land on a dedicatory mission. Fellow Apostle John E. Page was also called to undertake this mission, and the two left Illinois on April 15, 1840. Elders Hyde and Page parted company in Cincinnati, Ohio, and for reasons that are not entirely clear, Elder Page did not travel to the Holy Land.

After many long months of travel across the United States, to the British Isles, through central Europe, and then on to Constantinople and Beirut, Elder Hyde finally neared the end of his journey in mid-October 1841 as he set sail across the Mediterranean Sea for Jaffa, the biblical seaport anciently known as Joppa. In 1841, Jaffa was part of the Ottoman Empire. The empire was ruled by a sultan and an attendant bureaucracy. At its peak, in the sixteenth century, the Ottoman

Empire had been one of the most dominant and powerful empires the world had known. Modern Turkey, Syria, Lebanon, Jordan, Israel, the West Bank, and the Gaza Strip made up only part of the Ottoman Empire. It was a predominantly Islamic empire that, because of self-imposed isolation, had been bypassed by the technological developments of the West. Beginning in about 1830, leaders recognized the need for advanced technologies, and a movement began that embraced almost any technology from the West in an effort to "catch up." This opened the area even more to European influences, and a flood of Westerners—tourists, merchants, and missionaries like Orson Hyde—entered the region.

Nevertheless, Christians in the empire—whether the indigenous Armenians of eastern Asia Minor or the Greek Christians of the Constantinople ghettos—were second-class citizens treated with apathy at best, scorn and persecution at worst. Subsequent chapters will show that this enmity was keenly felt by Latter-day Saint missionaries serving in the Ottoman Empire.

By the time Orson Hyde landed at Jaffa on October 19, 1841, the heretofore grand Ottoman Empire was commonly known as "the sick man of Europe." The empire had straggled behind in almost every conceivable way: communication, education, economics, science, warfare, technology, and civic infrastructure. From his correspondence and other writings, it seems apparent that Orson Hyde was quite aware of the downward slide of the Ottoman Empire but generally unfamiliar with the causes and subsequent tensions associated with the decline.

JERUSALEM, THE HOLY CITY, OCTOBER 1841

The very next day after his arrival in Jaffa, Elder Hyde traveled southeast on a two-day journey of forty miles up to Jerusalem—a climb of 2,500 feet to the top of the Judean hills. He traveled with some Englishmen who had come to Jaffa for business. They were protected from marauders by several armed servants. On his second day of travel, he probably passed through Kirjath-Jearim (also known as Abu Gosh), where Abinadab had lived and kept the ark of the covenant for twenty years (see 1 Sam. 7:1–2). It was here that pilgrims coming from the west would get their first glimpse of the Holy City.

Tears flowed down Orson Hyde's cheeks as he saw Jerusalem for the first time with his natural eyes—precisely according to the vision he had seen. He said, "I saw no one with me in the vision; and although Elder Page was appointed to accompany me there, yet I found myself there alone."[8]

After eighteen long and difficult months of travel, Elder Hyde finally stood before the west gate of the city. The date was October 21, 1841. He was thrilled as he contemplated walking across the "stage upon which so many scenes of wonder had been acted, where prophets were stoned, and the Savior of sinners slain."[9]

In describing Jerusalem, Elder Hyde explained that

> the city is situated in the southeastern extremity of an inclined plain, with the valley of Kedron [Kidron] on the east, and the vallies [sic] of Hinnom and Gihon on the south and west, all converging to a point in the valley of Jehosaphat, south-east of the city; from the eastern gate of the city to the top of Mount Olivet, as you pass through the Valley of the Kidron, is just about one English mile.[10]

He further explained that the walls of the city, mounted by many cannons, were ten feet thick on the sides that would be most exposed, and four or five feet where the descent from the wall was vertical. Within the walls were about twenty thousand inhabitants: seven thousand Jews, plus Turks and Arabs.[11] Elder Hyde said, "Many of the Jews who are old go to this place to die, and many are coming from Europe into this Eastern world."[12]

In addition, he observed that "the customs and manners of the people of the east are so similar to what they were in the days of our Saviour, that almost everything which the traveler beholds is a standing illustration of some portion of scripture."[13] He saw two women grinding wheat with a small stone grinder, which reminded him of the Savior's words: "Two women shall be grinding at the mill; one shall be taken and the other left; and for ought I know, these two I saw were the identical ones."[14]

In the Old City of Jerusalem, Elder Hyde called upon several people. One of the first was George Backus Whiting, an American missionary, to whom he gave a letter of introduction for the consular agent at Jaffa. Whiting helped Hyde find board and lodging at the Latin Convent.[15] That same day, Charles Selden Sherman, an American missionary, and one Mr. Gager, an American licentiate from the Presbyterian Church, called on Orson Hyde. Elder Hyde explained to them his mission to Jerusalem and asked for their "cooperation" and "friendly aid." This they agreed to give.

After a much-needed rest, Elder Hyde met again with his three new missionary acquaintances and read to them the document containing the object of his mission. He then told them of the rise of the Church and its doctrine. Elder Hyde boldly told the three missionaries they were wasting their time in Jerusalem, since no one would listen to them. He then bore his testimony and asked them to introduce him to Jewish leaders. They were reluctant to do this, so he procured a valet de place, or lackey, to introduce him to a Mr. Simons, a very respectable Jew who had recently, with his family, become one of the four Jewish converts to the Church of England in Jerusalem.

Simons was very friendly and proceeded to invite two ministers of the Church of England to join the discussion. The ministers questioned the propriety of Hyde's undertaking because he claimed that God had sent him. Elder Hyde later concluded: "If, indeed, I had gone to Jerusalem under the direction of some missionary board, or society, and left God out of the question altogether, I should have been received as a celestial messenger."[16] The ministers, while courteous, reiterated the old argument that miracles, visions, and prophecy had ceased. Orson Hyde summarized their "sectarian notions" with these words:

> That which was looked upon by the ancient saints, as among the greatest favours and blessings, viz., Revelation from God and communion with him by dreams and by visions, is now looked upon by the religious world as the height of presumption and folly. The ancient saints considered their condition most deplorable when Jehovah would not speak to them; but the most orthodox religionists of this age deem it quite heterodox to even admit the probability that he ever will speak again. O, my soul! language

fails to paint the absurdity and abomination of such heaven-opposing, and truth-excluding dogmas.[17]

The ministers' poor reception of his message did not stop Elder Hyde. He challenged Mr. Simons to be baptized, explaining that his baptism in the Church of England was not valid. Hyde preached, but his audience did not share his feelings. He was a little discouraged with his efforts to convert Mr. Simons, a Christian-Jew, and said:

> there is more hope of those Jews receiving the fulness of the gospel, whose minds have never been poisoned by the bane of modern sectarianism, which closes the mouth of deity, and shuts up in heaven all the angels, visions and prophesyings.[18]

Elder Hyde felt that if the so-called Christians of the Crusades and down through the following seven hundred years had been the example of Christianity, then why would a Jew ever believe it? Still, Elder Hyde said he found many Jews who listened with intense interest.

Elder Hyde greatly desired that their interest would bloom and that the Lord would effect a change in the land. He expressed this yearning in these words: "As I walked about the environs of the town [Jerusalem], my spirit struggled within me in earnest prayer to the God of Abraham, Isaac, and Jacob, that he would not only revolutionize this country, but renovate and make it glorious."[19]

After returning from his walk, his legs were completely coated with dust. The whole country was like an ash bed for lack of rain. Elder Hyde commented that it must have been easy for the ancient disciples to fulfill an injunction of the Savior to "shake off the dust of your feet." And Elder Hyde was about to do just the opposite by leaving an apostolic blessing on the land. As one reads Elder Hyde's dedicatory prayer, one may consider the temporal and spiritual ramifications of the blessing for the Jews and the house of Israel in general.

ORSON HYDE'S DEDICATORY PRAYER, OCTOBER 24, 1841

Those who have stood on top of the Mount of Olives just prior to sunrise know that it is a singular experience. Often there is a peculiar stillness about the spot that evokes deep thought and contemplation. The dull light of the impending dawn already adds a hue of gold to the ancient walls of the Old City, while sheep and shepherds stir in the Kidron Valley below. One can smell the antiquity of the surroundings. In a simple yet sublime way, one feels a sense of elevation as the eyes are drawn across the brook-carved valley toward the Temple Mount and as one reflects upon sacred events that unfolded in the Holy City. Melchizedek, Abraham, Isaac, Isaiah, Lehi, Jeremiah, Jesus, Peter, and Paul, among others, all cross the landscape of the mind. And as a result of his ascent up the mount to dedicate the land for the return of the Jews, Latter-day Saints include Orson Hyde in this group of Jerusalem's foreordained spiritual caretakers.

Elder Hyde's own account explains:

> On Sunday morning, October 24th [1841], a good while before
> day, I arose from sleep, and went out of the city as soon as the

The Old City of Jerusalem as seen from the Mount of Olives.

The Mount of Olives

gates were opened, crossed the brook Cedron, and went upon the Mount of Olives, and there in solemn silence, with pen, ink, and paper, just as I saw in the vision, offered up the following prayer to Him who lives for ever and ever.[20]

Elder Hyde's prayer, the first dedication of the Holy Land in modern times, proceeded as follows:

O Thou! who art from everlasting to everlasting, eternally and unchangeably the same, even the God who rules in the heavens above, and controls the destinies of men on the earth, wilt Thou condescend, through thine infinite goodness and royal favour, to listen to the prayer of thy servant which he this day offers up unto thee in the name of thy holy child Jesus, upon this land where the Sun of Righteousness sat in blood, and thine *Anointed One* expired.

Be pleased, O Lord, to forgive all the follies, weakness, vanities, and sins of thy servant, and strengthen him to resist all future temptations. Give him prudence and discernment that he may avoid the evil, and a heart to choose the good; give him fortitude to bear up under trying and adverse circumstances, and grace to endure all things for thy name's sake, until the end shall come, when all the saints shall rest in peace.

Now, O Lord! thy servant has been obedient to the heavenly vision which thou gavest him in his native land; and under the shadow of thine outstretched arm, he has safely arrived in this place to dedicate and consecrate this land unto Thee, for the gathering together of Judah's scattered remnants, according to the predictions of the holy prophets—for the building up of Jerusalem again after it has been trodden down by the Gentiles so long, and for rearing a temple in honour of thy name. Everlasting thanks be ascribed unto thee, O Father! Lord of heaven and earth, that thou hast preserved thy servant from the dangers of the seas, and from the plague and pestilence which have caused the land to mourn. The violence of man has also been restrained, and thy providential care by night and by day has been exercised over thine unworthy servant. Accept, therefore, O Lord, the tribute of a grateful heart for all past favours, and be pleased to continue thy kindness and mercy towards a needy worm of the dust.

O Thou, who did'st covenant with Abraham thy friend, and who did'st renew that covenant with Isaac, and confirm the same with Jacob with an oath, that thou would'st not only give them this land for an everlasting inheritance, but that thou would'st also remember their seed for ever. Abraham, Isaac, and Jacob, have long since closed their eyes in death, and made the grave their mansion. Their children are scattered and dispersed abroad among the nations of the Gentiles like sheep that have no shepherd, and are still looking forward for the fulfilment of those promises which thou did'st make concerning them; and even this land, which once poured forth nature's richest bounty, and flowed, as it were, with milk and honey, has, to a certain extent, been smitten with barrenness and sterility since it drank from murderous hands the blood of Him who never sinned.

Grant, therefore, O Lord, in the name of thy well-beloved Son, Jesus Christ, to remove the barrenness and sterility of this land, and let springs of living water break forth to water its thirsty soil. Let the vine and the olive produce in their strength, and the fig-tree bloom and flourish. Let the land become abundantly fruitful when possessed by its rightful heirs; let it again flow with plenty to feed the returning prodigals who come home with a spirit of grace and supplication; upon it let the clouds distill virtue and richness, and let the fields smile with plenty. Let the flocks and the herds greatly increase and multiply upon the mountains and the hills; and let thy great kindness conquer and subdue the unbelief of thy people. Do thou take from them their stony heart, and give them a heart of flesh; and may the sun of thy favour dispel the cold mists of darkness which have beclouded their atmosphere. Incline them to gather in upon this land according to thy word. Let them come like clouds and like doves to their windows. Let the large ships of the nations bring them from the distant isles; and let kings become their nursing fathers, and queens with motherly fondness, wipe the tear of sorrow from their eye.

Thou, O Lord, did once move upon the heart of Cyrus to shew favor unto Jerusalem and her children. Do thou now also be pleased to inspire the hearts of kings and the powers of the earth to look with a friendly eye towards this place, and with a desire to see thy righteous purposes executed in relation thereto. Let them know that it is thy good pleasure to restore the kingdom unto Israel—raise up Jerusalem as its capital, and constitute her people a distinct nation and government, with David thy servant, even a descendant from the loins of ancient David, to be their king.

Let that nation or that people who shall take an active part in behalf of Abraham's children, and in the raising up of Jerusalem, find favour in thy sight. Let not their enemies prevail against them, neither let pestilence or famine overcome them, but let the glory of Israel overshadow them, and the power of the highest protect them; while that nation or kingdom that will not serve

thee in this glorious work must perish, according to thy word—
"Yea, those nations shall be utterly wasted."

Though thy servant is now far from his home, and from the land
bedewed with his earliest tear, yet he remembers, O Lord, his
friends who are there, and family, whom for thy sake he has left.
Though poverty and privation be our earthly lot, yet ah! do Thou
richly endow us with an inheritance where moth and rust do not
corrupt, and where thieves do not break through and steal.

The hands that have fed, clothed, or shown favour unto the
family of thy servant in his absence, or that shall hereafter do so,
let them not lose their reward, but let a special blessing rest upon
them, and in thy kingdom let them have an inheritance when
thou shalt come to be glorified in this society.

Do Thou also look with favour upon all those through whose
liberality I have been enabled to come to this island; and in the
day when thou shalt reward all people according to thy works, let
these also not be past by or forgotten, but in time let them be in
readiness to enjoy the glory of those mansions which Jesus has
gone to prepare. Particularly do thou bless the stranger in
Philadelphia, whom I never saw, but who sent me gold, with a
request that I should pray for him in Jerusalem. Now, O Lord, let
blessings come upon him from an unexpected quarter, and let his
basket be filled, and his storehouse abound with plenty, and let
not the good things of the earth be his only portion but let him
be found among those to whom it shall be said, "Thou has been
faithful over a few things, and I will make thee ruler over many."

O my Father in heaven! I now ask thee in the name of Jesus to
remember Zion, with all her stakes, and with all her assemblies.
She has been grievously afflicted and smitten; she has mourned;
she has wept; her enemies have triumphed, and have said, "Ah,
where is thy God?" Her priests and prophets have groaned in
chains and fetters within the gloomy walls of prisons, while

many were slain, and now sleep in the arms of death. How long, O Lord, shall iniquity triumph, and sin go unpunished?

Do Thou arise in the majesty of thy strength, and make bare thine arm in behalf of thy people. Redress their wrongs, and turn their sorrow into joy. Pour the spirit of light and knowledge, grace and wisdom, into the hearts of her prophets, and clothe her priests with salvation. Let light and knowledge march forth through the empire of darkness, and may the honest in heart flow to their standard, and join the march to go forth to meet the Bridegroom.

Let a peculiar blessing rest upon the Presidency of thy Church, for at them are the arrows of the enemy directed. Be thou to them a sun and shield, their strong tower and hiding-place; and in the time of distress or danger be thou near to deliver. Also the quorum of the twelve, do thou be pleased to stand by, for thou knowest the obstacles which we have to encounter, the temptations to which we are exposed, and the privations which we must suffer. Give us, therefore, strength according to our day, and help us to bear a faithful testimony of Jesus and his gospel, and to finish with fidelity and honour the work which thou hast given us to do, and then give us a place in thy glorious kingdom. And let this blessing rest upon every faithful officer and member in thy church. And all the glory and honour will we ascribe unto God and the Lamb for ever and ever. Amen.[21]

Elder Hyde accomplished his mission to dedicate and consecrate the Holy Land unto the Lord for the gathering place of Judah's scattered remnants. Jerusalem was to be rebuilt again after having been trodden down by the Gentiles so long, and a temple was to be built in Jerusalem to honor the name of the Lord. The Holy Land was given to Abraham's descendants for an everlasting inheritance and was to become abundantly fruitful.

As a part of his covenant-making prayer on the Mount of Olives that October morning, Elder Hyde erected a pile of stones "as a witness according to the ancient custom."[22] This act is significant on

Orson Hyde erected a pile of stones on the Mount of Olives to commemorate his dedicatory prayer. Perhaps that monument looked something like this re-creation, with the Dome of the Rock seen in the background.

many levels. For example, one meaning of the word *witness* in Hebrew is "to repeat" what has been seen or heard. By extension, the word denotes such things as stones erected as memorials of an agreement or event. Jacob raised a heap of stones as "the heap of witness" between him and Laban that they would not pass "over the heap" to harm each other (Gen. 31:44–55). Joshua set up a stone as evidence of the allegiance Israel promised to God (Josh. 22:27; 24:26–27).[23] Elder Hyde erected a similar monument as a tangible memorial of the covenant renewed between the Lord and His people.

THE IMPORTANCE OF ORSON HYDE'S MISSION TO THE HOLY LAND, 1840—1842

With the dedication complete, Elder Hyde explained in a letter to Elder Parley P. Pratt that "the great wheel is unquestionably in motion, and the word of the Almighty has declared that it shall roll. I have not time to write particulars now, but suffice it to say that my mission has been quite as prosperous as I could expect."[24]

Elder Orson Hyde knew from visions, special blessings, and revelations directed to him that his mission to the Holy Land was unique. From April 15, 1840, to December 7, 1842, he traveled throughout the eastern United States, England, Europe, and the Near East—thirty-two long months of separation from his wife and children, plus the added hardship of traveling approximately twenty thousand miles, generally alone.

Though long, lonely, and perilous, his mission was divinely appointed and the ramifications far-reaching. It was certainly a bold and startling pronouncement when Elder Hyde said that he was one of the "two sons" Isaiah prophesied would take Jerusalem by the hand and lead her as she was awaking after drinking from the cup of the fury of the Lord.[25] He believed that his prayer of dedication and pleadings with the Lord on the Mount of Olives would be the force that would start the "gathering of Judah" to the Holy Land from the four corners of the earth.

It is not now possible to understand all the ramifications of Orson Hyde's mission, but perhaps one can get a clearer picture of its importance from a letter written by the Prophet Joseph Smith in Nauvoo, Illinois, to Elders Orson Hyde and John E. Page, dated May 14, 1840.

> It is a great and important mission, and one that is worthy for those intelligences who surround the throne of Jehovah to be engaged in. Although it appears great at present, yet you have but just begun to realize the greatness, the extent and glory of the same. . . . Brethren, you are in the pathway to eternal fame, and immortal glory.[26]

Orson Hyde's "pathway to eternal fame" was given additional prominence on October 24, 1979, when President Spencer W. Kimball dedicated a beautiful five-and-a-half-acre park on the Mount of Olives that was named after Elder Hyde: the Orson Hyde Memorial Garden.

For Latter-day Saints, Orson Hyde's unprecedented journey to the Near East was revolutionary for its time, yet it did not remain an isolated event. Historical records indicate that the Holy Land has been formally dedicated for the return of Judah and the house of Israel on eleven different occasions in this dispensation. For the purposes of this book, a formal dedication includes the presence and approval of at least one member of the Quorum of the Twelve Apostles or First Presidency of the Church. In addition to Orson Hyde's prayer and ten subsequent dedications that will be described throughout this book, there have been numerous prayers offered by apostles and prophets that, while sacred and significant, did not employ the specific language typical for dedicatory prayers.

THE SECOND, THIRD, AND FOURTH DEDICATIONS, 1873

During the 1872 October general conference, President George A. Smith, first counselor to Brigham Young in the First Presidency, announced, "I am about to go abroad on a visit to the Holy Land. I expect to start in the course of a few days. The contemplated journey will cost $3000 in gold . . . an amount which I am unable to raise without difficulty, and I thought of inviting the Bishops and my friends generally . . . all who feel disposed to do so . . . to donate something towards the expenses of this pilgrimage to the Holy Land."[27] This mission was heartily endorsed by President Brigham Young, and George A. Smith would become the first member of a First Presidency to walk in the Holy Land since the days of Jesus' Apostles.

George A. Smith became the first member of the First Presidency to travel to the Holy Land.

On October 15, 1872, the day George A. Smith was to depart, President Young gave him a letter indicating that the First Presidency felt that a Latter-day Saint presence in the Holy Land was essential.

> We desire that you observe closely what openings now exist, or where they may be effected, for the introduction of the gospel into the various countries you shall visit. . . . We wish you to dedicate and consecrate that land to the Lord, that it may be blessed with the fruitfulness, preparatory to the return of the

Elder Albert Carrington of the Quorum of the Twelve Apostles.

Eliza R. Snow, general Relief Society president.

Salt Lake City businessman Feramorz Little.

Clara Little, daughter of Feramorz Little and the traveling companion of Eliza R. Snow on the dedicatory mission. This picture was taken in 1873.

Jews in fulfillment of prophecy, and the accomplishment of the purposes of our Heavenly Father.[28]

Joining President George A. Smith were seven other members of the 1872–73 dedicatory party: Elders Lorenzo Snow and Albert Carrington of the Twelve, general Relief Society president Eliza R. Snow, her traveling companion Clara Little, linguist Paul Schettler, prominent Salt Lake City businessman Feramorz Little, and Salt Lake City treasurer Thomas Jennings.

When the group arrived in the Holy Land, their initial impression of the area was bleak. Their ship landed at the small

Elder Lorenzo Snow of the Quorum of the Twelve Apostles.

port at Jaffa, whose poor condition reflected the rest of the Ottoman Empire. Jaffa's streets were narrow, crooked, filthy, and stifling. After one night's stay, the group began their two-day journey up to Jerusalem, and their disappointment turned to wonder and awe at the prospect of actually walking where the Savior walked. Lorenzo Snow wrote:

> The morning lovely as ever dawned upon the Holy land of Palestine. We felt that we were passing over the land once occupied by the children of Abraham, the plains once trod by the kings of Israel with their marshalled hosts, the land of the apostles and prophets. We were in Palestine! The consciousness of the fact was inspiring.[29]

The journey to Jerusalem was a rigorous ride on horseback.[30] Nevertheless, on the afternoon of February 25, 1873, they caught their first glimpses of the Mount of Olives and the city walls of Jerusalem.[31] Lorenzo Snow again captured the emotion of the group as they approached Jerusalem.

> Away to the right is Mount Zion, the city of David. Off to our left that lofty eminence, with an aspect so barren, is the Mount

of Olives once the favorite resort of our Saviour, and the spot last pressed by his sacred feet before He ascended into the presence of His Father. These interesting historic scenes, with all their sacred associations, inspire thoughts and reflections impressive and solemn. Yes, there is Jerusalem! Where Jesus lived and taught, and was crucified, where he cried "It is finished," and bowed his head and died![32]

Sunday morning, March 2, 1873, was cool and breezy as the small group of Latter-day Saints, except Clara Little, who remained at camp, ascended the Mount of Olives on horseback. On the Mount of Olives, their guide pitched a tent for their privacy and laid a carpet on the ground about one hundred feet northeast of the Church of Ascension, which had been transformed into a mosque in A.D. 1187. At approximately 10:00 A.M. Albert Carrington opened the meeting with a prayer. He dedicated the ground, the tent, and the land of Israel generally.[33] After this prayer was offered, Elder Carrington and Thomas Jennings stood outside the tent to keep watch, since they had not brought their temple clothing with them.[34] The remaining members of the party then "engaged in divine worship" in the order of the Holy Priesthood on the mount.[35] Elder Snow offered the next prayer, wherein "the same dedicatory sentiments were contained."[36] Following this prayer, President George A. Smith offered up his own. Eliza R. Snow recalls his dedicatory prayer as follows:

> President Smith leading in humble, fervent supplication, dedicating the land of Palestine for the gathering of the Jews and the rebuilding of Jerusalem, and returning heartfelt thanks and gratitude to God for the fulness of the gospel and the blessings bestowed on the Latter-day Saints. Other brethren led in turn, and we had a very interesting season; to me it seemed the crowning point of the whole tour, realizing as I did that we were worshiping on the summit of the sacred Mount, once the frequent resort of the Prince of Life.[37]

President George A. Smith described what followed:

Looking east atop the Mount of Olives. The Church of Ascension, a mosque since A.D. 1187, in the foreground, with the Russian Tower of Ascension in the background. George A. Smith, Lorenzo Snow, and Albert Carrington offered dedicatory prayers in a tent pitched about one hundred feet northeast of the mosque.

With our faces bowed toward Jerusalem, we lifted our prayers to
God that he would preserve [Israel] and confound [her] enemies.
We felt in our hearts that Zion was onward and upward, and that
no power could stay her progress; that the day was not far distant
when Israel would gather, and those lands would begin to teem
with a people who would worship God and keep his commandments; that plenty and the blessings of eternity would be poured
out bounteously upon that desert land, and that all the prophecies concerning the restoration of the house of Israel would be
fulfilled.[38]

Other accounts of the dedication mention the promise that the
land would be redeemed from its sterility and that its historic fruitfulness would abound.[39] Additionally, President Smith prophesied that
Jerusalem would be rebuilt due to a hastened gathering of the Jews in
the last days.[40]

President Smith makes it clear in his journal that the three
Apostles present each dedicated the land of Israel for the return of the
Jews. Including Elder Orson Hyde's 1841 prayer, apostolic keys had
now been turned in four different instances, beseeching the Lord on
behalf of Judah and the land of Israel. Elder B. H. Roberts said of
apostolic dedications that they unlock a great work—"how great, men
at present know not."[41] Without question, this was a sacred moment
in the history of the Church.

Following the dedicatory prayers, Lorenzo Snow prayed again.
Then George A. Smith offered a benediction at 10:34 A.M., and "all
engaged felt greatly blessed of the Lord."[42] The party repaired to their
camp, arriving there just before noon.[43]

Two days later the chief rabbi in Jerusalem, Abraham Askenasi,
visited the Latter-day Saint delegation at their camp. He expressed to
the group the Jews' firm belief in the redemption of Israel and in the
return of the ten lost tribes. The Latter-day Saints found the visit very
pleasant and interesting.[44]

The question is sometimes asked if the members of the party ever
tried to proselytize their new friends in Palestine. President Smith
expressly affirmed that theirs was not a proselytizing mission, which
was an advantage to the group's purpose. He explained that

> we visited many countries, and had an opportunity of acquiring
> information and extending acquaintances into lands which
> heretofore have been barred against visits from our Elders, as the
> Elders, when they were abroad went expressly to preach, and
> were frequently prohibited from entering these countries, or if
> permitted to enter were not allowed to speak of the gospel. We,
> having means to travel, of course passed along as other travelers,
> for not being on a mission for preaching were not interrupted
> and this enabled us to acquire a knowledge of the laws and
> customs of the various countries we visited, and a variety of
> information that we had heretofore only got by reading.[45]

On March 5, 1873, the group mounted their horses, passed by
the city walls, and climbed Mount Scopus (the northern end of the
Mount of Olives), where they took their final views of the Holy City.
Eliza Snow shared that their visit brought "bright prophetic anticipation for the future," giving them "a feeling of reluctance at bidding a
final adieu."[46] Their journey home took them through various countries, and on May 28 they arrived in London, where they boarded the
Wisconsin and sailed for America.

Each member of this company felt a deep sense of gratitude for
the high honor of traveling to the Holy Land and for the safety they
experienced on their 25,000-mile journey. Eliza R. Snow expressed
the feeling this way:

> To those who have an eye to see and a heart to understand, the
> hand of God has been manifest in dispensing blessings to us as
> tourists: From calamities and dangers by storms at sea, in front
> and rear, we have escaped; and without any interruption worthy
> of note either by sea or land, for which we feel truly grateful.[47]

The dedicatory mission of 1872–73 stands tall in Church history.
Not since the great missions to England of the 1830s had so many
high-ranking leaders traveled together abroad. The dedicatory prayers
stand next to Orson Hyde's 1841 prayer as further confirmation that
"in the mouth of two or three witnesses every word may be established" (Matt. 18:16). While it would still be some time before

missionaries were sent to preach the restored gospel, these repeated dedications are evidence of the Church's long-term interest in the Holy Land.

Notes to Chapter 1

1. F. Brown, S. Driver, and C. Briggs, *The Brown-Driver-Briggs Hebrew and English Lexicon* (Peabody, MA: Hendrickson, 2000), 975. See also Ernst Jenni and Claus Westerman, *Theological Lexicon of the Old Testament,* trans. Mark E. Biddle (Peabody, MA: Hendrickson, 1997), 2:581–84.

2. Victor L. Ludlow, *Isaiah: Prophet, Seer, and Poet* (Salt Lake City: Deseret Book, 1982), 363–64. See also Daniel C. Peterson, *Abraham Divided* (Salt Lake City: Aspen Books, 1995), 4–6.

3. Bruce R. McConkie, *A New Witness for the Articles of Faith* (Salt Lake City: Deseret Book, 1985), 527.

4. Joseph Fielding Smith, *Answers to Gospel Questions* (Salt Lake City: Deseret Book, 1960), 3:153.

5. For more on Orson Hyde's background, see B. H. Roberts, ed., *History of The Church of Jesus Christ of Latter-day Saints,* 7 vols., 2nd ed. rev. (Salt Lake City: Deseret Book, 1949), 2:240, 283; 4:12 (hereafter cited as *HC*). Orson Hyde, "History of Orson Hyde," *Millennial Star,* November 19, 1864, 742, 744; Marvin Sidney Hill, "An Historical Study of the Life of Orson Hyde, 1805–1852" (master's thesis, Brigham Young University, 1955), 4–9; Andrew Jenson, *Latter-day Saint Biographical Encyclopedia* (Salt Lake City: Andrew Jenson Company, 1901), 1:80–83; "Orson Hyde," *The Utah Genealogical and Historical Magazine* 4 (April 1913): 53–64; Howard Baron, *Orson Hyde* (Salt Lake City: Horizon, 1977); Myrtle S. Hyde, *Orson Hyde: The Olive Branch of Israel* (Salt Lake City: Agreka Books, 2000), 3–65.

6. *HC,* 4:375. See also Nephi L. Morris, *Prophecies of Joseph Smith and Their Fulfilment* (Salt Lake City: Deseret Book, 1926), 261; and David B. Galbraith, D. Kelly Ogden, and Andrew C. Skinner, *Jerusalem, the Eternal City* (Salt Lake City: Deseret Book, 1996), 331.

7. *HC,* 4:201–2.

8. *HC,* 4:455; See also Orson Hyde, *A Sketch of the Travels and Ministry of Elder Orson Hyde* (Salt Lake City: Deseret News, 1869), 27.

9. Hyde, *Sketch,* 7.

10. Ibid., 16.

11. Ibid.

12. Ibid., 32.

13. Ibid., 18.

14. Ibid.

15. We have visited the building that was once the Latin Convent. In the 1840s it served, in part, as a hostel for pilgrims visiting Jerusalem. The building still stands, but it is no longer a hostel. However, there is a door there that may very well date back to the 1840s into which some visitors carved their names or initials. Just beneath the keyhole on this door is carved the name HYDE in large block print. It may be that Orson Hyde left his signature on the door, as so many other pilgrims had done before him.

16. Hyde, *Sketch,* 12.

17. Ibid., 13.

18. Ibid., 14.

19. Ibid., 19.

20. Ibid., 28–29; see also *HC,* 4:456.

21. Ibid., 29–32; see also *HC,* 4:456–59.

22. Ibid., 32.

23. Jenni and Westermann, *Theological Lexicon of the Old Testament,* 2:838–46.

24. *HC,* 4:459.

25. *Times and Seasons,* vol. 1, no. 10, August 1840, 156–57.

26. *HC,* 4:128–29.

27. Zora J. Smith, *Ancestry, Biography, and Family of George A. Smith* (Provo, UT: Brigham Young University Press, 1962), 249.

28. This letter is found in *Correspondence of Palestine Tourists* (Salt Lake City: Deseret News Steam Printing Establishment, 1875), 1–2. This book was compiled by Eliza R. Snow and contains letters written by George A. Smith, Lorenzo Snow, Paul A. Schettler, and Eliza R. Snow as they traveled through America, Europe, Asia, and Africa in the years 1872 and 1873. See also B. H. Roberts, *A Comprehensive History of The Church of Jesus Christ of Latter-day Saints,* 6 vols. (Salt Lake City: Deseret News Press, 1930), 5:474–75. See also Eliza R. Snow, *Biography and Family Record of Lorenzo Snow* (Salt Lake City: Deseret News Company, 1884), 496 97.

29. Lorenzo Snow, in *Tourists,* 203.

30. Lorenzo Snow reported that they planned to stay in the Holy Land for approximately four weeks and that travel within Palestine would be done entirely upon horseback until January 19, 1873. See Paul Schettler, *Tourists,* 146; see also 120.

31. Paul Schettler, in *Tourists,* 209.

32. Lorenzo Snow, in *Tourists,* 203.

33. Journal of George A. Smith, 1873, 4, LDS Church Archives.

34. This detail is found in the Journals of Albert Carrington, March 2, 1873, LDS Church Archives. It can also be found in Zora J. Smith, *Ancestry, Biography, and Family of George A. Smith,* 252.

35. *Millennial Star,* April 1, 1873, 201. See also Eliza R. Snow, in *Tourists,* 260.

36. Journal of George A. Smith, 1873, 4.

37. Eliza R. Snow, in *Tourists,* 260.

38. *Journal of Discourses,* ed. George D. Watt, 26 vols. (Liverpool: F. D. Richards, 1855), 16:102.

39. *Millennial Star,* April 1, 1873, 201.

40. Ezra Sampson, "George A. Smith," *The Contributor,* vol. 4, May 1885, 312.

41. B. H. Roberts, "The Rise and Fall of Nauvoo," *The Contributor,* vol. 8, March 1887, 162.

42. *Millennial Star,* April 1, 1873, 201.

43. Journals of Albert Carrington, March 2, 1873.

44. George A. Smith, in *Tourists,* 225.

45. *Journal of Discourses,* 16:88.

46. Eliza R. Snow, in *Tourists,* 261.

47. Ibid., 379.

CHAPTER TWO

The Pioneering Years of the Turkish Mission

1884–1890

The advent of Latter-day Saint missionaries in the Near East is a chapter in Church history replete with revelation, miracles, and manifestations—fulfilling the teachings of ancient and modern prophets. Missionaries for the Church did not formally enter the Holy Land, however, until 1884, approximately eleven years after the 1873 dedication. However, the story does not begin in Jerusalem, Jaffa, or Haifa—but, rather, in Constantinople (now known as Istanbul).

In the late nineteenth century, Constantinople was the capital of the crumbling Ottoman Empire. At the peak of the empire's prowess in the sixteenth century, there would have been little toleration for Western cultural infusions within the capital city. However, as the empire declined, the "sick man of Europe" began to look to the West as a source of vitality and new life. Ottoman officials were sent to Europe for training in language, warfare, science, medicine, and economics. More and more Europeans found a niche in the Ottoman capital serving as intermediaries between the Ottomans and everything Western. By the time the first Latter-day Saint missionary arrived in Constantinople in 1884, there was a significant European Christian population, and it was among these people that the Latter-day Saint missionaries proselytized.

Because the Ottoman Empire was an Islamic dynasty, missionary work within its borders was, at best, challenging. However, during the nineteenth century the Church would often promote proselytizing efforts wherever an interest was expressed and the resources were available to organize a missionary force. Nevertheless, the creation of a mission within the borders of the predominantly Islamic empire may have been the boldest proselytizing undertaking since the organization of the Church in 1830.

Even so, the Latter-day Saints were not the first Western missionaries to preach Christianity in the empire. Protestant missionaries were laboring there as early as 1820. By the end of the nineteenth century, they had established churches, primary schools, universities, and hospitals in many different areas.[1] But Christians were still not treated on equal terms with their Muslim counterparts. Religious affairs for non-Muslims were administered through a "millet system" that required all citizens to deal with the government through a formally recognized religious organization. If one's religion was not recognized by the Ottoman government, that person was subject to higher taxes, loss of employment, limitation of education, and even imprisonment. Although the Protestants had gained recognition in 1850, the Latter-day Saints had not. Consequently, new converts to the Church remained under the direct control of their former religious leaders, who were often prone to make life miserable for them through a variety of persecutions and penalties.[2] One Latter-day Saint mission president who served under this millet system explained that individuals

> who had been thus converted were at once ostracized, excommunicated and condemned by their mother church, they did not only lose all their civil and religious rights, the rights of Christian burial and the protection of the law, but were made the target of bitter persecution, having no religious head to represent them at the seat of government, they became outlaws.[3]

Furthermore, publishing religious tracts was illegal, and travel to the interior of the country was frequently stifled or entirely forbidden. In Constantinople, the missionaries could teach the gospel to the Europeans and Armenians, but they were not allowed free access to the Muslims. This was agreeable, since the primary thrust of the missionary effort was directed toward Christians.

Not long after the first missionaries labored in Constantinople, it became evident that success in the sprawling city would be limited. The work gradually shifted from people in the large cities of the coastal region to the Armenian Christians in cities in central Turkey and northern Syria, such as Sivas, Aintab, Marash (Maras), and Aleppo. On occasion, missionaries would travel to Palestine and preach primarily among European immigrants in Haifa, Jaffa, and Jerusalem. The remainder of this chapter will describe these introductory missionary efforts in the Near East.

JACOB SPORI AND THE ADVENT OF THE TURKISH MISSION

In 1884, Elder John Henry Smith of the Quorum of the Twelve Apostles was serving as president of the European Mission, headquartered in Liverpool, England. He received correspondence from Hagop T. Vartooguian, an Armenian living in Constantinople, who had investigated Mormonism on his own. Vartooguian wrote to President Smith in hopes that Latter-day Saint elders would be sent to Constantinople so that he might join the Church.[4] President Smith received word from President John Taylor to call upon Elder Jacob Spori, who had recently arrived from Utah in the Swiss-German Mission, to travel to Constantinople and introduce the gospel into Turkey.[5]

Jacob Spori was a large man. He stood "six foot three in his stocking feet and had an average weight of 200 pounds."[6] His faith, however, was even larger than his frame. He was born in the Swiss village of Oberwil on March 26, 1847. A man of letters, he studied extensively and was a gifted linguist, mastering ten different languages in his lifetime.[7] He married his sweetheart, Magdalena Roschi, on September 16, 1875, and shortly thereafter accepted the principalship of his alma mater, the high school at Oberwil, while also being appointed as auditor, assessor, and treasurer of the canton of Bern in

Switzerland.[8] At twenty-eight years old, Jacob Spori had attained positions of trust and prominence that few attain during a lifetime. He represented Switzerland's finest.

Jacob Spori and his wife, Magdalena Roschi, on their wedding day, September 16, 1875.

While studying at Heidelberg University, Jacob Spori met a fellow Lutheran named Karl G. Maeser. The two academicians discussed the absence of the fullness of the gospel of Jesus Christ on earth. Later, while Spori was visiting Florence, Italy, he received a parcel from Brother Maeser containing a book with a note scrawled on the inside cover: "This is the Truth."[9] Upon close inspection of this Book of Mormon, Jacob Spori firmly believed it was true and sought baptism at the hands of the Latter-day Saint elders.

Enormous pressures bore upon Spori in an effort to dissuade him from joining the Church. But no degree of compulsion could keep him from following his heartfelt promptings, and finally Jacob Spori was baptized. Although the school system in Oberwil was technically separate from religious interests, it was still viewed as an outgrowth of the community's religious values. While greatly respected as a scholar and thinker, Spori now belonged to a foreign church whose beliefs led to what many considered a conflict of interest: he could not simultaneously be a Latter-day Saint and the leader of the local educational system. Therefore, he was ultimately relieved of his duties as school principal, and his contract was not renewed.[10] Over time, he also lost his civic positions because of his new faith.[11]

Jacob Spori was jobless but still had his wife and children by his side. Eventually, he felt impressed to join the Saints in Utah. He was alone in his feelings, however, and when he finally left for Zion in 1879, Magdalena chose not to accompany him. Instead, she took the children to live with her parents.[12] He left Switzerland alone in 1879 to travel to Utah, although he maintained contact with his wife and children.[13]

In September 1884, Jacob Spori was called to serve in the Swiss-German Mission.[14] After a short layover in England, he was granted permission to travel to Switzerland to be reunited with his family for a time. He spent several weeks with his wife and children before he began his missionary service. During that time, he baptized Magdalena, his most important convert.[15]

Jacob Spori, the first Latter-day Saint missionary to serve in the Near East.

After his two-and-a-half-year mission, Spori rejoined Magdalena and their children and led a group of Latter-day Saint emigrants to Utah, sailing from England on May 26, 1888.[16] Spori was eventually appointed to serve as the first principal of a new academy that would later become Ricks College, now known as Brigham Young University–Idaho. From the day that the academy opened on November 12, 1888, until the day of his death on September 27, 1903, Jacob Spori was a pioneer in education in southeastern Idaho.[17]

The faith and devotion Elder Spori manifested throughout his life would serve him well as he became the first authorized servant of the Lord to preach the gospel in the Near East in modern times.[18] Upon his arrival in Constantinople on Wednesday, December 31, 1884, Elder Spori proceeded to locate Hagop Vartooguian, whom he described as an elderly looking gentleman, middle sized, little gray, clear hazel eyes, brown beard, red cap, clean clothing, deliberate in speech, quiet in motion, very well posted in history and the different religious denominations, speaks Turkish and Armenian fluently, pretty good English and some French.[19]

During their first meeting, Elder Spori suggested that he sleep in a corner of Hagop's home rather than spend the equivalent of one dollar per day at a hotel. Since the Vartooguians were a family of little means, Spori would use the dollar saved to feed himself and the entire Vartooguian family. Hagop agreed with Elder Spori, and then the two men knelt and had a Spirit-filled prayer together. Later that day, Hagop requested baptism at the earliest possible moment for himself, his wife, and two of his children who had reached baptismal age.[20] Elder Spori and the Vartooguians became quick friends as he taught the family the gospel, and after a short time the family was baptized. Brother Vartooguian served temporarily as Elder Spori's missionary companion and language tutor.

Armenia and Its People

To better understand Hagop Vartooguian and his Armenian contemporaries in the Ottoman Empire, it would be helpful to know something of the Armenian geography and culture.[21] Armenia is a mountainous region lying southeast of the Black Sea and southwest of the Caspian Sea. Its diverse geography results in a harsh and rigorous climate.[22] Politically, the Armenian people have always been challenged, as Armenia has served as a crossroads for conquerors down through the ages. Nevertheless, the Armenian people have managed to maintain a national and ethnic spirit of their own.

In A.D. 276, Armenian ruler Prince Tiridates converted to Christianity, causing Armenia to be the first nation to embrace Christianity en masse.[23] Thus, the Armenian Church is one of the longest-standing branches of Christianity. Even so, Armenia is geographically removed from the holy cities of Christianity in Palestine and Europe. Of this island of Christianity, one writer noted that the Armenians "were a people without a country; the only Christians without a useful proximity to Christendom; scattered and industrious and frequently poor, debarred by their faith and customs from full Ottoman citizenship, but lacking champions abroad."[24]

In the 1830s, Protestant missionaries, mainly from the American Board of Commissioners for Foreign Missions, first approached the Armenian people. Their intent was to stimulate fresh life in the Armenian Church rather than to convert members to Protestantism. Hence, they translated the Bible into the vernacular and opened schools for the Armenian children. Conservatives in the Armenian Church were troubled by this outside intrusion, and in 1846 the Armenian patriarch in Constantinople excommunicated members who followed the foreign missionaries. As a result, evangelical churches were formed to accommodate those who had been cut off. Latter-day Saint missionaries worked almost exclusively among these peoples. By the time Latter-day Saint missionaries began their work in the 1880s, the tensions between the Armenian Church and these evangelical churches were, to some degree, relieved.[25]

Elder Spori reported that the Armenians were "tall and powerful, with dark eyes and hair, and they are intelligent. My impression is that the Spirit of God is working with them."[26] Although many Armenians had ascended to important positions in banking and business in Constantinople, most worked as weavers in the large but antiquated textile industry in the inland cities. Generally, they lived very modest, if not impoverished, lives. Altogether, there were approximately two million Armenians in the Ottoman Empire when Jacob Spori arrived in 1885.

Missionary Work in Constantinople

The first meeting of The Church of Jesus Christ of Latter-day Saints in Turkey was held in Constantinople at the Vartooguian home on Sunday, January 18, 1885. Although both preached, Elder Spori remarked in his journal that "Brother Vartooguian has been a preacher and is still full of old sectarian notions."[27] Unfortunately, as time passed, Hagop Vartooguian became less and less enthusiastic about the gospel and ultimately apostatized.[28]

This left Elder Spori companionless. However, because his residence was in Pera, a veritable melting pot of European peoples located on the European side of Constantinople, he could often speak their languages, and when he couldn't, he took lessons to learn. In fact, giving and taking language lessons was an important medium by which Jacob Spori met people.[29]

In time, Elder Spori became better known in the community; this exposure led to a wide variety of missionary experiences, both positive and negative. For example, a woman in her seventies was very ill. Her body was swollen excessively on one side, and she was pale and in great pain. Her family had hired all the doctors and priests in the area, all of whom were perplexed by her condition and had basically left her to die. An elderly woman recommended to the family that they call for the Latter-day Saint missionary, explaining that if he were to pray over her, she would rise up from her bed and walk. Elder Spori was summoned immediately.

On April 7, 1885, Elder Spori paid a visit to the sick woman. With great anticipation, the family members asked, "Can you do anything for our poor grandma?" Elder Spori explained that he could pray over her but that he seldom administered to people who were not members of the Church. However, their pleadings moved Elder Spori, and he administered to her. Three days later he visited the woman and found her much improved.[30] After another three days, on April 13, 1885, the old woman was out of her bed and was perfectly well. Of this healing Spori wrote: "This result caused a veritable Turkish astonishment. A doctor called upon her to convince himself, and she told him a few words for which the Lord will bless her."[31]

This miracle and others assisted Elder Spori in spreading the gospel and was partially responsible for the many friends he made in Constantinople. Some of these friends would not only defend Elder Spori but would also defend his Latter-day Saint faith. Such was the case with Haritioun Mavian. At one point a group of Methodists was secretly spreading rumors that misrepresented Elder Spori and the Latter-day Saints. To a degree, their lies were successful in drawing away a few from Elder Spori's preaching. However, Elder Spori noted that Haritioun Mavian's soul was expanded by the Spirit of the Lord, causing him to defend the doctrines of the Church "manfully, regardless of the trying consequences under which he thereby place[d] himself."[32]

Jacob Spori also became fast friends with a Russian couple who had come to Constantinople after being expelled from their homeland. Elder Spori taught the couple, and the woman was particularly moved by the doctrine of eternal marriage. These doctrines worked upon her heart so powerfully that she became a strong advocate for the restored gospel and defended the Church in numerous settings, as Mavian had. Elder Spori reported her saying, "I am acquainted with one of the Mormons; he is a friend of my husband, and I see nothing wrong in his talk nor behavior, and if there is a true Church, then it must be this." Elder Spori ended his account of the woman's zeal by writing: "What a happy thought to be a Mormon missionary!"[33]

In contrast to these examples, however, people were more frequently ambivalent toward the truth; over time, Spori found this response taxing on his nerves and frustrating to his spirit.[34] One man told him, "I know you Mormons are closer to the truth than all other preachers; but as I have stolen no oxen, nor committed murder, I think I can stand the chance as well as the rest without being baptized."[35]

Opposition greeted Elder Spori at every turn. The following examples illustrate not only this adversity but also the integrity, honor, and Christlike example that Elder Spori displayed before the Christian people of Constantinople.

In April 1885, at about the same time as the miraculous healing of the old woman, Elder Spori was asked to help interview some young French ladies from the Scutari Institute because of his fluency in their language. Spori related that he was directly warned by a feeling to beware of the engagement, and he responded that he would "be happy to meet these ladies, only they must bring their fathers, brothers or teachers with them." As it turned out, the whole arrangement was a trap set by several Protestant ministers in the area looking to create a damning scandal in the life of a scandal-free man.

Another example occurred later that year. A group of men were proselytizing in the area, claiming to be Latter-day Saint missionaries. They would knock on people's doors, declare their faith as "Mormons," preach a sermon, and then request financial alms to help the great Latter-day Saint work roll on. One woman whom they contacted shared her experience with Elder Spori's Russian defender, mentioned previously. She immediately identified the men as impostors, explaining that "they cannot be Mormons; there is only one here and he asks no alms." And as is so often the outcome with opposition, the woman then requested an audience with the real Latter-day Saint missionary, Elder Jacob Spori.[36]

A third example relates to a German newspaper in Constantinople, the *Berliner Tagblatt,* which printed an article that Elder Spori described as "most bitter and fiendish" and that "bore its fruits for a while"; in fact, he was still refuting it in public discourse almost one year after its publication.[37] At the close of one such meeting, one reporter explained that "we never saw the accusations against you Mormons denied, so we took them for true, but we are glad to hear the other side also!"[38] An editor of another newspaper was so favorably impressed that he printed a report of the evening's events with the following introduction: "As we have published several rumors and accusations against the Mormon people, we deem it right to publish the following sketch also."[39] Hence, slowly but surely, the honest in heart began to recognize the uprightness of the Mormons.

A New Companion

After serving as the first and only Latter-day Saint missionary in the Near East for eleven months, Elder Spori was joined in Constantinople by Elder Joseph M. Tanner on Sunday, December 6, 1885. Because Elder Tanner had an incorrect address for the residence of his new companion, he did not find Elder Spori for almost two whole days. Their rendezvous was a joyous one—Elder Tanner was no longer lost in a large city, and Elder Spori was no longer the only active Latter-day Saint in Constantinople.[40] The elders quickly secured a room in the German section of Pera, where they held small meetings and received calls throughout the day.[41]

In addition to their teaching responsibilities, the missionaries also traveled about to determine potential fields of labor for the near and distant future. As part of this ongoing inquiry, Joseph Tanner left Constantinople in the spring of 1886 with Elder Francis M. Lyman of the Quorum of the Twelve Apostles for Greece, Egypt, and Palestine.[42] A significant result of this tour would be Elder Spori's eventual assignment to preach the gospel in Palestine.

When Elder Lyman and Elder Tanner arrived in Palestine, which was controlled by Ottoman authority, they encountered nine colonies of German immigrants known as *Tempelgesellschaft* (Temple Society). These Christians believed themselves to be the beginning of the foreseen redemption of the promised land and felt that, as a people, their goodness constituted a divine temple—hence their common name, Templers.[43] They abolished the priesthood, the sacrament, and other holy ordinances because they recognized that they lacked authority and therefore could not be in line with the commandments of the Savior.[44] Perceived as apostates from the Protestant Church, they fled persecution in Germany and moved to Palestine in hopes of establishing a small-scale "Kingdom of God" on earth.[45]

Joseph M. Tanner

Unfortunately, due to their successful vineyards, some Templers became drunkards, and as a result, disunity arose among the colonists, causing the more exemplary members to look elsewhere for spiritual guidance in 1886. They were like the 1830 "seekers" in America, who were also searching for the full gospel organization as described in the New Testament—a group which included such converts to the Church as Brigham Young, Heber C. Kimball, Parley P. Pratt, Sidney Rigdon, and Wilford Woodruff.[46] Generally speaking, these individuals would worship God with the religious denomination where they felt most comfortable but were ultimately waiting for a fullness of the gospel. Elders Lyman and Tanner felt that there were promising possibilities among these German colonists in Palestine.[47]

On May 2, 1886, Elder Tanner was back in Constantinople. He and Elder Spori discussed the possibility of leaving Constantinople to preach among the Germans in Palestine. They decided that the move would be prudent, but they struggled to know in which German settlement the work should begin. During these considerations, they corresponded with Daniel H. Wells, president of the European Mission, and on June 29, 1886, President Wells sent written approval authorizing the elders to labor among the German colonists in Palestine.[48]

Money was scarce for the missionaries, and it became obvious that only one of them would be able to make the trip. After a prayerful night, strong impressions came to Elder Tanner that Elder Spori should undertake the mission. The next morning, Elder Tanner turned to his companion and asked him how he felt about the hardships he would surely encounter as the first Latter-day Saint missionary in the Holy Land. A smile crossed Elder Spori's face, and he said:

> I had a vision in the night and was told to begin my labors in the town of Haifa. In this vision I saw a man with a short coal black beard. He was a blacksmith and as I passed his shop he came out to meet me. I was further told that he would be notified of my coming and that he and his family should be prepared to receive me and to receive the message I had for them. I shall know the man if ever I see him.[49]

Elder Spori left Constantinople on July 29, 1886, and arrived in Haifa on August 16, 1886.[50] Upon his arrival, Jacob Spori made his way through the streets of the city. Although he had never been to Haifa, he was able to find the exact street he had seen in his vision. As he walked down that street, he could hear the ringing of an anvil. Staying his course in the middle of the road, he continued walking until he was directly outside the door of a blacksmith's shop, where the owner, Johann Georg Grau, was working. Grau looked up from his work to see the Latter-day Saint missionary standing in the street and immediately dropped his hammer and tongs and raced to the side of Jacob Spori as if he were a long-lost friend. The night before, Grau had received a dream from God wherein he was shown that this very missionary would share a divine message with his family. Johann Georg Grau took Jacob Spori to his home and treated him very well.[51]

The visions of both men were fulfilled as Jacob Spori taught the restored gospel of Jesus Christ to the Grau family. On Sunday, August 29,

1886, Johann was baptized by Elder Spori at Haifa in the Bay of Acre.[52] This was the first modern authorized baptism in the Holy Land. On September 3, 1886, Brother Grau received the Melchizedek Priesthood and was ordained to the office of elder, and later that month, he baptized his wife, Magdalena Frey Grau.[53] Both were anxious to spread the message of their newfound faith.

PREACHING IN THE COASTAL CITIES AND JERUSALEM

Shortly after Magdalena's baptism, Jacob Spori extended what he called "necessary instructions" to Johann Georg Grau and then left for Jaffa, Gaza, and Jerusalem.[54] With less than one month of experience in the Church, Grau became the presiding authority of the Church in Haifa. Jacob Spori's departure is an indication of his faith in the Grau family, as well as his determination to teach the gospel throughout Palestine.

Elder Spori vigorously sought opportunities to preach among Europeans in Palestine, such as the Templers, as well as the Arab peoples of the land. In fact, Joseph Tanner had great hopes that Elder Spori's missionary work in Palestine would open a great avenue to the conversion of the Arab population that generally adhered to the tenets of Islam.[55] President John Taylor, however, countered any thought of taking the gospel to the Jewish people prior to the Second Coming. This stance was clearly expressed by John Taylor's predecessor, Brigham Young. One example of his teachings on the subject occurred twenty years prior to Elder Spori's mission to Palestine. Speaking to the Saints in the Tabernacle on December 23, 1866, President Brigham Young said:

> We do not want [the Jews] to believe our doctrine. . . . We have a great desire for their welfare, and are looking for the time soon to come when they will gather to Jerusalem, build up the city and the land of Palestine, and prepare for the coming of the Messiah. . . . When the Savior visits Jerusalem, and the Jews look upon him, and see the wounds in his hands and in his side and in his feet, they will then know that they have persecuted and put to death the true Messiah, and then they will acknowledge him, but not till then.[56]

While not all presidents of the Church have shared this opinion—and it certainly is not the doctrinal stance of the Church today—given President Brigham Young's instructions at the time, it should come as no surprise to find minimal missionary contact between Elder Spori and the Jews living in Palestine in 1886.[57]

Jacob Spori did seek opportunities to teach the Arabs, and he traveled up and down the Mediterranean coast from Haifa to Gaza. In Ashdod, the Arab citizens listened to Elder Spori with great interest, and many claimed to see in Mormonism the fulfillment of prophecies found in the Koran.[58] From Ashdod, Elder Spori traveled to Gaza and then back to Jaffa. He traveled alone, on foot, and sometimes at night. In all of these travels along the coastline, he was treated very well and was consistently fed by the local Arabs, who occasionally gave him rest from walking by offering their camels for him to ride on.[59]

From Jaffa he departed for Jerusalem, which in 1886 was a thinly populated city of 25,000. The census of the day identifies 13,000 Muslims, 8,000 Christians, and 4,000 Jews.[60] Spori preached among the Europeans and met with the leaders of the German Templer Society, who treated him very kindly. They had fond recollections of entertaining President George A. Smith some thirteen years earlier in 1873,[61] but in response to Elder Spori's invitations to join the Church, the Templers explained:

> We could not become Mormons thus far; for we cannot believe in the appearance of angels. We did away with baptism, as nobody seems to be worthy of administering this ordinance, and we consider a person should show evidence first that he really wants to serve God before he receives baptism. But we know that the Mormons have good principles and that they are badly misrepresented; we do not despise you.[62]

From Jerusalem Elder Spori traveled back to Jaffa, where people witnessed marvelous signs in the heavens. He recorded that "not far from Jaffa wonderful signs were seen one afternoon by many people. Soldiers and horsemen were seen in the air." This was not unlike the experience of Heber C. Kimball, Brigham Young, and others who beheld great wonders in the skies over Mendon, New York, on September 22, 1827. They beheld mighty armies engaged in battle in the heavens and believed it was a sign from the Almighty that a new gospel order was to be introduced to the world prior to the coming of the Son of Man. Interestingly, that manifestation occurred on the same night that Moroni appeared to Joseph Smith to inform him about the Nephite record buried in the Hill Cumorah.[63] This precedent may imply that the hosts of eternity not only were anxious for the gospel to be preached again in the Holy Land but also were allowed to heighten the interest of the honest in heart through signs in the heavens. Elder Spori felt that there was a great spirit of investigation brooding over Palestine at this time.[64] Without question, as Jacob Spori traveled and preached throughout the region, he was encouraged and felt that his prospects for success were fair.

On December 13, 1886, Elder Spori traveled to Beirut to spread the gospel, before returning to Haifa. Truth continued to gain a firmer foothold in Haifa; in fact, during Jacob Spori's absence, one person was baptized into the Church. As the work progressed, Elder Spori declared that "many are getting the conviction that Mormonism is a growing power not to be overthrown any more."[65]

Before leaving Haifa, Spori baptized German-born Maria Siebel on January 3, 1887, another indication that Spori preached primarily among the Germans in Palestine.[66] In fact, Jacob Spori had introduced the gospel in every German community in Palestine.[67] After five months in the Holy Land, he departed for Constantinople to rejoin Elder Tanner.

MISCHA MARKOW

Mischa Markow was single, thirty-two years old, and searching for the Church of Christ as described in the New Testament.[68] Deeply religious in temperament, he was haunted by the fact that he did not possess the fullness that Christianity surely offered. He traveled to the Holy Land seeking spiritual rejuvenation, and from there he drifted to Alexandria, Egypt, where he opened a barber shop. Here, a messenger of the Lord appeared to Mischa in a night dream and communicated a very clear message: he was to sell his barber shop immediately and sail on the next available ship bound for Constantinople.

Mischa Markow had great faith in the dream and followed the messenger's instructions to the letter. In fact, as he purchased passage on the next steamer to Constantinople, the ticket agent tried vigorously to persuade Mischa to wait for the next ship, explaining that the

seas would be rough and the next steamer would provide a much more comfortable journey. When this reasoning failed, the ticket agent reduced the ticket price on the later voyage by half. Still, Mischa was unmoved. He boarded the vessel and sailed for Constantinople as planned with a scheduled stop at Jaffa, Palestine.

In Palestine, Jacob Spori boarded that very steamer early in January 1887 and was greeted by an animated argument between a group of Arabs and a young foreigner over the price of some small service that they had rendered.

Mischa Markow

Spori chose to intervene in order to protect the foreigner. When the scrap was settled, the grateful foreigner introduced himself to Spori as Mischa Markow and explained that he had just left Alexandria, Egypt, and was on his way to Constantinople. The two became fast friends, and Jacob Spori taught him the gospel in German throughout their voyage. Elder Spori held the fullness of truth that Mischa had longed for over the past several years.[69] He was baptized in the Marmara Sea on Tuesday, February 1, 1887, by Elder Ferdinand Hintze, who had recently arrived from Utah as the third missionary in the Turkish Mission.[70]

Elder Spori labored in Constantinople for three additional months until he received his release and began his journey home on March 23, 1887. Ferdinand Hintze recorded his high regard for Jacob Spori, explaining that he was "an honest and unassuming man, highly educated; yet he can adapt himself to all classes of people and to all kinds of circumstances. God bless him for the faithful labors he has performed."[71]

A FOREORDAINED COMPANIONSHIP

Following Jacob Spori's departure, Ferdinand Hintze and Joseph Tanner served as missionary companions for only eleven days while Elder Tanner prepared to journey to Palestine. However short their time together may have been, it was manifested to Elder Hintze that the companionship was inspired and foreordained. The following story illustrates.

On March 25, 1887, Elders Hintze and Tanner were greatly honored by being entertained by grand vizier Kamil Pasha, the second most powerful man in the Ottoman Empire. Because his home was situated on the banks of the Bosporus, the elders were required to journey there on a small paddleboat. The leader was kind and generally inquired about the beliefs and lifestyle of the Latter-day Saint people. The elders asked permission to present him with a copy of some of the standard works of the Church. He accepted their gift, and arrangements were made to formally present the books to Kamil Pasha at a later date.[72] Needless to say, he became a helpful acquaintance for the Saints.

Earlier in his life, while serving in a different mission, Elder Hintze had had a dream wherein he was shown a specific village that he would one day visit as a missionary, as well as the companion that would be serving with him. As the two elders traveled up the strait toward the home of the grand vizier, Elder Hintze realized that this was the village he had seen in his dream and that Elder Tanner was the very companion shown to him. Elder Hintze was left to conclude that "God had sent him; for this mission appeared contemplated by the powers above long before it was made known by the authorities here below."[73]

JOSEPH M. TANNER IN PALESTINE

On April 4, 1887, Joseph Tanner left Elder Hintze alone in Constantinople while he traveled to Palestine to continue Spori's efforts among the Templer colonists.[74] The spirit of investigation Elder Spori had witnessed in Palestine was reconfirmed during Elder Tanner's visit. While laboring in Palestine for five months, Joseph Tanner was responsible for nine people joining the Church.[75]

One of those nine converts was Friederich Dieterle. The stepson of Johann Georg Grau, Brother Dieterle went on to serve as a missionary in the Turkish Mission, laboring primarily in Aintab, Turkey (present-day Gaziantep). He played a key role in sustaining and adding stability to the fledgling Church in Palestine and Turkey and will be spoken of again later in this chapter.[76] With such individuals coming to the fold, it is no wonder that Elder Tanner referred to his time in Palestine as the happiest hours of his life.[77]

Elder Tanner had his fair share of adventure. Early one morning in 1887, he was traveling back to Jaffa with a new convert, a young man whom he had baptized the night before. They were confronted by a band of eight bedouin, who proceeded to rob them and treat them very roughly. Joseph explained that in the midst of the mugging, God softened the heart of one of the robbers, who stopped and defended the missionaries. This unknown bedouin used his strong arm to seize a lance that was about to be thrust at Elder Tanner and then proceeded to return some of the stolen items. As the skirmish ended, Joseph turned to his young companion and said "that notwithstanding our loss, I felt afterwards like singing for joy."[78]

On August 18, 1887, Joseph Tanner received his release as a missionary and spent the next three weeks preparing to depart for home. Finally, on September 6, 1887, Elder Tanner boarded a ship and left Palestine. But he was destined to return to the Near East.

When Elder Tanner left Palestine, the burden of leadership in the Near East rested solely on the shoulders of Ferdinand Hintze. From those early days spent alone, the Spirit moved Elder Hintze to labor among the Armenian people. He began learning Turkish and Armenian and had his testimony translated into Armenian and printed on Articles of Faith leaflets.[79] These efforts blossomed into full-time service among these people—his vigor and persistence among them eventually earned him the title of Father of the Armenian and Turkish Missions.[80]

Ferdinand Friis Hintze Continues the Work

Like Jacob Spori, Ferdinand Hintze was a giant of a man. He was powerfully built and stood six feet four inches tall. Born in Roskilde, Denmark, on May 13, 1854, he was baptized on his eighth birthday and emigrated to Utah with his parents at age ten. Prior to his labors in the Near East, Ferdinand Hintze filled missions to Nebraska and Iowa (1877–78); Michigan, Illinois, Iowa, and Nebraska (1879–80); and Scandinavia (1885–86). Following his mission to Scandinavia, Hintze was called to travel to Turkey, where he joined Joseph Tanner and Jacob Spori in January 1887. Later that year he was called as president of the Turkish Mission (1887–90)—serving a total of five missions in his lifetime. He directed the translation of the Book of Mormon and portions of the Doctrine and Covenants into the Turkish language. During his second mission to Turkey, Hintze traveled to Palestine with Elder Anthon H. Lund of the Twelve and rededicated it for the gathering of Judah and Israel (see appendix E).

Ferdinand Friis Hintze introduced the restored gospel to the Armenian people.

Ferdinand Hintze was strong willed and very confident. Both traits would prove essential in his pioneering efforts as the mission president in Turkey. He had four wives and thirty-two children. He would die at age seventy-three on March 9, 1928.[81]

Elder Hintze faced formidable challenges in Turkey. Previous converts such as Hagop T. Vartooguian had become quite inactive, which meant that Elder Hintze was left to work alone.[82] Nevertheless, on May 17, 1887, Ferdinand Hintze baptized a one-legged man named Hohannes Minasian.[83] The day after the baptism, Elder Hintze noted that Hohannes was frustrated that his leg had not been miraculously restored. Hintze was quick to point out that "the Lord had not promised any such signs."[84]

On September 1, 1887, Elder Hintze received word from Elder George Teasdale, an Apostle and president of the European Mission, that Elder Joseph Tanner had been released. In this letter Elder Hintze also received his formal calling to preside over the Turkish Mission.[85]

President Teasdale's letter indicated continued concern on the part of Church leaders for the Turkish Mission. After acknowledging some of the difficulties faced by Hintze, such as frustrations in preaching in Constantinople and a severe lack of monetary support, President Teasdale promised that he would send a considerable number of publications and scriptures to be used in Constantinople. These would come at a substantial monetary sacrifice the mission could not logically justify. President Teasdale then explained:

> If I did not have any faith in the mission I certainly should not think of taking the course I am. I stand by it and pray for its success. I feel you have a peculiar situation and my sympathies are with you. You are a servant of God and you have the word of the Lord unto that people and if they reject you they will reject God who sent you. You are not on your own business you are on His and as your fellow servant I am aiding all I can for the accomplishment of His purposes. God bless you, my dear brother. Be faithful [and] seek earnestly the revelations of the Father to guide and direct you and He will do so.[86]

President Teasdale's support was important, because the Turkish Mission was not proving to be a productive field of labor. The Ottoman government generally refused to allow any Latter-day Saint tracts to be published, and many of the tracts President Hintze did possess were confiscated by state officials. Although Hintze was progressing in his fluency, the language was still a significant barrier. Very few visitors called to discuss the gospel; the mission was destitute, largely because many converts immediately emigrated to Zion; and President Hintze was mostly alone in his labors. Almost a year after his arrival in Constantinople, President Hintze became somewhat displeased with the mission's lack of progress.

Near the end of 1887, President Teasdale transferred Elder George Clove of Payson, Utah, from Copenhagen to Constantinople to join President Hintze. Elder Clove was twenty-one years old, well educated, and anxious to shoulder some of the burdens that had been borne exclusively by the president.[87] His companionship and assistance became invaluable to President Hintze.

On August 21, 1888, President Hintze received a letter from President Teasdale containing twenty pounds sterling (one hundred dollars) and directions for Hintze to travel to the Holy Land and labor for a time.[88] One purpose of the journey was to proselytize. In fact, the German colonists had been requesting missionaries for months.[89] Brother Grau was busy upholding the Church in Haifa. His wife, Magdalena, had died on May 5, 1888,[90] leaving him alone; but he continued to preach, and on May 31, he baptized a woman named Aleyzandera Levonava at Haifa. A success like this seemed to justify further missionary activity in Palestine. A second purpose for the journey stemmed out of the first. If missionaries were to be sent to Palestine in the future, then President Hintze needed to acquire a better feel for what their needs would be during a full-time proselytizing experience in the Holy Land.[91]

Hintze left for Palestine a mere eight days after receiving President Teasdale's directive. However, during that eight days President Hintze and Elder Clove baptized Demetri G. Sarafoff and Marer Seferian. President Hintze baptized both men and confirmed Brother Sarafoff, while Elder Clove confirmed Brother Seferian.[92] The following Sunday, both men were ordained to the Aaronic Priesthood.

President Hintze left Constantinople on August 29, 1888.[93] However, he did not arrive in Palestine until late December 1888. For Ferdinand Hintze, the road to Palestine went through Sivas, a city of central Turkey.

BOUND FOR PALESTINE VIA SIVAS

Leaving Constantinople, Hintze sailed the Black Sea on the French steamship *Anatolia* on August 29, 1888.[94] After two days at sea, he landed at Samsun on the thirty-first and started the five-day journey inland toward Sivas. These travels were done by team in company with a Kurd and a Turk. The journey took them through Amasya and Tokat, and they arrived in Sivas on September 12, 1888.[95]

The primary reason President Hintze was traveling through Sivas was a man named Dekran Shahabian. In the latter part of 1887, Hintze had preached the gospel to Dekran in Constantinople. Dekran had been favorably impressed but had not joined the Church at that time. Later, in June 1888, Hintze had received a letter from Dekran. Elder Hintze had noted in the mission record:

> I received my first letter in the Turkish language, but Armenian
> characters. It was written by a man at Sivas, in the interior of
> Asia Minor, by the name of Dekran Shahabian. He was here
> some time ago to see me and was very favorably impressed with
> what I said and now has written me a letter wherein he gives me
> an invitation to come to Sivas to learn the language and teach
> him the gospel.[96]

The invitation would prove to be significant in the mission of
Ferdinand Hintze and for the Church in the Near East for several
reasons. First, Elder Hintze was struggling to learn the Turkish and
Armenian languages, so an offer to be taught and tutored on a
personal basis seemed heaven sent. Second, this invitation ultimately
took Hintze into the interior of Turkey, where he would become
successful in finding converts. Additionally, circumstances would arise
in 1889 that created a need for these Turkish Armenian Saints to have
a direct connection with the Holy Land; as a result, Ferdinand Hintze
would eventually propose a Mormon colony in Palestine as a gathering place for persecuted Armenians. All these events would be insti-
gated by the invitation to Sivas.

When President Hintze arrived in Sivas, Dekran was there to
greet him "with a kiss and every demonstration of love and respect
and took him to his home."[97] After two days of instruction from
President Hintze, Dekran Shahabian and his wife, Lucia, were
baptized on September 14, 1888. On the sixteenth, Hintze blessed
the Shahabians' two children and ordained Dekran a priest.[98]

President Hintze was eager to introduce the gospel to all of central
Anatolia. He began preaching with vigor. Ten days after the first two
baptisms in Sivas, a schoolteacher named Haig Jevahirdjian joined the
Church. Haig would later become Hintze's scribe as Hintze translated
the Book of Mormon and Doctrine and Covenants into Turkish.[99]
After so little success in coastal cities such as Constantinople, it was
exhilarating for Ferdinand Hintze to be preaching to congregations of
over one hundred. These congregations and investigators were mostly
Armenians. During this visit, he lived with Dekran, and there was
hardly a moment when some interested soul was not knocking at the
Shahabians' door in search of the Latter-day Saint missionary.

Thirty-six miles east of Sivas was the village of Zara. President Hintze and Dekran felt impressed to travel to Zara and introduce the gospel. Hintze ordained Dekran an elder, and later the two departed on their journey. Although they were in Zara for only ten days, they were able to baptize two men as a result of divine manifestations.

The two men were Nigogos Sherinian and Nishan Sherinian. As explained earlier, Nigogos Sherinian joined the Church upon hearing the message of Elder Hintze.[100] His son-in-law, Nishan Sherinian, on the other hand, did not decide to join the Church based solely on the teachings of the missionaries. As Nishan was taught by Hintze and Shahabian, the gospel message sounded promising, but the Lord sent additional witnesses of the truth whose teachings ultimately led to his baptism. When Nishan went to sleep at night, he was taught in his dreams. According to the account recorded in the history of the Turkish Mission, the dreams commenced immediately after the arrival of President Hintze and Elder Shahabian and continued until Nishan had been baptized. Nishan shared one of the dreams with the missionaries. In his dream, he had been visited by an unnamed prophet of God who reviewed with Nishan all the teachings of President Hintze and Elder Shahabian. The prophet then proceeded to verify all their words by opening to passages in the Bible and explaining to Nishan how the gospel in the last dispensation meshed perfectly with the gospel message as taught by the Savior when He was on the earth.[101] Nigogos was baptized, confirmed, and ordained an elder on October 4, 1888. In response to his impressive dreams and challenges from Hintze, Nishan was baptized, confirmed, and ordained a priest on October 5.[102]

As Hintze left the village to return to Sivas, he noted in his journal that "Zara is a filthy place and it caused me to thank God that we were permitted to take a better knowledge to Zara."[103] After one month in Sivas, President Hintze parted company with Dekran Shahabian and continued his journey toward Palestine on horseback.[104] Traveling in this region of Asia Minor was dangerous. The countryside was so infested with robbers that Hintze joined company with a courier, but additional hazards were posed by the mountainous and unforgiving terrain.

On November 13, Hintze arrived in Marash, where he enjoyed his first warm bath since arriving in Turkey almost two years earlier.[105]

Shortly thereafter he journeyed to Aintab, where the Armenian people flocked around the Latter-day Saint elder to hear his message. The Armenians of these cities had been introduced to the restored gospel by Brother Shahabian, who, upon returning home from his initial visits with Hintze in Constantinople eighteen months earlier, had taught the gospel to his neighbors and friends. Their interest was greatly heightened by the time President Hintze finally arrived in their region of Anatolia.[106] Hintze preached from the early hours of the morning until late in the evening; thereafter, two individuals demanded to be baptized. President Hintze's stay was so hurried that he declined their request and counseled them to continue in study and prayer and await his arrival in the city again the next spring.[107] The success was so striking that Hintze requested that more missionaries be sent to Turkey.[108]

From Aintab, he traveled through Aleppo, Alexandretta, and Beirut, where he was briefly imprisoned for not having an appropriate visa.[109] Finally, on Thursday, December 20, 1888, Elder Hintze arrived in Haifa, where he was warmly greeted by Johann Georg Grau.[110] He had a letter waiting there from President Teasdale, informing him that two other elders had been appointed to serve with him in the Turkish Mission, namely Janne M. Sjodahl and Charles U. Locander. President Hintze was particularly pleased with the pending arrival of Elder Sjodahl because they had first met during Hintze's mission to Norway (1885–86). He wrote: "I first met Brother Sjodahl a little more than two and one-half years ago, in Christiana, Norway, and there bore my testimony to him, and now he comes to be my fellow-laborer. Is not that a great blessing? I rejoice at the prospect of meeting him."[111] Elder Locander's arrival in the mission also made an immediate impact, since he could speak several languages.[112] President Hintze learned that Elder Sjodahl would land in Haifa in late January, which would make it possible for him to meet Sjodahl as he arrived in the Holy Land.

In the meantime, President Hintze continued to consider Palestine as a field of labor for the Latter-day Saint missionaries. From his observations, it seemed apparent that the work in Haifa would continue to grow. He noted that there were fourteen baptisms in 1888. However, during 1887 and 1888 sixteen members had emigrated, leaving a total of fifteen members in Haifa under the leadership of Brother Grau.[113] The work was encouraging, despite the high percentage of emigration among new converts; and the baptism of a Russian woman, whom Elder Hintze met upon his arrival in Haifa, added to that encouragement. She expressed a fervent and enthusiastic desire to travel from Haifa to Jerusalem to share the gospel message with the thousands of Russian visitors in the Holy City, whom she claimed were good-hearted but hindered in spiritual growth by centuries of false traditions.[114] While the missionary work in Haifa was still in its infancy, there was great reason to hope. These budding circumstances attended the arrival of Elder Sjodahl in Haifa on January 23, 1889.

FROM MANTI TO HAIFA

Elder Janne Sjodahl was a Baptist minister prior to his conversion to the Church. After his conversion, he married, and for three months he and his bride settled into their newfound lives in Manti, Utah. Then a letter arrived directly from President Wilford Woodruff, calling him to serve in the Turkish Mission. One day later, he replied that he "was perfectly willing" to serve and that he had the unconditional support of his new bride, who was expecting their first child.[115]

Janne M. Sjodahl

On November 14, 1888, Elder Sjodahl left Utah for the Holy Land. In fact, Elder Sjodahl became the first Latter-day Saint missionary to spend his entire mission experience laboring in Palestine.[116] President Hintze was waiting in Haifa to meet him, and the two were exceedingly pleased to be reunited. In a letter to the Saints in Utah, Elder Sjodahl recorded his initial impressions of the city, describing the streets as narrow, dirty, and lined with "houses built in a style of architecture common to American packing boxes."[117] Elder Sjodahl also provided a valuable description of the German colony in Haifa. He explained that it gives one a very good impression. Its houses are mostly surrounded by gardens, and everything is clean and neat. The colony now has some four hundred inhabitants and these live mostly by agriculture. They have also some industrial enterprises. A soap factory makes a very pure soap and has found a market for this chiefly on the American continent. They have also a windmill and a steam mill, both in good condition. Prominent is the culture of the vine. Most of the settlers have their vine-"bergs," and also seem to be very fond of their wine. It is well understood by the colonists that the temporal prospects of the colony are not great. It seems to be difficult for the growing generation to find employment here, and they have to look to foreign countries for a livelihood. A feeling is prevalent that the founding of the colonies here, although done with the best of intentions, was a planless undertaking, with no definitive purpose in view. I hope that an acknowledgment of this will lead to prepare the colonists for the acceptance of the gospel of Jesus Christ. Morally the colony stands on a very high level. I am told that in all the years it has existed here not more than two cases of unlawful intercourse have been known. No drunkenness is to be seen in the streets. No swearing is heard, no fighting, no gambling. When you enter a house, the first thing that attracts your attention is a verse from the Bible put as a motto over the door. [Note: These mottos are still visible.] Inside everything bears a religious stamp of the old pietistic color. The people (even the young girls) are dressed plainly, with no regard for the requirements of an ever-changing fashion, not even for the tasteful. The meals are good, but simple, and it appears that no one is too busy to find time after each meal to pray to God or to read a few verses from the Bible and a Psalm, all arranged in a little book to be used, one piece each day in the year. All this is good and commendable. Were there more intelligence, more spiritual life, more understanding of the Word of God, the Servian colony in Haifa would be an admirable place, not often found on this sinful globe of ours.[118]

Elder Sjodahl closed his letter with expressions of optimism and hopefulness regarding his work in Palestine. He said that "right here in the Holy Land and in the adjacent countries is a vast field of missionary labor which, rightly cultivated will yield an abundant harvest."[119]

Two days after Elder Sjodahl's arrival, on January 23, 1889, a council meeting was held in which Johann Georg Grau was called to serve as Elder Sjodahl's missionary companion as circumstances would allow.[120] The importance of Brother Grau remaining faithful to the Church since his baptism almost three years before cannot be overstated. He served as a great strength to the Haifa Branch during these pioneering missionary efforts. Of his devotion, President Hintze wrote:

> We have some members in the colony, among whom Brother G. Grau deserves honorable mention. He is laboring for the good of his fellowman, and is liberal with his means for the upbuilding of the Kingdom of God. God grant that we may find many such men. They are jewels for any community to possess.[121]

After settling into his new field of labor, Elder Sjodahl, in company with Ferdinand Hintze and Johann Georg Grau, toured the Holy Land for approximately three weeks.

ELDER CHARLES U. LOCANDER

While the three men toured, Elder Charles U. Locander arrived in Palestine. Elder Locander had started out the journey with Sjodahl several months earlier, but his route to the Holy Land was somewhat less than direct. After parting company with Sjodahl in Paris, he received permission to visit relatives in the southern part of France. From there he traveled to Italy, where he decided, for pure diversion, that he would visit Greece and the wonders of Egypt. From Alexandria he took a steamer to Jaffa, but because of fierce weather the boat could not land. Instead, it sailed on to Beirut, where the weather was so rough that the boatmen charged ten francs to row passengers from the steamer to shore (the entire passage from Egypt was thirteen francs). Once in Beirut, however, he did not have enough money to sail back to Jaffa when the weather cleared.[122] He was forced to make arrangements for the delivery of his valise to

Haifa, notify Hintze and Sjodahl of his delay, and start his southward journey to Haifa on foot.

While traveling between Beirut and Haifa, Elder Locander was robbed of several personal items. When he approached a local law enforcement officer in a nearby village, the officer listened to the missionary's story and then proceeded to rob him of his shoes.[123] Weatherbeaten, broke, and shoeless, Elder Locander must have presented quite a picture as he walked into Haifa in early 1889.

In conversations with German ministers, Elder Locander learned that the colony members attending their respective congregations were forbidden to patronize the Latter-day Saint gatherings. Nevertheless, while waiting for his fellow missionaries to return to Haifa, Elder Locander held two Sunday morning meetings, two Sunday evening meetings, and two weekday meetings. His initial report of the Saints in Haifa was that they were doing "quite well."[124] On March 9, 1889, Hintze, Sjodahl, and Grau returned from their tour of the Holy Land, and Elder Locander happily welcomed the trio. Two weeks later, another member of the Haifa Branch, Friederich Dieterle, was called to serve as Elder Locander's companion. Their field of labor would be Aintab, Turkey.[125]

Altogether there were now four American missionaries serving in the Turkish Mission: Elders Hintze, Clove, Sjodahl, and Locander. Three local missionaries were also serving: Elders Minassian, Dieterle, and Grau.[126] The arrival of Elders Sjodahl and Locander infused the mission with a renewed sense of hope and vitality.

ELDER SJODAHL IN THE HOLY LAND, 1889

Elder Sjodahl immediately went to work learning Arabic, and initially his prospects appeared to be good in the colony. However, as his work progressed in Palestine, Sjodahl felt overwhelmed by the fact that he was face-to-face with millions of Arabs who had never heard the latter-day message. In a letter to President Wilford Woodruff, Elder Sjodahl explained that he constantly pled to God that doors would be opened so the work could progress among the Arab people.[127] And he felt his prayers were being answered, as many Arabs requested to be taught the gospel, some even asking for baptism.[128] Since he felt it best to go slowly with these individuals, he established a daily Bible class. If they proved faithful in this, they could eventually receive baptism.

From his earliest days in Palestine, Janne Sjodahl looked upon his Arab friends with respect, referring to them as "men of bright intellects" who merely lacked sufficient information.[129] In a letter to the *Deseret Weekly*, Elder Sjodahl concluded that because of the Palestinian Arabs' trustworthiness and kindness, many of them must be fellow descendants of Israel. He also spoke favorably of Islam: "it teaches men to worship *one* God and to hate idolatry. In this respect Islam is far ahead of Catholicism at least."[130]

On the other hand, Elder Sjodahl made no progress among the German colonists, which he found disappointing, since he had anticipated a bountiful harvest among these European Christians.[131] Moreover, he was perplexed by the light persecutions the Saints were receiving in Haifa. Eventually, he learned the source of the difficulty. According to Elder Sjodahl, one Reverend Illif, a Methodist clergyman who claimed to be from Utah, had written an anti-Mormon tract that had been distributed among the German colonists in Haifa. The tract, titled "The Mormon," spread lies such as: Joseph Smith was dishonest in character; the Mormons were driven from state to state because of their godless and corrupt way of life; Joseph Smith claimed to be the fifth member of the Godhead; Mormons sanctioned murder through secret organizations such as the Danites, who executed those who appeared to be suspicious; and the women of Utah were bound as slaves.[132] With such propaganda being spread, it is no wonder the work slowed in Haifa. Elder Sjodahl eventually moved to Jaffa.[133]

Although Elder Sjodahl had arrived in Palestine in January 1889 and had spent most of his time proselytizing, it was not until May 14, 1889, that he witnessed his first baptism in the Holy Land. He later said that "it is no small thing to become a 'Mormon' in this country."[134] The name of the convert was Joseph Ludescher, born in Austria on September 22, 1857.[135] As a young man he had subscribed to the Catholic faith but was exposed to so much fanaticism and bigotry that he nearly came to a point of denying the existence of God. During this period of doubt and consternation, an unexplainable feeling moved upon him to leave Europe and journey to the

Holy Land. Although the decision defied all common sense, he made the pilgrimage and there met Elders Sjodahl and Grau and accepted their message. He was baptized on a moonlit night in the gentle breakers of the Mediterranean Sea.[136] His conversion lifted Elder Sjodahl's spirits. Elder Sjodahl wrote to President Woodruff just over one month later, "I am alive and happy in the discharge of my duties."[137]

Even in Jaffa, a large portion of Elder Sjodahl's duties dealt with misperceptions about the Church—misperceptions often sewn by the most unlikely of villains. The following story illustrates.

A member of the Church was admitted to the German hospital in Jaffa with a life-threatening illness. His condition worsened, and it became apparent that he would not live. The American vice-consul, quartered in Jaffa, heard that a Latter-day Saint was on the brink of death in the nearby hospital and felt duty-bound to assess the well-being of the "deceived" man's soul. He came to the man's hospital bed and explained that if the man would deny "Mormonism" and apostatize from his faith, he would probably enjoy an immediate healing. In response, the dying Latter-day Saint raised his hand toward the heavens and declared with emphasis on every word, "Mormonism is the eternal truth!"

The man died the very next day, faithful to his testimony. Elder Sjodahl explained that the vice-consul, on the other hand, "instead of getting the credit of having turned a righteous man from God— as was his purpose—obtained a testimony the rejection of which will in the eternities cause him bitter sorrow."[138] For some unknown reason, possibly to protect family members from potential backlash, Elder Sjodahl withheld the name of the dying man in his account. Even so, Elder Sjodahl explained that he related these details as he heard them from the mouth of the unnamed Latter-day Saint shortly before his death.

Three New Missionaries and Three Historic Baptisms

On June 6, 1889, Elders Frederick Stauffer and Edgar D. Simmons, both of Salt Lake City, and Elder William H. Smart of Franklin, Idaho, arrived in Constantinople. Elders Simmons and Smart were assigned to serve with Elder Charles Locander in Aintab.[139] Later that summer, Elder Locander journeyed to Palestine to join

Elder Sjodahl in Jaffa, study Arabic, and preach the gospel among the Arab people. He brought Simmons and Smart as traveling companions, although they would stay in Palestine for only a short time and then return to Turkey.[140] Just as during his walk from Beirut to Haifa in early 1889, Elder Locander was for a second time robbed by a bedouin, and for the second time that year he was left destitute. When President Teasdale heard of Elder Locander's misfortunes, he was anything but sympathetic. In a letter to President Hintze he wrote:

> I understand Bros. Smart and Simmons followed Bro. Locander to Palestine. I do not understand such missionary business. By letter from you I understood they were laboring in Turkey. Bro. Locander got into all his trouble through leaving his field of labor. I suppose he had no faith in the mission and so he went off to seek employment and fell amongst thieves who robbed him of everything.[141]

Improprieties aside, the missionaries' arrival in Jaffa was fortuitously timed. Elders Locander, Sjodahl, Simmons, and Smart had the privilege of witnessing the first modern baptisms of Arabs in the Holy Land. The converts were two young men named Salim Inzil and Pharez Randure. Both had consistently attended Janne Sjodahl's Bible class for three months, but Sjodahl had postponed their baptisms until he was sure these two men had been taught clearly and thoroughly.[142] Finally, on September 21, 1889, the sacred ordinances were performed. Elder Sjodahl presided at the service and directed Elder Locander to perform both baptisms in the Mediterranean Sea at Jaffa. Then the party retired to a room in the *khan* (inn), where Elder Smart confirmed Salim and Elder Sjodahl confirmed Pharez. In retrospect, Elder Sjodahl testified that "the occasion was a solemn one. God was present."[143]

About three weeks after these historic baptisms, the first Arab woman joined the Church—Jaffa resident Louise Khayat. Elder Sjodahl performed the baptism in her home. Louise Khayat was described as a refined lady and well educated. A mere two years after joining the Church, Sister Khayat died, true to the faith, at Jaffa in September 1891.[144]

Sjodahl's Final Days in Palestine

Correspondence from Elder Sjodahl during the last quarter of 1889 is scant. At the end of November, Elder Sjodahl explained why he had written so little during this time. He had been sick with an ailment known as *abu al-rukab,* which literally means "the father of the knees." This feverish malady spread through all parts of Palestine, and cases were reported in Damascus, Beirut, and as far away as Constantinople. Elder Sjodahl explained that the sickness began with a headache that increased in intensity until the pain resulted in partial paralysis of the extremities. The headaches were accompanied by a fever, the greater effects of which were felt in the form of weakness in the knees—hence the name.[145]

In a letter from President Teasdale dated November 12, 1889, President Hintze was informed that Janne Sjodahl had requested a release from the Turkish Mission.[146] Elder Sjodahl received the requested release and was called upon to travel to Bern, Switzerland, to supervise the creation of a hymnbook to be used by the German and Swiss Saints.[147]

Eleven days before his departure for Switzerland, Elder Sjodahl penned some final thoughts regarding his labors among the peoples of Palestine. He noted the prophetic significance of the Jews gathering to Palestine and causing the land to become fruitful at their hands; he explained that the world was generally unaware of the miraculous gathering and that even the Jews themselves failed to comprehend the significance of these movements. In light of this observation, he suggested that

> a mission to the Jews, therefore, the object of which would be to enlighten the scattered nation upon the subject of gathering, as foretold by their ancient prophets, would be a work of vast importance just at this time. . . . The Jews need messengers from the Lord, and they will have them; for the time is at hand.[148]

Elder Sjodahl left Palestine on January 1, 1890. In one year he had baptized four individuals. As mentioned earlier, he was the first missionary to spend his entire proselytizing mission in Palestine.

President Hintze and
Missionary Activity in Turkey, 1889

After President Hintze welcomed Elder Sjodahl to Haifa in January 1889, the missionary group toured Palestine and returned to Haifa. While touring, Hintze kept his finger on the pulse of the proselytizing efforts in the mission and gave this report in March 1889:

> The Turkish Mission is moving on slowly, but we hope surely. Many of our brethren interested in its progress have perhaps wondered at its stubborn refusal to shine out brightly; but there are many reasons. Much has to be learned by the Elders formerly unacquainted with a language not easily acquired, and there are no publications for distribution to assist in combating the many wilful lies so studiously circulated by the missionaries of so-called "Christian" denominations. Still we have a membership of about twenty, with four Elders from Zion and a small local force in the field.[149]

On March 22, 1889, Hintze, Locander, and Dieterle sailed for Adana, Turkey, about twenty-five miles east of Tarsus.[150] These elders spent about two months laboring there among the Armenians, whose interest was high; they received visitors at their flat as early as 6:00 A.M. and as late as 10:30 P.M.[151] The elders were in even greater demand among the fleas living in their apartment. The problem was so acute that it occasionally affected their ability to do the work. President Hintze recorded in his journal that "today we have had a full room [of investigators] from early morning till late at night, hardly finding time to eat we have been so busy talking. I was not in so good a trim for talking, because of fleas bothering us so at night, we slept but little. Brother Locander killed 53 fleas, I also killed many."[152]

Near the end of April, President Hintze moved further east to Aintab, continuing his tour of the mission. A lack of productivity, coupled with persecutions, led him to shift his missionary efforts away from the European community in Constantinople to the Armenians in central Turkey. The move to Aintab, facilitating this emphasis, is a benchmark date in the history of the mission.

President Hintze loved the Armenians he encountered in central Turkey. His description of their temperament, however, leads us to conclude that doing missionary work among them was anything but easy.

> The Armenian is smart, is imitative, has a splendid memory, has a strong desire to be the same as "Christian" nations in Europe in all matters. . . . As a nation they are distrustful and doubtful. They do not believe even one another. . . . They will loom up and appear wonderful in speech and determination only to collapse into the most frivolous excuses, always complaining of their circumstances and rulers. On religious questions they are interesting and argumentative. . . . So long as they are ruled with an iron hand they are obedient and useful, being active, and full of resources, but when left to themselves they melt away nationally and individually. And in the Church membership we have many good and honorable persons, so far as we know them, but we have had some whom we did not know when we thought we did.[153]

Elder Locander offered an interesting description of the challenges the missionaries faced as they taught among the Armenians. He wrote that

> when we explain a principle of the gospel they smile, and even laugh. "Why, how simple and easy to understand," they say. That is just what everybody else ought to believe. With them it seems to be thus: Hearing they hear in very deed, but do not understand. They have faith but no depth of soul. Very few weeds, if any, choke them, but they have no moisture. . . . The Armenians, with three or four exceptions out of as many hundreds are not opposed to Mormonism, nor in favor of it, being lukewarm. They sometimes ask "How much will you pay me if I am baptized?"[154]

These descriptions must be read in the context of the day. Armenian Christians had been oppressed, second-class citizens for centuries and were constantly under the scrutinizing eye of the Ottoman Empire due to their national aspirations as a people. Suspicion, maneuvering, and intrigue were a part of their lives because of their political standing in the predominantly Islamic government. Given this background, any success had by the Latter-day Saint missionaries among the Armenian people is quite remarkable. It must be remembered that religious freedoms in the Ottoman Empire were greatly inhibited. For example, the missionaries had no real opportunity to distribute their views in print. Religious tracts were generally confiscated by the government, and while President Hintze spent a great deal of his time attempting to procure government permits to publish accurate information about the Church, he rarely succeeded. The missionaries were constantly at a disadvantage. The following examples illustrate this point.

One Turkish and one Armenian newspaper reported the "alarming" news that

> two expatriated "Mormon" Elders fleeing from America landed on these hospitable shores and dared, under the very shadow of the Ottoman Crescent, to elude its officers, and are now wending their way to the interior of this unspotted land to besmear it with their polluting doctrine! The officers are tracing them to the center of this peninsula, whence they will be carried beyond the Turkish frontier, which they so cunningly crossed over.[155]

In another instance, two Armenian men were arrested, bound in chains, and led off to Constantinople for trial. Their names were Havadis and Salek, and their crime was that of falling under the influence of Mormonism. Although it was freely acknowledged that the two men were among the most highly esteemed gentlemen of their community, the harassment was tolerated by officials. General sentiments could be represented by the widely wired editorial comments of the *Levant Herald,* a French newspaper, that declared: "Nobody here needs to repent; consequently 'Mormonism' must go!"[156]

In Sivas two Armenian brethren were arrested for carrying a sign containing the painted inscription, "Repent, for the Kingdom of God is at hand." Crowds gathered in agitation and curiosity, and the brethren were eventually arrested, possibly on the grounds that the slogans were meant to have some kind of political meaning.[157]

Finally, in late April, President Hintze received word that persecutions had become so severe in Constantinople that many had apostatized, and Elder Clove was very discouraged.[158] It goes without saying that presiding over this mission would tax the greatest and most committed of spiritual men. Yet Hintze pressed on. He was creative and willing to be innovative to get his message to a broader audience. For example, one problem he faced was that Ottoman society was segregated. Women were not in the habit of attending public meetings with men, so few women heard the missionaries' message. To ease the disparity, President Hintze organized a ladies' meeting in Aintab. The turnout was fair, and Hintze and Locander were encouraged.[159] However, it was at this general time (late spring and early summer 1889) that the Ottoman government issued a decree making it illegal for the Latter-day Saints to hold public meetings. Again President Hintze was frustrated by the government's hindrance.

Despite these many difficulties, the honest in heart continued to seek out the missionaries. On May 5, 1889, President Hintze baptized Nersis Garabetian in Aintab, and on June 25, Elder Locander baptized a young medical student named George Viserian.[160]

Brother Viserian became a very important member of the Church in Aintab. On one occasion in the summer of 1889, his intervention may have saved the missionaries' lives. The story goes as follows: While introducing the doctrine of marriage for time and eternity, the missionaries shared the doctrine of a Heavenly Mother. The idea was considered offensive and repugnant by many people in the city. Hintze wrote in his journal that the whole city was in a stir over the doctrine. The agitation was heightened by the unbelievers in the city who were seeking for offenses. The other churches in the area combined against the Latter-day Saints in an effort to keep their own members from becoming converted. The sentiments against the Saints rose to a feverish pitch, until the lives of the elders became endangered. The problem was so serious that President Hintze and the other missionaries were preparing to flee in late June, when George Viserian stood boldly as a witness for the truth. This new convert fearlessly acknowledged the veracity of all that the missionaries had taught. His testimony calmed the crowds and brought the strife to an end.[161]

RETURN TO MISSION HEADQUARTERS

On July 9, 1889, Elders Simmons and Smart arrived in Aintab. Before then, the Ottoman government had confiscated "every book, pamphlet, memento, photograph-souvenir and scrap of printed matter they had."[162] Nevertheless, they were healthy and anxious to assume their missionary duties in the area. Brother Friederich Dieterle (stepson of Johann Georg Grau) of Palestine was there to serve with them. The presence of these three missionaries in Aintab made it possible for President Hintze to return to Constantinople after his four-month visit in Aintab. Altogether, Hintze toured the Turkish Mission for eleven months, traveling over three thousand miles.[163] Reflecting on his experiences, he wrote:

> God has been with me. I have borne testimony to thousands and baptized seven persons. . . . I have learned the wants of the mission better and I hope and pray that God will give me strength and favor so that I may put my experience to good use. From some of those baptized I have good reports, from others not so good. . . . The people are willing to receive the truth, but the difficulties are so many that they despair.[164]

Now alone in Constantinople, President Hintze observed that the work had "collapsed" because the missionaries were not wanted there. As early as the spring of 1889, he had been looking more seriously into expanding the proselytizing effort in the smaller, rural communities of central Anatolia, and by the fall he had sent all his missionaries out to the country. It seems he came to the decision to move while touring the mission, because when he returned to Constantinople, the missionaries' attention suddenly turned away from the Europeans to focus almost solely on the Armenians.[165] Years later, Brother Hintze explained some of the reasons why this move seemed practical. He wrote:

> The Greeks . . . said they had a lineally descended priesthood and authority from the Apostle Paul, even as the Romans claimed they had from St. Peter. . . . So what use would they have for any new revelation or church when they had it all? . . .

The Turks [Muslims], on the other hand, claimed to be the only true and faithful nation whom Allah loved. They had all truth as embodied in the Law of Moses, the Psalms, the Prophets and the gospel. So they would hear nothing of us. The Turks . . . forbade us preaching to them . . . but they were willing we should convert any Christian Armenians. . . . They felt that such work would break up Armenian unity and thus make it easier to govern them. So it came about that we did most of our work among the Armenians.[166]

Much to his chagrin, President Hintze had to remain alone in the city to broker the affairs between the Church and the Ottoman government—which he described as despotic because of its treatment of "unrecognized" religions.[167]

Changes in the Missionary Force

Elders Clove, Minassian, and Locander were all released in August 1889, leaving only the inexperienced elders serving in Turkey. Therefore, President Hintze concluded that the work would be at a virtual standstill for approximately one year until these new missionaries could effectively speak the Armenian and Turkish languages. Beyond this, new converts were exposed to grievous formal and informal persecutions and became candidates for imprisonment, immediate and permanent expulsion from the empire, and higher taxes—all this in addition "to the usual hatred and persecution common to the cause of truth everywhere."[168] Describing the burden of overseeing the Turkish Mission at this time, President Hintze wrote:

Yesterday morning was to me very depressing. I felt low spirited because the work seemed to be against me, although . . . I feel the good spirit whisper that this is the work of the Lord and that He will bring it through all right, and I feel to take hold with new zeal and vigor and hope in God for a brighter future. I have experienced of late that when . . . a spirit of darkness seems to seize me and present everything so darkly and so impossible . . . I pray . . . and soon something turns up whereby . . . my mind is enlightened.[169]

Ferdinand Hintze served as a great example of perseverance and determination in serving the Lord in spite of the work's extreme difficulty. Well aware of the taxing nature of Hintze's service, President Teasdale communicated feelings of love and concern for his fellow laborer and let him know that his service was coming to an end.

> Now Bro. Hintze you have been away from home about three years and I do not think it right to impose on good nature. I was in hopes you would have someone to succeed you in the charge of that mission but as things are shaping up I cannot see how we can spare you until the spring. I should be pleased to learn your feelings in this matter, and what you propose to do that you think would be for the benefit of that mission and it shall have my careful consideration.[170]

Concerning his release, President Hintze left the matter entirely up to President Teasdale.[171] The president acted quickly, and Ferdinand Hintze received a formal letter of release on December 14, 1889. Four days later he left Constantinople for his home in Zion, arriving in Salt Lake City on January 28, 1890.[172] Once home, Hintze reflected fondly on his mission, explaining that he saw

> the power of God largely made manifest in our behalf. . . . Though I have traveled daily through very dangerous parts of the country, I have always been preserved from danger in a most remarkable manner. Caravans and individuals have been stopped and robbed before and behind both me and my brethren, but through the blessing and providence of God we have escaped molestation. . . . I shall always look back with feelings of pleasure and satisfaction upon my late mission.[173]

A New Mission President

At the close of 1889, Frederick Stauffer, who was serving in Sivas, was called to preside over the Turkish Mission.[174] Hintze's quick departure suggests a great deal of confidence in the new mission president.[175] Unfortunately, President Stauffer's first major trial as a mission president was coping with the death of one of his elders.

Elder Smart had been released from his mission for health reasons in November 1889, leaving only two elders in Aintab, Elders

Simmons and Dieterle.[176] Ferdinand Hintze later noted that these two elders worked well together and had a strong bond of affection and friendship.[177] Tragically, on January 22, 1890, Elder Simmons showed the first visible symptoms of smallpox. The disease advanced quickly, and soon his face and body were full of marks and his skin began to slough away. Elder Dieterle reported that by a week later, Elder Simmons was consumed by intense pain, which never subsided throughout the illness. He became so weak that he could not stand or speak, although he never became completely incoherent.

Edgar D. Simmons

Finally, on February 4, 1890, Elder Simmons died.[178] He had served in Aintab, where he essentially began his mission, since July 9, 1889.

Since the Church was not a recognized religion in the Ottoman Empire, Elder Dieterle did not know the proper burial protocol. Would he need governmental permission and permits to obtain a burial plot and conduct a service? At this point, Brother Vezerian approached Budville Krihor, the most prominent Protestant minister in Aintab, and requested assistance. Although there had been many times when local Protestant ministers had shown great animosity toward the Saints, this was not such an occasion. Reverend Krihor was a kind man and offered his help freely. He suggested there was no need to approach the government because he would allow the burial to take place in the Protestant Armenian Cemetery in Aintab. Furthermore, he offered to preach the funeral sermon. Since Elder Dieterle's command of the language was still limited, he accepted the offer.[179]

Of the death and burial of his companion, Elder Dieterle wrote:

> This blow strikes hard not only to the Church but also the rela-
> tives of the deceased; we have, however, to give way to the will of

God; for what God does is done well. . . . May God permit Brother Simmons' remains to rest in peace in the grave until the resurrection and comfort his relatives.[180]

The grave is at the northwest edge of the cemetery near the graves of some other Americans and is marked by a large black basalt monument. Engraved on the stone are these words:

EDGAR D. SIMMONS
DIED AT THE POST OF HIS OFFICE
FEB. 4, 1890, 27 YEARS OLD.[181]

Elder Dieterle took the death of his companion hard and wrote to President Teasdale for advice regarding his mission. In the meantime, he received a telegram from his father-in-law, Johann Georg Grau, instructing him to join him in Palestine at the earliest possible moment.[182] Elder Dieterle's departure in the first quarter of 1890 meant that President Stauffer was the lone full-time missionary in the Turkish Mission. However, he would not be alone for long.

*The gravestone of Elder Edgar Dilworth Simmons in the
Protestant Armenian Cemetery in Aintab.*

Conclusion

Missionary work in the Near East from 1885 to early 1890 was a time of astounding discovery. The miraculous visions and dreams of Jacob Spori, Johann Georg Grau, and Mischa Markow, the baptism of the first Arabs in modern times, and the unparalleled patience and perseverance of Ferdinand Hintze as he struggled to spread the gospel among Armenians in the waning Ottoman Empire—all constitute a compelling catalog of pioneering effort and faith. The marvelous work in the Near East may best be capsulized in the actions of the new convert from the Holy Land, Friederich Dieterle, as he dealt with the death of his companion with the steadiness and composure of a mature member of the Church. This chapter in Church history provides simple yet powerful examples of how gospel truths refine and expand the souls of men and women who accept them.

Notes to Chapter 2

1. Kenneth Scott Latourette, *A History of Christianity,* vol. 2, *Reformation to the Present* (Peabody, MA: Prince, 2003), 1205–25. See also James A. Toronto, "Early Missions to Ottoman Turkey, Syria, and Palestine," in *Out of Obscurity: The LDS Church in the Twentieth Century* (Salt Lake City: Deseret Book, 2000), 340.

2. Rao H. Lindsay, "The Dream of a Mormon Colony in the Near East," *Dialogue* 1.4 (winter 1966): 51–52.

3. Papers of Anthon H. Lund, August 10, 1900, LDS Church Archives.

4. Andrew Jenson, comp. and ed., "The Manuscript History of the Palestine-Syrian Mission," LDS Church Archives. See also Ivan J. Barrett, "The Story of the Mormons in the Holy Land," unpublished manuscript, 1977, 35. Copy in authors' possession.

5. Jacob Spori's daughters point out that "President John Taylor, with his eye on Jacob Spori as possible timber for starting an academy in the Snake River country, called him to open the Turkish Mission for the L.D.S. Church." This note is taken from "Jacob Spori, First Administrator of Bannock Stake Academy," written by Jacob Spori's daughters, Elizabeth Stowell and Annie Kerr. The full document was read at the Ricks College seventy-second homecoming in the fall of 1960. Transcript in authors' possession.

6. Elizabeth S. Stowell, *The History of Jacob Spori by His Daughter, Elizabeth S. Stowell,* written for the Daughters of the Snake River Pioneers, November 16, 1926, 12.

7. Ibid., 5. Sister Stowell documents that her father spoke German, French, English, Latin, Greek, Turkish, Armenian, Syrian, Hebrew, and Arabic. In an *Ensign* article titled "Istanbul and Rexburg: Jacob Spori's Mission Field," June 1980, 26, Denton Y. Brewerton noted that Jacob Spori learned to read and write three additional languages, bringing the total to thirteen. We note that "fluency" may have different meaning for different users; however, it may be safely stated that Jacob Spori possessed a gift for languages.

8. Stowell, *History of Jacob Spori*, 2.

9. This information comes from an interview conducted with Elizabeth S. Stowell (daughter of Jacob Spori) by LaMar C. Berrett, April 17, 1976, Rexburg, Idaho. Transcript in authors' possession.

10. Stowell, *History of Jacob Spori*, 12.

11. Ibid.

12. The parting of Jacob Spori and his wife, Magdalena, is generally accounted for in two different ways: First, his daughter, Elizabeth Stowell, explained that Magdalena's father was adamantly opposed to Mormonism and was so upset by Jacob's conversion that he firmly persuaded his daughter to leave Jacob and bring the children to his home while Jacob was left to pursue his fantastic dream in "Zion." Magdalena was embarrassed and disgraced by her husband's conversion and therefore conceded to her father's demands. See Stowell and Kerr, "Jacob Spori, First Administrator of Bannock Stake Academy." Second, James Christianson, on the other hand, explained that Magdalena, in addition to her unwillingness to join the Church, was potentially an heiress to her father's estate. Practicality moved her to stay behind. See James R. Christianson, "Jacob Spori: Swiss Missionary, Educator, and Kingdom Builder," in *Supporting Saints: Life Stories of Nineteenth-Century Mormons*, ed. Donald Q. Cannon and David J. Whitaker (Provo, UT: Religious Studies Center, Brigham Young University, 1985), 349. We feel that Spori's daughters convey excessive strain between Jacob and Magdalena. They describe a woman that loved her father more than her husband. We cannot entirely accept this because historical records show that the two consistently correspond in tones of love for each other and their children throughout Jacob's move to Zion and subsequent missionary efforts in Turkey and Palestine. On the other hand, we cannot totally agree with Christianson because he places Magdalena's pragmatism above her love for her husband. In 1888, Magdalena immigrated to America and settled in the remote Snake River Valley of Idaho to be with her husband. This suggests that Magdalena deeply loved Jacob Spori and was willing to sacrifice land and fortune to be with him. We believe that there was a strain on the relationship when Jacob joined the Church, but the strain did not drive a permanent wedge between the two, nor did it induce Magdalena to simply wave off her husband for the sake of an inheritance.

13. Brewerton, "Istanbul and Rexburg," 26.

14. Christianson, "Jacob Spori: Swiss Missionary," 351.

15. Ibid. See also Stowell and Kerr, "Jacob Spori, First Administrator of Bannock Stake Academy." It should be noted that the accounts of Magdalena's conversion to the gospel do not all agree. For example, Elizabeth Stowell explains that six years after he left his family for Utah and during his mission in Turkey, Elder Spori received word from Magdalena that Katherine, their oldest daughter, had died on February 27, 1885, from injuries sustained in a fall from a swing. Magdalena was heartbroken and despondent. Jacob wrote her a tender letter filled with Latter-day Saint doctrines relating to life after death and the hope of a glorious reunion at a future day with their daughter. The truths contained in the letter sunk deep into her heart, and Magdalena chose to investigate and join the Church. She was baptized at night to avoid the sure persecution from her father. Stowell, interview by LaMar Berrett, April 17, 1976, Rexburg, Idaho. We acknowledge Elizabeth Stowell's account of Magdalena's baptism but recommend Christianson's rendering. Historical records and general historical observations support his account.

16. Christianson, "Jacob Spori: Swiss Missionary," 360–61.

17. At one point, the school in Rexburg was on the verge of financial collapse and the Church seriously considered closing the academy. To make matters worse, there was a horrible crop failure in 1889. These two factors meant that teachers couldn't be paid and few students could afford tuition. Upon hearing that the school might be closed, Jacob Spori wrote to Karl G. Maeser and asked for some vacation time. With this time off, Jacob went to work on the railroad in order to pay the salaries of the two other teachers. Because of Jacob Spori's vision and tenacity, the school remained open. See Brewerton, "Istanbul and Rexburg," 26.

18. *Millennial Star*, December 15, 1884, 793.

19. Ibid., January 12, 1885, 27–28.

20. Ibid., 28. Elder Spori's proposal to sleep on the floor of the Vartooguian home was not practical, since it was a one-room dwelling for a family of six. A search was begun for a small home for Elder Spori, and he noted in his journal that on February 4, 1885, he rented a room in the new quarter of Pera. He continued to eat his meals with Hagop and his family. Pera was the section of Constantinople north of the Golden Horn and was heavily populated by Europeans. In a letter written by Joseph M. Tanner to Franklin D. Richards, Elder Tanner explained that Constantinople was divided into two distinct sections: Turkish and European. Jacob Spori initially desired lodging in the Turkish side of the city but was not given access. Therefore, he settled in Pera, the more European side of the sprawling city. In *Journal History*, vol. 31, August 31, 1886, 4.

21. Some of the following information is gleaned from the *Millennial Star*, January 19, 1885, 43–44, which was written in January 1885. This provides a

fair representation of how Jacob Spori and subsequent missionaries would have viewed the Armenian Christians among whom they labored.

22. Yohanan Aharoni and Michael Avi-Yonah, *The Macmillan Bible Atlas* (New York: Macmillan, 1977).

23. Incidentally, the Old City of Jerusalem is divided into four quarters: Armenian, Christian, Muslim, and Jewish. The Armenians have maintained a long-standing presence in the Old City.

24. Jason Goodwin, *Lords of the Horizons* (New York: Owl Book, 1988), 306.

25. Latourette, *Reformation to the Present,* 1209.

26. *Millennial Star,* January 12, 1885, 27–28.

27. Jenson, "The Manuscript History of the Palestine-Syrian Mission."

28. Ibid.

29. Jacob Spori taught German, French, and English to anyone who desired to learn. The Armenian people lacked the means to pay for such lessons, and since Elder Spori did not charge, he taught many bright Armenian students. Furthermore, a Russian Jew gave Spori Russian lessons. Jacob Spori explained that the language would be impossible to learn without such help. *Millennial Star,* August 21, 1885, 605–6.

30. *Millennial Star,* May 4, 1885, 286.

31. Ibid., May 18, 1885, 317.

32. Ibid., November 30, 1885, 764.

33. Ibid., 765.

34. Joseph M. Tanner shares this observation in a letter written to Apostle Franklin D. Richards. *Journal History,* vol. 31, 4.

35. *Millennial Star,* September 21, 1885, 605.

36. Ibid., November 30, 1885, 765–66. Elder Spori did not sit idly by upon hearing this report. He immediately informed the three leading newspapers circulated among Europeans in Constantinople of the fraudulent scheme. Furthermore, he provided his own address and personal information so that people could contact the legitimate Latter-day Saint elder at their earliest convenience.

37. Ibid., February 15, 1886, 108–9.

38. Ibid.

39. Ibid.

40. Joseph M. Tanner, *Millennial Star,* January 11, 1886, 29.

41. Ibid., January 8, 1886, 75–76. Elder Tanner explained that the rents in Constantinople were quite high but that the cost of food was reasonable.

42. Journal of Francis M. Lyman, March 9, 1886, LDS Church Archives.

43. The title "Templer" is of secondary derivation, not unlike the appellation "Mormon" for members of The Church of Jesus Christ of Latter-day Saints.

There is no connection between Templers and *Templars,* the group of twelfth-century knights who vowed to guard pilgrims in the Holy Land.

44. This synopsis of the Templers is taken from a life sketch written on March 21, 1892, by Friederich and Elizabeth Raile, who were Templers in Palestine but converted to Mormonism after being taught the gospel by Elder Jacob Spori in 1887. LDS Church Archives. See also Yehoshua Ben-Arieh, *Jerusalem in the Nineteenth Century* (New York: St. Martin's Press, 1986), 127.

45. *Encyclopedia Judaica,* ed. Cecil Roth (Jerusalem: Keter Publishing House, n.d.), 15:994–96. See also Ben-Arieh, *Jerusalem in the Nineteenth Century,* 127.

46. For further examples on this point, we recommend such publications as Lucy Mack Smith, *Joseph Smith and His Progenitors* (Lamoni, IA: The Reorganized Church of Jesus Christ of Latter Day Saints, 1912); Orson F. Whitney, *The Life of Heber C. Kimball* (Salt Lake City: Bookcraft, 1945); *The Autobiography of Parley P. Pratt* (Salt Lake City: Deseret Book, 1985); and *Regional Studies in Church History: New York* (Provo, UT: The Department of Church History and Doctrine, Brigham Young University, 1992).

47. Joseph M. Tanner, *Millennial Star,* July 12, 1886, 443.

48. Ibid., July 26, 1886, 479.

49. Mission Record, Turkish Mission, September 6, 1887, 9, LDS Church Archives.

50. Ibid., July 31, 1886, and August 8, 15, 1886; *Millennial Star,* August 30, 1886, 555.

51. Mission Record, Turkish Mission, September 6, 1887, 9.

52. Ibid. See also Rao H. Lindsay, "A History of the Missionary Activity of The Church of Jesus Christ of Latter-day Saints in the Near East, 1884–1929," master's thesis, Brigham Young University, 1958, 20.

53. Mission Record, Turkish Mission, September 6, 1887, 9.

54. *Millennial Star,* November 15, 1886, 731.

55. Joseph M. Tanner, *Millennial Star,* October 4, 1886, 636.

56. *Journal of Discourses,* ed. George D. Watt, 26 vols. (Liverpool: F. D. Richards, 1855), 11:279.

57. For a more detailed discussion of Latter-day Saint thought concerning the gospel and the Jews, see Arnold H. Green, "Gathering and Election: Israelite Descent and Universalism in Mormon Discourse," *Journal of Mormon History* 25.1 (spring 1999): 195–228.

58. *Millennial Star,* January 3, 1887, 14.

59. Ibid.

60. Julius Debrincke, "Jerusalem Once and Now," *The Contributor,* July 1886, 375–81.

61. *Millennial Star,* January 3, 1887, 14.

62. Ibid., November 15, 1886, 731.

63. Whitney, *The Life of Heber C. Kimball,* 15–18. See also Ronald K. Esplin, "Conversion and Transformation: Brigham Young's New York Roots and the Search for Bible Religion," in *Regional Studies in Latter-day Saint Church History: New York,* 176–77.

64. *Millennial Star,* November 15, 1886, 731.

65. Ibid.

66. Mission Record, Turkish Mission, January 3, 1887, 3.

67. Christianson, "Jacob Spori: Swiss Missionary," 358.

68. For additional readings on Mischa Markow, see Lindsay, "Missionary Activity in the Near East," 20; Richard O. Cowan, "Mischa Markow: Mormon Missionary to the Balkans," *BYU Studies* 10.1 (fall 1970): 92–99; Christianson, "Jacob Spori: Swiss Missionary," 358–59; and William Hale Kehr, "Missionary to the Balkans: Mischa Markow," *Ensign,* June 1980, 29–32.

69. The details of Mischa Markow's journey to Constantinople and subsequent conversion are taken from the account provided by George Q. Cannon, "An Interesting Occurrence," *Juvenile Instructor,* May 1, 1889, 204–5, as found in Lindsay, "Missionary Activity in the Near East," 21–22. Two other versions of this meeting between Spori and Markow exist: Brewerton, "Istanbul and Rexburg," 26–27; and Kehr, "Missionary to the Balkans," 30–31. We feel that George Q. Cannon's 1889 account is the most accurate.

70. Lindsay, "Missionary Activity in the Near East," 22.

71. Mission Record, Turkish Mission, February 1, 1887, 5.

72. Ferdinand Hintze, "Turkey and Its People," *Juvenile Instructor,* May 15, 1894, 300–301. Copies of the Book of Mormon, Doctrine and Covenants, and *A Voice of Warning* were sent to Elder Hintze from the mission office in Europe to be presented to the grand vizier. See Mission Record, Turkish Mission, August 26, 1887, 7.

73. Hintze, "Turkey and Its People," 300.

74. Mission Record, Turkish Mission, February 1, 1887, 6.

75. Their names are Friederich and Elizabeth Raile, Fred and Christiana Kegel, Samuel and Maria Kopp, Daniel and Friedericha Reski, and Friederich S. Dieterle. These names are recorded in Mission Record, Turkish Mission, April 21, May 21, July 5, July 6, and August 13, 1887. Rao H. Lindsay notes that Joseph Tanner baptized seven people during this period. However, apparently he does not reference the baptisms noted in the Mission Record on July 6 and August 13, 1887.

76. Ferdinand Hintze, *Deseret Weekly,* March 22, 1890, 411.

77. *Millennial Star,* October 3, 1887, 637.

78. Ibid.

79. Mission Record, Turkish Mission, April 10, 1887, 9.

80. Ibid., September 6, 1887, 9.

81. *Scandinavian Jubilee Album* (Salt Lake City: n.p., 1900), 120. See also Evelyn Mackay Frandsen, "A History of My Grandfather, Ferdinand F. Hintze," 1962. Additionally, see A. J. Hansen, "Ferdinand Friis Hintze," 1928, an eleven-page document written by Hansen, a lifelong friend to Hintze, in Rexburg, Idaho, May 10, 1928, LDS Church Archives. Frandsen reports that Ferdinand Hintze practiced plural marriage, marrying his first two wives, Minnie Madsen and Augusta Matilda Hall, in 1876 and 1878, respectively. He took a third wife, Marie Sophia Jensen, in 1882, and a fourth, Nora Mikkelsen, in 1898.

82. Mission Record, Turkish Mission, February 5, 1887, 5.

83. Ibid., May 17, 1887, 7.

84. Ibid., May 18, 1887, 7.

85. Ibid., September 1, 1887, 7.

86. George Teasdale to Ferdinand Hintze, July 7, 1887, Papers of Anthon H. Lund.

87. Mission Record, Turkish Mission, November 7, 1887, 10.

88. Ibid., August 21, 1888, 12.

89. Letters were received by Joseph Tanner in Provo, Utah, from the colonists requesting that missionaries be sent back to Palestine. These pleas were forwarded to Ferdinand Hintze in Constantinople. See Joseph M. Tanner to Elder Hintze, March 15, 1888, Papers of Anthon H. Lund.

90. Magdalena Frey Grau is buried in the German Templer and Military Cemetery in Haifa. Her tombstone is unmistakably Mormon, portraying an angel (presumably Moroni) flying triumphantly through the air and carrying a scroll representing the everlasting gospel. Revelation 14:6 is inscribed on the tombstone beneath the angel. See LaMar C. Berrett and D. Kelly Ogden, *Discovering the World of the Bible* (Provo, UT: Grandin Book, 1996), 157.

91. President Teasdale encouraged Ferdinand Hintze to go to Palestine in letters dated July, August, and October 1888, although Hintze had already left for Palestine in late August.

92. Mission Record, Turkish Mission, August 24, 1888, 12.

93. Ibid., August 29, 1888, 13.

94. Ibid.

95. Ibid., September 12, 1888, 13.

96. Ibid., June 20, 1887, 7.

97. Ibid., September 12, 1888, 13.

98. Ibid., September 14 and 16, 1888, 13.

99. Ibid., September 24, 1888, 13.

100. In the mission record, Nigogos is referred to, in this instance, as Niccais. We are unsure of the reason behind the different name renderings. However, we are satisfied, based on multiple accounts of these conversion experiences, that Nigogos and Niccais are the same person.

101. Mission Record, Turkish Mission, October 9, 1888, 13.

102. Ibid.

103. Ibid.

104. Ferdinand Hintze, *Millennial Star,* January 14, 1889, 28.

105. Mission Record, Turkish Mission, November 23, 1888, 14.

106. Ferdinand Hintze, *Millennial Star,* January 14, 1889, 28.

107. Ibid. See also Ferdinand Hintze, *Deseret Weekly,* February 9, 1889, 200.

108. Ibid.

109. Mission Record, Turkish Mission, December 17, 1888, 15. See also Lindsay, "Missionary Activity in the Near East," 32.

110. Mission Record, Turkish Mission, December 20, 1888, 15.

111. Ferdinand Hintze, *Millennial Star,* January 14, 1889, 28.

112. George Teasdale, Apostle, to Ferdinand Hintze, November 15, 1888, Papers of Anthon H. Lund.

113. Lindsay, "Missionary Activity in the Near East," 32.

114. Ferdinand Hintze, *Millennial Star,* January 14, 1889, 28.

115. Janne M. Sjodahl to Wilford Woodruff, September 22, 1888, Sjodahl's letter file, Church Historian's Office, Salt Lake City, as found in Bernt G. Lundgren, "Janne Mattson Sjodahl—Baptist Minister, Convert to Mormonism, Editor, Author, and Missionary," master's thesis, Brigham Young University, 1971. See also Mission Record, Turkish Mission, January 23, 1889, 17.

116. Janne M. Sjodahl, *Deseret Weekly,* March 16, 1889, 378.

117. Ibid.

118. Ibid.

119. Ibid., 380.

120. Mission Record, Turkish Mission, January 25, 1889, 18. See also George Teasdale to Ferdinand Hintze, February 21, 1889, Papers of Anthon H. Lund.

121. Ferdinand Hintze, *Deseret Weekly,* February 9, 1889, 216.

122. Lindsay, "Missionary Activity in the Near East," 33.

123. Charles U. Locander, *Deseret Weekly,* April 6, 1889, 479.

124. Ibid.

125. Mission Record, Turkish Mission, March 17, 1889, 18.

126. Lindsay, "Missionary Activity in the Near East," 33.

127. Janne M. Sjodahl to Wilford Woodruff, June 23, 1889, Papers of Janne M. Sjodahl, LDS Church Archives.

128. Ibid.

129. Ibid.

130. Janne M. Sjodahl, *Deseret Weekly*, July 17, 1889, 289.

131. Ibid., February 1, 1889, 380.

132. Mission Record, Turkish Mission, February 13, 1889, 18. See also Janne M. Sjodahl, *Journal History*, February 13, 1889, as cited in Lundgren, "Janne Mattson Sjodahl," 37–39.

133. Janne M. Sjodahl, *Journal History*, July 1, 1889, 5.

134. Janne M. Sjodahl to Wilford Woodruff, June 23, 1889, Papers of Janne M. Sjodahl.

135. Mission Record, Turkish Mission, May 15, 1889, 19.

136. Janne M. Sjodahl, *Deseret Weekly*, July 27, 1889, 129–30. See also Janne M. Sjodahl, *Journal History*, May 15, 1889, 8–9.

137. Janne M. Sjodahl to Wilford Woodruff, June 23, 1889, Papers of Janne M. Sjodahl.

138. Janne M. Sjodahl, *Deseret Weekly*, October 12, 1889, 492.

139. Mission Record, Turkish Mission, June 6, 1889, 20; see also July 9, 1889, 21.

140. President Teasdale to President Hintze, November 12, 1889, Papers of Anthon H. Lund.

141. Ibid. See also Ferdinand F. Hintze, *Deseret Weekly*, December 7, 1889, 763. In this letter, President Hintze records that Elders Simmons and Smart had returned to Aintab to continue their service in Turkey.

142. *Deseret Weekly*, November 2, 1889, 582.

143. Ibid. See also Janne M. Sjodahl, *Juvenile Instructor*, June 15, 1892, 363.

144. Mission Record, Turkish Mission, October 11, 1889, 23. See also Sjodahl, *Juvenile Instructor*, June 15, 1892, 363. It should be noted that the mission record explains that the baptism took place at Haifa. However, at the end of the entry is written "Jaffa Record." Furthermore, the *Juvenile Instructor* article referenced herein clearly identifies Jaffa as the place of Louise Khayat's baptism. We believe that the mission record is inaccurate in this instance.

145. Sjodahl, *Deseret Weekly*, November 27, 1889, 92. *Abu al-rukab* is also known as dengue, or breakbone fever.

146. President Teasdale to President Hintze, November 12, 1889, Papers of Anthon H. Lund.

147. *Deseret Weekly*, July 5, 1890, 56.

148. Sjodahl, *Deseret Weekly*, December 20, 1889, 239.

149. Ferdinand F. Hintze, *Journal History*, April 19, 1889, 6.

150. Mission Record, Turkish Mission, March 17, 1889, 18; see also April 26, 1889, 19. See also Charles U. Locander, *Deseret Weekly*, May 18, 1889, 644.

151. Charles U. Locander, *Deseret Weekly*, May 18, 1889, 644.

152. Mission Record, Turkish Mission, April 8, 1889, 19.

153. Ferdinand F. Hintze, *Deseret Weekly*, May 15, 1889; quoted in Lindsay, "Missionary Activity in the Near East," 38.

154. Charles U. Locander, *Deseret Weekly*, July 6, 1889, 53.

155. Ibid., May 18, 1889, 644.

156. Ibid. See also Mission Record, Turkish Mission, April 1, 1889, 18.

157. Janne M. Sjodahl, *Journal History*, May 15, 1889, 8–9.

158. Mission Record, Turkish Mission, April 8, 1889, 19.

159. Ibid., June 3, 1889, 19.

160. Ibid., May 5, 1889, 19. This entry is a record of the baptism of Nersis Garabetian. For an account of the baptism of George Viserian, see ibid., June 25, 1889, 20.

161. Ibid., June 9, 1889, 20–21, and accompanying footnote.

162. Charles U. Locander, *Deseret Weekly*, August 24, 1889, 283.

163. Ferdinand F. Hintze, *Deseret Weekly*, September 28, 1889, 418.

164. Mission Record, Turkish Mission, July 26, 1889, 21. See also Ferdinand F. Hintze, *Deseret Weekly*, December 7, 1889, 763.

165. President George Teasdale to President Hintze, August 7, 1889, Papers of Anthon H. Lund. See also Ferdinand F. Hintze, *Deseret Weekly*, December 7, 1889, 763; and Lindsay, "Missionary Activity in the Near East," 37.

166. Ferdinand F. Hintze, "The Gospel in Armenia," *Relief Society Magazine,* June 1921, 367.

167. Ibid.

168. Ferdinand F. Hintze, *Deseret Weekly*, September 28, 1889, 418.

169. Mission Record, Turkish Mission, September 6, 1889, 22.

170. Letter from President Teasdale to President Hintze, November 12, 1889, Papers of Anthon H. Lund.

171. Mission Record, Turkish Mission, November 6, 1889, 24.

172. Ibid., December 18, 1889, 24.

173. Ferdinand F. Hintze, *Deseret Weekly*, March 15, 1890, 408.

174. Mission Record, Turkish Mission, December 31, 1889, 24.

175. Frederick Stauffer was born October 24, 1866, in Willard, Utah. He was the son of John and Elizabeth Mussler Stauffer.

176. President Teasdale to President Hintze, November 12, 1889, Papers of Anthon H. Lund.

177. Ferdinand F. Hintze, *Deseret Weekly,* March 22, 1890, 411.

178. The details concerning the sickness and death of Elder Edgar Simmons were passed on to Ferdinand Hintze by Elder Dieterle two days after the death of Elder Simmons and one day after his burial. Brother Hintze submitted the letter in full for publication in *Deseret Weekly,* March 22, 1890, 411.

179. Ibid. See also Joseph W. Booth, "Four Heroes Far Away," *Improvement Era,* September 1909, 902–3.

180. *Deseret Weekly,* March 22, 1890, 411.

181. Booth, "Four Heroes Far Away," 902–3; and *Millennial Star,* March 3, 1890, 411.

182. *Deseret Weekly,* March 22, 1890, 411. See also Friederich Dieterle, *Millennial Star,* March 3, 1890, 139.

CHAPTER THREE

Planting, Watering, and Harvesting

1890—1896

After beginning his duties as president of the Turkish Mission in December 1889, Frederick Stauffer wrote his first letter to European Mission president George Teasdale. He noted that "considering the few missionaries that have labored here, the principles of the gospel have spread exceedingly fast. It seems that in every village and city something is known of us."[1] This progress is astonishing. One would not think that such a small group of Latter-day Saints (there were never more than two hundred in the mission at any given time from 1884 to 1928) could be making a name for themselves among the Armenian people of the Ottoman Empire. Nevertheless, such was the case.

This chapter describes the growth and progress of the Church in the Near East from 1890 to 1896. During these few years, four men presided over the Turkish Mission. Eventually, the mission was closed in 1896 due to vicious strife among the peoples of Turkey. Furthermore, three missionaries (including Elder Simmons) died while engaged in the work of the Lord. Yet, most important, several of the honest in heart accepted baptism and were numbered among the Lord's people at the hands of a small group of faithful servants who labored diligently in that part of the world.

Ministering in Anatolia

During the winter of 1890, President Frederick Stauffer continued to improve his language skills as he traveled to different parts of Anatolia. In the spring he paid a ten-day visit to Zara. There, he was sought out by two young, well-educated men, Oskan Dilsizian and Mirijan Baghdadliyan.[2] Within a few days President Stauffer had taught them the basic principles of the gospel, and shortly thereafter they were baptized and confirmed members of the Church. These baptisms were important for two reasons. First, the two young men would bolster the infant Church in Zara. Second, they were proof that the Spirit of the Lord could still pierce through the emerging bias against the Latter-day Saints.

As previously mentioned, antagonism toward the Latter-day Saints was generated, in large measure, by the uncomely conduct of other Christian faiths in the predominantly Muslim region. Since the Latter-day Saints were not a recognized religion in the Ottoman Empire, they were frequently lumped in with their Protestant contemporaries, and no group generated more animosity among the locals than the Protestants. Protestant ministers in Anatolia were generally very kind. The tender aid offered by Reverend Krihor at the death of Elder Simmons is a good example of how benevolent these men could be toward the Saints. However, there were occasions when ministers could be quite cantankerous.[3] Their disrespect appears to have been a matter of general knowledge among the people of the region. In fact, the Latter-day Saint missionaries reported that the disrespect was so strong in some circles that certain locals were prone to say, "No, my son has not become a Protestant; thank God that he has commenced drinking instead!"[4]

Occasionally, even the Protestants would tire of their own faith and congregations and investigate alternatives. This deserves an illustration. One Sunday morning, early in June 1890, President Stauffer and Elder Nishan Sherinian, a local elder who had been called to serve by President Hintze and had joined President Stauffer in April 1890,[5] attended a Protestant service at Mersivan, a village in central

Anatolia. The minister was in the middle of his sermon as the elders entered the back of the church and sat down. Upon seeing the missionaries, he immediately changed the subject of his preaching and mounted an all-out attack against the Latter-day Saints.

After the service, the two missionaries left quietly, only to be followed by the Protestant congregation, who by now had had their interest piqued concerning this new church and wanted to hear more from "actual Mormons" and not from their fiery minister. The host stayed close on the heels of the missionaries and followed them out of the churchyard to the shade of a large walnut tree, where the elders were pressed upon to preach. President Stauffer and Elder Sherinian explained the principles of the gospel to this large congregation in the open air. So far as can be deduced, no baptisms resulted from this day's preaching. However, once again, an anti-Mormon tirade led to greater understanding of the Church among the common people.

With such curiosity being generated throughout the countryside about Mormonism, why were there not more baptisms? President Stauffer explained that their preaching frequently resulted in convincing their hearers of the truth, "but on account of the natural weakness of the people, and the increase of slander as well as on account of bigoted superstitions concerning us we had not the privilege of performing [many] baptisms."[6] Beyond these socioreligious biases, the government was also a source of consistent consternation. The Latter-day Saints were still denied the right to hold any public meetings.[7] Additionally, during this time period, President Stauffer reported that a law had been passed prohibiting most citizens from leaving the empire.[8] This became one more complexity the missionaries had to deal with as they worked to gather the Saints to Zion.

Despite these and other challenges, the work continued. For example, President Stauffer received word from Johann Georg Grau, in Palestine, that he had baptized Karl August Kiel in Haifa. The entry in the mission record says that "this was the nineteenth baptism by divine authority since the Mission had been opened in Palestine."[9]

On June 2, 1890, the elders arrived in Mersivan. They took a room at a *khan* (inn) and began receiving callers. So much had been written of the Mormons—most of it negative—that the curious Christians of Mersivan were more than anxious to meet the missionaries and hear their doctrines in person. So many people visited Stauffer and Sherinian that the proprietor of the khan ordered them to leave at once.[10] Once in other quarters, the missionaries received so many interested callers that they scarcely had time for morning and afternoon meals.[11] Again, however, President Stauffer lamented in a letter to President Teasdale that despite their curiosity, the people were too satisfied with their old ways of life to make the sacrifices associated with joining the Church. Additionally, President Stauffer pointed out that without the Book of Mormon or any written tracts to distribute, actual baptisms would be slow at best.[12]

President Stauffer and Elder Sherinian labored in Mersivan for about seven weeks, until opposition became too intense. Those opposing the work justified their position by claiming pity on those who might be deceived by the doctrines espoused by the missionaries. Before leaving the city, both elders felt satisfied that the gospel had been introduced in Mersivan sufficiently to let the word of God work upon the souls who had heard it. Therefore, they "left them to ponder upon the things which we had laid before them, and we hope that after having 'planted and watered,' that God will, in His own due time, 'give the increase.'"[13]

Because of circumstances at home, Elder Nishan Sherinian was honorably released in August 1890. Given the unsettled political conditions and the health risks in that region of Turkey during the heat of the summer, President Stauffer was counseled to return to Sivas and resume his work there.[14] He explained to President Teasdale that he was willing to work alone but that a companion would be a great comfort to him, if it could be arranged.[15]

In Sivas, President Stauffer worked to translate tracts for the Saints to read. At this time there were a few solid members in Sivas, including three local elders. Aintab, on the other hand, had no one to officiate in the ordinances and administration of the Church. President Stauffer felt that his next proselytizing visit would need to be in Aintab.[16]

Harassed, Arrested, Jailed—but Ever Preaching

President Stauffer's journey to Aintab was anything but dull. Because of an outbreak of cholera in Aleppo, the roads were quarantined between

Adana and Aintab, and a detour to Marash became inevitable. The inconvenience was nearly unbearable at the time but would prove quite providential in hindsight. President Stauffer entered Marash on October 4, 1890, and took a room at an inn before venturing out to see the people. While walking through the streets, he was arrested, and all the books he was carrying were confiscated for inspection. The only complaint brought against him to justify his imprisonment was that he was stirring up the Armenians to war. His case was not to be reviewed for ten days.

Fortunately, he had left a favorable impression in the mind of the innkeeper, who offered himself as a bond for President Stauffer's freedom until the review of his case. This left him free to teach and bear testimony to all who came to hear his message. One of those visitors was a Christian minister named Astur Partamian. He had been an itinerant preacher for years but had never attached himself to any specific sect or religion. The teachings of President Stauffer moved him deeply. He applied for baptism at the hands of the Latter-day Saint accused of insurrection. President Stauffer baptized and confirmed him and welcomed him into the Church on October 11, 1890.[17]

On October 15, Elder Stauffer's case was reviewed by a judge in Marash. He found no grounds for the charges levied against Stauffer and promised safe passage to Aintab under guard. He took the one-day journey on horseback, but upon his arrival he was turned over to authorities and was confined. For two days and two nights he was imprisoned and then learned that a judge in Aintab wanted the case to be reviewed by a judge in Aleppo. The orders were given, and Elder Stauffer arrived in Aleppo under guard three days later.[18] His books and belongings were taken for inspection, and he was imprisoned for two nights and a day with no possibility for bail.

Ultimately, the judge in Aleppo found nothing wrong with President Stauffer's activities and ordered his release. After seventeen days of detention, Stauffer demanded further explanation to justify the Ottoman government's actions against him. He wrote:

> On asking the judge the reason of my having been arrested, he replied that there was nothing, merely some Government matters that could not be told. Thus, after seventeen days, I was set free

without fine or punishment, only having been put to five dollars extra expenses for traveling.[19]

Needless to say, the work in the Turkish Mission could be aggravating when the government got involved.

Aintab: A People Prepared

When President Stauffer finally arrived in Aintab, he was greeted by Brothers Vizerian and Garutch, two local members who had been true to their newfound faith and had maintained the Church in Aintab despite the absence of elders and seasoned Church leadership. After Elder Simmons's death in 1890, the missionaries had left Aintab, and the city went for about eight months without priesthood authority.

However, the absence of elders did not keep Brothers Vizerian and Garutch from teaching the gospel. They converted two others to the faith. When the Armenian Latter-day Saints explained that they did not hold the proper authority to baptize, the new converts joined in the preaching of the gospel as if they had been baptized. They, in turn, convinced a few more individuals of the truthfulness of the restored gospel. In fact, they were so convinced of the gospel's truth that they had been attending weekly meetings and paying their tithing while they waited for an elder to arrive.[20]

We can only imagine President Stauffer's delight when he came to Aintab and found about seven souls awaiting baptism.[21] With such a foundation laid, he scheduled a meeting at the local khan for Sunday, November 2, 1890. The room was packed, with about 150 people in attendance, and the meeting lasted for several hours. Several days later, President Stauffer ordained Brothers Vizerian and Garutch elders in the Melchizedek Priesthood, and they immediately traveled to a nearby river, where Brother Vizerian baptized Sarkis Negoghosian. Certainly, great blessings of stability were being poured out upon the few members of the Church in this city.[22]

Progress in the kingdom of God always faces opposition, however. At Aintab the ministers of several Protestant churches rose up to oppose the newly returned missionary and his new converts. One particularly prominent minister of the Congregational Church in Aintab challenged President Stauffer to a debate on Monday, December 1, 1890.

The invitation was accepted, and word swept through the city. At the appointed time, the minister arrived at President Stauffer's room. A huge crowd gathered, filling the room to capacity. Once the room was full, people gathered on the lawn outside, where, once the windows of the room were opened, the crowds were able to hear the meeting with relative ease. Two hundred people in all listened intently for three hours. The subject of the debate was the apostasy of the primitive Church and the restoration of the gospel in latter times by the Prophet Joseph Smith.[23]

The general mood of the discussion weighed heavily in the favor of the Latter-day Saints. Many of the two hundred gathered that day later sought out President Stauffer and his companions to be taught more fully. In fact, the following Friday, December 5, 1890, the elders accompanied five baptismal candidates to a small pond at the edge of the city. There, President Stauffer baptized Levon Negoghosian, Simon Saatjiian, Hatin Polasijian, Kirkor Meneshian, and Hatin Kurkjiian. Later that evening, they were confirmed members of the Church by President Stauffer, Elder Garutch, and Elder Vizerian.[24]

Although the Saints had to gather at different locations from meeting to meeting to avoid their opponents, the year ended successfully once again. With a total of ten baptisms, there were twenty-five Saints between the two branches in Aintab and Sivas.[25]

In a letter to Brigham Young Jr. (who had recently replaced George Teasdale as president of the British Mission), President Stauffer shared four overriding thoughts. First, he praised the local elders and gave them credit for the fact that "the work [was] making progress in spite of [the] disadvantages."[26] Second, he pled for more elders to be sent to the Turkish Mission, emphasizing that there were "many people anxious to hear the gospel in various cities."[27] Third, he expressed the need for a Mormon colony in the Near East. And finally, he desired to have the Book of Mormon translated into Turkish. He felt that the Book of Mormon "would be the greatest help [they] could have"[28] and would bring a new power to their labors.

Final Year in the Near East

The year 1891 was to be President Stauffer's final one in the Turkish Mission. He spent the first few months teaching the gospel, despite the onslaught of falsehoods promoted by anti-Mormon sentiment. Originating mainly from the Protestant ministers, these accusations constituted the same old harangue—the Mormons were plotting to overthrow the government, they taught the heresy of blood atonement, and Joseph Smith was a fraud and a charlatan.[29] But seekers of truth continued to find the elders and lay hold upon the pearl of great price. On February 14, 1891, a man named Garabed was baptized and confirmed in spite of this opposition, partially deflating a great deal of the anti-Mormon effort in Aintab during the opening weeks of that year.

Because it was illegal for Church members to formally convene as a congregation, sharing the gospel in this area required more energy than in almost any other mission in the Church at the time. Further complicating the situation, President Stauffer explained:

> On account of the peculiarities of the people and country, it is impossible for us to travel from house to house, or from city to city, or to preach as freely as missionaries in other countries, so we have to stay in one city, and talk whenever we get the chance, to those who may be desirous of hearing us.[30]

When President Stauffer felt impressed to travel to a particular city, he was only able to rent a room and pray that those interested would hear from shopkeepers and other townspeople that a Mormon was in the city and seek him out. The only element of certainty in this kind of missionary work was the uncertainty.

An example of this is found in one of President Stauffer's journeys through a town called Nezik. Before nightfall, nearly every Christian who had heard that Stauffer was in town had knocked on his door and received a short tract on the Articles of Faith. When exhaustion had overtaken him and he finally fell asleep, he was quickly awakened by a knock at the door informing him that a number of Christian men had gathered together in order to hear him preach. Despite his taxing journey and great need for rest, President Stauffer cheerfully arose and went to address the people. The discussion continued late into the night, after which he was able to get a little sleep.[31] Although the rigor and difficulty of these situations would have brought any other work to a grinding halt, President Stauffer served on and succeeded.

On Sunday, March 29, 1891, President Stauffer met with the Saints to worship and bid them farewell. His selfless service among these Saints had won him their admiration, respect, and trust. They pledged all their efforts to continue the missionary effort in Aintab after his departure.[32]

On April 6, President Stauffer left for Palestine and spent several days in Jerusalem preaching, distributing tracts, and sightseeing. His presence piqued the curiosity of members of the community, and many families invited him to their homes for additional discussions beyond those taking place in the streets and halls of the city. In fact, a Jewish family requested baptism, but President Stauffer felt impressed to limit his associations with the Jews to teaching only. He gently invited them and others to await a future day when those ordinances could be administered.[33]

After a stay of three weeks, President Stauffer left Jerusalem and traveled to Jaffa, where he strengthened the sole member living there at that time, David Thiel. He then went on to Haifa, where he was greeted for the first time by Elders Johann Georg Grau and Grau's son-in-law, Friederich Dieterle. President Stauffer's stay there was also brief, and soon he sailed for Constantinople, where he spent the entire summer and fall of 1891.

Upon his arrival, his first order of business was to obtain the personal belongings of Elder Simmons, who had died sixteen months earlier. One of President Stauffer's first experiences as a mission president was grappling with this terrible loss, and he felt duty-bound to obtain and return this elder's personal belongings to his family.[34] Following the funeral, Elder Dieterle had mailed Elder Simmons's small valise, but it had been detained in the customs house at Constantinople. The customs agent at first refused to release the suitcase, which contained books and moth-eaten clothes, to President Stauffer. Finally, after surrendering a large baksheesh (tip), President Stauffer obtained the belongings of his deceased elder. He planned to take the belongings with him back to Utah once he was released from the mission.

With this first objective accomplished, President Stauffer undertook a second. Though laws prohibiting public meetings for unrecognized religions were enforced more strictly in Constantinople than in Sivas, Aintab, and other inland cities of Anatolia, President Stauffer set out to do missionary work in the sprawling city, coupling his teaching efforts with an attempt to print much-needed literature that accurately described the restored gospel. Recalling the years of frustrating arbitration that President Ferdinand Hintze went through (without success) to receive governmental approval to print Latter-day Saint literature, President Stauffer decided to contract a printer without the necessary permits. He found a willing printer and paid him just over 950 piasters to print the unapproved gospel tracts.

Unfortunately, his efforts were discovered, and he was sued for the attempt. The court ruled that Latter-day Saints did not have the right to publish religious tracts in the empire.[35] On September 14, 1891, President Stauffer spent the day at court seeking to resolve the immediate problem posed between the Church and the printer. An agreement was reached through arbitration, wherein the printer received 477.50 piasters to cover his expenses, while President Stauffer received 477.50 piasters, constituting the other half of the initial agreed price for printing.[36] In short, valuable time was lost, nothing was printed, the expense was considerable, and the vexation was high.

However, President Stauffer was not about to give up. He appealed the decision of the lower court to a higher court of the Ottoman Empire, and the decision was overturned, guaranteeing the right of the Saints to publish their own literature.

This decision resulted in a new wave of anti-Mormon sensationalism among the Protestant sects who wanted to sway the high court against the Church. Their primary claim in this instance was that the Latter-day Saints anxiously favored and encouraged rebellions against the Ottoman government.[37] Given his experience with such outcries, President Stauffer was quick to point out in his letters home that all the rumblings and persecution would do nothing but hasten the work.[38] He was right.

In spite of the spirited attacks from the local clergy, the work continued to progress in Constantinople and Aintab. President Stauffer received a letter from Brother Vizerian, who was called as president of the branch in Aintab in March 1891 and was now busily working.[39] He reported that the branch had grown to twenty-one members, including five women. At the end of 1890 there had been twenty-five members in the Aintab and Sivas Branches combined. Additionally, there were several people earnestly investigating the restored gospel at the time, and the congregation was poised to grow even more in the near future.[40]

Throughout the summer and fall of 1891, President Stauffer received companionship and assistance from an investigator named Binyad Daniel. They served together until October 6, when Elder Albert Herman and Elder Joseph F. Schoenfeld arrived in Constantinople from America.[41] President Stauffer rejoiced to see American elders again in the mission. He had spent the better part of eighteen months as the only Latter-day Saint missionary from the West in the entire Near East. President Stauffer spent October, the last month of his mission, orienting the new missionaries to their field of labor and teaching them the Turkish and Armenian languages.

On November 6, 1891, President Stauffer was released after two and one-half years of faithful service,[42] with the total number of members in the Turkish Mission at thirty-nine.[43] His departure came on the heels of his final baptism, two days earlier, on November 4, 1891. Binyad Daniel, President Stauffer's helper and companion during the summer and fall, was received into the fold.[44] President Stauffer remarked, "Though I experienced many hardships, I enjoyed my mission better than any other period of my life."[45] The fraternity formed among those who served in the Turkish Mission a great boon to those still in the field. This group of men supported one another in their common experiences and continued to care for the well-being of the mission, the missionaries, and the converts. President Stauffer said of this support, "I felt discouraged many a time but through the encouraging letters of the former President Hintze who after more than three years of long, faithful labor had been released, I felt every time strengthened and determined to remain there and fulfill my duties."[46]

Two New Presidents

President Joseph F. Schoenfeld was called to replace President Stauffer at the close of 1891. He had served in the mission for only three months when he learned that the climate of Constantinople was less than therapeutic for his health.[47] After only getting sicker, Joseph Schoenfeld was released on February 29, 1892, and was transferred to

Adolf Haag

the Swiss and German Mission, where the climate would be more tolerable. At the same time, Elder Don Musser, who had been laboring in the Swiss and German Mission for ten months, was called to preside over the mission.[48] He was transferred to the Turkish Mission with Elder Adolf Haag, and they traveled to Constantinople together.

In the summer of 1892, President Musser directed Elder Adolf Haag to preach in Palestine. Within two weeks, the twenty-seven-year-old elder was deathly ill, suffering dramatic weight loss, heart problems, constant exhaustion, and a body temperature that had reached 108 degrees.

He had contracted typhoid fever and felt that it was a contest between life and death.[49] He was taken to the hospital at Mount Carmel in Haifa, but his condition worsened to the point that he was released on September 16. He returned to Haifa and the home of the Hilts, an investigator family who had become good friends of the missionaries.[50] They gently attended to him until he died at 4:05 A.M. on October 3, 1892.[51]

Because of the excessive heat, Elder Haag's funeral could not be delayed, and he was buried at 5:00 P.M. that day in the small German Templer Cemetery in Haifa. Word of the missionary's death spread quickly through the city, and a great number of people, including the mayor of Haifa, gathered to pay their respects.[52] Elder Adolf Haag's grave is now marked by a large marble block supporting a white, broken marble column—signifying the abrupt and seemingly premature end to his life.[53]

The grave of Elder Adolf Haag in the German Templer Cemetery in Haifa.
LaMar C. Berrett is standing by the monument.

The trauma of Elder Haag's death was not easily forgotten in the mission. But with investigators attending meetings and seeking greater understanding, President Don Musser pressed forward in the work. Shortly thereafter, he baptized Magdalena and Karoline Hilt at Haifa. Ten days later, Brother Johann Georg Grau baptized Jacob Hilt at the same location.[54]

President Musser spent the rest of the year proselytizing, but his success was limited by his investigators' fears of social isolation and persecution, which were sure to follow baptism on account of the displeasure of friends and family members. For example, when Louise Khayat, the first Arab woman baptized in Palestine, passed on in the fall of 1892 after having been a member for three years, Brother and

Sister Dieterle, who had been good friends to her, explained that "she died faithful notwithstanding much persecution."[55]

In other cases, a fear of physical harm or even death attended the consideration of baptism. One case in point will suffice. President Musser met and conversed with a Jew in Jaffa who claimed (rather unbelievably) to have never before met a Christian. He inquired regarding the Church, and President Musser read him the thirteen Articles of Faith. At that point, the gentleman invited President Musser to dinner at his home and expressed a sincere desire that his family be taught the gospel. That teaching led to conviction, which turned into a desire to enter the waters of baptism. However, the man feared the persecution that would surely follow, explaining to President Musser that "his life and the lives of his children would be endangered by his being baptized." President Musser explained that persecution had always been the lot of those who chose to follow Jesus Christ, but to no avail; the man would not consent to be baptized. President Musser's final comments on the matter describe the challenge of bringing souls in the Near East to the Savior. Concerning the man, he wrote, "Though he believed all, he had not the courage to forsake the world by becoming a Latter-day Saint. This is only one instance in many."[56] Nevertheless, there were those who would proceed and join the Church, despite the perceived and real hazards.

In April 1893, Brother Johann Georg Grau and his family emigrated to Utah. He had been the anchor of the Church in Haifa since his baptism at the hands of Jacob Spori in 1886.[57] Fortunately, the newly converted Hilt family assumed the role that the Graus had played for so long. Their home served as the focal point of the Church in Haifa, and they opened their doors to any missionary or Latter-day Saint passing through.[58] Later, Ferdinand Hintze would refer to this family as the mainstay of the branch.[59]

To further bolster the missionary force, Elder Frederick A. Huish was called to serve in the Turkish Mission, arriving in Aintab on August 30, 1893.[60] Additionally, in the latter half of 1893, Elder Albert Herman was sent to establish the Church in Damascus. Because proselytizing Muslims was illegal, Elder Herman did not see much success in the area. He eventually began teaching two people who were seriously considering baptism, but his work came to an immediate halt when the Ottoman governor in Syria banished him from the region for preaching to "Mohammedans."[61] Following his expulsion from Damascus, Elder Herman traveled to Haifa, where he spent the remainder of the year.[62]

As 1893 drew to a close, Elder Huish reported that the Aintab Branch was flourishing. Likewise, Brother Vizerian, who was the presiding elder in Aleppo, reported that membership was growing there as well, due to the diligent efforts of the members. President Musser described the branches in Aintab and Aleppo as "bright and full of promise."[63] The final report of 1893 claimed fifty members of the Church in the Turkish Mission.[64] As a conclusion to the year, President Musser wrote, "The mission is progressing nicely, and I trust we are doing some good, though at times matters look rather discouraging."[65]

TROUBLE IN ALEPPO

Despite the progress of the mission, the year 1894 started off with discouraging news indeed. President Musser received a report of inappropriate conduct in the Aleppo Branch, and Albert Herman was sent to set the affairs of the branch in order. He arrived on March 24, 1894, and over time it became evident to him that Brother George Vizerian was in serious trouble.[66] Brother Vizerian acknowledged that he had been stealing from the tithing funds of the branch. At this discovery, he was severely limited in his authority to perform ordinances and conduct the affairs of the Church in Aleppo. In response to this discipline, he rose up with a rebellious spirit and defied the authority of Elder Herman. After he had met with the elders of the branch and showed nothing but contempt for them, it was decided that he should be disfellowshipped.

It was thought prudent to let the First Presidency review this case. Their response was appropriately acute—excommunicate Brother Vizerian unless he repents. Elder Herman relayed the First Presidency's message to George Vizerian and gave him the opportunity to telegraph the Brethren at Church headquarters with his perspective and feelings. He quickly refused the chance and defiantly claimed no desire to confess his faults or repent of his wrongdoings. Subsequently, on May 20, 1894, he was excommunicated.[67]

To further compound the troubles in Aleppo, Brother Vizerian, like so many apostates, found his way out of the Church but then could not leave the Church alone. He became a bitter enemy of the Restoration and endeavored to poison the minds of the local Saints in an effort to initiate their apostasy. He even created a scheme to steal the records of the Church in Aleppo. The plot was successful, and Elder Herman called upon local law enforcement officers to reclaim the stolen property.[68] Prior to his excommunication, George Vizerian had done so much good, but the devil worked hard to claim this new convert for his own.

Four years later, in 1898, Vizerian had conversations with Apostle Anthon H. Lund that shed light on the errant path on which Satan had led this good man to eventual excommunication. He told Elder Lund that God had given him permission through revelations to steal the sacred tithing funds of the branch. Furthermore, he had been praying that the Lord would choose him and a partner, George Nazarian, to become the two prophets to be murdered in the streets of Jerusalem just prior to the Second Coming. Elder Lund noted in his journal that Brother Vizerian seemed "to have a screw loose."[69] Brother Vizerian's mistakes and eventual dismissal from the Church were heavy blows to the branch in Aleppo. Nevertheless, the work continued to progress.

Appointment of a New President

President Wilford Woodruff, mindful of President Musser's service, recommended that he be released to return to his family after his calling of two and a half years. President Musser was formally released on July 23, 1894, and Edward Robinson was appointed to serve as the new mission president. After entering the mission field, President Robinson took a few weeks to assess the condition of the mission and then reported back to Elder Lund: "We are too few Elders here . . . for so expansive a field. . . . It is a hard and expensive mission and requires Elders that are able to bear the expenses and who are equal to the task of learning a very difficult language. . . . This field is one in which it takes a prayerful heart and a humble spirit to keep alive the spirituality that must attend a successful missionary."[70]

ELDER HUISH DESCRIBES ALEPPO

President Robinson also informed Elder Lund that Elder Herman was extremely sick and that he planned to release him. Soon Elder Huish took his place in Aleppo. In the fall of 1894, the elder provided a valuable description of the city to the Saints in Utah. Elder Huish explained that Aleppo was a centuries-old stronghold of the Muslim faith. In fact, he was told that not many years prior to his arrival, Christians were obliged to walk in the middle of the streets with the animals, not being allowed to traverse the city using sidewalks. By 1894, however, Christians, while still second-class citizens in the empire, enjoyed many of the basic rights that Muslims enjoyed.

Aleppo served as the center of commerce for the region of northern Syria. It was built around an ancient fortress in the center of the city. The area spreading out from this central spot was where the two hundred thousand occupants of the city resided. Elder Huish described Aleppo as one continuous house, because the buildings were so close together and the roofs were flat, making it possible to walk from one edifice to another. The streets of the city were so

A view of the city of Aleppo from the Citadel, looking west toward the Great Mosque.

narrow that if a pedestrian and a camel were walking through the same street, the pedestrian would be forced up against the wall as the beast of burden passed by. Elder Huish also noted the filth of Aleppo. Garbage was strewn about everywhere, despite the fact that men were employed as street cleaners. In fact, as one walked through the city streets, it was prudent to keep an eye overhead, as housewives were ever dumping their garbage and other waste down onto the streets below.

The city was divided into quarters of Muslims, Jews, and Christians. The three groups did not interact with one another except when it was absolutely essential. Intermarrying was entirely forbidden.[71]

Elder Huish's description is valuable because in many ways Aleppo was typical of Ottoman cities of the day. The lack of homogeneity among the different sects, language barriers, cultural distinctiveness, and staunch loyalty to centuries-old traditions all combined to make missionary work in these fields very challenging and sometimes perilous. As we have seen time and time again, converting to a different religion could be life-threatening and would, at the very least, bring persecution and misery which few were willing to endure.

Elder John A. Clark

Given these circumstances, Elder Fred Huish was happy to be joined by President Robinson, who had been in Palestine with Elder John A. Clark since late August. President Robinson arrived in Aleppo on October 24, 1894, and remained there until the winter of 1895.[72]

THE DEATH OF ELDER JOHN A. CLARK

Elder John Clark had been transferred from the Swiss-German Mission to labor in Haifa, Palestine. He arrived on August 29, 1894. One week after his arrival, he wrote a letter to family members at home. The entire letter is included here for two principal reasons. First, it provides a portrait of Elder John Clark, his enthusiasm for the work, his struggle with the German language, and the spiritual influences that moved him to serve diligently. Second, it provides an animated description of

Haifa, Mt. Carmel, and the general economy of the German colony in 1894. The letter is presented here just as it was written, including the original spelling and grammar. Also, we have attempted to preserve the general format of the handwritten letter, which fills two full pages on 8.5x11-inch paper. The letter reads as follows:

Haifa, Palestine
Sept. 5" 1894.

Edward and Wealthy

Dear Brother and Sister,

With pleasure do I address you. This is really September. The Summer will soon be gone and I can scarcely realize it. Am still looking as it were for haying and harvesting to begin. The gathering of grapes is the principal business here and Mt. Carmel yet looks beautiful with the side which is towards me clothed with vineyards and its back hidden in shrubery still green. The fig and olive and sycamore are growing at its feet and above amongst the grape vines. If all Carmel is as lovely as this section here it indeed excelled Isiah (C. XXXV v. 2) said, in predicting the futures of Israel and their country that to this desert which should rejoice and blossom as the rose, should be given the "excellency of Mt. Carmel." The Mt. is about twenty miles long, one thousand eight hundred feet high at the end running seaward and six hundred feet high at the other end. It is very rocky and many walls have been put up in forming the terraces on which the fruit is growing. On the uncultivated land there are still to be seen the thorns and briers referred to by Isiah and the curse pronounced by Amos (II, 2) [sic—this should be Amos 1:2] is at present time traceable. I love to gaze from my open window on these hills where Elijah, also others of the Lord's prophets, worked myracles, which they were, as we now are preaching the gospel of Christ. One thinks he can feel the influence of other departed spirits prompting him to greater diligence in serving the Lord. Although it has not rained during the Summer months much of the vegetation is yet fresh and green. The weather still remains warm, the nights are cooler than they have been. My health is good, sea-bathing is delightsome and I indulge myself nearly every morning. Am enjoying very much my labors here. Am training as best I can my mouth and tongue and throat to the Deutsche language. The throat is principally concerned. It is said that during the confusion of tongues at the tower of Babel a gob of mud, dropped from an elevation of considerable height into a man's mouth. The noise introduced in expelling it received the name German language. I have all the practice I desire, in fact it is seldom that I speak English to anybody beside myself. But I'm having a pleasant time and a good experience, the latter I prize for it is a great privilege to serve the Lord in this part of His vineyard.

I trust you are all well. Shall be very pleased to hear from you.

> Your Aff. Brother
> J. A. Clark
> Haifa
> Palestine

P.S. Please have my "weekly news" directed to Haifa
by J. Hilt
German Colony

I enclose a few leaves
and some seeds   —John[73]

About one week later, Elder Clark wrote another letter home. His excitement for the Holy Land is again evident. "Sixteen days have passed since . . . I was permitted to step on soil of the Holy Land. With thought I gazed in reverence to God for His divine mercies; with my sense for sight I gazed in awe on the land. . . . Am thankful to be a messenger of the gospel of eternal life."[74]

While he traveled to Haifa with President Robinson, he was soon left companionless when, as mentioned before, President Robinson left for Aleppo. Elder Clark stayed with the Hilt family and visited daily with the inhabitants of the city, improving his German and his Arabic. On November 10, 1894, he wrote:

Though I am alone [without a companion] I am having an enjoyable time. I have learned the German language well enough to explain the principles of the gospel to the German colony here. I have carried a tract to nearly every family and, where allowed, have explained to the people the gospel which I have been sent here to preach. On each tract I wrote the time and place of our meetings. Some have read their tracts and made the request for books to read, which I have complied with as nearly as possible. I have written to Bern for some more books and tracts. Getting out among the people appears to be the only way of reaching them, although I believe they would attend our meetings if held in a public place. I intend to try them by this method when I think that the best time has come. In the meantime I shall learn the language better, labor in a quiet way, and also continue my studies in Arabic.[75]

Elder Clark's daily contact with the people had tragic, unforeseen consequences. Later in 1895, a smallpox epidemic raged through Haifa. Unaware that the city was in the early stages of infestation by disease, Elder Clark continued his labors among the people, and by the end of January he showed his first symptoms of the dreaded disease. Although his condition worsened rapidly, Elder Clark received every possible comfort and aid available in the Hilts' home. A physician attended to Elder

The gravestones of Elder John A. Clark (foreground) and Elder Adolf Haag (background).

Clark on February 7 and suggested that while the young man's condition was serious, there was a good possibility that he would pull
through.[76] However, at 1:00 A.M. on February 8, 1895, the twenty-three-
year-old missionary passed away.[77] He was buried on February 9, just ten
days after contracting the deadly disease.

As with the deaths of past missionaries, the tragedy of John
Clark's passing cannot be overstated. Highly esteemed as a missionary
among his peers, he was praised by one mission president for his
"engaging manners," and he said that "the pleasant spirit he was in
possession of endeared him to the Elders." In a telegram to President
Wilford Woodruff, European Mission president Anthon H. Lund
described Elder Clark as "an excellent young man, worthy of the high
confidence placed in him."[78] Elder John Clark was buried in the
German Templer Cemetery in Haifa within twenty feet of Elder
Adolf Haag's grave, and their marble pillar monuments are identical.[79]

THE MISSION CLOSES

President Robinson had already made a plea to the Brethren to send
him more missionaries, and the death of Elder Clark only made that
need more acute. On May 18, 1895, Elder Neils G. Christiansen arrived
at Aleppo and became the presiding officer over that branch, at which
time Elder Huish was extended an honorable release. This brought the
total of American missionaries in the Turkish Mission to two.[80]

Conditions for the Church within the Ottoman Empire worsened
during 1895. After successfully printing some two thousand Arabic
tracts in Beirut, President Robinson returned home with them to
Haifa, only to have them confiscated.[81] Although he reclaimed them
the next day by "tipping" the inspector, he was still required to appear
before a spiteful governor. Indicative of President Robinson's persistence and kindness as a missionary, the governor "afterwards cooled
off and I gave him a tract to read stating that I hoped to baptize him.
At this he laughed, but promised to read the tract."[82]

After paying off the debts occasioned by the death of Elder John
Clark, Robinson stayed an additional week in Haifa to design and order
the distinctive monuments that still stand over the graves of Elders
Haag and Clark.[83] In his personal writings, he gives an interpretation of
the broken pillar design, explaining that it signifies "lives broken off in

their prime."[84] His trip was cut short, however, when he received a telegram from President Lund, reading: "Place Hagopian in charge. You and Christiansen come here [Liverpool]. Answer."[85] The missionaries' lives were in danger. They were being pulled out of the Ottoman Empire, and the Turkish Mission was to be closed indefinitely.

The decision to close the mission was necessitated by mounting political tensions in the Ottoman Empire. As the empire increasingly waned, the nationalistic spirit of the Armenian people waxed stronger. Although they were not the only group within the empire to exult, their national aspirations posed the greatest threat. Any success on their part meant the likely doom of the already dying empire. Like a wounded lion, the empire savagely lashed out against its own subjects, and thousands of Armenians were slaughtered. Unfortunately, conditions worsened before they improved.[86]

These incidents of violence and murder were avoided by the elders, but they posed obvious concerns in the minds of the leaders of the Church regarding the future of the mission. President Robinson and Elder Christiansen were counseled to avoid conversations that might lead to political discussions of any sort. Obviously, such threatening conditions among the Armenian people hindered the progress of the missionary labors. But the elders faithfully persisted, until violence erupted again during October and November 1895.

During this second wave of violence, twenty thousand Armenians were massacred, according to the consulate in Constantinople. The Saints in Zara were in grave danger.[87] While evil men gathered, "sharpening their knives," the Saints determined to fast and pray for seven days for protection from the Almighty. "The result was God raised up a few staunch friends just in time and saved the city. . . . They believed God would save them, and He did."[88]

Meanwhile, a man in Aintab had asked to be baptized in secret, because he could not stand the shame of openly embracing Mormonism. Brother Sarkis Negoghosian counseled him to join the true Church no matter what the cost, but at that moment the man did not have the courage. However, the Spirit of the Lord worked on his heart over the next few days, and he soon determined that he would join the Church. Unfortunately, he would not have the opportunity to be baptized in this life, for shortly after his decision he was dragged out in the street and told that if he would become a Mohammedan and deny Christ his life would be spared. This man who had been so afraid of the opinions of men at this moment proved himself to be a true martyr. He answered the Turk: "How can I deny Jesus when I know he is my redeemer?" A blow, and his white hair was colored with his blood.[89]

Upon hearing of this man's death, President Lund made a special request that his temple work be performed at the earliest possible moment following Lund's return to Salt Lake City.

As this instance suggests, many Christians did not escape, and the slaughter was wholesale. President Robinson noted in his journal that

all but two of the Armenian cities in six provinces had been pillaged. Thousands are starving. Dr. Post, who has been here 30 years came while I was there [at the consulate] and asked the Consul to take joint action with the mission to ask America for immediate protection. There is every indication of trouble throughout all the empire, and I think it is for this reason I have been so suddenly called to England.[90]

It seems apparent from President Robinson's journal entry that President Woodruff in Salt Lake City was more aware of the danger in the Ottoman Empire than Robinson was while in Beirut. President Woodruff immediately sent a telegram to President Lund that said: "Elders in Turkey must not remain. In Danger."[91] President Lund then sent the previously mentioned telegram to President Robinson in Beirut, instructing him to call immediately for Elder Christiansen to leave Turkey, put Brother Hagopian in charge of the branch at Aleppo, and close the Turkish Mission.

Departing in Haste

At the time of the massacres, President Robinson was relatively safe in Haifa and then Beirut. However, Elder Neils Christiansen was in the heart of the difficulties in Aleppo. In fact, a letter from President Lund to President Woodruff indicates the serious danger Elder Christiansen faced in Aleppo. He wrote, "I feel anxious to hear from the brethren there [at Aleppo], as the dispatches from Aleppo give accounts of many having been massacred in that neighborhood."[92]

Elder Christiansen did manage to escape from Turkey, arriving in Beirut on December 9, 1895. But when he stepped off the boat, he was terribly ill. His companion, President Robinson, said he looked like a shadow. As it turned out, he had malaria.[93] He got sicker and sicker, until a physician was called who suggested that Elder Christiansen be immediately admitted into a hospital. His condition was never life-threatening; he simply needed time to recuperate in the warmth of the hospital ward. President Robinson explained that it was impossible to maintain a warm temperature in their rented room during the winter.[94]

Elder Christiansen recovered, and on January 6, 1896, he took a steamer for Liverpool via Gibraltar. He arrived in Liverpool in early February, ready to continue his labors as a missionary. President Lund reassigned him to serve out the rest of his mission in Denmark.[95]

Unfortunately, President Edward Robinson did not travel with his companion to Liverpool as previously planned. Money was the problem. At the time he had been told to close the mission, President Robinson was broke. He had immediately requested funds from Elder Lund and soon thereafter received 875 francs from the mission office to balance the accounts and an additional fifty dollars to purchase tickets for transport to England for the two missionaries. Furthermore, Sister Robinson sent fifty dollars, and Elder Christiansen's mother sent twenty-five to offset expenses.[96] All of this money was used to pay hospital bills, however, leaving only enough for one elder to sail to Liverpool. Elder Christiansen received the ticket. To further complicate the situation, the unstable political environment made it impossible for President Robinson to cash a check, making him literally destitute.[97] He wrote: "This being 'broke' among strangers is a hard lot, but like other things it will pass away."[98] President Robinson made his way to Jerusalem and Jaffa, where he was finally able to depart the mission on Tuesday, January 29, 1896.[99] He arrived in Liverpool on February 8, 1896.[100]

President Robinson closed the mission and reported that there were three branches (Aleppo, Aintab, and Haifa), forty-six members, one excommunication, and one death. There was only one baptism in the mission in 1895.[101] Upon his arrival in Liverpool, President Robinson gave a detailed report of conditions in the mission to President Lund. After carefully considering President Robinson's explanation of conditions in Turkey, President Lund wrote that "in the Turkish Mission the condition is not as I would wish."[102]

The Church in the Turkish Mission during 1896 and 1897

Prior to his departure from Aleppo, Elder Neils Christiansen had ordained Brother Armenag D. Hagopian an elder and called him to preside over the branch, as well as over missionary activity in the former Turkish Mission. Brother Hagopian did so faithfully.[103] This responsibility was no small undertaking for an Armenian, because "the Saints at Aleppo are very jealous, and it [is] hard for them to submit to a local man."[104] Indeed, the condition of the Church in Aleppo was shaky, and in early February 1896 Brother Hagopian felt that there were several members in the branch that ought to be excommunicated because they were not paying their tithing, attending meetings, or acknowledging his authority. Of the existing fifteen members, Brother Hagopian explained that only five, including himself, were worthy to maintain their membership.[105] President Lund instructed Brother Hagopian not to cut any off from the fold without his first reviewing the case in question.

In early 1896, President Lund wrote to President Woodruff, explaining that "without our Elders from home there would be but little progress in the better established missions, and this can be more emphasized still in regard to the work in Turkey."[106] The stabilizing effect that missionaries from Utah provided for the fledgling branches became evident. The most telling statistic is the number of excommunications during their absence, which reached fourteen in 1896.[107] Without the leadership and experience of Utah elders, people joined the Church but found it difficult to be active Saints.

Notes to Chapter 3

1.   Frederick Stauffer, *Millennial Star,* March 10, 1890, 157.

2.   Mission Record, Turkish Mission, May 7, 1890, 25, LDS Church Archives.

3.   While it is true that a Protestant minister aided Elder Dieterle greatly at the

passing of Elder Simmons, this camaraderie appears to be the exception and not the rule of the day in Turkey.

4. Stauffer, *Deseret Weekly*, July 19, 1890, 120.

5. Rao H. Lindsay, "A History of the Missionary Activity of The Church of Jesus Christ of Latter-day Saints in the Near East, 1884–1929," master's thesis, Brigham Young University, 1958, 50. Brother Sherinian was ordained an elder by Frederick Stauffer on May 7, 1890. See Mission Record, Turkish Mission, May 11, 1890, 25.

6. Stauffer, *Deseret Weekly*, October 4, 1890, 489.

7. Stauffer, *Millennial Star*, March 10, 1890, 157.

8. Ibid., May 17, 1890, 395; see also *Deseret Weekly*, May 17, 1890, 120.

9. Mission Record, Turkish Mission, August 21, 1890, 26.

10. Stauffer, *Millennial Star*, June 30, 1890, 413.

11. Ibid.

12. Ibid.

13. Ibid., September 8, 1890, 570–71.

14. Ibid., 571.

15. Ibid., June 23, 1890, 395.

16. Ibid., September 8, 1890, 571.

17. Ibid., October 30, 1890, 763–64. See also Mission Record, Turkish Mission, October 24, 1890, 27.

18. Mission Record, Turkish Mission, October 24, 1890, 27.

19. Stauffer, *Millennial Star*, October 30, 1890, 764.

20. Ibid.

21. Ibid., February 16, 1891, 107.

22. Mission Record, Turkish Mission, November 6, 1890, 27.

23. Stauffer, *Millennial Star*, February 16, 1891, 107–8.

24. Ibid.; see also Mission Record, Turkish Mission, December 31, 1890, 27.

25. Mission Record, Turkish Mission, December 31, 1890, 28.

26. Stauffer, *Millennial Star*, February 16, 1891, 108.

27. Ibid.

28. Stauffer, *Millennial Star*, October 30, 1890, 764.

29. Mission Record, Turkish Mission, January 10, 1891, 28.

30. Stauffer, *Millennial Star*, March 10, 1890, 157.

31. Mission Record, Turkish Mission, March 19, 1891, 29.

32. Ibid., March 29, 1891, 29.

33. Ibid., April 15, 1891, 30.

34. Ibid., August 24, 1891, 30.

35. Stauffer, *Millennial Star,* December 7, 1891, 777.

36. Mission Record, Turkish Mission, September 14, 1891, 31; see also Stauffer, *Deseret Weekly,* January 2, 1892, 53.

37. *Millennial Star,* December 7, 1891, 777.

38. Ibid.

39. Mission Record, Turkish Mission, November 6, 1891, 32.

40. Ibid., September 30, 1891, 31.

41. Ibid., October 6, 1891, 31.

42. *Millennial Star,* December 18, 1891, 797.

43. Mission Record, Turkish Mission, December 31, 1891, 33.

44. Ibid., November 4, 1891, 31.

45. Stauffer, *Deseret Weekly,* January 2, 1892, 53.

46. Mission Record, Turkish Mission, November 6, 1891, 33.

47. Ibid., December 31, 1891, 33. See also Stauffer, *Deseret Weekly,* January 2, 1892, 53.

48. *Millennial Star,* July 23, 1894, 475.

49. *Deseret Weekly,* October 22, 1892, 565.

50. Joseph W. Booth, "Four Heroes Far Away," *Improvement Era,* September 1909, 903.

51. Ibid. See also Lindsay, "Missionary Activity in the Near East," 57.

52. Lindsay, "Missionary Activity in the Near East," 57. Furthermore, about twenty of the Templers became converts to The Church of Jesus Christ of Latter-day Saints, and a branch of the Church was organized in Haifa. Seven Latter-day Saints are buried in the German Templer Cemetery. See also LaMar C. Berrett and D. Kelly Ogden, *Discovering the World of the Bible* (Provo, UT: Grandin Book, 1996), 156–57.

53. Booth, "Four Heroes Far Away," 903.

54. Mission Record, Turkish Mission, October 13, 1892, 34. See also Mission Record, Turkish Mission, October 23, 1892, 34.

55. *Deseret Weekly,* October 8, 1892, 512.

56. Ibid., January 14, 1893, 97.

57. Mission Record, Turkish Mission, April 1893, 34.

58. Lindsay, "Missionary Activity in the Near East," 58. On October 10, 1894, Brother Johann Georg Grau left Salt Lake City for a mission to Germany. Grau's missionary experience there was grievous for everyone involved. George Naegle, Grau's mission president, reported to Elder Anthon H. Lund of the European Mission that Grau had to be released because "his conduct is so outrageous that the Saints will not have him in their houses. He holds meetings and preaches

socialism. The police were seeking him. He advertized in the papers his lectures and gives a variety of subjects among others: 'Mystery' 'The Wife' etc. A paper commenting on this says: 'It is said that this man from Haifa is from Utah, and is a Mormon. This explains his reason for choosing such subjects.' The brethren who have labored with him are afraid he will ruin the branch and give them much trouble with the authorities. He wants to go to Haifa, and I fear he will do harm there. He seems to be not quite right in his mind." Elder Lund to President Woodruff, January 9, 1895, Papers of Anthon H. Lund, LDS Church Archives. Interestingly, Brother Grau traveled from Germany to Haifa to continue his service as a missionary. The mission record entry dated December 31, 1896, states, "Bro. Johan Grau, who had returned to Palestine as a missionary, resided in Haifa attending to temporal matters. He was a great assistance to the little branch, being generous and paying a liberal tithing" (p. 37).

59.   Papers of Anthon H. Lund, October 11, 1898.

60.   Frederick A. Huish, *Deseret Weekly,* August 26, 1893, 300–301. Mission Record, Turkish Mission, August 30, 1893, 34.

61.   Donald C. Musser, *Deseret Weekly,* December 2, 1893, 749. See also Musser, *Millennial Star,* December 25, 1893, 834.

62.   Musser, *Deseret Weekly,* December 2, 1893, 749. See also Mission Record, Turkish Mission, March 24, 1894, 35.

63.   Musser, *Deseret Weekly,* December 2, 1893, 749.

64.   Mission Record, Turkish Mission, December 31, 1893, 34.

65.   Musser, *Millennial Star,* December 25, 1893, 834.

66.   To this point in the historical records, Brother Vizerian is known as Kevork. Hereafter, he is more commonly referred to by the English equivalent George.

67.   Mission Record, Turkish Mission, May 20, 1894, 35.

68.   Ibid.

69.   Journal of Anthon H. Lund, March 16, 1898, LDS Church Archives.

70.   Papers of Anthon H. Lund, August 18, 1894.

71.   Frederick A. Huish, *Millennial Star,* October 8, 1894, 644–46.

72.   Mission Record, Turkish Mission, October 24, 1894, 35.

73.   We received a copy of John Clark's handwritten letter and a careful transcription of the letter from D. Kelly Ogden of Brigham Young University. He received his copy from Wayne W. Clark of Brigham Young University, who owns the original document. (Dr. Clark is the grandson of Edward—one of the two addressees of the 1894 letter—and former associate director of the Jerusalem Center for Near Eastern Studies.) We confirmed this information through conversations with Wayne W. Clark.

74.   John A. Clark, *Juvenile Instructor,* April 15, 1895, 246, 248. This letter was dated September 13, 1894.

75. *Millennial Star,* March 7, 1895, 154–55.

76. *Deseret Weekly,* March 9, 1895, 358.

77. *Millennial Star,* March 7, 1895, 154. The content of this letter was written by President George Naegle, who was serving in Stuttgart, Germany. President Robinson was unavailable because he was traveling, and Sister Kegel, of Haifa, did not have the home address of Elder Clark. She therefore sent news of Elder Clark's death to President Naegle, who reported the news to Church leaders. George Naegle had served previously as a missionary in the Turkish Mission.

78. *Deseret Weekly,* March 9, 1895, 367.

79. Booth, "Four Heroes Far Away," 905. Elder John Clark's grave is located in the German Templer Cemetery, row 4, grave 4, on the right. See Berrett and Ogden, *Discovering the World of the Bible,* 156–57; and Journal of Edward Williams Robinson, vol. 2, November 22, 1895, LDS Church Archives.

80. Mission Record, Turkish Mission, May 18, 1895, 35.

81. Journal of Edward Williams Robinson, vol. 2, November 1, 1895.

82. Ibid., November 12, 1895.

83. Ibid., November 13–14, 1895.

84. Ibid., November 22, 1895.

85. Ibid., November 23, 1895. See also Mission Record, Turkish Mission, December 1895, 37.

86. Robert E. Speer, *Missions and Modern History* (New York: Fleming H. Revell Company, 1904), 441–85.

87. Journal of Edward Williams Robinson, vol. 2, November 26, 1895.

88. Ferdinand Hintze, *Deseret Weekly,* May 21, 1898, 723.

89. Anthon H. Lund, *Improvement Era,* July 1898, 682–83.

90. Journal of Edward Williams Robinson, vol. 2, November 26, 1895; and Lund, *Improvement Era,* July 1898, 682–83.

91. Papers of Anthon H. Lund, November 20, 1895.

92. Ibid.

93. Ibid., December 31, 1895.

94. Journal of Edward Williams Robinson, vol. 2, December 9 and 18, 1895.

95. Papers of Anthon H. Lund, February 15, 1896.

96. Journal of Edward Williams Robinson, vol. 2, December 18, 1895, January 15, 1896.

97. Papers of Anthon H. Lund, February 15, 1896.

98. Journal of Edward Williams Robinson, vol. 2, January 28, 1896.

99. Ibid.

100. Mission Record, Turkish Mission, January 3, 1896, 36.

101. Ibid., December 31, 1895, 37.

102. Journal of Anthon H. Lund, 1896; as found in Mission Record, Turkish Mission, 36.

103. Mission Record, Turkish Mission, December 1895, 37.

104. Papers of Anthon H. Lund, March 28, 1896.

105. Ibid., February 15, 1896.

106. Ibid.

107. Mission Record, Turkish Mission, December 31, 1896, 37.

CHAPTER FOUR

Aintab, Aleppo, Antioch, Alexandria, and Athens: The Work Expands

---

1897–1899

Despite the many internal difficulties and potential dangers in Turkey, members of the First Presidency never wavered in their resolve to get missionaries back into this part of the world as soon as possible. Thus, with a cautious hopefulness, the Turkish mission reopened in 1897. The ensuing three years, from 1897 to 1899, were critical in determining the continued feasibility of missionary work within the Ottoman Empire. During this short time period, the First Presidency sent Apostle Anthon H. Lund in company with Ferdinand Hintze to reopen the mission, organize the Saints, and select a site for a Mormon colony in the Near East. These men also dedicated Palestine again for the return of Judah and the gathering of Israel. Furthermore, the gospel was introduced to Egypt and Greece, and the first authorized latter-day baptism in Jerusalem was performed. These three years set the pace that would carry the Church in the Near East into the twentieth century.

Reopening the Turkish Mission

Two missionaries, Elders Philip Maycock and Andrew L. Larson, were selected to travel to the Near East and serve in the newly reopened Turkish Mission. They had been laboring in the Swiss-German Mission, Elder Maycock for about one year and Elder Larson for six weeks. Elder Maycock was called as president of the new Turkish Mission.[1] On September 8, 1897, they arrived in Haifa, where they received a hearty welcome from Johann Georg Grau and the rest of the Haifa Saints.[2] After a three-week stay in Palestine, they visited the Saints in Aleppo, arriving on October 5, 1897.[3] Brother Hagopian and the Aleppo Saints were so anxious to greet the elders that they met the carriage outside the city limits and escorted it into town.[4]

President Maycock and Elder Larson made an earnest study of the culture and the Armenian and Turkish languages. As with the other missionaries sent to Turkey, this endeavor took the better part of a year.[5] As 1897 drew to a close, there were 130 members of the Church in the three branches of the Turkish Mission. Ten baptisms had been performed, and some of the fourteen individuals that were excommunicated in 1896 now desired to be rebaptized.[6] The most compelling developments regarding the work in the Near East, however, were transpiring in Salt Lake City, Utah.

The Return of Ferdinand Hintze

On December 29, 1897, the First Presidency called Elder Hintze to travel in company with Elder Anthon H. Lund of the Quorum of the Twelve Apostles to the Near East and serve in the newly reopened Turkish Mission. The letter extending the call described the specific objectives of the mission laid out by the First Presidency. Elder Hintze would be "visiting the Saints there, learning their true condition, and taking such measures as you may deem necessary to organize them more effectively than they are at present; and also to extend the gospel to other peoples in any of the regions that you may visit."

In reference to the strict emigration laws that governed this region of the world, Elder Hintze and Elder Lund were also told:

> When you have made yourselves familiar with the conditions
> which exist in those lands, we desire you to visit such parts of

Palestine that you may think suitable in which to select a place of settlement for the oriental [meaning Near Eastern] members of the Church. . . . We feel led to endeavor to select a place of gathering for the Latter-day Saints in the Holy Land. We feel that it would be better for the people themselves, in view of their traditions and habits and their surroundings, as well as in view of the predictions of the holy prophets, that there should be a place of gathering selected at some suitable point in Palestine. This is really the great object to be accomplished by you.[7]

Elder Hintze was set apart under the hands of the First Presidency (Wilford Woodruff, George Q. Cannon, and Joseph F. Smith) on December 29, 1897. President Cannon was voice and blessed Elder Hintze with the assistance of angels to shield him from every harm and with power to work miracles and do all the work necessary for him to have an influence in the midst of the Turkish people.[8] He and Apostle Anthon H. Lund left Utah the next day on a train bound for Chicago.

In Chicago they were joined by an Armenian convert, Hagop Gagosian, who had emigrated to Utah. In returning to the Near East, he hoped to be reunited with his wife and family and bring them back to Salt Lake City.[9] One of the great challenges of this journey was to see if Hagop Gagosian would be able to enter the

Elder Anthon H. Lund of the Quorum of the Twelve Apostles.

Ottoman Empire and be rejoined with his family. Due to the Armenian troubles, the Ottoman government was more than hesitant to allow Armenians back into the country. Moreover, Brother Gagosian began his journey without the paperwork needed to do so. It was believed by the three Latter-day Saints that God would somehow prepare the way, and in this regard, Brother Gagosian was traveling by faith.

The three then traveled to Washington, D.C., where they met with Utah's delegates to Congress in hopes of securing letters of introduction

and endorsement from the government of the United States to Ottoman government officials. The object of such letters would be to
"remove prejudice and prevent the throwing of obstacles in their [the
missionaries'] way."[10]

When the group eventually arrived in Jaffa on February 17, 1898,
the Church's travel agent came aboard their vessel and walked all
three off the boat. Fortunately, they did not have to show their papers
to the customs officers. Once on land, the agent went to work and
somehow obtained a proper passport for Brother Gagosian. The
group's prayers had been answered, to everyone's great relief.

The trio then took transport to Haifa on horseback, allowing them
to view the Jewish colonies up close and consider the work and effort
that a "Mormon colony" would one day require. On February 22,
Hintze recorded that Johann Georg Grau was rebaptized and underwent a review of his covenants. Given his previous struggles while
serving as a missionary to Germany, this was a joyous occasion.[11]

REUNION AT AINTAB

The next day, Hintze, Lund, and Gagosian departed for Aintab,
Turkey. Elder Hintze was particularly anxious to visit Aintab, since he
was the first missionary to introduce the fullness of the gospel in that
region of Anatolia. They arrived on March 1, 1898, and were
welcomed into the open arms of Sarkis Negoghosian, branch president of the thirty members in Aintab.[12] On this occasion, Elder
Hintze explained: "Tears of joy rolled down our cheeks when we met.
Your humble servant felt blessed indeed. Nine years ago or more he
arrived in this city without a friend or acquaintance to bid him
welcome, and now there was a branch of thirty souls."[13]

Brother Negoghosian had diligently taught the gospel to his peers
during the long absence of elders in Aintab. In a letter to the First
Presidency, Elder Lund expressed gratitude that this man had "been
led by inspiration of the Spirit in keeping the people together"[14] and
had "been raised up by the Lord specially for that place [Aintab].
During the trials and hardships through which the Saints have passed
he has ever been staunch and true, and unwavering in his faith, and
has been an inspiration to the Saints to be faithful. They had full
confidence in him."[15]

Brother Negoghosian proved worthy of this confidence by baptizing six individuals prior to the arrival of the missionaries in 1898. Since he did not hold the Melchizedek Priesthood, these converts were in need of confirmation. Above and beyond these individuals were seventeen others (four men and thirteen women) who were anxious to be baptized.[16] Elder Lund interviewed and carefully questioned each of the baptismal candidates and found them well prepared to receive the ordinance. Arrangements for the baptisms were made immediately.

A friend of Sarkis Negoghosian offered the use of his courtyard fountain for the baptismal service. Accordingly, on Friday evening, March 4, 1898, the Saints and baptismal candidates gathered in the courtyard for the sacred service, and each of the seventeen candidates was baptized under the brilliant light of the moon.[17] The joy of adding seventeen souls to the young Aintab Branch made this evening most memorable to all present.

The next afternoon, President Philip Maycock and Elder Andrew Larson arrived in Aintab from Aleppo. Armenag Hagopian, medical doctor and branch president in Aleppo, accompanied them. After retiring to their beds that night, their sleep was interrupted at 4:00 A.M. by Elder Hintze, who gathered all the missionaries together for the early Sunday morning baptism of a Sister Ozunian, the wife of Artyn Ozunian.[18] The early hour was chosen because the courtyard fountain used Friday was not made available to the Saints and the river was some distance from the city; this left the missionaries with only one option—the public bath. The early hour afforded some privacy that could not be had during the day.[19]

Later that morning, the Saints convened for sacrament meeting. Hundreds of people gathered to see the service, but the small home could accommodate only a small fraction of the crowd, leaving about five hundred people outside. Many of these onlookers tried to peer in through windows to catch a glimpse of the proceedings. With all of the baptisms in the past few days, there was a total of twenty-four souls who were confirmed members of the Church that day.[20] On the heels of these confirmations came the blessing of twenty-two babies, the administration of the sacrament, and the long-awaited ordination of Sarkis Negoghosian as an elder under the hands of Apostle Lund. As if that were not enough, later that evening three more young men were baptized by Elder Hintze and confirmed immediately afterwards.[21]

During these first few days in Aintab, the work progressed at a dizzying pace. Brother Hintze explained that their arrival had "certainly made a great stir. Men of fifty years of age say they have not in all their time seen the like. In every direction there is investigation."[22] Elder Lund recorded that "some evenings we had to divide up in three parties in order to satisfy the people in different parts of the city."[23] The interest was so prevalent that it became necessary to obtain a larger meeting hall, the elders sometimes cramming seventy-five persons into a fourteen-by-sixteen-foot room.[24] Although many landlords did not dare rent their property to the Latter-day Saints because of the great crowds they attracted, a man who had met with the Saints on several different occasions enthusiastically came forward and offered his fine hall for twelve dollars a month and himself as a security officer. Elder Lund illustrates how valuable this added service was. "Our meetings last Sunday passed off peaceably [a rarity]. Our new landlord is a man of great moral courage, and he kept the mobocrats in the street. We had nearly a hundred strangers at each meeting."[25]

"The Devil Is Mad"

This spirit of investigation did not go without opposition. As Elder Lund put it, "There are many investigating and the Devil is mad."[26] One manifestation of this anger related to the temporal welfare of the members, many of whom were weavers and dyers of cloth. Over time, Elder Lund learned that they were among the best weavers in town. Nevertheless, they were threatened with the loss of work if they continued to pursue their interest in the Church.[27]

The Church was also the subject of many sermons preached by ministers in Aintab Protestant churches, who sought to stem the rising tide of this new religion in their community.[28] On one occasion, Sarkis Negoghosian confronted a local minister concerning the horrible assertions he was making about the Latter-day Saint people, to which the minister replied, "Oh, I do not mean your members here, for they are exemplary men and women; but I refer to those in Utah."[29]

Furthermore, the professors from the Central Turkish College of Aintab (sponsored by the American mission in Turkey) published five tracts on Mormonism attempting to prove, from the Bible, that the religion was a fraud. The literature attacked from a variety of angles such topics as polygamy, blood atonement, and the Mountain Meadows Massacre.[30]

Finally, the children of the Saints were forbidden to attend school in Aintab on account of their religious beliefs. In response to this prejudice in the community, Elder Lund recommended that "it may be well to start a school of our own in which our children can be taught the principles of the gospel."[31]

At times the persecutions were so severe that it became necessary to cancel some Sunday meetings, meaning that the Saints met only once on the Sabbath, very early in the morning. Even then, people lined the streets to see them going to and from their meetings, occasionally throwing stones. If the elders were invited into a home, a crowd of ruffians would pound on the door or throw stones at the house until they were admitted or the elders were excused. The Saints were forced to call upon the governor of the city for protection, which helped somewhat.[32]

Opposition was not new to the small body of Saints in Aintab. The adversary was working against investigators even before the missionaries arrived in 1898. When Brother Negoghosian was alone as branch president, he had taught a young single woman who became convinced of the truthfulness of the gospel and desired baptism. Her father was much opposed and had instead arranged her marriage to a local ruffian. She had begged her father not to compel her to marry the man, but he would not comply. The local priest had advised the father to have the young man rape his daughter, which would force the marriage and make it impossible for the young woman to associate with the Saints. The father had agreed with this evil plot, and it was carried out. The marriage had occurred according to plan, and the men in her life had never allowed her to return to the faith she had embraced. Unfortunately, this was not an isolated incident. Brother Negoghosian explained that this tactic was used by more than one father to dissuade children from joining the Latter-day Saint congregation.[33]

It is important to note that these events were the culmination of many long years of anti-Mormon sentiment in Aintab, and some Saints felt they could not bear to live there any longer. At this time, the Lord sent relief through an unexpected venue—the missionaries were invited by one Professor Hohannes, from the aforementioned college, to meet with him in a public setting to debate the truths of the restored gospel. The hall was filled to capacity. Elder Lund assigned Ferdinand Hintze, Dr. Hagopian, and President Maycock to represent the Church in this setting.

The subject chosen for the debate was authority, and the elders explained the principles of divine authority from the Bible in a clear and straightforward fashion. Hohannes answered by quoting from vicious, ridiculous, and libelous tracts of anti-Mormon literature in a way that lacked any semblance of credibility. Later, Ferdinand Hintze wrote, "As you may imagine, this was a complete vindication for us. Our new members became stronger, the honest admitted the weakness of the opposition, and altogether had a good influence over the people."[34]

THE SAINTS IN AINTAB

When Elders Lund, Hintze, and Brother Hagop Gagosian had arrived in Aintab, they had immediately sent word to Gagosian's cousin in Sivas, Nishan Sherinian, to join them. After nearly a month, Elders Dekran Shahabian and Nishan Sherinian finally arrived. Unfortunately, harsh weather made their journey from Sivas anything but easy. Tensions regarding their delay were eased, however, when Ferdinand Hintze dreamt that the brethren would arrive safely. Indeed, two days later they did.[35] Hintze recorded:

> When we met we embraced and wept with joy, the most impres-
> sive being the meeting of Brother Hagop and his cousin Nishan.
> They embraced and kissed and cried like children. Brother
> Hagop particularly gave way and cried until he had to be paci-
> fied. For nearly three years they had not met. Brother Hagop had
> been in Zion and was now returning . . . and Brother Nishan
> had closed up his business to come to meet us two hundred miles
> and to see an Apostle of the Lord Jesus Christ. . . . Brother
> Nishan is a genuine Latter-day Saint; for over seven years the

Saints in his town have not seen an Elder and all the time God
has protected them, and led them by His Spirit.[36]

It will be remembered that former branch president George
Vizerian had been excommunicated on May 20, 1894, due to his
involvement in the stealing of tithing funds. On March 16, 1898,
George Vizerian and another excommunicated member, George
Nazarian, sought out Elder Lund and his companions in Aintab,
where Vizerian declared that he "had not come to talk but wanted
money." He wanted money for food, which the elders quickly gave
him.[37] One week later, Elder Lund had a long conversation with
Brothers Vizerian and Nazarian, during which the two explained how
they had felt that they would be martyrs for the kingdom. Elder Lund
spoke with them for some time, after which they both admitted their
errors.[38] Brother Vizerian made an open request for baptism for
himself and Brother Nazarian. While they were not baptized at this
time, as will be seen, the eventual rebaptisms of these men proved to
be historically significant.[39]

Before leaving Aintab, Elder Lund presided over the first conference of the Turkish Mission, where two organizational developments
transpired: first, a Sunday School was organized in Aintab; and
second, Ferdinand Hintze was called and sustained as pastor of the
Turkish Mission.[40]

Although the calling of a pastor is anomalous in the organization
of The Church of Jesus Christ of Latter-day Saints, it is not unlike that
of a bishop and might be somewhat parallel to that of a district president. He is an overseer charged with the duty to maintain the general
welfare of the Saints in a given area (see Jer. 2:8; 3:15; 1 Ne. 1:21;
Eph. 4:11; A of F 6). Under the direction of an Apostle of the Lord,
Ferdinand Hintze was given a post in the mission with significant
responsibility beyond basic proselytizing duties. It is unclear exactly
what those responsibilities were. President Maycock once referred to
Ferdinand Hintze as possessing a "roving commission" in the field.[41] As
will be seen shortly, at the invitation of Elder Lund, Hintze was
invited, as pastor of the mission, to act as voice in a prayer of dedication on the Mount of Olives. This action alone is significant, since
such prayers are usually reserved for apostolic witnesses.

Elder Anthon H. Lund was most favorably impressed with the Saints in Aintab. He strongly recommended to President Maycock that the headquarters of the mission be relocated to that city, as there were now sixty adult members of the Church in the Aintab Branch. He also expressed a firm desire to see the young children of the branch be taught by a faithful Latter-day Saint instead of antagonistic Protestants. The fulfillment of this desire was hastened when a qualified schoolteacher who had investigated the restored gospel just prior to Elder Lund's visit was united to the fold. As a result of his membership in the Church, he lost his job as a teacher. Elder Lund recommended that he could be the headmaster of a new Latter-day Saint school.[42] This is but one example of Elder Lund's desire to care for his new friends in Aintab. He loved these new members of the Church and felt that the Saints in Aintab were full of life and energy.[43] His enthusiasm for the faithful Saints in Aintab was also felt in later council meetings with his Brethren in the Quorum of the Twelve as they discussed the needs of the Saints in Turkey.

A Tour of the Mission

On the morning of Tuesday, March 29, 1898, Elder Lund, President Maycock, Elder Larson, Pastor Hintze, and Nishan Sherinian made their way out of Aintab and traveled south to Aleppo, where they would stay for a week.[44] One pressing issue that Elder Lund felt needed to be resolved concerned the excommunication of Brother Vizerian. Elder Lund met with him and requested the records of the Church that he had in his possession, which he had refused to turn over at the time of his excommunication. This he now did. Brother Vizerian again repeated his request to be rebaptized, but Elder Lund "refused his application for rebaptism as he did not wish to baptize him in his sin."[45]

The five men went on to visit Damascus and then Beirut, and by mid-April they traveled to Palestine. There, they continued to search out possible colony sites in the Galilee region. Their search led them to Tiberias, where they immediately hired a boatman to row them to the southern end of the Sea of Galilee, where the Jordan exits the lake and flows down to the Dead Sea. After two hours of rowing on smooth waters, the party arrived at their destination.

It was now quite hot, and Pastor Hintze suggested a swim from the lake into the river. The rest of the story is related in a sheepish third-person by the nearly drowned pastor himself.

> The water was delightful. Soon one [Hintze] suggested a swim through the outlet down the river. The invitation was accepted and one of our party [Hintze] with confidence in his ability to swim through all right started down smiling, the other two being ahead. Now the water leaves the lake at a fall of about three or four feet to the hundred yards, so the current was quite strong and at one place it flowed quite swiftly. The river is open, and as it was seen that everything was clear for a long way down the river, no danger was suspected. So down went the three Yankees. But an old Arab boatman yelled at the top of his voice not to go and succeeded in stopping the two who crawled out and began yelling also. By that time the third [Hintze] was going down the swiftest place smiling at the sport, saying in Turkish, "Never mind, it's all right." All the time pushing ahead. The old man by this time was nearly wild. He did not understand that it was intentional. He believed that the stream had carried our man off. Now, however, a serious moment arrived, our man swam down all right, but when the swift point was passed and he desired to land he saw a large whirl pool off to the left. He missed the point of landing and quickly surveying the situation he determined on a move for the other side. By this time the calling was terrible and for a moment our man [Hintze] became confused and in the turn lost confidence and felt as though he was sinking. Then he began to cry out to the ferryboat on the opposite side, gel, gel (come, come). This started brother Lund and now everybody except the donkey in the ferryboat, were excited. The donkey was perfectly cool and got an extra ride. All the time treating the matter indifferently. The ferryboat came on to the rescue but fortunately it was not needed. For at the most critical moment, our brother asked himself a question, "Have I come to drown in Jordan?" To which the response was no. Confidence and strength returned and he swam to a place of safety in the river. The old gent was by this time too mad, that while our man stood on the

Front row, left to right: Ferdinand Hintze, Elder Anthon H. Lund, Nishan Sherinian.
Back row, left to right: Philip Maycock, Andrew Larson.
This picture was taken in Palestine on May 9, 1898.

bar, waist deep in water, he flung a great stone at him. . . . An Arab had by this time stripped and came out at full speed not knowing that it was an intentional swim he insisted on dragging our swimmer on shore. But he was not allowed it as our brother after a pause swam to another point up the stream where he was met by Brother Lund and one of the boatman in our own boat and the excitement was over.[46]

A DEDICATORY PRAYER AND BAPTISMS IN JERUSALEM

On May 1, 1898, the five Latter-day Saints left for Jerusalem, where they stayed for eleven days before returning to Haifa. Two extraordinary highlights of this visit to the Holy City took place on the successive dates of May 8 and 9, 1898, the first being the rededication of Palestine, and the second, the first Latter-day Saint baptisms in Jerusalem.

Twenty-five years had passed since the dedications by George A. Smith, Lorenzo Snow, and Albert Carrington. The passage of time had not improved conditions for the Ottoman Empire. In 1898 the empire was on the verge of collapse. A series of economic downturns, capped off by the Crimean War (1853–1856), had compelled the empire to take out loans from Western countries. Over the next two decades, more and more foreign loans were needed. Ultimately, the weight of retaining the sultanate's autocracy and adopting forms of Western bureaucracy, together with the debt, forced the Ottoman Empire to declare bankruptcy in 1875. As one writer observed: "The Turks had lost the benefit of their old ways without mastering the advantages of the new."[47] In December 1876, the Young Ottomans succeeded in drafting a constitution and calling an assembly of representatives under the watchful eye of Sultan Abdulhamid II. The assembly convened for the first time in March 1877, but when war broke out with Russia six months later, the sultan did away with the constitution and the assembly altogether. This resulted in a return to the sultanate exclusively, and the machinery of the massive empire continued to grind to a painful halt.

Between 1878 and 1898, the empire lost large tracts of land to Russia, Britain, Greece, and France. With the land went some seven million Muslims, thus changing the demographic makeup of the empire. For example, the Russo-Turkish Treaty of San Stefano (1878) awarded an interest over the Armenians in eastern Anatolia to Russia. This stirred among the Armenians aspirations for independence, which simmered until the mid-1890s, when the Ottoman Turks, alarmed to the point of action, carried out the massacres in eastern Anatolia. Conditions of complete instability prevailed.

Palestine was part of this complex scenario. Fortunately, conditions in and around Jerusalem were relatively calm as Elder Lund, President Maycock, Elder Larson, Pastor Hintze, and Nishan Sherinian arrived in the region for the fifth dedication. Accounts of this dedication are comparatively sparse, but the following provides a brief overview of the 1898 dedicatory prayer.

Elder Andrew L. Larson noted in his diary that the party ascended

the slopes of the Mount of Olives on May 8, 1898. They climbed to the top of the mount, stopping at the Russian Tower of Ascension (a bell tower referred to in the journal entries of the party as the Belvedere Tower). They were permitted to climb to the top of the bell tower, where they were able to see for miles around. Back at the base of the tower, they walked to the east and found seclusion in a grove of olive trees. The group knelt and prayed, with Ferdinand Hintze as voice, and under the direction of Elder Lund the land of Israel was dedicated for the return of Judah and the house of Israel.[48] The 1898 dedication of the Holy Land confirms, once again, that Palestine ranked as a high priority of the Brethren as the nineteenth century came to a close. First and foremost, priest-

The Russian Tower of Ascension atop the Mount of Olives. Ferdinand Hintze, under the direction of Elder Lund, dedicated the Holy Land for the fifth time at a spot just east of this tower.

hood keys were turned again in behalf of Judah and scattered Israel as well as the land itself.

The second highlight of the visit was the rebaptism of George Vizerian and George Nazarian. The men had traveled all the way from Aleppo to see Elder Lund and to plead for rebaptism. To this request Elder Lund felt impressed to give his consent. The two men "were entirely overjoyed to think that again they were to be admitted into heaven."[49]

There had never been a baptism in Jerusalem by members of the Church in the latter days, and therefore, Elder Lund gave Pastor Ferdinand Hintze the assignment of performing the baptisms. Elders Lund, Hintze, and Larson, along with the two baptismal candidates and Nishan Sherinian, went in search of a suitable location to perform the ordinance.

Their first impression was that the baptisms could be performed in the Pool of Siloam. (Still known by this name, the pool serves as the collecting reservoir for waters that have flowed through Hezekiah's Tunnel. It is located near the convergence of the Hinnom, Tyropoeon, and Kidron Valleys.) Upon their arrival at the pool, they found that the waters were much too low. They continued their search, walking around the City of David and up the Kidron Valley to the Pool of Bethesda near the north end of the Temple Mount. On the way they came across St. Mary's Spring, or Fountain of the Virgin, where, as it is traditionally held, Mary washed Jesus' clothes in the spring water.[50] (Contemporary visitors to Jerusalem may know this location as the Gihon Spring, or the starting point of Hezekiah's Tunnel. At the headwaters of this spring, where steps lead down to the water, there is a substantial pool which is bridged today. In the late nineteenth century, visitors would have had to wade through this deep pool prior to entering Hezekiah's Tunnel.) The group determined that there was sufficient water in the pool at St. Mary's Spring and prepared to baptize Brothers Vizerian and Nazarian.

Women were coming to and from the pool for water, and in order to ensure privacy, baksheesh was given to a local Arab man, who stood watch while Pastor Hintze baptized the two men. They were confirmed that evening at the Lloyd Hotel.[51]

Pastor Hintze's description of St. Mary's Spring is interesting. He recorded:

We baptized two men . . . in Jerusalem. The ordinance was
performed in the well of St. Mary in the valley of Jehosaphat
[Kidron]. The well is underground about fifty feet. It being
reached by substantial steps. I have baptized many before on the
surface of the earth, but not many under the surface. We have
thus proved by this, the first ordinance of the kind in this dispensation in Jerusalem, that there is water enough to baptize by
immersion, although it is a dryer country now than ever before.[52]

Departures from the Holy Land

Elder Lund and his four companions spent five weeks in the Holy
Land searching for possible colony sites, then combined their impressions in a report to be reviewed by President Wilford Woodruff and
the First Presidency. Before leaving for America on May 15, 1898,
Elder Lund wrote a letter to President Wilford Woodruff, wherein he
explained: "We find many obstacles in the way of making a settlement
in this land, but if the Lord's time has come for the accomplishment of
this I know he will help us to overcome them."[53]

The impact of Elder Lund's tour of the mission cannot be overstated. Soon after Elder Lund's departure, President Maycock wrote:

The mission has a promising outlook. The visit of the brethren has
inspired the Saints to new endeavors, and they now feel they are
really part of the brotherhood. Before, they felt that they had been
somewhat neglected. Brother Larson and I too, rejoice that we have
been so much assisted by the labors of the brethren, and we feel a
renewed desire to forge ahead in carrying the banner of truth.[54]

From Palestine, President Maycock traveled to Aintab, while
Pastor Hintze, Elder Larson, and Nishan Sherinian arrived in Aleppo
on May 22, 1898. There had been some contentions among the
Saints since the elders had last departed Aleppo, which Pastor Hintze
attributed to the fact that they were leaderless. Elder Larson was
called to preside in Aleppo.

Beyond the internal strife, there had been external persecutions.
On four different occasions, stones came crashing through the

windows of the meeting hall while the Saints were worshiping. Nevertheless, President Maycock believed that the stonings did far more good than harm, saying: "Of course, if the stone-throwing becomes serious, we shall have to appeal for protection, but so long as it keeps within limits, it is rather a good advertisement for us."[55]

Despite the difficulties, within one week there were eight baptisms in Aleppo.[56] Following these baptisms, Hintze wrote: "It is a great joy to me to see the work of God go on as it does. I have now baptized 36 persons since I came here."[57]

THE CALL OF JOSEPH WILFORD BOOTH

Ferdinand Hintze is known as the father of the Turkish and Armenian missionary effort. Given his two terms of missionary service in the Near East, he deserves an honored place in the history of the Church in that part of the world. However, he is not the missionary with the longest terms of service in the Near East. That honor falls to Joseph Wilford Booth.

The Booths were a prominent yet modest family. Joseph Booth's parents were Richard T. and Elsie Edge Booth, who, in their simple home in Alpine, Utah, reared nine of their ten children (one son died while crossing the plains in 1857). All but two of the Booth children attended either the Brigham Young Academy or the University of Utah. Two became lawyers, four taught school (Joseph Booth included), one daughter married Apostle James E. Talmage, four of the sons served missions for the Church, and two of those four missionaries died in the mission field.[58]

Joseph Wilford Booth

Joseph Booth was born August 14, 1866, in Alpine. He married Mary Rebecca (Reba) Moyle on May 28, 1890, and eight years later he was called on his first of three missions to the Near East over a

The Richard T. and Elsie Edge Booth family, around 1890.
Joseph W. Booth is standing on the back row, second from the right.

time frame spanning eighteen years. Joseph Booth was set apart for a mission to the Near East in early August 1898. He left Salt Lake City in company with Levon Negoghosian, the son of Sarkis Negoghosian of Aintab. Levon had been under the watchful care of Elder Lund, receiving every benefit of education and training the Saints could offer, the hope being that he would return to Aintab and labor to build up the Church. These two men were set apart as missionaries in the Turkish Mission together. Although hopes for the young Armenian were high, when the two reached the Eastern seaboard, Levon abandoned his mission, traveled to meet a friend in Connecticut, and left Booth companionless.[59] In a letter to Elder Hintze, Anthon H. Lund expressed his feelings over losing Levon.

In talking about going home he wanted to know if the Church could give him employment. He said he had understood you to say that the Church would give him work and pay him. I told him to go trusting in the Lord and He would provide. I was not pleased with the question though I did not let him know this. I thought when he got home and interested in the work he would not let temporal matters drive away the spiritual. I am sorry for him. He lacks true stability of character and is not what we fondly hoped he would be. He made the mistake of his life.[60]

Joseph Wilford and Rebecca Moyle Booth

With the hope now gone to have missionaries from their own lands preaching to their own people, Elder Lund keenly felt the loss of Elder Negoghosian. In fact, in another letter to Pastor Ferdinand Hintze, Elder Lund wrote that Levon's staying in America "is certainly a riddle to me. I fear it will have a bad effect on the Aintab Mormons."[61] Unfortunately, Elder Lund's fears would prove to be well founded.

PASTOR HINTZE'S TRAVELS IN CONSTANTINOPLE AND BEYOND

As Joseph Wilford Booth was traveling to the Near East, Pastor Hintze was doing all in his power to gain recognition for the Church by the Ottoman government. Eleven years earlier, during his first mission to Turkey, Hintze had been blocked at every turn by bureaucratic maneuvers against the Saints that resulted in a failure to acquire recognition. On August 29, 1898, Pastor Hintze visited the U.S. legation in Constantinople to follow up on his earlier efforts to gain recognition. He was told that eleven years earlier, the Ottoman government had received notification from representatives of the government of the United States that "the Mormons were not a statutorily recognized people at home [in the United States] and that their religion was a disgrace and they would do all they could to help them suppress 'Mormonism.'"[62] The result of this report was that the consul general was ordered to investigate "one Hintze, an alleged American citizen, who had published a tract without permission."[63] His investigation led to the repeal of the order to arrest Elder Hintze, but all the tracts belonging to the Latter-day Saints were confiscated. It was interesting for Hintze to discover, so many years later, the reasoning behind the Turkish persecution aimed at him over a decade earlier. With more positive relations with the Ottoman government, Pastor Hintze anticipated the eventual approval of the petition to grant the Saints recognition as a church. Such recognition would allow for many privileges, the most important being the ability to hold public meetings freely and to print and distribute tracts and scriptures legally and without harassment.

On September 1, 1898, Pastor Hintze sent a report to the First Presidency regarding his petitions for recognition. He also asked questions regarding possible colonization sites in areas other than Palestine and submitted a request for more missionaries to be sent to the Turkish Mission. With this last request, he sent a recommendation. He suggested that native elders be paired up with missionaries from Utah whenever possible.[64] After submitting the report, he departed for Haifa, arriving on September 12.

In Haifa, Pastor Hintze received word that President Wilford Woodruff had died. On September 22, 1898, Hintze wrote, "President Woodruff's faithful testimonies will long be remembered by the Saints. He was one of the most honorable of the earth, a truthful and unassuming man, much respected and beloved by the people."[65] President Woodruff's successor was Lorenzo Snow, who possessed deep feelings for the Near East, as he had traveled to Palestine and dedicated the Holy Land in 1873.

Over the next six weeks, Pastor Ferdinand Hintze labored from Haifa to Jerusalem. Not much progress was made, as the German colonists in Haifa would not even grant Pastor Hintze an audience. He wrote that "the people of the colony here do not want to see me. I have on several occasions tried to converse with people, but they do not want the disgrace of being seen with a Mormon."[66] While in Jerusalem investigating avenues for land purchases, Hintze learned that the Ottoman government had sent an order from Constantinople to banish him from the empire. By this time, the United States government had sent a positive endorsement regarding Hintze, making it possible for U.S. officials to protect Hintze without apology.[67]

The problem centered around Pastor Hintze's *teskere* (what we might call a passport). It was so plastered with stamps from Armenia that Ottoman officials assumed he must be an Armenian spy. The U.S. consul strongly advised Hintze to obtain a new teskere. When he finally received one early in November, he claimed that with the new teskere he would be "like a new man in the land."[68]

Not all of his travel woes were solved by the acquisition of new documents. Pastor Hintze left Haifa for Beirut on November 7, 1898, with the intention of investigating colony sites. After he had spent nine days in Beirut, the police approached the lone Latter-day Saint and issued an eviction from the city on account of his knowing too many languages. Of this outrageous action, Hintze wrote: "Such rubbish! What little I know may shine alongside of their opaque minds, but otherwise it is to nobody's hurt."[69] Despite his fervent opposition to the action, he had no choice but to leave that very day. He made his way back to Constantinople via Aleppo. He arrived in Aleppo on Sunday, November 20, 1898.

Once in Aleppo, Pastor Hintze was greeted by Elder Larson and the rest of the Saints. The following Thursday (November 24, 1898), Armenag Hagopian presented the Church's petition for recognition to the governor in Aleppo for review. Despite the assurances given Hintze in Constantinople, the governor, or *vali,* immediately rejected the petition, stating that he had been told by officials in Constantinople to anticipate its presentation and to deny it without hesitation. Pastor Hintze noted that "this news was a backset to me, but showed how treacherous this government is; they treated me so nicely and seemed so willing, but sent word to the Vali (Governor) at Aleppo not to accept the petition. I forwarded a report on this matter to President Lorenzo Snow and counselors in the First Presidency."[70]

The Latter-day Saints were also informed that any colonization efforts involving Armenians would not be allowed. The governor explained that if the Armenian people began to gather together in one body as Latter-day Saints, he would move to disperse them.[71] This, too, was a great setback.

While in Aleppo, Pastor Hintze received a letter from Elder Anthon H. Lund. In the letter, Elder Lund discussed the possibility of purchasing weaving looms for the Saints to start a business venture on their own.[72] Many of the Saints in Aleppo and Aintab were gifted weavers. According to Elder Lund, providing seed money for a business venture would most likely infuse the Saints with a greater degree of independence in the work force. This was needed, because many Armenian Saints had either taken pay cuts or lost their jobs entirely when they joined the Church. In addition, it would give the leaders of the Church in Turkey and America the opportunity to see if the Armenian Saints could be relied on and prove their worth as future settlers in Utah.[73] By late November and early December, with Hohannes Boyagian appointed as manager, the enterprise was underway, and the Saints began making cloth. A similar company was formed in Aintab on January 9, 1899, since wages for a Latter-day Saint weaver had been reduced as much as thirty percent in that city. Brother Zadyk Aposian was named manager of this second weaving enterprise.[74]

From Aleppo, Pastor Hintze traveled to Aintab to greet the Saints and spend time with President Maycock. Of the progress being made in Aintab, Hintze was most pleased with the fact that "the best gain in the season's work is the grounding of the Saints more firmly in the gospel as I perceive an increase of faith."[75] This must have been particularly refreshing, since so much of the pastor's time was taken up not by proselytizing efforts but by regulating the affairs of the Church.

For example, just prior to his departure from Aleppo, Pastor Hintze learned that recently rebaptized Brothers Vizerian and Nazarian had been in jail for over three months for preaching the gospel and were now being transferred from an outlying jail to a jail in Aleppo. Learning that posting bail would secure their temporary release, Pastor Hintze sent Brother Hagopian on the errand of buying their freedom. The two joined a meeting of the Saints and bore testimony that they had been imprisoned for the gospel's sake and their afflictions had given them opportunities to teach many in prison.

While Hintze acknowledged that they had been imprisoned for their public witnesses, he also noted that "they had been indiscreet and disobeyed council."[76] It was in Aintab that Elder Joseph Booth would finally catch up with Pastor Hintze.

ELDER BOOTH'S ARRIVAL

Elder Booth had arrived in Constantinople on September 30, 1898, just two weeks after Pastor Hintze had left for Haifa.[77] Entirely alone in the city and waiting for word from Pastor Hintze, Elder Booth decided to prepare to serve by studying languages and scripture. After eight full days of lonely study, Elder Booth turned to the Lord more completely through a special fast in hopes of hastening contact with other missionaries. After five days of fasting, he wrote: "Five long days and nights have passed and still I am waiting patiently on the Lord." On Sunday, October 16, 1898, Elder Booth ended an eight-day fast, recording in his journal that

> at 2 p.m. I retired to my room and although alone so far as human beings were concerned I held divine services and sang and prayed and partook of the sacrament in remembrance of the Lord Jesus. I felt to Glorify the name of the Lord who has been so merciful unto me and I felt that he had accepted of my fasting and prayers and will continue his blessing toward me. About 3:30 o-clock I broke my long fast, eating a plain dinner.[78]

Elder Booth waited eight more weeks before he heard from Pastor Ferdinand Hintze. During that time, he held meetings, taught the gospel to people in his boarding house, and studied as diligently as he knew how. Finally, a letter arrived from Pastor Hintze instructing Elder Booth to travel to Aleppo. Booth arrived on December 14, 1898, where he was warmly greeted by Elder Larson and Armenag Hagopian—the first members of the Church whom Elder Booth had seen since he had left London over three months earlier.

Elder Larson and Brother Hagopian informed Elder Booth that Ferdinand Hintze had traveled to Aintab to labor. And so, after three weeks in Aleppo, Booth made his way to Aintab, where he was finally embraced by Pastor Hintze and President Maycock on January 5, 1899.

Of this experience, Joseph Booth recorded:

> We came in sight of Aintab about sunset and just off to the right
> on a little hill top we spied two men who, answering to a wave of
> my hat and an American "yell" rushed down to meet us and
> there had the pleasure of shaking the hands of Pres. F. F. Hintze
> and Pres. Philip S. Maycock. They received me with a warm
> welcome.[79]

The three missionaries were together in Aintab for only five days,
after which Pastor Hintze departed for Aleppo, leaving President
Maycock and Elder Booth to plant and harvest in Aintab. They determined to increase their number of contacts, which proved challenging, since door-to-door contacting was forbidden in Turkey. They
could only hope that interested persons would call at their flat or
voluntarily attend meetings. In a letter, President Maycock explained
why Turkish customs prohibited door-to-door contacts, and how the
elders increased their pool of potential contacts despite this challenge.

> The reason of this particular prohibition is plain. The women
> and children are left at home during the day . . . and if they were
> seen holding much converse with men, especially with strangers,
> they would be charged with base motives; so also would those
> with whom they conversed. Among the Mohammedans, with
> whom this subjection of the women is fanatically severe, there
> would be positive danger for one who would call indiscrimi-
> nately from door to door. . . . Lately, however, we have begun the
> practice of going from shop to shop, where the men are at work
> weaving. It requires no inconsiderable force of lungs to make a
> louder noise than a group of looms, but we generally succeed. A
> crowd soon gathers, for Orientals are nothing if not curious, and
> we have some interesting and at times exciting occurrences.[80]

March 13, 1899, was Shrove Monday—an Armenian Memorial
Day of sorts that preceded Ash Wednesday and served as the first day of
Lent. On this day, tradition called for the people to gather in cemeteries
to picnic and commemorate the lives of those who had died.[81] While

hundreds of people gathered in the Aintab Cemetery, President Maycock and Elder Booth determined that they would go out among the people and seek an opportunity to preach the gospel. Maneuvering through the crowds of picnickers, they were greeted coolly with the familiar cry of "Mor-r-r," which is the word for the color purple but became a common way for antagonists to mock the Mormon missionaries in Aintab. After a group of men extended an invitation to preach to them, a large crowd quickly gathered around the elders. Soon the number of the press reached several hundred, and they were so boisterous as to make communication impossible. Maycock and Booth were attempting to quiet the crowd when an Armenian teacher roused the group to a feverish pitch culminating in vile name calling and stone throwing. The situation had so quickly become dangerous that several Muslim police officers had to whisk the elders away to safety, all the while defending them by throwing rocks back at the angry mob. Hordes of additional onlookers rushed down the road to behold the spectacle.

The instigators of the whole affair took complete advantage of the situation and spread the rumor among the gathering crowds that the Latter-day Saints had been arrested by the police after committing grievous offenses and were being led off to prison. Therefore, the elders were met with disgusted glances from the misled crowds, and the entire city was in an uproar. Certain members in the countryside who heard of the "apprehension" of the elders armed themselves and came racing to their defense, only to find the missionaries safely resting in their flat.

After relating this experience, President Maycock wrote that

> it is a significant comment on the so-called Christianity of to-day that the professed followers of Him who taught good-will to all men should have to be restrained in their mobbish intention to injure fellow-Christians by the disciples of him whom they regard as a barbarous impostor. It isn't the first time, either, that Mohammedans have had to prevent Christians from committing barbarous excesses.[82]

It is impossible to determine exactly why such hostilities were unleashed upon the Saints this day in Aintab by fellow Christians. However, David P. Charles offers the following possibilities:

Assuming that the "Christian mob" was composed exclusively of Armenians, the agitators might have been one of these groups: Armenian Orthodox objecting to the threat posed by Western missionaries and their divisive influence on the Armenian Church and Armenian people; Protestant Armenians incited by anti-Mormon rumors circulating at the time; a mixed crowd simply protesting against these Mormon trespassers (because burials were under the jurisdiction of each millet, cemeteries generally were segregated according to religion); or any combination of these.[83]

Opposition from Within

Such doses of anti-Mormonism in Aintab in the early days of his mission led Elder Booth to conclude:

> Mormonism is being vigorously opposed by our enemies, but the opposers use oil instead of water to extinguish the flames soon destined to consume the evils of this world. The ministers are the chief agitators, the great fire brigade, against the Mormon confla-gration, and some of them ignorantly stand with the very nozzle of the hose in their hand directing their inflamable liquid of hatred against this ever living fire of truth.[84]

Persecution from without is the legacy of believers; however, a much more insidious form of opposition came from within the Church body. The branch president in Aintab, Sarkis Negoghosian, apostatized and left the Church—and he did not leave peacefully. Instead, he refused to cooperate and insisted on retaining some money that clearly belonged to the branch. Brother Negoghosian was excommunicated, along with three other young men.

The apparent cause of this formerly stalwart member's apostasy originated with his son Levon. Levon (the benefactor of Elder Lund's generosity) had written defamatory letters to his father, as well as other branch members at Aintab, claiming that he had had to leave his home in Bridgeport, Connecticut, because the Latter-day Saints were pursuing him.[85] Of course, nothing could be further from the truth. Additionally, reports had been spread in Aintab claiming that President Maycock and Elder Booth were immoral men.[86]

Fortunately, the character of these two men was above reproach, the spirit of truth triumphed, and many Saints became more faithful to their duties than ever before.[87]

Nevertheless, persecution in the Turkish Mission was so severe that Pastor Hintze called for a general fast day throughout all the branches of the Church. The purpose of the fast was to supplicate the Lord for greater success in the mission (particularly, the right to print religious tracts and scriptures) and to petition for relief from the suffocating persecution that persisted against the Church throughout Turkey. The prayers of the Saints were answered positively on at least one front—Pastor Hintze's labors were hastened in Constantinople with unexpected speed.

New Fields in Egypt, Antioch, and Athens

The Prophet Isaiah apparently foresaw the future of the Egyptian peoples and indicated that the Lord would heal them and they would "return even to the Lord. . . . Blessed be Egypt my people" (Isa. 19:22, 25), although the timing of this prophecy may be "soon," in the "last days," or even during the "millennial era."[88] When these prophecies are eventually fulfilled, 1899 may prove to have been a benchmark year of small beginnings. It was in this year that a mission in Egypt was first proposed to the President of the Church. It all came about because a Near Eastern Saint, being denied entrance to a port in Palestine, was subsequently sent to Egypt.

On October 16, 1898, Armenian Saints Haig Kjevahirdjian and his wife had arrived in Haifa from Sivas. The Kjevahirdjians, who had joined the Church in the late 1880s and were among the very faithful members of the Church in central Turkey, were denied entrance at the port in Haifa. Ferdinand Hintze, who was in Haifa at the time, had tried to intervene but was unsuccessful.[89] Subsequently, he sent the Kjevahirdjians to Alexandria, Egypt, to begin missionary work in that nation. While the Kjevahirdjians traveled to Egypt, Hintze traveled to Aleppo, where he received exciting news from Alexandria in January 1899. Haig Kjevahirdjian was laboring diligently and had prepared three or possibly four Egyptians for baptism.

Another promising possibility was Antioch, Syria, as George Boyadjian, a new convert in Aleppo, had relatives living there. Upon further investigation, Pastor Hintze believed that Antioch would be a fruitful field of labor, as it had been anciently.[90] One problem stood in the way of Church growth in Egypt and Antioch—a shortfall of missionaries.

Ferdinand Hintze immediately penned a letter to Church President Lorenzo Snow requesting that fifteen elders be sent and recommending that a new mission be opened in Egypt so that the elders could monitor the work already accomplished by the Kjevahirdjians.[91]

Meanwhile, Pastor Hintze ordained George Boyadjian a deacon, and the two departed to preach in Antioch. Large crowds of mostly Armenians gathered to hear the missionaries, which caused an uproar among the local Protestant churches. They threatened to have the missionaries physically removed from the region with the aid of Ottoman officials. Fortunately, on this occasion, the government did not pay attention to the wishes of these citizens. In fact, they did quite the opposite, sending a soldier to guard the missionaries. However, Pastor Hintze dismissed him, as he felt they were safe and among friends.[92]

Under these conditions, the missionaries were allowed to preach for the better part of the month of February. However, on March 1 the governor of Antioch told the elders that he had just received a telegram from the Ottoman government ordering him to prohibit any preaching by Mormons in his jurisdiction. A seasoned veteran in such matters, Hintze refused to obey this order, claiming the right of freedom of speech granted by a treaty between the Ottoman Empire and the United States. The governor backed down in the face of Hintze's boldness and shortly thereafter confessed that there never was a telegram sent. Rather, he was working in concert with the local Protestants who wanted the Saints evicted from the region. Commenting on this experience, Ferdinand Hintze wrote: "The whole affair [was] a Protestant trick; they are unable to withstand us with the Bible, so they call in the Turkish Government to help them."[93]

Elder Hintze left Antioch the next day for Alexandretta, where he sent word to Elder Larson at Aleppo to travel immediately to Antioch and follow up with the contacts that had been made in that city. But travel to Antioch for Elder Larson was impossible, since his travel papers were rendered completely useless by Ottoman officials.[94] Elder

Hintze then approached the U.S. consul in Alexandretta, who intervened to clear the way for Elder Larson to travel to Antioch.[95]

ATHENS

To complement the expansion in Antioch and Egypt, Pastor Hintze received a letter from Church headquarters notifying him that there were several people in Athens, Greece, who were waiting to join the Church. The introduction of the gospel into this ancient land in modern times can be traced back to two men: Rigas Pofantis and Nicholas Malavetis.[96] Pofantis was an affluent bachelor, well known in the city of 120,000. The forty-four-year-old Athenian owned a stationery business/printing press and was respected by all who knew him. Malavetis, a man of humbler means, was also in his early forties and married to a woman named Andromache.

In 1894, these two men were searching for Christ's original Church as described in the New Testament but had concluded that such an authorized body of Saints did not exist in Athens. They were so certain that all Christian sects in Greece were wrong that in 1895 they published a small tract, wherein they announced that the Savior's true Church was not in Athens, and delivered these tracts to every friend, minister, and clergyman they could contact. In the meantime, they prayed to find the fullness of the Lord's gospel.

At this time, Nicholas Malavetis had a dream in which he was reading from a Greek newspaper called *O Aster Tes Anatoles* (The Star of the East). He was clearly shown that the year of the publication was 1859. Believing that the dream was from God, he approached the front office of the publisher and obtained the 1859 bound volume of the newspaper. As he pored over that volume, he came upon a translated interview with Brigham Young dated September 19, 1859. A young editor by the name of Kalapothakes had discovered the interview in an American newspaper and felt that this description of one of the American West's most famous citizens might prove entertaining to his readers. Therefore, he had the piece translated and published in Greek, which Malavetis read some forty-six years later.

The article described a church with Apostles, baptism by restored authority, gifts of the Spirit, temple ordinances, no paid clergy, and a prophet of God. Malavetis and Pofantis believed that this was a partial answer to their many prayers, yet they continued to pray for additional guidance from the Lord. These prayers resulted in another dream, this time granted to Pofantis.

In his dream, Pofantis saw a man dressed in normal European apparel with the exception of the Turkish cap (*fez*). The stranger asked him what kind of machinery he had in his printing shop. He showed the stranger the old and worn machinery in his possession, whereupon the stranger bade Pofantis to follow him. The two walked to the harbor, where they saw the most beautiful ocean liner imaginable. Within the ship was the most updated, efficient machinery known to man. In fact, the ship was perfect in form and function. Then the dream ended.

Rigas Pofantis interpreted this dream to mean that the true Church would come to him from Turkey (hence the fez) but not by a Turk (hence the Western apparel). Furthermore, he determined that the ship was the perfect and true Church that would carry him back to the Master.

With this interpretation in hand, the two immediately made inquiries among all they knew concerning a church in Turkey that mirrored the Savior's ancient Church. When they shared their religious ideas one day with an American acquaintance named George J. Webster, he declared, "You believe as the Mormons do." His comment captured his friends' attention and, not knowing English, they begged George to write to the Mormon Church on their behalf, submitting their request for baptism at once. Webster was a Quaker and was quite uncomfortable with their request, but Pofantis and Malavetis would not be denied. The letter was written. Eventually, Ferdinand Hintze received the assignment from Salt Lake to travel to Athens, teach these men, and open a branch if possible.[97]

On March 23, 1899, Hintze landed at Athens and immediately sought out Pofantis and Malavetis. The moment Pofantis laid eyes on Ferdinand Hintze, he identified him as the man from his dream (Hintze was wearing a suit but not a fez). Although he shared as much as he could with them about the Restoration on this first visit, they were no closer to baptism than they were when Elder Hintze was in Turkey. Hintze reported that the men held such strange ideas regarding religion that he was unable to work with them. They were anxious to hear the message of the restored gospel but unwilling to change.[98] As he explained it, they believed that men once converted could not sin. They based this on a passage or two in 1 John. They claimed to be guided by the spirit of revelation. Now these men also possessed good intentions . . . but they were hid away behind so much rubbish that none but those holding the Priesthood and a knowledge of God's plans could do anything with them.[99]

Malavetis explained to Hintze that while they had been commanded by God to join the Mormon faith, they were also commanded not to join the Church until ten years had passed since they discovered that the true Church was not in Greece (about 1895).

Under these circumstances, Hintze could do nothing. He left some literature with them and promised that he would see them again over the next few days to answer any of their questions. After meeting with Hintze a number of times, their feelings changed, and they came to rejoice in the doctrines of the Restoration and begged to be baptized. Then Elder Hintze was inspired to ask the men about their feelings regarding marriage. To this Malavetis explained that he believed that God Himself had married him to his wife. Elder Hintze then explained that he could not be baptized until he was legally and lawfully married. In his journal, Hintze wrote:

I have been very careful with them so as not to push them off, if God has raised them up. . . . If they do not reject the opportunity, but continue to move on in the truth, the Lord will make them instrumental in His hands in doing good and in being the first to receive the gospel in this land.[100]

Malavetis would not yield, and neither man was baptized. Having been rejected in such a bizarre way by the men who went to so much effort to see that he came, Pastor Hintze graciously gave Pofantis and Malavetis the benefit of the doubt by concluding that "it takes persons different from the common run to make the start, and these people may have been raised up to break the ice."[101] As will be seen, this initial rejection of Pastor Hintze cost Nicholas Malavetis the opportunity of being baptized in this lifetime by one holding authority.[102] He died before being reunited with any Latter-day Saint elders.

Pastor Hintze basked in the freedom of religion he enjoyed as a missionary in Greece, which stood as a stark contrast to his usual grind in Turkey. On April 1, 1899, he departed for Constantinople, where he planned to negotiate once again with government officials for the right to print religious tracts.

Meanwhile, the Brethren in Salt Lake were trying to act on Hintze's request for more missionaries in Turkey. The First Presidency felt it would be unwise to send the amount requested; however, the decision had been made to send five elders as soon as possible.[103]

Apostle Anthon H. Lund had been on holiday at Bear Lake, where he met with two veterans of the Turkish Mission: Jacob Spori and Albert Herman. Brother Herman explained to Elder Lund that if the Brethren felt impressed to call him to serve another mission to Turkey, he would be willing to go. Herman did not feel that he had filled his mission completely because of a companion who had been interested more in sightseeing than in teaching the gospel.[104] Furthermore, he had had to leave the mission because of poor health. Given these circumstances, his willingness to return to the Turkish Mission is understandable. Under the inspiration of the Lord, he was not called to return immediately. However, about ten years after this meeting with Elder Lund, Albert Herman would serve for a second time as a missionary in the Near East.

Printing the Word of the Lord

After a great deal of labor and considerable amounts of money spent for baksheesh, Pastor Hintze received permission to print the Articles of Faith in Turkish on May 9, 1899. This was only two days after the general fast mentioned earlier which was dedicated to stemming the tide of anti-Mormon sentiment. Hintze was thrilled beyond description with the news.[105] A short nine days later, permission was granted to print the Articles of Faith in Armenian as well.[106]

Pastor Hintze immediately contracted with a printer to produce five thousand copies of the Articles of Faith in Turkish and five thousand in Armenian. These tracts also included many key scriptural references.[107] The ten thousand tracts were completed on June 3, 1899, and Pastor Hintze immediately sent them to the missionaries and branches in the mission.[108]

The greatest blessing the Church received from this newfound freedom was the possibility of printing Latter-day Saint scripture in Turkish and Armenian. Pastor Hintze soon requested permission from the President of the Church to translate and print the Book of Mormon and selected sections of the Doctrine and Covenants. President Lorenzo Snow felt confident that it would be a great boon to the work and authorized Pastor Hintze to proceed under the direction of Elder Anthon H. Lund.[109] Hintze spent the better part of the summer of 1899 working on this endeavor, as well as a variety of tracts in Turkish and Armenian.

Unfortunately, by late summer it became evident that publication of these scriptures would be impossible for a time because of the Church's poor financial condition. This caused almost all of President Snow's labors to revolve around releasing the Church from its burdensome debt and urging the Saints to observe the law of the tithe.[110] Nevertheless, because of Ferdinand Hintze's diligence, twenty-eight sections of the Doctrine and Covenants were already translated into Turkish, and he began the translation of the Book of Mormon.[111]

Releases and New Arrivals

President Philip Maycock anxiously awaited every mail delivery in the spring and summer of 1899, hoping for news of more elders being sent to the Turkish Mission.[112] But he had no idea that one of the letters received on June 24 would contain his release. The departure of President Maycock was particularly painful to Elder Booth. He was left entirely alone in Aintab, and the total number of missionaries in Turkey dropped to three—Hintze, Larson, and Booth. Knowing that his letter would be published in the *Millennial Star,* Booth penned his feelings at this time and added an earnest plea to be joined by fellow laborers.

> There is a great work to be done among this people, but we can not make much headway with only three missionaries in all Turkey. "Come over and help us" has been the cry for many months, but we can hear of no response yet. We will do all we can and patiently wait for more reapers.[113]

With the departure of Philip Maycock, Pastor Hintze assumed the responsibilities of president of the Turkish Mission.[114] By the end of 1899, Hintze had printed ten different tracts (including "The Joseph Smith Story" and "Pre-existence and Salvation for the Dead"). The combined number of copies had reached 29,000.[115] The value of this work was incalculable.

Thomas P. Page

During the fall of 1899, two new missionaries—Elders J. Alma Holdaway and Thomas P. Page— were appointed to serve in the Turkish Mission. After spending some time in Constantinople training and studying with President Hintze, Elder Holdaway carried a parcel full of tracts to Aleppo, where he was called to serve as the new branch president. He arrived in December 1899.[116]

Elder Thomas P. Page was appointed to labor with Elder Booth in Aintab.[117] President Hintze described Page as a man possessing "a pleasing manner."[118] He had formerly operated a large mercantile business in Riverton, Utah, called the Page-Hansen Company, until his call to the Turkish Mission in 1899.[119] His business skills would prove valuable to the mission and the Saints in Turkey.

Throughout the fall of 1899, President Hintze expected to be released from service in the Turkish Mission. He wrote to his son Royal, "I cannot tell you when I can be home to see you all. I have been expecting to get my release every week but it has not yet arrived."[120] The simple truth was that the Brethren were finding it very difficult to locate a suitable replacement for President Hintze. Soon, however, the First Presidency felt impressed to release him immediately, and on December 20, 1899, President Hintze received his release, with a generous expression of gratitude from President

Snow and his counselors.[121] Although he yearned to see his wife and family in Utah, leaving Turkey was painful for Hintze because so much of his life was invested there in the work. The Turks call Constantinople the "Gate of Happiness," and while the city was the site of great vexation and aggravation, it was also a place of great joy for Ferdinand Hintze.[122]

THE END OF A YEAR AND A CENTURY

At the close of 1899, the statistical report of the mission indicates that there were four elders from Utah serving in the mission: Elders Booth, Larson, and Holdaway, with Elder Thomas P. Page still en route to Constantinople. In fact, the paths of Elder Page and Ferdinand Hintze crossed in Hamburg, Germany: President Hintze was traveling home and Elder Page was traveling to Constantinople. In Hamburg, President Hintze assigned Elder Page to labor in Aintab with Joseph Booth. Prior to his departure, President Hintze assigned Elder Larson to labor in Zara, Elder Holdaway to serve as the president of the branch at Aleppo, and Elder Booth to remain at Aintab.

In the year 1899 there were 102 members of record in the Turkish Mission, with an additional fifty children under eight years of age. During the year, forty-five souls had been baptized, and four members had been excommunicated.

The Turkish Mission had survived the test. The Brethren had hoped that the mission could remain open and be productive despite the ever-present difficulties within the Ottoman Empire. With new missionaries in the field and a forthcoming call to a new mission president, the Church in the Near East could now look toward a new century of anticipated growth.

NOTES TO CHAPTER 4

1. Mission Record, Turkish Mission, September 8, 1897, 37, LDS Church Archives.
2. Andrew L. Larson, *Millennial Star,* December 9, 1897, 782. See also Mission Record, Turkish Mission, September 8, 1897, 38.
3. Mission Record, Turkish Mission, September 8, 1897, 38. The entry under this date includes details from September 8, 1897, through October 5, 1897.

4. Larson, *Millennial Star,* December 9, 1897, 782–83.

5. Mission Record, Turkish Mission, October 5, 1897, 38.

6. Rao H. Lindsay, "A History of the Missionary Activity of The Church of Jesus Christ of Latter-day Saints in the Near East, 1884–1929," master's thesis, Brigham Young University, 1958, 68.

7. Papers of Anthon H. Lund, February 15, 1896, LDS Church Archives. This letter to Elder Anthon H. Lund and Ferdinand Hintze was signed by Wilford Woodruff, George Q. Cannon, and Joseph F. Smith, First Presidency.

8. Papers of Anthon H. Lund, December 29, 1897.

9. Mission Record, Turkish Mission, February 19, 1898, 38.

10. The First Presidency to Senator F. J. Cannon, January 4, 1898, Wilford Woodruff letterbook #1352, vol. 21, pp. 544–45, LDS Church Archives.

11. Mission Record, Turkish Mission, February 22, 1898, 39. See also Journal of Anthon H. Lund, February 20, 1898.

12. Mission Record, Turkish Mission, February 22, 1898, 39.

13. Ferdinand F. Hintze, *Deseret Weekly,* May 21, 1898, 723.

14. Papers of Anthon H. Lund, March 9, 1898. See also Anthon H. Lund, *Millennial Star,* April 21, 1898, 242.

15. Anthon H. Lund, *Millennial Star,* April 21, 1898, 242.

16. Mission Record, Turkish Mission, March 3, 1898, 39.

17. Diary of Anthon H. Lund (May 1896–August 1903), March 4, 1898, LDS Church Archives. This entry in the record is actually noted as March 3—an obvious error that is limited to this entry only.

18. Ibid., March 6, 1898.

19. Ibid. See also Mission Record, Turkish Mission, March 5, 1898, 39.

20. Diary of Anthon H. Lund (May 1896–August 1903), March 6, 1898; Mission Record, Turkish Mission, March 5, 1898, 39.

21. Ibid.

22. Hintze, *Deseret Weekly,* May 21, 1898, 722.

23. Lund, *Millennial Star,* April 21, 1898, 243.

24. Mission Record, Turkish Mission, March 13, 1898, 40.

25. Lund, *Millennial Star,* April 21, 1898, 244.

26. Diary of Anthon H. Lund (May 1896–August 1903), March 6, 1898.

27. Ibid., March 17, 1898.

28. Ibid.; see also March 15, 1898.

29. Lund, *Millennial Star,* April 21, 1898, 242.

30. Ibid. See also Diary of Anthon H. Lund (May 1896–August 1903), March 9, 1898; Mission Record, Turkish Mission, March 18, 1898, 40.

31. Papers of Anthon H. Lund, March 9, 1898.

32. Lund, *Millennial Star,* April 21, 1898, 242. See also Diary of Anthon H. Lund (May 1896–August 1903), March 9, 1898.

33. Diary of Anthon H. Lund (March 24, 1898–September 4, 1898), March 25, 1898, LDS Church Archives.

34. Hintze, *Deseret Weekly,* May 21, 1898, 722.

35. Diary of Anthon H. Lund (May 1896–August 1903), March 21, 1898.

36. Hintze, *Deseret Weekly,* May 21, 1898, 723.

37. Diary of Anthon H. Lund (May 1896–August 1903), March 16, 1898. See also Mission Record, Turkish Mission, March 19, 1898, 40.

38. Mission Record, Turkish Mission, March 19, 1898, 40.

39. Diary of Anthon H. Lund (May 1896–August 1903), March 23, 1898.

40. Lund, *Millennial Star,* April 21, 1898, 244.

41. Philip Maycock, *Millennial Star,* March 23, 1899, 190.

42. Lund, *Millennial Star,* May 5, 1898, 278.

43. Diary of Anthon H. Lund (May 1896–August 1903), March 31, 1898.

44. Lund, *Millennial Star,* May 5, 1898, 279.

45. Mission Record, Turkish Mission, April 1, 1898, 41.

46. Hintze, *Deseret Weekly,* June 25, 1898, 49–50.

47. Jason Goodwin, *Lords of the Horizons* (New York: Owl Book, 1998), 309.

48. Diary of Andrew Larson, 1898, LDS Church Archives. See also Francis M. Lyman to President Joseph F. Smith, May 5, 1902, LDS Church Archives: "I presume President Snow would be pleased to know that I had traversed those sacred precincts where he and President George A. Smith together visited and prayed, as President Hyde had done, and as President Lund did later." See also LaMar C. Berrett and D. Kelly Ogden, *Discovering the World of the Bible* (Provo, UT: Grandin Book, 1996), 44; and A. J. Hansen, "Ferdinand Friis Hintze," May 10, 1928, 7, LDS Church Archives. Referring to the May 5, 1898, dedication, Hansen, a lifelong friend of Brother Hintze, writes that "at this time also, as on former occasions, the home land of scattered Israel was again dedicated by an Apostle of the Lord for the gathering of that people, which is now being fulfilled."

49. Diary of Andrew L. Larson, May 8, 1898.

50. LaMar C. Berrett, *Discovering the World of the Bible* (Provo, UT: Brigham Young University Press, 1973), 277–79.

51. Diary of Andrew L. Larson, May 9, 1898.

52. Hintze, *Deseret Weekly,* June 25, 1898, 52.

53. Papers of Anthon H. Lund, May 15, 1898.

54. Maycock and Hintze, *Deseret Weekly,* July 16, 1898, 145–46.

55. Ibid.
56. Mission Record, Turkish Mission, May 29, 1898, 43.
57. Ibid.
58. For a thorough overview of Joseph W. Booth's life, see Journal of Joseph W. Booth, L. Tom Perry Special Collections, Harold B. Lee Library, Brigham Young University, Provo, UT.
59. Papers of Anthon H. Lund, August 19, 1898.
60. Ibid., September 8, 1898.
61. Ibid., September 9, 1898.
62. Mission Record, Turkish Mission, August 29, 1898, 48.
63. Ibid.
64. Ibid., September 1, 1898, 48.
65. Ibid., September 22, 1898, 48.
66. Ibid., September 27, 1898, 49.
67. Ibid., October 22, 1898, 49.
68. Papers of Anthon H. Lund, November 10, 1898.
69. Mission Record, Turkish Mission, November 16, 1898, 50.
70. Ibid., November 20, 1898, 50.
71. Ibid.
72. Ibid., November 27, 1898, 50.
73. Papers of Anthon H. Lund, December 27, 1898.
74. Mission Record, Turkish Mission, January 9, 1899, 52.
75. Ibid., December 8, 1898, 51.
76. Ibid., December 5, 1898, 51.
77. Events surrounding the arrival and eventual meeting of Elder Booth and Ferdinand Hintze have been taken from the journals of Elder Booth, as cited in Lindsay, "Missionary Activity in the Near East," 73–74.
78. Journal of Joseph W. Booth, October 16, 1898.
79. Mission Record, Turkish Mission, January 5, 1899, 52.
80. Maycock, *Millennial Star,* March 23, 1899, 191.
81. Lindsay, "Missionary Activity in the Near East," 76. See also David P. Charles, "The Day the 'Brave Sons of Mohamed' Saved a Group of Mormons," *BYU Studies* 40.4 (2001): 237–54.
82. Maycock, *Millennial Star,* April 20, 1899, 246–47.
83. Charles, "The 'Brave Sons of Mohamed,'" 245.
84. Booth, *Millennial Star,* May 25, 1899, 330–31.
85. Mission Record, Turkish Mission, May 29, 1899, 57.

86. Ibid.

87. Ibid.

88. For additional insights regarding this series of prophecies from Isaiah, see Donald W. Parry, Jay A. Parry, and Tina M. Peterson, *Understanding Isaiah* (Salt Lake City: Deseret Book, 1998). See also Daniel C. Peterson, *Abraham Divided* (Salt Lake City: Aspen Books, 1995); and Victor L. Ludlow, *Isaiah: Prophet, Seer, Poet* (Salt Lake City: Deseret Book, 1982).

89. Mission Record, Turkish Mission, October 16, 1898, 49.

90. Antioch was where believers in Christ were first called "Christians," according to Acts 11:26.

91. Mission Record, Turkish Mission, January 21, 1899, 53. See also Hintze, *Millennial Star,* February 23, 1899, 126. For President Maycock's plea for additional missionaries at this time of expansion, see *Millennial Star,* January 5, 1899, 11.

92. Mission Record, Turkish Mission, February 6, 1899, 53.

93. Ibid., March 1, 1899, 53.

94. Larson, *Millennial Star,* April 20, 1899, 246.

95. Mission Record, Turkish Mission, March 12, 1899, 54.

96. This description of the gospel being introduced to Greece, unless otherwise cited, is drawn from a series of articles written by Joseph Wilford Booth in 1906 and published in the *Millennial Star,* February 22, March 1, March 8, 1906, 114–17, 129–33, 146–49.

97. Mission Record, Turkish Mission, March 2, 1898, 53.

98. Ibid., March 23, 1899, 54.

99. Hintze, *Journal History,* May 1, 1899, 7.

100. Mission Record, Turkish Mission, April 1, 1899, 55.

101. Hintze, May 15, 1898, Papers of Anthon H. Lund.

102. Ibid. See also Mission Record, Turkish Mission, April 1, 1899, 55.

103. Lund, March 10, 1899, Papers of Anthon H. Lund.

104. Ibid.

105. Mission Record, Turkish Mission, May 9, 1899, 56.

106. Ibid., May 18, 1899, 56.

107. Ibid. See also Mission Record, Turkish Mission, May 9, 1899, 56.

108. Ibid., June 3, 1899, 57.

109. Papers of Anthon H. Lund, June 27, 1899; see also July 25, 1899.

110. Ibid., September 7, 1899; see also June 27, 1899; July 25, 1899.

111. *Millennial Star,* January 5, 1899, 74.

112. Maycock, *Millennial Star,* March 23, 1899, 192.

113. Joseph W. Booth, *Millennial Star,* July 27, 1899, 474–75.

114. Mission Record, Turkish Mission, December 31, 1899, 59. See also Lindsay, "Missionary Activity in the Near East," 80.

115. Mission Record, Turkish Mission, September 30, 1899, 58. See also Papers of Anthon H. Lund, November 17, 1899. These tracts were enormously helpful to the elders, especially during those times when the Turkish government limited the interaction of the missionaries with the people. For example, on September 1, 1899, President Hintze received word from Elder Booth that the government had prohibited the members from meeting as a congregation in Aintab. Prior to the publication of tracts, these restrictions rendered the missionaries virtually useless. But given tracts, Elder Booth reported that even without open meetings "the Elders were doing much active work." Mission Record, Turkish Mission, September 12, 1899, 58.

116. Autobiography of Joseph Alma Holdaway, 1, LDS Church Archives.

117. Mission Record, Turkish Mission, December 23, 1899, 59.

118. Ibid.

119. Maud Page Butterfield, "Entry No. 6 in Journal's Famous Character Contest: Thomas Phillip Page," *Midvale Journal,* February 15–April 12, 1929, LDS Church Archives.

120. Papers of Anthon H. Lund, November 17, 1899.

121. Mission Record, Turkish Mission, December 20, 1899, 59.

122. Hintze, *Juvenile Instructor,* December 1, 1899, 729.

CHAPTER FIVE

Ebbs and Flows:
The First Decade of the Twentieth Century

1900–1909

A Turkish Book of Mormon, a switch of mission headquarters, and three Holy Land dedications—these are just a few of the elements that make the first decade of the twentieth century in the Near East particularly rich in Church history. Due to horrific violence occurring within the Ottoman Empire, this decade also necessitated the closing of the Turkish Mission for the safety of the missionaries. Beyond these occurrences, however, this decade is significant because of the developing organization of The Church of Jesus Christ of Latter-day Saints in the Near East.

A NEW YEAR AND A NEAR DEATH

Elder Joseph Alma Holdaway was notably apprehensive about his new assignment as branch president in Aleppo. Knowing that he would not be near any other elders from Utah, he asked President Hintze a hypothetical question: "What should I do if Elder Booth contracts smallpox and sends for me to come to Aintab?" President Hintze quickly replied: "Don't talk of smallpox, we have had enough smallpox here already."[1]

Elder Holdaway had been in Aleppo for only about two months when he received a letter from Joseph Booth explaining that he was sick and requesting a visit. After arriving in Aintab at sundown a few days later, Holdaway found Booth in his apartment, laid out on a mattress on the floor, afflicted with black smallpox. Holdaway was shocked because Elder Booth had not "prepared me for his condition."

> Had I known before there is a doubt whether I would have gone or not, but after being exposed I could do no more than stay and nurse him through. I had been led to believe all my life if one was exposed to small pox there was nothing else to do only "take it" so I expected I would "take it" also. . . . After I was passed the time for taking the disease I really enjoyed looking after him and noting the love and devotion of the saints to him. They used to come in ten or fifteen a day and shake hands with him and then come and shake hands with me.[2]

Elder Booth noted that he was grievously ill for twenty-two days. The arrival of Elder Holdaway was timely but came after the worst stage of the disease had already passed, a time through which the Aintab Saints waited on him faithfully. In an expression of gratitude, Joseph Booth wrote, "I feel truly thankful to our Heavenly Father for sparing me to continue the pleasant work of teaching the gospel to His children."[3]

The Turkish Mission in 1900: An Overview

The first six months of the new century were filled with change, travel, miracles, and conversions. An overview of missionary activity during this time includes marketing in Aintab, a miraculous delivery in Aleppo, a triumph in Zara, and the arrival of President Albert Herman. These examples will illustrate that the mercies and blessings of the Lord were being deeply felt by the elders and Saints in the mission.

Aintab

After his recovery, Elder Booth spent several more weeks in Aintab and was there when Elder Thomas P. Page arrived on March 1. Page was favorably impressed with the city, writing:

> I am of the opinion that the opportunities for the spread of the gospel are greater here than any other mission of the Church. . . . The reason for my belief is that here we have a people well acquainted with the Scriptures and believe implicitly in the same, but who are to quite an extent dissatisfied with the prevailing forms of Christianity.[4]

Because of the extreme poverty among Aintab Saints at the turn of the century, the arrival of Elder Page and his great business expertise was very providential. Elder Booth noted that the branch was well spiritually but that they were not being redeemed temporally. He recorded:

> Frequently we find our own brethren without food or fuel, and no work whatever to do. Only yesterday one of them came in for assistance, sat for an hour or so, got up and bid us good-bye and then stood at the door, too modest to make his wants known, until he was asked to come in again and say what he wanted. He had nothing to eat for his family, and had been walking the streets nearly all day in a rain storm trying to sell his only coat, offering it for less than a shilling, but could find no buyer.[5]

Elder Page put his business acumen to work immediately. He recognized that Turkey was flooded with cheap goods from Europe, making it almost impossible for the local artisan weavers to make a living. Knowing that additional markets were essential if the small LDS weaving enterprise was to succeed, Elder Page chose to expand into Salt Lake City. He used the frequently published correspondence from missionaries in the Near East as his first forum for advertising. The following extract from a letter will illustrate his marketing strategy:

> The people here make beautiful Turkish rugs, by a slow, laborious process, some of them being works of art . . . [and] they are nearly indestructible. . . . We heard of some carpets being sold a short time ago that were 190 years old. No extra charge for special designs or any name you wish wove in the carpet.

We are also preparing to make a carpet to be presented to the Salt Lake Temple, by the Saints of Aintab, with the design of the Temple and the information that it is a present from the Saints here, as a pattern on the carpet.[6]

Over several years, and with the help of others, many Turkish rugs were carried by ZCMI and sold to the Saints in Utah.

Aleppo

Elder Holdaway soon left Aintab and in April traveled back to the branch in Aleppo. On April 15, 1900, following Sunday School, Elder Holdaway was on one of his usual walks outside the city when he saw a large number of peculiarly dressed people forming a line on the road leading into Aleppo. He soon learned that this line, stretching more than one mile, was formed to commemorate the triumphal entry of Muhammad into the city. As he passed through the line of people to get to the other side, the Muslim participants were incensed to see a Christian do so and yelled, "Gaur, gaur," which means "gentile." At this moment, the irate crowd began throwing stones, and yet, Elder Holdaway reported,

the stones rolled by and over me like hail. There were none of them striking me. I did not run as I should, perhaps, just walked along as though nothing was the matter. I seemed to have no fear, strange for me. . . . I must have walked 45 yards in this manner when I heard one running behind me, heard him puff and heard a spat as though a stone had struck bare flesh. I heard the stone fall to the ground but I felt no shock. At that instant I was coming near a police stand and one stepped out and motioned the rabil [sic] back. I was allowed to walk on peaceably to my home.

When I arrived at my quarters it being high noon and quite warm I removed my coat which was black with a velvety finish and there was the dust spot of the large stone as large as my two fists that I had heard spat on my coat and fall to the ground. I had walked out with my coat clean. I am sure that nothing but the stone could have made the dust spot. One could see the mark of the edge of the stone and all.

Others may doubt or think nothing of such a circumstance like that but to me it was wonderful. The feeling of security with the lack of fear or retaliation. The joy I felt then and the comfort of the remembrances of it all gives me that "joy unspeakable."[7]

ZARA

While Elders Booth, Page, and Holdaway served in their respective fields, Elder Andrew Larson was laboring in Zara, forty miles northeast of Sivas. Unfortunately, some inhabitants of Zara believed that the Church paid people to join its ranks and thereafter continued paying the new convert a monthly stipend. Elder Larson was approached by one man who claimed to know a convert to the Church who was receiving sixty piasters a month. As earnestly as Elder Larson endeavored to debunk this myth, the man was equally earnest in his resolve to believe it.[8]

Such perceptions led to heightened persecutions for the Saints from their Christian contemporaries. The most prominent opponent to the cause had been a leading Protestant in town named Luke. During this most recent round of harassment, however, Luke was conspicuously absent. New trouble began when a member got engaged to a young Campbellite woman. The local Christians found this marriage unacceptable and convinced the authorities that Elder Larson should be arrested, interrogated, and detained in order to stall the nuptial. Elder Larson was taken before the police commissioner and the mayor for an investigation, during which crowds had gathered with expectations of formal banishment or some other severe restriction. In this they were sorely disappointed, for Larson related that he was treated with utmost respect by these gentlemen, who, after a friendly chat, released him to freely pursue his personal interests in their city.

As Elder Larson made his way through the disappointed crowd, he was approached by Luke, his granddaughter, and the newlywed bride, all of whom requested immediate baptism at the hands of Elder Larson. They discreetly made their way to the banks of the Red River and were baptized. Of this occasion Elder Larson wrote, "You may be sure there was joy in Zion's camp that night. . . . There are now 23 members and 13 children [in Zara]."[9] Near the end of May that year, Elder Larson was released from his faithful service of nearly three years.

President Albert Herman and New Setbacks

In the spring of 1900, about ten years after expressing to Elder Lund a willingness to return to the Near East, Albert Herman was called to serve as the president of the Turkish Mission. After arriving in Constantinople in July, he traveled to Aintab on a bicycle.[10] Here, he faced his first administrative challenge as president of the mission.

Prior to his departure, President Hintze had encouraged Elder Booth to find a cheaper meeting hall for the branch and school. Booth found a member of the branch who suggested that he could build a second story on his large home and rent the upper floor to the branch for considerably less than they were then paying. Contracts were drawn up and construction began.

By the fall, the outer walls of the structure were almost completed when the builder frantically told Booth that the neighbors were in an uproar that a "Mormon church" was being built. The rumor had it that the building would be tall enough so that the elders could sit atop the structure and command a desecrating view of the young women of the city.

With this news, a petition was circulated and brought before the city council, which ordered the building to be knocked to the ground. President Herman wrote that

> strange men came, and with a whoop and yell, rocks and timber went a flying in all directions, not only the new, but also the lower story of the old part was torn down to the very ground, incurring a complete loss of the money paid by the Church and depriving the builder of his own home. What could be done?—the builder lamented over the loss of his money. To make the best of the end, Bro. [Booth] yielded to the pitiful coaxing of the unfortunate man, and waded a little deeper by giving him more money to get a new permit and build an inferior building of a smaller size.[11]

The destruction of their meetinghouse was difficult for Booth, for it seemed that progress was blocked at every turn. However, his frustrations were partially soothed by the arrival of President Herman and Elder Willis Lester Mangum, bringing the number of missionaries to five.

On October 31, 1900, President Herman and Elders Booth and Page departed for a tour of the Holy Land on bicycle. Elders already attracted attention when entering a town, but Latter-day Saint missionaries on bicycles were quite a spectacle. They experienced many adventures, such as carrying their bikes over treacherous mountain passes, camping out with bedouin, crashing numerous times and getting bloody scrapes, and surviving on whatever foods they found along the way, including sheep's-head soup and buffalo milk.[12] The threesome finally arrived in Haifa on December 10, 1900.[13] After a short visit, Elders Booth and Page were stricken with malaria. They had hoped to visit Jerusalem, but their condition was too poor. After sufficient recuperation, they boarded a ship bound for Alexandretta and then traveled inland to Aintab.[14] Thus ended the first-ever bicycle tour of Latter-day Saint missionaries in the Near East.

For Elder Thomas P. Page, the price of their visit to Palestine was high. He never fully recovered from his bout with malaria and was released in the spring of 1901.[15] Upon his release, Joseph Booth wrote, "We had hoped [he] would be one of the long staying missionaries to do much good in the field but now we think the Lord has work for him at home, still in the interest of the Turkish Mission."[16] Indeed, his labors for the Armenian Saints continued in Utah in the form of placing carpet orders for the weaving Saints in Aintab and Aleppo. His experience in the Near East was so valuable to the Brethren that he would eventually return to the Turkish Mission on a special assignment from the First Presidency of the Church.

Page's departure dropped the number of missionaries to four. They were spread so thin that the work at times seemed to overwhelm them. Nevertheless, they faithfully plodded on, as evidenced in the closing line of Elder Mangum's letter dated April 3, 1901. "The sky is a little cloudy just now, but we are hopeful, and are patiently looking for the silver lining."[17]

President Herman's Analysis of Conditions

Following the bicycle tour, President Herman was still in Haifa when Johann Georg Grau died suddenly on June 9, 1901—the first man baptized by the authority of the priesthood in Palestine since the

days of Jesus' Apostles. Brother Grau had served diligently in the Haifa Branch for many years and was buried in the Templer Cemetery at the foot of Mt. Carmel in Haifa.[18]

In late July 1901, President Herman apologetically wrote to Elder Lund, explaining that he had mistakenly overestimated the advances the Turkish

The tombstone of Johann Georg Grau, located in the German Templer Cemetery in Haifa.

Mission would make up to that point. The difficulties of the times moved Brother Herman to be blunt in his report to the Brethren, which shed light on two important issues: the ever-fluctuating relationship between the Church and the Ottoman government, and the condition of the Saints in Turkey and Syria. With the question of Latter-day Saint colonization in the Near East or emigration to join the Saints in Utah, the character and fortitude of the Turkish Saints was a consistent query put forth by the Brethren.

President Herman asks, "Who is to blame for the wretchedly slow progress in Turkey—where is the fault?" In the report, he answers this question himself.

> The fault lies in the administrative government that exists by the will of God. Sultan Hamid and his precarious government labor under a guilty conscience that is haunted by every innovation as the terminating stroke to its existence, and every book school and missionary is fearfully looked upon as a phantom ghost presaging its end. We have no rights, no privileges no protection as a religious organization in Turkey. . . . We may travel as U.S. citizens, and as such have protection, but not as Mormon

Missionaries. In fact, I am the only L.D.S. missionary here in this land, the balance of our brethren have their religious designation on their passports and papers as Protestants, the name Mormon being refused them even on their papers.[19]

The members of the Church in the Ottoman Empire did not receive a glowing report from President Herman either. In the late nineteenth century and early twentieth century, the Church was in dire straits financially. It will be remembered that, in these difficult conditions, the Brethren were making consistent efforts to assist the impoverished Saints in Turkey by carefully channeling tithing funds to work projects such as rug weaving. While the project was valuable, there was not enough work and resources to supply all the needs. Rather, President Herman found that jealousy and backbiting, instead of gratitude and industry, were the frequent fruits of the weaving enterprise.

While these difficulties persisted, the missionaries continued to search for more effective ways to introduce the gospel to the people of the region, with a particular focus on the Armenians. Just prior to the bicycle tour to Palestine, President Herman assigned Elders Booth and Holdaway to make a lengthy four-month tour of the mission. This proselytizing strategy was geared more toward public relations than baptizing Turks and was inspired by the sparse number of elders in the mission. Toward the end of the summer of 1901, two months into their tour, Elder Holdaway reported that they had made many friends with both Christians and Muslims, seeds they hoped later would be harvested.[20]

Late in 1901, President Herman intercepted the traveling elders in Zara and announced a reassignment. Elder Alma Holdaway would finish the tour with President Herman and then proceed directly to Aintab to preside over the branch. Elder Booth, on the other hand, received the assignment to remain in Zara through the winter, assisting Nishan Sherinian in bolstering the branch members in the faith. He also agreed to teach school for the children of the branch.[21] This would allow Elder Mangum the opportunity to serve away from the established centers of the Church in Turkey.

President Herman advised Elder Mangum to prepare for an entirely new field of labor. Even with that warning, Elder Mangum manifested a good deal of shock when he received his assignment. He was called to travel to the east side of the Euphrates and preach the gospel to people who had never seen a Latter-day Saint elder. President Herman explained that there were not enough elders in the field for him to have a companion, and therefore he would be entirely alone in his work. Upon learning that he would be companionless, Elder Mangum wrote, "If I did not realize that there is a great shortage of Elders, I might think we were neglected to be thus compelled to labor alone in such difficult fields."[22]

Yet, just as Mangum penned these words, there were two elders from Utah en route. Elders Henry and Charles Teuscher had accepted calls to serve in Turkey.[23] They arrived in Liverpool on November 14, 1901, and from there traveled to Turkey.[24] Furthermore, a convert from the Turkish Mission would soon make his way toward Asia Minor. By midyear 1903, Mischa Markow would be preaching the gospel in the Turkish Mission.

A letter from Elder Mangum to Ferdinand Hintze at the close of this year preserves a valuable picture of conditions in Turkey at the time. He reported that there were forty members and children in Aleppo, eighty in Aintab, and thirty-five in Zara. Under the leadership of Nishan Sherinian, the small group of Saints in Zara was flourishing. Aleppo, on the other hand, was deemed "asleep" to the restored gospel, and Elder Mangum stated that the Saints in Aintab were also struggling with commitment. "If their acts corresponded to their knowledge, our portion of Aintab would be a modern 'City of Enoch.'"[25]

As can be seen, there were ebbs and flows to the proselytizing work in the Turkish Mission. At times the missionaries were certain that they were on the verge of baptizing hundreds and creating a latter-day "City of Enoch," and not long thereafter the same missionaries in the same areas would describe the Armenian Saints as "lying low" or "asleep." While there were many successes throughout the years, they never culminated in a large body of Saints in the region. In fact, during the first three decades of the twentieth century, there were never more than two hundred members of the Church in the Near East.[26] However, the enthusiastic reports should not be viewed as misleading. Rather, they serve to illustrate the great desires and yearnings of the missionaries, the potential they saw in the Armenian people, and the general optimism that accompanies work grounded in faith.

A MISSION TOUR AND NEW DEDICATORY PRAYERS

Elder Francis M. Lyman, president of the European Mission, and Sylvester Q. Cannon, president of the Netherlands and Belgium Mission, were assigned to tour and report on the Turkish Mission. On February 26, 1902, President Herman met them in Jaffa and served as their guide. Before detailing their brief tour, however, it is important first to explain Elder Lyman's personal preparation for this assignment.

Elder Lyman had served as an Apostle for just over twenty-one years. During that time, he had had several dreams or visions regarding a future mission to the Holy Land, during which he was visited and instructed by brethren who shared a keen interest in the affairs of Palestine. In one dream, he visited the Holy Land with *Elder Francis M. Lyman of the Quorum of the Twelve Apostles.*

President Joseph F. Smith and the late George Q. Cannon. In another dream or vision, he traversed Palestine with President Joseph F. Smith and Anthon H. Lund. The dream that moved Elder Lyman most strongly took place in September 1901. In the dream, he stood before President Lorenzo Snow and President Joseph F. Smith. The two prophets discussed a very difficult mission that needed to be performed in the Holy Land but were undecided as to who should fill the assignment. Elder Lyman felt impressed to step forward and volunteer, saying, "I will undertake it and do the best I can." To this President Snow said, "We don't want to wear you out that way." Elder Lyman then replied, "I shall wear out and shall not rust out."[27] Elder Lyman felt that these spiritual manifestations served as the needed endorsement to undertake a mission to the Holy Land in 1902.[28]

At the time of this last dream, Elder Lyman was presiding over the European Mission. He was pleasantly and mildly surprised to receive an assignment from the First Presidency to tour the Turkish Mission. To Elder Lyman, this calling was but a fulfilling of his prophetic dreams.[29] On February 5, 1902, Elder Lyman was joined by Sylvester Q. Cannon in Paris, and the next day the two sailed for Alexandria, Egypt, from Marseille.[30]

Sylvester Q. Cannon, son of George Q. Cannon, was serving as the president of the Netherlands and Belgium Mission in 1899 when the call came to accompany Elder Lyman on this tour.[31] In addition to their ecclesiastical relationship, Brother Cannon also served as Elder Lyman's guide and interpreter, speaking fluent Dutch, French, and German. In a letter to Joseph F. Smith, Elder Lyman wrote that "Sylvester is master of three languages beside English, and I could think of no one that could take the place as well as he."[32]

On Sunday, March 2, 1902, Elder Lyman, in company with mission presidents Cannon and Herman, retired to the Mount of Olives to perform the sacred duty of dedicating Palestine for the gathering of Judah. Elder Lyman was desirous to know in what part of the mount Elders Hyde, Smith, Snow, Carrington, and Lund had offered up their dedicatory supplications, but such knowledge was unavailable to the party.[33] As they searched for a suitable spot to pray, Elder Lyman recorded:

> It seemed as if the elements all combined to prevent us. We could have ascended the Russian tower to have a good survey of the city and the hills of Judea, but the winds were so furious it seemed as if the tower, 200 feet high, would certainly be blown down. The mount is so occupied that we could not decide where a suitable spot could be had where we could be undisturbed. We felt clearly impressed to appoint Tuesday, March 4 for a second trip with the design to find a suitable place for us to appear before the Lord upon that sacred mount.[34]

Later that night, they retired to their rooms at the Casa Nova Hospice, which is near the New Gate of the Old City of Jerusalem.

Elder Lyman called Presidents Cannon and Herman to his room, where they knelt and prayed. During his prayer, Elder Lyman dedicated the Holy Land for the sixth time in latter-day history. Sylvester Q. Cannon described the dedication that night in his personal journal. He wrote that "apostle Lyman, in praying this evening, prayed fervently for the restoration of fruitfulness and prosperity to the land and the people, and pronounced a renewal of dedication and a blessing upon the land for the gathering of Judah and Israel."[35]

Two days later, on March 4, the Holy Land was dedicated again by Elder Lyman. Previously, the weather had been wet and the grounds in Jerusalem muddy. But Tuesday, March 4, was beautiful and clear. In the early afternoon, they ascended the Mount of Olives in search of a peaceful location where the dedication could be performed. Elder Lyman noted that the mount was crawling with locals "hungry like wolves after backshish [money]."[36] They came to the base of the Russian tower on the Russian grounds on the top of the Mount of Olives. Throughout the compound were groves of cypress trees. One particular grove, fifty yards east from the base of the tower, caught their attention.[37] It was grassy, shady, peaceful, and would be identifiable as long as the tower would stand. Elder Lyman felt impressed that this was to be the spot, if permission could be obtained. The three men approached the priest of the church and the gardener over the grounds and explained that they would like to kneel and pray in the cypress grove. Permission was immediately granted, and the brethren repaired to the chosen spot.

Elder Lyman spread his heavy Irish rug on the grass to avoid the moisture of the ground. As they prayed, they faced west—toward the Temple Mount, the temples of the Most High on the western continent, and Zion in the everlasting hills.[38] Elder Lyman began praying at 3:30 P.M., and all present noted that a most profound silence and spirit of peacefulness fell over the entire Mount of Olives, which persisted throughout the duration of the thirty-minute prayer.[39]

In his prayer, Elder Lyman remembered the prayers of dedication which had preceded his and pled with the Lord that they might be fulfilled, causing the lost ten tribes to be gathered, with Judah returning to Jerusalem. He recalled the prophecies of Isaiah, the Savior, and others, and he begged for a fulfillment of their prophetic utterances regarding the Holy City. He noted President Joseph Smith's prophetic feelings for scattered Israel and prayed for a fulfillment of his words. Elder Lyman then blessed the land itself that fruitfulness would return. He then blessed scattered and gathered Israel, supplicating the Lord for their best interests—particularly that the gospel would be preached in all nations. Elder Lyman prayed for the rebuilding of Jerusalem and the building of a temple. He also beseeched the Lord to hasten the building of temples in the stakes of Zion. Finally, Elder Lyman prayed for the First Presidency, the Quorum of the Twelve, and all the missionaries throughout the world. He finished praying at 4:00 P.M.[40] This was the seventh time the Holy Land had been dedicated.

In his letter to the First Presidency, Elder Lyman described his satisfaction of mind and spirit as the dedication was completed. He wrote, "Our souls were full of gratitude and great joy. We felt that one prime object of our coming at this time was accomplished. We have been particularly light and joyous in our spirits ever since."[41]

The group left Jerusalem for Jaffa on March 8. From Jaffa they took a carriage to Haifa, where they visited points of interest in northern Palestine, such as Nazareth, Cana, and Capernaum on the north shore of the Sea of Galilee. Back in Haifa, they waited for a steamer to take them to Beirut and Alexandretta, Syria. The weather had been cloudy and wet until Sunday, March 16, 1902, when the skies cleared and the sun rose bright and warm over Mount Carmel. After an 11:00 A.M. sacrament meeting, Elder Lyman, with Presidents Cannon and Herman, ascended to Kaiser's Watch near the western point of Mount Carmel, where the view down upon the city and the sea was both breathtaking and inspiring.[42]

In climbing the mount, it was not Elder Lyman's design to dedicate the Holy Land again. However, as he reached the summit, the Spirit of the Lord bore powerfully down upon him, and he felt impressed to pray. In fact, as he approached the grounds of Kaiser's Watch, he was drawn to a grove of pine trees about seventy feet east of the obelisk. Elder Lyman knew "that it was just the very spot and occasion for us once more upon a sacred mount to supplicate the Lord, as we had done upon the Mount of Olives."[43] A profound silence fell across nature as the group knelt facing Jerusalem.[44] Elder Lyman prayed for over half an hour, supplicating the Lord for the

The view from Kaiser's Watch, high above the oldest section of the city of Haifa.

necessities of Judah, Jerusalem, Zion, and all the children of Israel. Elder Lyman explained:

> The Lord gave us copiously of his Spirit, and it was a season ever to be remembered. We seemed to remember everything in connection with the work and purposes of the Lord. The spot where we prayed is known as the "Kaiser Watch" and will always be known if destruction does not overtake it. The day seemed as if arranged specially for the occasion.[45]

The journal entry of Brother Cannon adds some interesting insights to the events on Mount Carmel. He writes that Elder Lyman prayed that the burdens of the land would be lightened and that fruitfulness would be restored. He also prayed that the people's hearts would be softened and become more susceptible to enlightenment from the Spirit. Furthermore, Elder Lyman prayed for each member of the party separately and "dedicated us all to the Lord—our time and our talents from this time henceforth." Brother Cannon noted,

"It was a powerful blessing."[46] Elder Lyman's prayer constituted the eighth dedicatory prayer of the Holy Land.

Elder Lyman described this mission as the "crowning journey for my life of travel."[47] Indeed, he continued to feel deep impressions regarding the dedicatory mission after his return to Utah. Several months later, in a letter to Albert Herman, Elder Lyman wrote, "Our tour through Palestine grows on me, and is of greater importance every time I think of it."[48] It is interesting to note that at the turn of the twentieth century the feelings of the prophets concerning the Holy Land had remained consistent since Joseph Smith first prophesied that Jerusalem would eventually be rebuilt to her former splendor and glory.

A Change in Assignment for Elder Booth

In addition to dedicating Palestine during their tour, the three-some traveled to Aintab and held a mission conference, where only Elder Booth was absent. He had traveled eleven and one-half hours through heavy rain and mud, only to arrive in Aintab just after their departure. The Saints and missionaries were thrilled to see Elder Booth, but he was, nevertheless, disappointed to have missed the visiting Church authorities.[49] Elder Lyman was also disappointed to have missed Booth, since he had a matter of important business he wanted to discuss with him personally. As it turned out, he gave the news to President Herman, who then passed it on to Elder Booth.

Booth discovered that he would be released immediately. He had served in the Turkish Mission for three and a half years since his arrival on September 30, 1898, during which time he had baptized seventeen persons. As in any missionary activity, Booth saw some of his converts flourish and others flounder.[50] In many instances, the strongest members emigrated to Utah, leaving the missionaries with the ever-present challenge of finding and training new leaders to fill the shoes of those who had departed. Although many of the Saints in Turkey wanted to travel to Utah with him, most were unable due to a lack of resources, an inability to acquire governmental permission, or failure to meet the quarantine requirements.[51] In spite of these diffi-culties, Joseph Booth was able to take several Armenians back to Utah. Caroline Hilt, daughter of the faithful Hilts of Haifa, was included in the party.[52] They arrived in Provo on May 23, 1902.

Booth traveled north to his home in Alpine, Utah, where he enjoyed a great reunion with his wife, Reba. He taught school for one year and noted that

> many promising positions were offered me, several were accepted and later canceled and finally a letter came from Box B asking me to call at the office of the First Presidency of the Church in Salt Lake City. I called, several letters were received and sent by me and several times I called and talked with Pres. Jos. F. Smith and counselors and the result was that before the fourth of July [1903] I was making preparations to fill another mission to Turkey in company with my wife.[53]

Joseph Booth was called as the new president of the Turkish Mission. Joseph and Reba were expected to be in Turkey by October 14, 1903, which was the day of President Albert Herman's release. They left Salt Lake City on August 5 and traveled in the company of Elder Reno Vance and Elder Mischa Markow. Markow had been called to serve another mission to the Balkans; but as it turned out, he spent the greater portion of this mission in Turkey under the leadership of President Joseph W. Booth.[54]

THE SERVICE OF MISCHA MARKOW

Since his baptism by Jacob Spori in Constantinople in 1887, Mischa Markow had served unceasingly in different fields of labor. Upon his ordination as an elder, he served a mission to Belgium, then emigrated to Utah in 1892. In 1899, Elder Markow was called to serve a mission to the Balkans until 1901.[55] He began preaching but was apprehended by the magistrate of the district court, who claimed that banishment was too good for a Mormon elder and that drowning in the Danube would be more fitting. Markow was instead imprisoned for a time and then put on a train bound for Hungary in June 1899.[56]

While preaching in Hungary, he was accused of being an anarchist, was imprisoned, and suffered abuses that surpassed those imposed upon him in Serbia (Belgrade).[57] Finally, he was evicted from the country and put on a train bound for Constantinople, where he was directed by the European Mission president, Francis M. Lyman, to serve with Ferdinand Hintze.[58] They proselyted together for a short time until Hintze sent Markow to Bucharest, Romania. In the Balkans, he baptized fourteen people, then finished his mission in Munich, Germany, in August 1901.

He lived in Salt Lake City until he was called to serve another mission to the Balkans in 1903. He traveled most of the way with the Booths and Elder Vance but parted company with the group in Liverpool and traveled to his respective field. It was not long, however, before Elder Markow was banished from the Balkans again. As before, he traveled to Turkey and spent the remainder of his time serving in the Turkish Mission under President Booth.[59]

President Joseph Wilford Booth

After reviewing the conditions of the mission with President Booth, Albert Herman left Turkey on October 14, 1903, accompanied by Elder Holdaway, who was released at the same time.[60] The new arrivals introduced into the mission an element that had not been seen for three

decades. Sister Reba Booth became the first Latter-day Saint woman from Utah to interact with the people of the Near East since Eliza Snow and Clara Little traversed the Holy Land in 1873. President Booth wrote, "Her presence is opening the door to a new class of people who, until this time, have been difficult to access."[61] Because men and women in Ottoman society at this time were generally segregated, male missionaries were not allowed to preach to a woman without the company of her husband, father, brother, or other male chaperone. Sister Booth, however, could interact directly with the women. She had a warm, caring, and tender personality. The

Sister Rebecca (Reba) Moyle Booth, the first woman to serve as a full-time missionary in the Near East.

Saints were drawn to her and adored her. She opened the door to more enriching experiences among the female members and investigators in the mission. Under her leadership, the women's organization of the Church, the Relief Society, was organized in the Turkish Mission.

President Booth began his stewardship over the Turkish Mission in late 1903 with only five elders and one sister (his wife). Early in 1904, President Booth reported that the prospects for success "are better than ever before in [Turkey]."[62] While prospects for spreading the gospel were good, the economic condition of the average Armenian Saint was dismal, as usual. Booth related:

> When I tell you the tithing of one man, whom I believe to pay a full and honest tithing, amounts to only $7 a year, and many earn much less than he does, you will get an idea of the poverty and scanty living that our poor Saints are accustomed to, and they are no worse off than the average people of the cities.[63]

President and Sister Booth spent most of 1904 traveling from city to city. The couple possessed an ability to reach out to the Saints in Turkey and strengthen them in the gospel. In addition to serving the members, President Booth was constantly considering new fields of labor; unfortunately, the work's limited progress stemmed from the minuscule missionary force in place. Henry Teuscher was released, leaving President Booth, Sister Booth, Mischa Markow, and Charles Teuscher as the only missionaries in the large Ottoman Empire.

The fortitude and determination of this small missionary force was astonishing. For example, Elder Markow (who seemed to be evicted from every field of labor that he entered) baptized five souls in Marash in August 1904: Sarkis Telekian, Sumbat Persheghiyan, Elmas Parseghian, Garabet Telekiyan, and Yepros Telekian. A branch was organized, and Elder Markow was called to serve as the president. The newly formed branch became the target of local Christian priests, and soon Elder Markow was driven from Marash back to Aintab.[64] The ever-persistent Markow then made his way to the seaport town of Alexandretta, where he met with immediate success, baptizing Shamoil Kyuchuch Georgiyan on October 23, 1904. A small branch was organized in that city, and Elder Markow presided.[65]

Even with these successes, the greatest source of frustration for President Booth was the shortage of missionaries. The Church in Turkey was gaining momentum, and more and more investigators were approaching the missionaries with a sincere desire to join the fold. One such investigator was Bagdasar Kaligeian, who lived in Kapu Kaya, Turkey. Bagdasar had written his Latter-day Saint friend, Hagop Gagosian, in the hope that Hagop would convince President Booth to send missionaries to Kapu Kaya to teach and baptize their congregation of believers. Bagdasar and over twenty other individuals had been investigating the Church on their own. Citing a portion of this letter will illustrate the sincerity of these hopeful disciples, as well as the anguish President Booth must have felt in not having enough elders to respond to requests such as these—for this was one of many.

> Wherever two or more of us were found together we were discussing the principles of Mormonism; and many were asking when your missionaries will come. . . . Both young and old seem to be moved by a light toward Christ. . . . Many have said that a Mormon missionary would come, but none has yet arrived, and we are awaiting that event. Now come, if you please . . . for there is a great work to be opened. I beg you do not delay . . . that we may be aroused from this deep slumber.[66]

President Booth later published this letter and a plea in the *Millennial Star:*

> With such calls as the above from earnest investigators can you wonder why we are always asking for more Elders. . . . [Four months have passed] since the invitation was sent, and others even precede that date. . . . We ought to have twenty Elders right now studying the three languages, Arabic, Turkish, and Armenian, in order to be ready for the work when the Book of Mormon comes, for which there are multitudes of people waiting and asking.[67]

President Booth finally started out himself to meet with Bagdasar Kaligeian in Kapu Kaya. While riding his bicycle from Charshambi to

Kapu Kaya, he was apprehended by four or five police officers, who ordered him to return to Charshambi. President Booth refused their orders unless they were willing to arrest him and then transport and house him, all at their expense. This they did. He was jailed in Charshambi and was never allowed to travel and meet with Brother Kaligeian. The stir over his arrest was noteworthy, since this part of Turkey had experienced little exposure to the Church. As Booth sailed away from Samsun on the Black Sea coast, he noted, "While I was not permitted to preach the gospel in Kapu Kaya, yet I am happy over the result of my endeavor, for the affair has made much talk and many friends for us. I think the next Elder that goes that way will receive better treatment."[68]

In his final report of the year to President Heber J. Grant, Joseph Booth wrote:

> After a journey of one hundred and forty-three days, and 2000 miles, I am home again at headquarters [Aintab]. . . . Never in all my life before were my hopes brighter for the advancement of Zion. . . . I could use forty Elders, and put them all in good fields right now. . . . I feel that for some wise purpose the Lord is holding back the Elders from this mission, for I cannot think that one or two or three Elders a year cannot be found for us.[69]

President Booth's missionary force continued to dwindle, for Elder Charles Teuscher was released the first day of the following year, January 1, 1905.

THE 1905 TOUR

In late spring 1905, during another mission tour, President and Sister Booth were visiting Marash when they were ordered by government officials to leave town immediately. In fact, the officials went to the trouble of imprisoning every Latter-day Saint in Marash, claiming that they would remain incarcerated until the Booths left town. Sister Booth's health was precarious, and it was imperative that she not travel more than three days at a time without rest. Therefore, the Booths refused to leave, and the officials had no choice but to release the Saints from prison.[70]

Knowing that such persecutions generally originated among fellow Christians, President Booth proposed to meet with an American missionary in Marash named Macallum in hopes of receiving some assistance. Pastor Macallum wrote him back, responding that "the society known as the Church of the Latter-day Saints is a most horrid and blasphemous society, opposed in every way to the truths of the gospel, and especially antagonistic to the sanctity of the family. Believing this, you will understand why I do not care to have an official representative and teacher of this society in my house."[71]

Ultimately, President and Sister Booth were banished from Marash. For safety, they traveled in a caravan of fifteen travelers and about fifty pack animals carrying valuable goods, bound for Sivas. One evening, camp had been established as usual, when all of a sudden the air was filled with yelling and whooping as nine armed bandits rode at breakneck pace toward the camp. President Booth gives the rest of the details. The bandits

> were from one to two hundred yards away when they began to fire. . . . The shooting kept up for about thirty minutes, and I think about forty shots were fired in all, when the thieves ran away into the darkness. . . . Under such circumstances we could only put our trust in the Lord, and while the bullets were whistling around us we were silently asking our Father to protect us. He gave us courage, and we were delivered from what might have been an awful fate.[72]

Establishing the Church in Greece

The next stop on the Booths' tour was Greece to visit Rigas Pofantis. They arrived in Athens on Sunday, October 1, 1905, and found the nucleus of believers the following day. They met at the home of Rigas Pofantis, where they were greeted by the enthusiastic "seekers," including one who had traveled over one hundred miles to meet them. With Rigas Pofantis were George Zdralis, Constantine Theodoseau, and Andromache Malavetis. Andromache was the widow of Nicholas Malavetis, who had been Rigas Pofantis's companion in the quest to find the true Church. As explained earlier, Nicholas Malavetis had died since the elders were in Athens and missed the chance to be baptized in this life. Later in October, one John Lazos joined this small group of initial believers, bringing their numbers to five.

In August 1905, the group had written to President Booth begging him to travel to Greece immediately and baptize their group of truth seekers. They had continued to meet regularly and discuss the principles of the gospel and had also translated three pamphlets in Charles W. Penrose's tract series "Rays of Living Light" that had been left with them. Rigas had proceeded to print the translated tracts—about one thousand copies of the first tract, five hundred copies of the second, and five hundred copies of the third.[73] By the time President Booth arrived in October 1905, numerous Latter-day Saint tracts had been distributed throughout Athens.[74]

The enthusiasm of this group of "new reformers" led President Booth to write:

> I feel that the day is not far distant when a mighty harvest will be gathered in from this Nation. . . . There may be many covered sins among the people here, but I believe that Athens can produce a greater percent of virtuous men and women than any other capital in Europe. I feel a spirit of purity in the very atmosphere, and see it in the modest life of the people. The Athenians are polite and mild and courteous.[75]

As President Booth taught and prepared these people for baptism, he was unsure if Greece had ever been dedicated for missionary labors; hence, he planned to dedicate the land at the exact time that the October 1905 general conference of the Church convened in Salt Lake City.[76] Accordingly, on October 6, 1905, he and Sister Booth ascended Areopagus (Mars Hill) and at 7:05 P.M. knelt and humbly asked God to turn the necessary keys "to open the gospel light to open the night-bound heart of Greece." The time of the dedication was significant because, as President Booth explained, there was nine hours and twenty-eight minutes' difference between Athens and Salt Lake City. Therefore, it was just after 10:30 A.M. in Salt Lake City, and the opening prayer of the conference was most likely being offered at the same time as the dedicatory prayer—spiritual light burning in both places at once.[77]

The first known public sermon by Latter-day Saint missionaries was preached in Greece on October 8, 1905. President Booth spoke to the Young Men's Christian Society and took for his text Acts 2:30–47. As Booth preached, there was some restlessness by those not sympathetic to the Latter-day Saint presence in Athens. An aged reverend named M. D. Kalapothakes interrupted Booth's sermon and

Prominent Latter-day Saint educator William E. Berrett
standing on Areopagus (Mars Hill) in Athens, Greece.

raised his voice against Mormonism, the first to do so in Greece. It is ironic to note that prior to becoming a reverend, the young Kalapothakes had been the editor of a newspaper called *O Aster Tes Anatoles* (The Star of the East), in which he had published an article about the Latter-day Saints in September of 1859. It was this publication that Nicholas Malavetis had seen in vision, leading to the introduction of the restored gospel in Greece. President Booth wrote, "Rev. Kalapothakes perhaps had little idea that night, that his action of forty-six years before had played an important part in bringing the doctrine of that same sect into his own city and to his own ears."[78]

The first Latter-day Saint baptisms in Greece were performed on October 22, 1905. All five of the truth seekers mentioned earlier were baptized about two miles beyond Old Phaleron in the Saronic Gulf. Following the confirmations, the new members participated in the first sacrament meeting in Greece in this dispensation. It was a time of great joy.[79] Several days later, seventy-five-year-old Marie Pechany was baptized, bringing the total Greek membership to six. There had as yet been no ordinations to the priesthood. Finally, in a sacrament meeting held on November 5, 1905, President Booth ordained Rigas Pofantis a priest. Immediately following his ordination, Rigas was invited to bless the sacrament.[80]

Four days later, the Booths left the Athens Branch in the capable hands of the newly ordained Rigas Pofantis until an elder could be sent to oversee the work in Greece. They arrived back in Aleppo on December 19, 1905, completing an eventful and productive year.[81] During their absence, two new missionaries had arrived in the mission. Elders Stephen B. Newman and John T. Woodbury began their service with Elder Reno Vance in Aintab.

The Publication of the Book of Mormon in Turkish

In July 1905, President Booth wrote the following:

> Seven years ago, when on my way here to Turkey, I expressed a desire to labor ten years in the mission field. That desire is coming about as fast as time can bring it. And now I have three more desires of my heart. One is to see the Book of Mormon among the people in their own language, the second is to get recognition from the [Ottoman] government for our Church, and the third is to see a colony established in this land for the Saints.[82]

There was a collective yearning to see the Book of Mormon in print in Turkish and Armenian. At the turn of the twentieth century, most Armenians living in the Ottoman Empire would have been bilingual in Armenian and Turkish. In 1899, Pastor Hintze had received permission from President Lorenzo Snow to translate and publish the Book of Mormon in Turkish as soon as possible. However, because of a lack of resources, the translation was not completed at that time.[83]

When Ferdinand Hintze returned to Utah, he continued working on the translation of the Book of Mormon into Turkish. He enlisted the service of his old friend, Haig Jevahirdjian, to assist in the translation.[84] Jevahirdjian, a convert from Sivas, had completed his missionary work in Egypt and then emigrated to Utah.

In 1905, President Booth and the Saints in Turkey knew that the translation of the Book of Mormon into the Turkish language was on the verge of being finished. Incidentally, the excitement over the prospects of having the Book of Mormon in Turkish moved a sister named Nuritza in the Zara Branch to forego her plans to emigrate to Utah so that she could finish her translation of the Book of Mormon into Armenian. She was the teacher in the school at Zara and was fluent in the English language. Sister Nuritza began her work of translation in the middle of May 1906.[85] Much of the expense of her work came from her own meager resources.[86]

By October 1905, the Turkish translation was finished, and the First Presidency of the Church decided to proceed with its publication. At their bidding, Ferdinand Hintze traveled to Boston early in 1906 to conduct final proofreading of the transcript and to oversee the printing. On February 7, Hintze wrote a letter to his former companion, Janne M. Sjodahl:

> I need not tell you that I have had many unlooked-for difficulties to overcome in doing a work in so strange and difficult a tongue as Turkish. But nevertheless the Lord has blessed me abundantly. . . . I was favored by obtaining the help of the Rev. Bool, B.D., an Armenian gentleman of talent and ability in both English and Turkish. With his help I am revising my translation, and it is put into modern Armeno-Turkish as well as the character of the work will permit and still retain its own style and originality.

> This latter will make it rather unique in style of literature among them. But it will help to introduce gospel thought from a highly Christianized book among the people and particularly in a nation which does not know Christ. I mean the Mohammedans. You will appreciate the difficulty of expressing great gospel truths from

atonement to eternal salvation in a language which has provided no such thought expressions. However, we are doing nicely, and shall be through with that part of the work soon. . . . Owing to the nature of the characters the book will contain about seven hundred pages, a little more than the standard size in English.[87]

The Turkish Mission history notes that "early in 1906 the [Turkish] Book of Mormon . . . was published by The Church of Jesus Christ of Latter-day Saints, in Boston, Mass, and entered in [the] Congressional Library in Washington D.C. that year."[88] At this time, Hintze placed five hundred copies of the Turkish Book of Mormon into two large boxes and sent them to Constantinople. President Booth assigned Elder Reno Vance and his companion, Elder Stephen B. Newman, to receive the parcels and forward them on to Alexandretta and then to mission headquarters in Aintab. The books arrived in Constantinople, and two copies were given to the missionaries for inspection. Elder Vance then obtained the appropriate authorizations and clearances to send the books to Alexandretta. With these essential tasks completed, Elder Vance wrote:

We are pleased to report success in the book of Mormon work here, for without any serious trouble the books passed the customs and were all stamped by the censor as desired. We were then able to ship them on to Alexandretta, from which place they will be forwarded to mission headquarters by an agent in Alexandretta, to whom we wrote regarding the matter. We thank the Lord for blessing us in this work, in answer to the prayers of all those interested in this special labor. Elder Hintze, who has been so faithful in the translation and publication of the Book of Mormon, is to be congratulated. We feel that it will be of much help in spreading the truth among our friends here in Turkey.[89]

THE BOOK OF MORMON EMBARGO

Elder Vance penned the above words in the latter part of 1906, but President Booth did not take delivery on the books until December 18, 1908, over two and one-half years after their printing and two years after they arrived in Turkey.[90] The copies of the Book of Mormon were sent to Alexandretta, but that is where they stopped. Even though the appropriate taxes had been paid and the customs agent in Constantinople had inspected and individually stamped each of the five hundred books, the port in Alexandretta refused to release the two boxes on the grounds that the Latter-day Saints were not a recognized religion in the Ottoman Empire, and therefore the missionaries did not have the right to receive the parcels.

After appealing to Jesse B. Jackson, the U.S. consul in Alexandretta, Booth traveled to Alexandretta in January 1907 in an attempt to obtain the books, but he was unsuccessful—as were the efforts of Jackson. President Booth then appealed to John G. Leishman, the American ambassador to Turkey, whose office was in Constantinople.

Months passed without word. More letters were exchanged, but the results never varied. Then, in the spring of 1908, President Booth learned that the blockade of Latter-day Saint literature in Turkey had reached the ears of Elihu Root, secretary of state of the United States of America, and that he was taking steps to resolve the difficulty.

Even with the secretary of state's involvement, the books were not released. Finally, in October 1908, President Booth wrote a fiery letter to Jackson (who was now the American consul in Aleppo) stating his belief that the embargo on the Latter-day Saint literature was nothing more than the fruits of embittered enemies of Mormonism. "Sir," he wrote, "we ask no ecclesiastical quarter at our American Consulate, we beg only that our rights as American citizens be no longer curtailed by the influence of religious opponents and with all charity towards our ministerial friends we suggest that one official sharp knock on the knuckles of bigotry, will release its grasp and our books will be delivered immediately."[91]

After one more month with no release of the books, Leishman communicated to Jesse Jackson that any further efforts to detain the two boxes of books would be considered a formal breach between the United States government and the Ottoman Empire.[92] This communiqué accomplished the task, and news of the release of the books reached President Booth on November 24, 1908. Of this occasion he noted that soon after breakfast I heard the pleasing sound from the outer door uttered by a man who entered the court. "There is a box" whereupon I rushed down and to my happy surprise the box of Books of Mormon was at our door—250 copies. The other box having been sent to Aleppo. We have had a long and hard fight to get this sacred record into the country but now we feel that the Lord has won this part of the battle and his cause will now gain impetus and strength and begin from the day of liberty, they arrived yesterday, to go on to a glorious triumph. My heart is full of praise and thanksgiving to God today.[93]

Finally, copies of the Book of Mormon were available to the Turkish people in their common language.

During the embargo, the work of translation had continued in Armenian, Arabic, and Greek. By August 1908, President Booth reported to President Lund that the Armenian and Arabic translations were ready for publication, while the Greek translation was progressing nicely under the direction of the missionaries and one Mr. Garsiatos, a local translator in Athens, but was not quite ready to go to press.[94]

NEW ELDERS AND A CONTINUANCE OF THE WORK

In December 1905, three elders were serving in Aintab: Elders Vance, Newman, and Woodbury. Then Vance and Newman traveled to Constantinople to oversee the arrival of the Book of Mormon, and Elder Woodbury received a new companion from Utah. Another missionary, Elder Joseph T. Thorup, traveled from Utah to Athens to carry out his first assignment in the small Greek Branch, where he arrived on March 19, 1906. By late spring, the need for elders in Turkey made it necessary for President Booth to transfer Elder Thorup to Turkey. He arrived, bearing the greetings of the Greek Saints, on May 16, 1906.[95]

Five other elders arrived in the Turkish Mission during this time period: Elders Clayton, Phelps, Stevenson, Shepherd, and Huber. While Elder Clayton left early on account of ill health,[96] just prior to his departure, President Booth received Elders Joseph O. Phelps and John David Stevenson into the mission on July 6, 1907.[97] The impact of the arrival of so many elders in the mission cannot be overestimated. Elders from Utah brought a sense of stability to whatever branches they served in.

Even so, the elders continued to encounter opposition, though they also found ways to deflect it. One Sabbath morning, the missionaries attended a Protestant worship service wherein the minister told blazing lies about the Latter-day Saints as a people and grand falsehoods regarding Church doctrines. The congregation was so infuriated against the Saints that, following the sermon, they turned on the missionaries and bodily threw them out of the building. According to Elder Woodbury, the two missionaries stood outside the church and told the congregation that

> we would willingly have left their church had they invited us to do so, but we thought it did not show the true Christian spirit when they used violence before finding out whether we would not peaceably comply with their wishes. The minister said in his sermon that the ideas of the heathen who come here from the East are not to be feared, but the false doctrines brought by the 'Mormons' from the West must be feared. Continuing, he said the 'Mormons' strip Jesus Christ of His Godhood or Divinity, and accept Him as a common man. In order to inform him of the mistake he had made regarding our doctrines, we waited after [the] meeting to talk to him. When we told him we accept Christ as God and the only Savior whereby mankind are saved, he contradicted us and said he found in the Book of Mormon what he told his congregation. We told him if he would show us where it was in the Book of Mormon we would make him a present of fifty dollars. Three weeks have passed, but he has not come to prove his assertion and claim the money.[98]

The new missionaries would face even more perilous challenges. Elder Huber arrived in Athens, Greece, on September 9, 1907, and was assigned to serve with Elder Joseph Shepherd, who had arrived just one month earlier. Then the two elders traveled to Alexandria, Egypt, where they spent about six months studying Arabic, preaching the gospel, and providing additional training for the few members in the branch at Alexandria. The two traveled to Turkey on March 14, 1908, and continued their service together in Aleppo.

One month later, Elder Huber began to experience severe headaches. Soon the headaches were accompanied by fever. Sister Booth was in Aleppo and immediately sent for President Booth to come from Aintab to Aleppo. Sister Booth watched over her sick missionary night and day for almost an entire week. During this time, one Dr. Altounyan, known as the best physician in Aleppo, was summoned to assess Elder Huber's condition. The diagnosis was conclusive: Elder Huber had contracted typhus fever.[99]

Emil J. Huber

Elder Huber was the recipient of priesthood blessings, and a special fast day was held in his behalf. Nevertheless, he continued to weaken, and on May 16, 1908, he died.[100] Elder Huber was from Switzerland, where his parents still resided. News of his passing was cabled to Liverpool and forwarded on to the Hubers in Europe. The First Presidency of the Church was also notified at the earliest possible moment. Prior to his departure for the Near East, Elder Huber was told to take his temple robes for burial because he would not be returning. The comment impressed Elder Huber in a singular way, and he included the sacred clothing in his packing. Now, Elder Huber's remains were clothed in the robes of the holy priesthood and two days later were laid to rest in a beautiful white-and-gold casket.[101] He was buried in a Protestant cemetery in Aleppo.[102]

During the last Sunday service that he attended, Elder Huber rose and bore a powerful witness of the truthfulness of the gospel. President Booth recorded part of this testimony as follows: "I know the gospel is true, and you cannot deny it, having heard it preached by a humble servant of the Lord." President Booth was so impressed with these words that he had them engraved around the base of Elder Huber's gravestone monument. The rest of the epitaph reads as follows:

IN MEMORY OF
EMIL J. HUBER,
MISSIONARY OF THE CHURCH OF JESUS CHRIST OF
LATTER-DAY SAINTS.
BORN IN PARIS, MARCH 7, 1885.
SET APART AT SALT LAKE CITY, JULY 23, 1907.
DIED IN ALEPPO, MAY 16, 1908.[103]

The news of Elder Huber's death shocked the entire mission. And as in the cases of other missionaries who had died while serving the Lord, Elder Huber's death struck deep chords in the hearts of the First Presidency of the Church. Anthon H. Lund penned the following words on behalf of the First Presidency to President Booth:

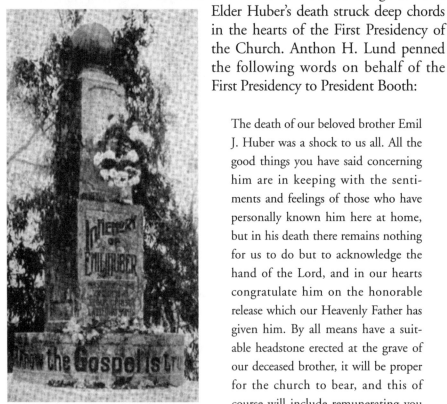

The gravestone of Elder Emil J. Huber in Aleppo, Syria.

The death of our beloved brother Emil J. Huber was a shock to us all. All the good things you have said concerning him are in keeping with the sentiments and feelings of those who have personally known him here at home, but in his death there remains nothing for us to do but to acknowledge the hand of the Lord, and in our hearts congratulate him on the honorable release which our Heavenly Father has given him. By all means have a suitable headstone erected at the grave of our deceased brother, it will be proper for the church to bear, and this of course will include remunerating you for the means you yourself advanced to him.[104]

CLOSING THE MISSION

Unfortunately, the unrest, violence, and massacres that necessitated the closure of the Turkish Mission in 1897 returned, beginning in the fall of 1908.[105] As has been mentioned, the Ottoman Empire, founded in the thirteenth century, reached its peak in the sixteenth century, and its subsequent decline was in part due to a rejection of Western advancements in warfare, technology, communications, economics, education, and so forth. These advancements were seen as the fruit of Christian infidels and deemed unacceptable for use within the Islamic empire; therefore, it fell behind in almost every conceivable way of life, from printing and weaving to banking and governance.

By the mid-nineteenth century, the Ottoman Empire had reappraised its view of the West and had begun a serious effort to modernize, borrowing money and technologies from Europe. Some political groups, such as the Young Ottomans, also turned to the West. The Young Ottomans favored a Western-style government within the Islamic Empire. Their movement gained momentum and culminated in reform during the first year that Sultan Abdulhamid II came to power in 1876. The Western-style constitution and representative governing assembly they created was possibly allowed by the sultan to serve as window dressing to appease the West and quell rising sentiments within the empire calling for even more democratic reforms. When the sultan took advantage of an emergency clause in the constitution in February 1878 which dissolved the elected assembly and ended constitutional reform, many members of the Young Ottoman movement were banished from the empire.

Years later, in an effort to build upon the efforts of the Young Ottomans, a political party known as the Young Turks was formed in 1889. It was their intention to promote Western advancements and government while remaining true to the tenets of Islam, and to achieve their goal, they planned to overthrow the sultan. The movement grew as a result of backroom meetings and underground newspapers published by exiled sympathizers and smuggled into Istanbul (Constantinople). In August of 1896, they plotted the sultan's overthrow. The plot was discovered, and many of the dissenters were exiled from the empire or banished to outlying regions such as Anatolia and Syria. These regions were populated by many Armenian Christians, and, given Armenian hopes for their own national interests, many of them gravitated toward the democratic views of the reformers.

In 1908, the Young Turk revolution came to a head. Organized and makeshift armies throughout the empire turned against the sultan and demanded that the constitution be restored at once. On July 23, 1908, Sultan Abdulhamid II capitulated, and the constitution was again granted legitimacy.

These actions did not come without an external and an internal price. Neighboring nations interpreted these internal struggles as a sign of weakness. Subsequently, Austria annexed Bosnia and Herzegovina, Bulgaria declared independence from the empire, and Crete allied herself with Greece. Internally, in what was left of "the sick old man of Europe," the revolution carried for many a deep sense of betrayal of Islamic values. A countermovement was mounted, claiming that the Shariat (governing laws based on the Koran, the scripture of Islam) was in danger due to the agenda of the Western-trained Young Turk leadership. As a result of this reaction, Ahmed Riza was removed from the speaker's chair of the governing assembly on April 15, 1909.

News of these developments quickly spread throughout the empire. In Anatolia, suspicions against those who had supported the Young Turks, especially Armenians, quickly rose to dangerous levels. These suspicions eventually led to violence and the massacre of thousands of Armenians by Ottoman Turks. Of this disaster, one writer noted that "responsibility for this was variously allocated. While Europe was appalled by Turkish brutality, Muslim opinion was shocked by what seemed to them the insolence of the Armenians and the hypocrisy of Christian Europe."[106]

It was reported to mission headquarters that there were skirmishes between Armenians and Turks in different quarters of the empire. By April 1909, there was considerable violence and killing at Marash, Adana, Alexandretta, and other major cities in Anatolia and Syria. The sale of rifles and revolvers escalated, and the prices matched the heightened fears of the people. The massacre at Adana involved the killing of one thousand people, including two non–Latter-day Saint American missionaries.[107] In Tarsus, the violence turned against the Christian quarter, and four thousand believers huddled into the college grounds under the protection of one Mr. Christi, a prominent American.[108]

Conditions were so troubling that President Booth purchased a revolver and seventy cartridges so as to be prepared for an emergency. Elders Newman and Phelps reported fourteen violent deaths and thirty-six injuries in Marash and Aintab, while the Christian village of Kasab, near Antioch, was burned to the ground.[109]

Needless to say, these reports reached Church leaders in Salt Lake City, provoking great concern for the missionaries and Saints in the Turkish Mission. On May 1, 1909, Elder Charles Penrose, president of the European Mission, sent a telegram to President Booth inquiring about the safety of the missionaries. President Booth replied, "All safe."

The difficulties subsided for a time, and all the elders gathered to Aleppo for a mission conference on July 4, 1909. By August, however, violence had erupted again, and the First Presidency of the Church moved to close the mission. President Booth received a letter of release for himself and Reba on July 28, 1909. The First Presidency instructed President Booth to release those elders who had served for substantial periods of time so they could return to their homes. Those who were newer in the field (such as Elder Don C. Loveland from Albion, Idaho, who had arrived in the mission one month earlier on June 28, 1909) were to be reassigned to other fields of labor (including Greece, which was not to be closed, and where Elders Ira O. Horsfall, Charles D. McAllister, and Loy Woods were assigned to work).[110] The reassignments were to be coordinated with President Charles Penrose of the European Mission. The First Presidency left the time of departure entirely up to the Booths. This gave them an opportunity to complete a small tour of the mission in order to bid farewell to the Saints and set in order the branches.

The preparations for departure were not easy for Brother and Sister Booth. President Booth wrote, "We are soon to vacate the field and leave the poor saints to drudge along alone with poverty and persecution, and hunger. Already gloom seems to be settling over them like a cloud and a hint of our departure, like a thunder bolt, is followed by a shower (of tears)."[111] Later he wrote, "It is 10 years, 8 mo. and 4 days since I first went to Aintab and nearly 6 years (lacking only 2 weeks) since Reba and I came on my second mission and naturally the thoughts of my long labor with the saints we are leaving, crowded upon my memory with pensive emotions."[112]

Finally, on October 1, 1909, the Booths left Aleppo with three families (the Orullians, Henryks, and Demirfiuns) who were emigrating to America. They took a train to Beirut, then sailed to Jaffa, Athens, Spain, and on to New York for the overland train ride to Utah.[113] President Booth published a partial report of the work accomplished from January through October.

> The conditions under which the elders labor in that country are so different from what they are in other parts of the European Mission that the figures do not give a proper conception of what has been done. However, about eight hundred meetings, outdoor and indoor, were held during the nine months that the work was going on, one hundred and thirty-five sessions of Sunday School, and forty Relief Society meetings; something over two hundred strangers' houses were visited by invitation and five hundred gospel conversations held. Ninety of the standard Church works were sold and upwards of five hundred tracts given out in various ways. Five new members and eighteen children of members were baptized and seventeen children blessed. There were thirteen elders all told in the mission during the year, but some of them were there only a short time.[114]

The mission would remain closed for twelve years. However, when the First Presidency of the Church determined to reopen the mission, Joseph Booth would be called up again.

Notes to Chapter 5

1. Autobiography of Joseph Alma Holdaway, 1, LDS Church Archives.

2. Ibid., 1–2. See also Mission Record, Turkish Mission, January 20 or 21, 1900, 59, LDS Church Archives.

3. Joseph W. Booth, *Millennial Star,* March 15, 1900, 165–66.

4. Thomas P. Page, *Journal History,* May 28, 1900, 12.

5. Booth, *Millennial Star,* July 27, 1899, 166.

6. Page, *Journal History,* May 28, 1900, 12. Apparently, this was not the first time a rug had been made for the temple by the Armenian Saints. In a letter from President Lorenzo Snow to Ferdinand Hintze dated December 13, 1899,

President Snow acknowledged receiving a rug at the temple from the Armenian Saints. He wrote: "I enclose a receipt for the rug sent by Sister Sherinian to the Temple with Brother Lund, who fears that the receipt has not been sent. If this has been sent before, this can be destroyed." Papers of Anthon H. Lund, LDS Church Archives.

7. Autobiography of Joseph Alma Holdaway, 2–3. See also Mission Record, Turkish Mission, April 15, 1900, 60.

8. Andrew L. Larson, *Millennial Star,* April 12, 1900, 236.

9. Ibid.

10. Rao H. Lindsay, "A History of the Missionary Activity of The Church of Jesus Christ of Latter-day Saints in the Near East, 1884–1929," master's thesis, Brigham Young University, 1958, 84.

11. Papers of Anthon H. Lund, October 16, 1900, 2.

12. Lindsay, "Missionary Activity in the Near East," 85. See also James A. Toronto, "Early Missions to Ottoman Turkey, Syria, and Palestine," in *Out of Obscurity: The LDS Church in the Twentieth Century* (Salt Lake City: Deseret Book, 2000), 352.

13. Journal of Joseph W. Booth, December 10, 1900, L. Tom Perry Special Collections, Harold B. Lee Library, Brigham Young University, Provo, UT. See also Thomas Philips Page, "Short Biography in Papers Preserved by His Daughter, Maud Page Butterfield," LDS Church Archives (also in the files of Darlene Hamilton Berrett, great-granddaughter of Thomas Philips Page and wife of author LaMar C. Berrett).

14. Maud Page Butterfield, "Entry No. 6 in Journal's Famous Character Contest: Thomas Phillip Page," *Midvale Journal,* February 15–April 12, 1929, LDS Church Archives. See also Papers of Anthon H. Lund, December 25, 1900, 2.

15. Lester Mangum, *Millennial Star,* April 18, 1901, 246. Elder Mangum claims that Page traveled home in March, while Elder Booth noted in his journal that Page left Turkey at noon on February 19, 1901. See Journal of Joseph W. Booth, February 19, 1901.

16. Journal of Joseph W. Booth, February 19, 1901.

17. Lester Mangum, *Millennial Star,* April 18, 1901, 247.

18. His tombstone is in the northwest corner of the cemetery, in the last row of graves (row ten), fifteenth grave on the left from the center aisle. See LaMar C. Berrett and D. Kelly Ogden, *Discovering the World of the Bible* (Provo, UT: Grandin Book, 1996), 156–57.

19. Papers of Anthon H. Lund, July 23, 1901.

20. J. Alma Holdaway, *Millennial Star,* August 15, 1901, 540.

21. Papers of Anthon H. Lund, October 13, 1901. See also *Journal History,* December 7, 1901, 4.

22. Mangum, *Millennial Star,* December 12, 1901.

23. Ibid.

24. Lindsay, "Missionary Activity in the Near East," 87. See also Journal of Joseph W. Booth, April 2, 1902.

25. Mangum, *Journal History,* December 7, 1901, 4.

26. Consult mission records from the Turkish Mission and the Armenian Mission. See also Toronto, "Early Missions to Ottoman Turkey, Syria, and Palestine," 341.

27. Francis M. Lyman to President Joseph F. Smith, May 5, 1902, LDS Church Archives.

28. Lyman, Letters Written by Francis M. Lyman: Excerpts, 1902, 8, LDS Church Archives.

29. Ibid.

30. Lyman, "President Lyman in the Holy Land," *Journal History,* March 16, 1902, 12.

31. Ibid. Sylvester Q. Cannon would eventually be called to serve as Presiding Bishop of the Church on June 4, 1925. He was ordained an Apostle on April 14, 1938, by Heber J. Grant.

32. Lyman, Letters Written by Francis M. Lyman: Excerpts, 2.

33. Lyman, "President Lyman in the Holy Land," 12.

34. Ibid.

35. Private Journal of Sylvester Q. Cannon, March 2, 1902, LDS Church Archives. See also Lyman, "President Lyman in the Holy Land," 12.

36. Lyman, "President Lyman in the Holy Land," 12.

37. Ibid.

38. Ibid.

39. Ibid. See also Sylvester Q. Cannon, "President Lyman's Tour," *Millennial Star,* April 3, 1902, 213.

40. This is a merging of the accounts of President Cannon ("President Lyman's Tour") and Elder Lyman ("President Lyman in the Holy Land"). See also Private Journal of Sylvester Q. Cannon, March 4, 1902.

41. Lyman, "President Lyman in the Holy Land," 12.

42. This is the place where Germany's Kaiser Wilhelm was brought for a panoramic view of the city of Haifa and the Bay of Acre on October 25, 1898. The German colonists in Haifa had labored to preserve the Carmel hillsides by terracing the slopes of the mount from top to bottom, planting vineyards in abundance. A six-foot-tall obelisk stands on the site to commemorate the visit. See Berrett and Ogden, *Discovering the World of the Bible,* 159. See also Lyman, "President Lyman in Jerusalem," *Deseret News,* April 19, 1902, 4.

43. Lyman, "President Lyman in Jerusalem," 4. See also Cannon, "President Lyman's Tour," 228.

44. Regarding the location of the site of dedication, Elder Lyman recorded that within a grove of seven hundred young pine trees were the remains of "a raised foundation of stone and earthwork upon which the German emperor stood and viewed Mt. Hermon." *Journal History,* March 17, 1902, 4. LaMar C. Berrett located this grove of pine trees and the remains of the small wall described in Elder Lyman's correspondence. This spot lies seventy feet east of the obelisk. See Berrett and Ogden, *Discovering the World of the Bible,* 159. This site was beautified by the city of Haifa and is located on the south side of the Panorama Road, northwest of the Dan Carmel Road, and directly above David Ben Gurion Street and the Baha'i Gardens. Both Elders Lyman and Talmage offered dedicatory prayers at this site.

45. Lyman, *Journal History,* March 17, 1902, 4.

46. Private Journal of Sylvester Q. Cannon, March 16, 1902.

47. Lyman, Letters Written by Francis M. Lyman: Excerpts, 4.

48. Ibid., 12.

49. Journal of Joseph W. Booth, April 2, 1902.

50. Ibid., April 3, 1902, and July 3, 1902.

51. Ibid., April 3, 1902. A list of those Armenian Saints who were planning to travel with Elder Booth was included in the *Journal History,* December 7, 1901, 4. They were Nishan Sherinian and family, Zaddik Aposian and family, Hosref Kulanjian, and three other young men. Listed as tentative members of the group were Artin Uzunian and family, as well as Esther Orullian.

52. Journal of Joseph W. Booth, April 29, 1904.

53. Ibid.

54. Ibid.; see also Lindsay, "Missionary Activity in the Near East," 93; and Richard O. Cowan, "Mischa Markow: Mormon Missionary to the Balkans," *BYU Studies* 10.1 (fall 1970): 92–99.

55. Mission Record, Turkish Mission, May 31, 1899, 57.

56. Ibid.

57. Ibid., June 1899, 57.

58. Lindsay, "Missionary Activity in the Near East," 93. See also Cowan, "Mischa Markow: Mormon Missionary to the Balkans," 92–99.

59. Lindsay, "Missionary Activity in the Near East," 93, 95. See also Cowan, "Mischa Markow: Mormon Missionary to the Balkans," 92–99.

60. Mission Record, Turkish Mission, October 14, 1903, 61.

61. Booth, *Millennial Star,* March 24, 1904, 179.

62. Ibid., February 11, 1904, 91.

63. Ibid., February 25, 1904, 125.

64. Mission Record, Turkish Mission, August 7, 1904, 61–62. Incidentally, the

spelling of these names comes from the mission record. Apparently, the surnames Telekian and Telekiyan, while similar in spelling, are two different names. See also Booth, *Millennial Star,* October 6, 1904, 636.

65. Booth, *Millennial Star,* January 12, 1905, 27.

66. Ibid., October 13, 1904, 655.

67. Ibid.

68. Ibid., November 24, 1904, 739.

69. Ibid., February 9, 1905, 93–94.

70. Ibid., July 13, 1905, 433–34.

71. Ibid., 434.

72. Ibid., 435.

73. Ibid., March 1, 1906, 131.

74. Ibid., September 7, 1905, 569. See also Booth, *Millennial Star,* September 21, 1905, 605; Booth, *Millennial Star,* October 26, 1905, 678.

75. Booth, *Millennial Star,* October 26, 1905, 679.

76. President Booth was unaware that Greece had been formerly dedicated and opened for missionary labors by Francis M. Lyman and Sylvester Q. Cannon as they returned from their tour of Palestine in 1902. See Lindsay, "Missionary Activity in the Near East," 191.

77. Booth, *Millennial Star,* October 26, 1905, 679.

78. Ibid., March 8, 1906, 146.

79. Ibid., 147. See also Journal of Joseph W. Booth, October 22, 1905.

80. Booth, *Millennial Star,* March 8, 1906, 149.

81. For details regarding their tour, see Booth, *Millennial Star,* January 11, 1906, 18–20. See also Booth, *Millennial Star,* January 18, 1906, 42–43.

82. Booth, *Millennial Star,* August 24, 1905, 541.

83. See Papers of Anthon H. Lund, June 27, 1899.

84. *Journal History,* October 5, 1905, 8.

85. Journal of Joseph W. Booth, December 10, 1907.

86. Booth, *Millennial Star,* August 24, 1905.

87. Ferdinand Hintze, *Millennial Star,* April 5, 1906, 214–15. The Church was able to keep the typeset plates for future printings. They were sent from Boston to Salt Lake City and were stored in the annex of the temple. See Letter to President Lund from the *Deseret News,* Papers of Anthon H. Lund. Incidentally, the phrase "Armeno-Turkish" in this citation may refer to a dialect of Turkish spoken by the Armenians in the Ottoman Empire at the time of translation.

88. Mission Record, Turkish Mission, 1906, 62.

89. Reno W. Vance, *Millennial Star,* November 22, 1906, 750.

90. President Booth did receive one copy of the Turkish Book of Mormon. Elder Vance sent one of the two copies given him for inspection at Constantinople to President Booth in Aintab. That book was delivered to President Booth on November 21, 1906. In his journal, Booth wrote: "In the evening as we were anxiously awaiting the mail the *Avedaper* only was brought at first but after dark Bro Messir Pilanyian came and brought what we have waited long for and prayed for. The first copy of the Book of Mormon to reach this city in the Turkish language." Journal of Joseph W. Booth, November 21, 1906.

91. Journal of Joseph W. Booth, October 28, 1908.

92. Ibid., November 22, 1908.

93. Ibid., December 18, 1908.

94. Papers of Anthon H. Lund, August 27, 1908. See also John T. Woodbury, *Millennial Star,* July 30, 1908, 495.

95. Journal of Joseph W. Booth, May 16, 1906. See also Joseph F. Thorup, *Millennial Star,* April 5, 1906, 219.

96. Journal of Joseph W. Booth, July 29, 1907.

97. Ibid., July 6, 1907.

98. John T. Woodbury, *Millennial Star,* October 17, 1907, 671.

99. Lindsay cites Booth's journal and explains that he learned from the doctor that Elder Huber had symptoms of typhoid and typhus and that typhus was the cause of death. This clarification is further substantiated in the *Improvement Era* article written by Joseph W. Booth in 1909, wherein he names typhus as the cause of death. Lindsay, "Missionary Activity in the Near East," 108. See also Booth, "Four Heroes Far Away," *Improvement Era,* September 1909, 906.

100. *Millennial Star,* June 11, 1908, 373–74. This article mistakenly places the date of Elder Huber's death on May 13, 1908, instead of May 16, 1908.

101. See Lindsay, "Missionary Activity in the Near East," 108.

102. In a subsequent chapter, we will discuss the reinterment of Elder Huber in the northeastern corner of the Armenian Evangelical Cemetery at Aleppo. For details regarding that burial site, refer to James A. Toronto, "Early Missions to Ottoman Turkey, Syria, and Palestine," 339.

103. Booth, "Four Heroes Far Away," 907.

104. Journal of Joseph W. Booth, August 10–11, 1908.

105. Details contained in this overview were gleaned from Bernard Lewis, *The Emergence of Modern Turkey,* 3rd ed. (Oxford: Oxford University Press, 2002); and Jason Goodwin, *Lords of the Horizons* (New York: Owl Books, 1998).

106. Lewis, *The Emergence of Modern Turkey,* 216.

107. President Booth records in his journal that one of these missionaries, a twenty-seven-year-old Mr. Rodger, was the son-in-law of a prominent American living

in Tarsus, surnamed Christi. The other was a Mennonite missionary. See Journal of Joseph W. Booth, April 28, 1909.

108. Journal of Joseph W. Booth, April 21, 1909.

109. Ibid., April 21–28, 1909.

110. Ibid., September 1, 1909. See also Lindsay, "Missionary Activity in the Near East," 200.

111. Journal of Joseph W. Booth, July 31, 1909.

112. Ibid., September 9, 1909.

113. Ibid., October 1, 1909.

114. Booth, *Millennial Star,* March 10, 1909, 156.

CHAPTER SIX

Transition after Transition—
But the Work Moves On

1921–1929

W hen the mission reopened in 1921, it did so under a new name: the Armenian Mission.[1] During the twelve-year closure of the mission, the few Saints in the Near East were located primarily in branches in Aleppo and Aintab. They endured the hardships attendant on grievous poverty, ethnic prejudice, and the ravages of a world war. In 1921 the Armenian Saints were, for all intents and purposes, refugees. Nevertheless, the hardy Armenians survived the times.

Not only had the name of the mission changed, but the political face of the region had also changed, and it continued to be altered dramatically as a result of World War I. British forces entered Constantinople on March 16, 1920. The Ottoman parliament held its last session four days later and was dissolved by the sultan three weeks after that. The empire was being carved and served up by the victorious Allies. The French received a mandate over Syria and the British a mandate over Palestine. The future of the region was largely in question. A variety of plans were considered, including a possible United States mandate over Turkey. Some Armenian Christians expressed delight in such a possibility. They had been second-class citizens for centuries, and the possibility of change mingled with a minimization of Islamic dominion would be welcomed. Needless to say, such feelings caused further suspicion in the minds of the Turks toward the Armenians. As these events were taking shape, vestiges of the Young Turks rallied to maintain a Turkish national identity and create their own nation. This resistance group, headquartered in the Anatolian city of Ankara, grew in numbers and power until, against the odds, the sultanate was dissolved and the Turkish Republic was established on July 24, 1923.[2] This was the general setting in which the mission was reopened.

The history of the Armenian Mission from 1921 to 1929 is mainly the story of the service of one man—Joseph Wilford Booth. There was not a great deal of proselytizing done during these years. However, Joseph Booth was a relief worker on behalf of the Armenian refugees who had lost everything during the war years. He labored tirelessly to rebuild the hopes of the people and reestablish the Church in an environment of extremity and difficulty. He labored alone from 1921 to 1924, with the exception of two short

President Joseph and Sister Rebecca Booth

periods of time when he had two different companions. The first served with President Booth for three months, and the second served for eight months. Eventually, President Booth's wife, Reba, was sent to join him in 1924. They labored together in behalf of the Armenian Saints with only rare visits from Latter-day Saints from Utah or from the European Mission headquarters.

During these years, the Booths' level of commitment to the Armenian people never waned. Significant events of faith and fortitude filled this historical period. David O. McKay, Apostle and future

President of the Church, toured the mission at its opening. He taught the beleaguered Saints, gave hope, and showed forth an apostolic example of priesthood leadership. Also, a reformation among the members was instituted, wherein the faithless and flagrantly disobedient members were removed from the body of the Church, which led to a renewed vivacity among the remaining Saints in the mission. Additionally, creating a colony for the beleaguered Armenian Saints was considered so carefully that the First Presidency of the Church once again sent an emissary to investigate the possibility. Finally, mission headquarters were moved from Aleppo, Syria, to Haifa, Palestine, and the entire focus of missionary labors was redirected under the watchful eye of first Elder James E. Talmage and then Elder John A. Widtsoe, both of the Quorum of the Twelve. Through all these developments, President Joseph W. Booth worked tirelessly.

PRELUDE TO RENEWED BEGINNINGS

In the spring of 1921, Emmeline B. Wells, general president of the Relief Society, received a touching letter from the sisters of Aintab that painted a partial picture of how difficult it was to live in Anatolia during the twelve years that the mission was closed.

Dear Sisters in the Gospel:

We have not heard from you for a long time, and we are somewhat disheartened, but yet we thank the Lord that we have been found worthy to hear the gospel in this world and accept the same. We think of you sisters continuously, and even if we do not meet in this life and see each other, face to face, we have the assurance that we shall meet in the Millennium. We thank the Lord that even though we are amidst great trials and tribulation, he has delivered us from many afflictions. We have been blessed with faith and for this blessing we are extremely thankful. Our condition at present is such that only we who have seen can make a person appreciative. Hunger, nakedness, and want are everywhere. We do not feel to burden you with our troubles, but ask you to remember us in your prayers to the One on high. We remain, your faithful sisters in the gospel.[3]

Understanding the cause of such desperate circumstances may be helpful. Armenian uprisings at crucial moments during the empire's decline and during World War I were blamed for the empire's military losses and the embarrassment of Ottoman leaders. While only a fraction of the Armenian population was guilty of conspiring against the empire, the long-held view that Armenians were a troublesome menace to the Ottomans was once again reaffirmed. The empire adopted a policy of deportation and murder of the Armenians. Estimates indicate that about two-thirds of the Armenian population were either killed or deported to concentration camps established in the deserts of Syria and the mountainous regions of Mesopotamia. While accurate counts are not available, it is estimated that between 600,000 to 1 million Armenians were murdered by mob or by government action during this campaign, while 750,000 were deported.[4]

Armenians who were not killed or deported were stripped of rights and properties to the point of absolute desolation described in the aforementioned letter. Other letters from the remaining Armenian Saints also described the extraordinary deprivations during the war years, such as insufficient shelter or inadequate clothing. At times they were so starved for food that they were forced to live on grass and leaves. Even more shocking was the news that the entire body of Saints in Marash had been killed.

For twelve years, letters like this were received by Armenian Saints who had emigrated to Utah. The appalling details related through correspondence, coupled with the pleadings of the Armenian members in Utah to send elders back to the Aleppo and Aintab Branches (every male member who held the Melchizedek Priesthood had emigrated to Utah), were significant factors in the decision to reopen the mission in 1921. As the mission record puts it:

> For twelve years, or until the autumn of 1921, the Armenian Saints were left to themselves, and during that period their frequent letters told of the distress they were in, and their pleadings were so earnest that at last the authorities moved to sympathetic action and the decision was made on August 19, 1921, to re-open the mission.[5]

The first public mention of missionaries returning to the Near East came at a Turkish Mission reunion held in Salt Lake City in October 1920. The speakers at the reunion included Elders Booth, Holdaway, and Newman, as well as Brother Orullian, who was the oldest Armenian member of the Church in Utah at the time. At this meeting, it was communicated to the large gathering that efforts were then being made to open the mission again.[6]

THE SEARCH FOR A NEW PRESIDENT

On August 19, 1921, eleven months after the mission reunion, Joseph Booth left his home in Alpine, Utah, and traveled to Salt Lake City with a bundle of letters from the Armenian Saints under his arm. These letters contained additional pleadings for advice, support, and a missionary presence in the Near East.

Upon his arrival at Church headquarters, Joseph Booth was ushered into the office of Elder George Albert Smith, an Apostle who had recently returned from presiding over the European Mission. The discussion immediately turned to the First Presidency's plan to reopen a mission in the Near East, and Elder Smith wanted to know who Brother Booth felt would be best suited to preside over the new mission. Brother Booth mentioned names of several persons, each of whom had already served faithfully in the Turkish Mission. After each of these suggestions, Elder Smith would request another recommendation, until finally Booth said that he would be willing to return to the Near East if his affairs could be put in order. Brother Booth had amassed some debt, and he had also signed a contract to teach school during the academic year beginning in just three weeks.

Apparently, this final recommendation was what Elder Smith had been waiting for. The Apostle excused himself and, unknown to Brother Booth, paid a visit to the office of Heber J. Grant, President of the Church. President Grant came directly to Joseph W. Booth and said, "Bro. Booth we want you to go to Turkey to carry help to the Saints there: the Church will assist you some in your financial difficulties, be ready as soon as you can." Booth replied, "I will be ready in a few weeks."[7] Joseph Booth was set apart as president of the Armenian Mission by President Heber J. Grant and his first counselor, President

Charles W. Penrose, on September 14, 1921.[8] This would be his third mission to the Near East. Unfortunately, Reba would not join him in the mission for over two years.

Opposition on the Way

President Booth wanted to be in Jerusalem by October 24 to commemorate the eightieth anniversary of Orson Hyde's dedicatory prayer and, even more important, to catch Elder David O. McKay and

Brother Hugh J. Cannon, who were touring the distant missions of the world; hence, Joseph Booth departed in haste.[9] Although no definite arrangements were made for a meeting, President Booth knew he needed to be in Palestine by early November to maximize his chances.

He felt that having Elder McKay tour the new Armenian Mission would serve at least three purposes: First, after twelve years of isolation, having an Apostle as the first visitor would communicate a high level of priority from the Brethren. Second, Elder Anthon H. Lund, long-time advocate for the Turkish Saints, had died in March 1921, so it would be very helpful to have Elder McKay see firsthand the condi-

Elder David O. McKay of the Quorum of the Twelve Apostles. This portrait was taken in the 1920s.

tions in the new mission. And third, Joseph Booth was carrying a large amount of money to be distributed among the needy Saints and was told that Elder McKay was to oversee this relief effort.

Travel went smoothly until Booth arrived in Rome, where a pick-pocket stole his wallet and all his travel money, leaving him stranded.

Although mission headquarters in Liverpool quickly wired funds, there was a mix-up in the transfer, and President Booth did not receive any money until October 27, causing him to miss the anniversary of Orson Hyde's dedication of the Holy Land in Jerusalem. President Booth did not arrive in Jerusalem until November 4, 1921, and began to search for Elder McKay and Brother Cannon with great intensity amidst the swarming crowds. Because the Lord needed him to find them, Booth labored in faith, despite the unlikelihood of success. Eventually, President Booth boarded the train that would take him to Haifa by about 12:30 P.M. that day.

In the meantime, Elder McKay and Brother Cannon needed to find President Booth. During their world tour, they had received word from President Grant that Joseph Booth had been called to preside over the Armenian Mission and that he was carrying a large sum of money collected from a special Church-wide fast for the benefit of the suffering Saints in Europe and Armenia. It was Elder McKay's assignment to distribute these funds appropriately. President Grant had written to Elder McKay in a tone that seemed to anticipate a miracle: "Brother Booth is sent to meet you *somewhere* with money for relief of the Saints in Armenia."[10] They also received a cable from Elder Orson F. Whitney, saying, "Brother Booth . . . will meet you *somewhere*."[11] After arriving in Jerusalem, they wired the United States consul in Aleppo in an effort to locate President Booth, but the return response read, "Informed Booth en route Aleppo. Do not know whereabouts."[12] The chances for a meeting between the three leaders appeared bleak.

Elder McKay and Brother Cannon turned to other important work to accomplish. The day after receiving the consul's message, they ascended the slope of the Mount of Olives and knelt down in a secluded spot, where Elder McKay offered up a prayer to God. Elder McKay noted in his personal writings that his prayer included seven distinct parts: (1) a request that the labors of the world mission tour would yield abundant fruit; (2) an expression of gratitude for being in the Holy Land at a time when they could witness the partial fulfillment of ancient prophecies; (3) a request that the memorials and buildings commemorating the Savior's ministry might reflect a true form of worship; (4) a request that the spirit of opposition and hatred between Muslims and Christians in the land could be overcome, particularly the opposition of Christians toward Jews who were returning to the Holy Land; (5) a plea that members of The Church of Jesus Christ of Latter-day Saints would be more earnest in keeping their covenants and living Christlike lives; (6) a request that the Church would receive special protection and guidance from the Lord; and (7) a request that the upcoming journeys through the Armenian Mission would be inspirational and successful.[13] Shortly after the prayer, while preparing to depart the Holy City, Elder McKay felt impressed that they should travel by train instead of by car, as previously planned. Elder McKay was quick to follow the prompting, and the appropriate arrangements were made.

On November 4, 1921, Elder McKay and Brother Cannon stepped onto a train heading for Haifa. Brother Cannon suddenly realized that he did not remember the name of their hotel in Haifa (Elder McKay noted that this was the first and last significant detail that Brother Cannon forgot on their entire world tour together). Consequently, when they arrived in Haifa, they had no idea where they would stay for the night, causing a delay that turned out to be most significant. Elder McKay asked his companion to watch their luggage while he inquired at the station office door for a suitable hotel for the night.

Joseph Booth had arrived at the station in Haifa, having unknowingly traveled on the same train as Elder McKay and Brother Cannon. He reported to the station office to inquire after a ship that would take him to Beirut. While searching for ship schedules, he turned around and saw a man inquiring after hotel accommodations. It was Elder McKay, whom he had tirelessly searched for and prayed to meet. President Booth tapped on Elder McKay's shoulder and said, "Isn't this Brother McKay?"[14] Elder McKay described the meeting thus:

> Astonished beyond expression to be thus addressed in so strange a town, I turned and recognized Elder Wilford Booth, the one man above all others whom we were most desirous of meeting. We had met, too, at the most opportune time and place. Having known nothing of our whereabouts he had come from the western part of the world, hoping in his heart to meet us. Knowing from the cablegram only that he was en route to Syria,

we had come from the eastern part of the world, traveling west-ward, praying that we might meet him; and there we had met at the very time and place best suited to our convenience and to the success of our mission to the Armenians. It could not have been better had we been planning it for weeks.

As we recounted to each other our experiences, we had no doubt that our coming together was the result of divine interposition. . . . Indeed, had it not been for our having met at Haifa, our trip to the Armenian Mission would have been, so far as human wisdom can tell, a total failure. As it was, among many duties and experi-ences, we organized the Armenian Mission, to take the place of the Turkish Mission.[15]

Rescuing the Saints in Aintab

The biggest concern these men felt with reopening the mission was the status of the Church in Aintab, and they immediately traveled there to meet with the Saints. Of the many members President Booth had left behind twelve years earlier, only thirty-five remained—and all Church records had been destroyed or lost. The city lay in ruins, and about two-thirds of the Christian population had been killed during the war. Elder McKay reported that although the Armenians of Aintab had previously been twenty-five thousand strong, they had been reduced by massacre or deportation to a mere five thousand.[16] The men listened in shock as the Aintab Saints described the horror they had seen. Conversely, when describing her joy at the arrival of the missionaries, one Armenian sister explained, "For seven years we have been in hell, but to-day we are in heaven!"[17]

Nonetheless, their joy was short-lived. The day the missionaries arrived in Aintab, the French announced that they would withdraw their forces from the city in two months—forces that had served as a buffer between the Muslim Turks and the Christian Armenians. With the announcement came renewed death threats from Turks, and the rumor spread through the city that "four hours after the French evac-uate the town, not an Armenian will be alive."[18] Church members were desperate to leave the city, but with the announced withdrawal, the French also prohibited Armenians from leaving. Remarkably, at this time of great alarm, the members brought the elders eighteen people who were prepared for baptism.[19]

Following the quick departure of Elder McKay and Brother Cannon, President Booth immediately went to work to free the Latter-day Saints trapped in Aintab. Securing passports for them consumed all of his time. He soon learned that the branch had begun an eight-day fast in hopes of freedom. As President Booth considered what else could be done, he received a particular impression to meet with General de Lamathe of the French army in Aleppo and boldly ask him to free the Aintab Saints and take them to Aleppo. Booth's account of their meeting serves as evidence that the Lord was keenly aware of His struggling little flock in Aintab.

> I was received with cordial greetings and presented my passport, and missionary certificate as well as my appointment as Relief worker. Thru the captain as my interpreter to the French Officer I emphasized the fact that I was a representative of the Mormon Church who has so liberally contributed to the fund of Relief for France and Belgium during the recent war, and I was delighted to learn that he had heard of it. . . . I then told him my mission and that we had about 50 members and relatives in Aintab who were poor and needed assistance also some 25 friends who are anxious to receive permission to come to this place, and begged him to grant us permission to bring them all here [from Aleppo to Aintab was a distance of eighty miles]. He at first gave an unfavorable reply stating that it would not be a good precedent for him to set as it would likely stir up strife. . . . I still urged that he allow us to bring the poor whom we could care for so much better here with the rest of our members in one group. I have prayed almost night and day for the Lord to open the way for us to rescue the Saints, and they in Aintab have fasted for 8 days so they wrote, and I surely felt to thank God for his answer to my prayers when the Gen. at last said, "We will grant you permission to bring the 50 and you may present the matter of the 25 to the Aintab authorities. If they see that your friends are in danger of their lives the passports will be given and they can be brought out." Further he said that

> if the Army had empty wagons etc. coming back from Aintab they would bring the Mormons with them. He asked me to furnish a list of the 50 and advised me to go to Aintab to arrange for their transportation. The General expressed his thanks for the friendship of the Americans and when I told him that I had relatives who died on the great war account, he replied that our friendship was the closer knit by the sadness of those deaths. The conference lasted about 30 minutes. I later prepared a list of all I could obtain of the saints and immediate relatives so as not to much exceed the 50.[20]

Over the next few days, President Booth continued to hear horrible news out of Aintab, but he thought it wise not to tell any of the Saints of the arrangements he was making. He privately prepared a list of all the Saints, their children, and as many of their immediate relatives as he could recall—the allotted fifty came all too quickly. He then submitted the list to General de Lamathe, who promised to forward it on to officials in Aintab, where Booth was going himself. Upon arrival, he went straight to the passport office, where the general had, as promised, forwarded the approved passports. Because children under eight did not require a passport, Booth was able to add more names of family members and friends of the Saints.

In one day's time, word had spread through Aintab that President Joseph Booth had made arrangements for the exodus of many individuals out of Turkey and safely into Syria. The result of this common knowledge was that President Booth was thronged by people of the city who begged for his assistance. Of course, adding more names to the passport list was not his prerogative. However, he was quick to point out in his journal entry of the day that these same people who begged his assistance in 1921 were the very men who, twenty-two years earlier, had persecuted Elder Booth and Elder Maycock and then driven them out of the city of Aintab.[21]

On December 8, all the Latter-day Saints gathered at the passport office with hundreds of people who hoped to receive permission to leave Turkey. Finally, an official approached the group with the list of names of those who would receive passports. President Booth described the tense moments that followed.

The roar of the tumult of the crowd below was hushed at once
on the harsh command of the man who appeared before the
multitude to read the names. There was a thrill of joy for every
one whose name was read out, but with a corresponding sadness
for all who were disappointed. About 150 names were read out
in a clear ringing tone and then the words, "Now come the
Mormons" was followed by the reading of 51 names of my list—
the remaining 7 were left for the next list tomorrow—which
ended the number of passports issued today. Within a few
minutes the 51 papers were in the hands of Bro. Moses
Hindonian who was with me to receive them. Though ours were
the last to be read we were ushered into the room and received
first consideration. Mormons were famous in Aintab today.[22]

President Booth rented two halls to accommodate the homeless
Armenians who arrived in Aleppo on December 16 after a difficult
journey of eighty miles through mud and rain. However, all arrived
safely and "were thankful to the Lord for deliverance from possible
death and destruction in Aintab."[23] This miraculous deliverance is
seen by the Armenian Saints as the single greatest event to have taken
place since the gospel was introduced to the Near East in the last
days. The anniversary of the exodus became a day of celebration and
thanksgiving, and they even wrote poetry and created pageants to
keep the memory alive. Indeed, this exodus was the spark for a religious revival among the Armenian Saints.[24]

THE QUEST FOR SELF-SUFFICIENCY

European Mission president Orson F. Whitney eventually
directed Booth to rebaptize all the members at the "Mormon Khan"
(as it was known) who would commit to keep their covenants and
strictly abide by the laws of the Church. Hence, all of Booth's efforts
became focused on this objective, and he hoped to have them
prepared by April 6, 1922.[25]

Their destitute living conditions, however, made discipleship
challenging. They had only eighteen rooms to serve between 100 and
120 individuals after the poorest Saints in Aleppo also moved into the
"Mormon Khan."[26] These close living quarters fueled many of the

frustrations Booth would face over the next seven years. The members of the community could rarely get along for more than a day or two before difficulties would flare up. Because President Booth was the common judge between the disputing parties, this friction weighed heavily on him.

Part of the problem was that the Armenian Saints had little or no work. President Booth looked for every opportunity to keep the Saints busy. He encouraged small business undertakings such as rug making and the production of carefully embroidered handkerchiefs and towels.[27] When necessary, he would loan the members small amounts of money to encourage an entrepreneurial spirit in the community. He described his intentions and plans in a letter to President Orson F. Whitney.

> You ask about my financial policy. I am carefully feeling my way out of the difficulty. Work is very scarce. I am advancing a little money to certain of our members and friends, to enable them to start up small industries of their own, so that they may furnish employment to members of the Church. If they succeed, I will extend similar aid to others. I hope before long to have the mission self-supporting.[28]

Unfortunately, self-sufficiency among the Armenian Saints was never seen by President Joseph Booth, making his labors as a relief worker imperative.

In the spring of 1922, while distributing a huge shipment of clothing from Salt Lake City, Booth found an overwhelming spirit of selfishness among the impoverished Armenians. For this and other reasons, the April 6 rebaptism date was postponed. His journal entry on April 6 conveys both his disappointment and his never-ending patience with his Armenian congregation.

> I have looked forward for several weeks hoping to see a new beginning in earnestness and devotion in the work of the Lord. . . . I expected to baptize some 60 people today . . . but in the past two or three days conditions have developed to warrant . . . a more careful preparation in faith and true repentance among the believers.[29]

President Booth had not seen a missionary since Elder McKay and Brother Cannon left Syria seven months earlier, so news that Elder Wilford Owen Woodruff would arrive from the Swiss-German Mission was met with great anticipation. Because Elder Woodruff had been denied entrance into Germany, he would be traveling through Aleppo sometime in late May or early June.[30]

On May 30, two days after Elder Woodruff arrived, the one hundred Saints in Aleppo resorted to a beautiful park to the northeast of town, where the much-anticipated rebaptismal service was held. Following some instruction from President Booth regarding the import of baptismal covenants, Elder Wilford Owen Woodruff dedicated the park and the water for the baptismal service. Then President Booth baptized forty-eight individuals, and Elder Woodruff baptized twenty-five more.[31] President Booth looked on this time as a sweet harvest following six long months of labor, stating, "It was indeed a day of great rejoicing for me to see the progress of the work of the Lord and the wonderful change in six months in this land."[32]

Unfortunately, the time came for Elder Woodruff to return to Europe. Shortly after his departure, President Booth wrote:

> Today I am a lone missionary in this land of Syria. We have 97 members enrolled all of Armenian stock here on the record of the Aleppo branch of the Church. . . . While they are generally of a poor and uneducated class yet many of them are dear good faithful souls and I love them as brethren and sisters in the gospel.[33]

Although the outpouring of the Spirit was great in the previous weeks, the Saints continued to struggle. President Booth was convinced that living together as a group was a big part of the problem, but the Saints' impoverished condition kept him from dissolving the "Mormon Khan." This meant that he had no choice but to continue his role as judge and arbitrator among his hundred-plus living companions.

During a particular Relief Society meeting, President Booth pointed out how much contention there had been in the branch and challenged them to mend their ways. Ironically, this brought two women in the congregation into a heated argument, and their ranting led to blows and hair pulling. The contention soon infected the men of the branch, who, later that night, initiated their own fights. This affair went from fists to cuffs, as President Booth was compelled to call upon the police to break it up. In Booth's words, "It was a disgraceful affair."[34]

Although contentions such as these were common, fortunately most of the troubles in the branch were caused by a relatively small number of people. In a letter to Elder David O. McKay, the new European Mission president since October 1922, President Booth provided a snapshot of many positive things that had happened during the year.[35] He reported that beyond the many baptisms performed, a Relief Society was fully organized, with forty-five members who met every Wednesday morning. In one of these meetings, President Booth noticed that all the women but eight were barefoot because of their extreme poverty. Ironically, the sisters had gathered that morning to help others in the city who were less fortunate than they.

In order to encourage such devoted discipleship, President Booth brought a high level of organization into the lives of the Armenian Saints. Much of their free time was spent meeting in some gospel context. For example, Sundays included Sunday School in the morning and sacrament meeting in the afternoon. Additionally, priesthood quorums met every Monday evening, and from the time those meetings began in early October 1922, only two men had been absent. Tuesday evening was occupied by singing practice from the hymns of Zion, in both Armenian and English. And finally, every Thursday evening the Saints gathered to hold a testimony meeting. Because of this, very little of President Booth's time was actually spent proselytizing. However, when considering the chaotic conditions among the Armenian Saints just twelve months earlier, his work in Aleppo is nothing short of remarkable.

Two Mission Companions in 1923

In the beginning of 1923, President Booth happily learned that Elder Earl B. Snell would serve as his companion in the Armenian Mission. The nature of his call was specific. Elder Snell was to make a thorough examination of the mission and create a detailed report for Elder McKay.[36]

This was a happy time for President Booth. Just prior to the arrival of Elder Snell, a baptismal service was held wherein eight people were added to the fold. In a letter published in the *Millennial Star,* President Booth described this day as "about the happiest day I ever spent in this mission of nearly twelve years' experience."[37] Add to this a companion to quench the loneliness of leadership, and President Booth was a very grateful servant of the Lord.

Sadly, Elder Snell possessed a sickly constitution, and he was frequently afflicted by fevers and serious kidney troubles. He served with President Booth for only eight months, yet they served well together and baptized fourteen persons during that time.[38]

The two missionaries also moved the mission home, which doubled as the "Mormon Khan."[39] On August 17, 1923, they moved into the building that had previously served as the British consulate. The new location was a great improvement.[40] President Booth explained that the grounds were much larger and "open to the sun and sky and air, and our visitors are glad to come out of the city to see our new home."[41] There was a great deal of work to be done to improve the property, but the two missionaries were diligent.

One month later, they took a break and celebrated the hundredth anniversary of the Angel Moroni's visit to Joseph Smith on September 21, 1823. The anniversary fell on a Friday, and the celebration included a dramatic pageant depicting the historical events surrounding the visitation of Moroni. Two young men reenacted the events from 1823 to 1827, when Moroni gave the plates to Joseph Smith. The pageant was two hours long and played Friday night and then, by popular demand, again on Sunday evening. Attendance at the play was 140 the first night and 202 the second.[42]

Elder Snell finished his detailed report for Elder McKay and mailed it on June 3, 1923. Unfortunately, his health necessitated his release at the beginning of December. It was suggested that either Booth's wife, Reba, be called to join him or that Booth be released to go home. That having been decided, Reba wrote her husband of her call to serve a second mission to the Near East, although he did not receive the letter until after she had left Utah on December 15. The year came to an end with the president serving alone once again.[43]

POLICY REGULATION

Sister Reba Booth arrived in Beirut on January 18, 1924, accompanied by European Mission president David O. McKay and his wife, Emma Ray, who also served as president of the Relief Society of the European Mission. As mentioned earlier, the presence of Sister Booth was a great boon to her husband and the work in the Near East. Specifically, one scholar notes that

> her presence helped the missionaries deal more effectively with one of their most complicated problems: how to help members overcome traditional Middle Eastern attitudes that severely limited women's status in public life. Contrary to accepted cultural practices of the time, the Booths insisted that the Armenian sisters participate fully and give speeches in Church meetings, establish active Relief Society and Young Women organizations to provide the sisters leadership and educational opportunities, and encouraged LDS families not to arrange marriages at a young age for their daughters but to send them to school.[44]

The McKays were warmly received during their short, six-day stay in Aleppo. It is evident that President McKay disclosed to Booth the First Presidency's three distinct conclusions according to Elder Snell's report. The first was to call Sister Reba Booth to serve with her husband in the Armenian Mission. The second recommendation dealt with colonization, which the Brethren felt was out of the question at that time. And the final regulation, which had the most immediate impact on the Booths' service, was the counsel to minimize proselytizing among the Armenian people. In the words of President Heber J. Grant and his two counselors, Charles W. Penrose and Anthony W. Ivins:

> Neither do we feel that it would be wisdom, under existing circumstances, for efforts to be made to bring new converts into the Church in any great number. Where it is certain that a person is thoroughly converted to the truths of the gospel, he should not be refused admission to the Church, but we feel that under the circumstances great care should be exercised in order

that our responsibility in caring for these people be not increased until circumstances change so that we can better provide for them. We must of necessity care for those who are already members of the Church, and this we will endeavor to do through any means or plan which you [President McKay] may suggest after having conferred with President Booth. . . . Please advise us of the means that it may be necessary to provide in order that this purpose may be accomplished.[45]

President and Sister McKay left Aleppo on January 24, 1924. A detailed discussion between President McKay and President Booth of the above regulation of proselytizing efforts would explain why Booth immediately traveled to Beirut to search out a new location for the Armenian Mission headquarters.[46]

Baptisms, a Move, and a New Mission President in Europe

In 1924 there were three baptisms in the Armenian Mission; of the three, one is particularly noteworthy. Twenty-one-year-old Hoyhannes Bassmadjian was studying at the prestigious Armenian school in Jerusalem in order to become a monk. However, during a school break spent in Aleppo visiting his mother, he first heard of the restored gospel. His investigation led to baptism and confirmation on August 9, 1924.

Four days after Hoyhannes was baptized, Elder David O. McKay sent a directive instructing President Booth to move from the large "Mormon Khan" into a smaller complex immediately. Apparently, this move was the result of previously mentioned deliberations intended to scale back the large role that the Church was playing to provide basic services to the Saints in Syria. It took just over one week to find a new location for mission headquarters and another week to complete the move.[47]

Another high moment occurred when Booth read in a belated copy of the *Deseret News* that Elder David O. McKay was released as president of the European Mission and that James E. Talmage of the Quorum of the Twelve Apostles had been called to take his place. Although sad to see Elder McKay go, the Booths found this change to be of particular interest, since President Talmage's wife, May, was Joseph Booth's sister.

And then, on November 19, a set of Armenian type arrived that President Booth had purchased in hopes of bringing a greater variety of gospel literature to the Armenian members. After printing several tracts, he dove headlong into their first major printing and binding job—the arduous process of printing and binding six hundred copies of a Latter-day Saint hymnal in Armenian. Up to this time, the Saints had used hand-copied hymnals in the branch.[48] In its finished form, the hymnal contained eighty-two hymns.

Finally, 1924 came to a close. Although Booth was an optimist and his journals do not detail a great number of the frustrations and trials experienced during this time, he did record that it was "the most unpleasant year of all my missionary experience."[49] His journal entries of 1925 explain why.

THE VINEYARD IS PRUNED BUT STILL BEARS FRUIT

In January 1925, President Booth wrote in his journal that "several families are in a state of apostasy and must be handled soon."[50] By the end of June, President Booth explained to the congregation that "out of the 145 baptized since I came we now have 40 on the list as not being so firm in the faith as we could wish and out of the 40 we had found that 14 of them had apostatized."[51]

Those fourteen members were excommunicated from the Church that day by a unanimous vote of the branch, and two weeks later, three more were cut off. By the end of the year, an additional eleven individuals lost their memberships. The first was for unchristian conduct, including domestic violence, and the remaining ten were cut off for apostasy.[52]

Given the fact that President Booth reported a total membership of 165 in June 1925, a loss of twenty-eight Armenian members from the Church constituted a substantial pruning. But the six convert baptisms in 1925 served to heal the branch somewhat. Because mission policy did not encourage additional proselytizing, these baptisms were extraordinary and welcome.[53]

Another boon during these difficult months was the Saints' dramatic performance of the first few chapters of the Book of Mormon. The title of the play was "Nephi," and it played for two nights. The first evening, over seven hundred people were in attendance. Most of those attending this night were members and friends. The second evening, the play was presented to the general public. For this showing, the title was changed to "The Death of a Drunkard and Five Marriages in One Night."[54] This curious title attracted the attention of the city, and about four hundred and fifty people enjoyed the performance.

Through all this, the pressure of overseeing the pruning and nurturing of the Armenian vineyard weighed heavily on President Booth, and in August 1925, he suffered a mild heart attack.[55] This heart attack caused President Booth's pace to slow for a time, but he never left his station as the presiding authority of the Armenian Mission.

Near the middle of 1926, President and Sister Booth received a letter from President Heber J. Grant. President Booth's time in the field and health were being considered by the First Presidency at Salt Lake City. President Heber J. Grant explained to the Booths that they could name the date of their release and return to Utah, and another president would be called to take their place, or they could choose to serve for two more years.[56] There is no indication from President Booth's journal entries that the option of going home was ever seriously entertained, even though he had been in the Near East (on this mission) since 1921.

Instead, President and Sister Booth continued their work of caring for their Armenian friends. They worked right through his sixtieth birthday on August 14, 1926. The rest of 1926 was comparatively uneventful, though during the year there were seven convert baptisms.[57]

THE HARRIS REPORT:
ASSESSING THE FUTURE OF THE ARMENIAN MISSION

The most important event in 1927 was the visit of Dr. Franklin S. Harris at the beginning of the year. He had been sent by the First Presidency to make a detailed report of the present condition of the Armenian Mission, and his impressions would largely determine the future of the Church's role in the Near East. He was an expert in agriculture and did a good deal of inspecting on behalf of the Church. At the time of his travels through the Near East, he was also president of Church-owned Brigham Young University.

For six straight days, Brother Harris visited the people, interviewed branch members, and gathered demographic data. His impressions were that the mission was "in prime shape with the members gradually getting on their feet financially."[58]

A major portion of the report, which was created in order to guide the First Presidency's decision concerning a colony in the Near East,

Franklin Stewart Harris atop a pyramid in Giza, Egypt. Brother Harris, president of Brigham Young University and an expert in agriculture, was assigned by the First Presidency to assess the feasibility of a colony for the Saints in the Near East.

dealt with the feasibility—and unfeasibility—of creating a colony for the Armenian Saints in Syria or Palestine. While key leaders such as Ferdinand Hintze and Joseph Booth yearned for this solution, the First Presidency chose not to colonize. Given this fact, the recommendations from this final section of the Harris report, six in all, are the most salient points to review here. The recommendations were to (1) move the mission headquarters to Haifa; (2) call local missionaries to assist the Saints with industrial undertakings that would lead to financial stability (these missionaries would be supported by the Church, but the cost would be a fraction of the expense the Church was funding at the time of the report); (3) call two English-speaking missionaries to serve in Palestine to expand the work among the European population; (4) keep the Booths in the field during these transitions for one to two years; (5) refocus attention on English-speaking peoples in Palestine until greater stability was established among the Saints of the

Near East; and (6) purchase a mission home in Haifa that could serve as both a comfortable residence and an efficient center of Church and mission business.[59]

Finally, Brother Harris noted:

> I find in Syria a body of members of the Church who have a comprehension of the gospel and its teachings which seems to me remarkable; it compares favourably with that in the wards of Zion. I am really astonished at the work that President Joseph W. Booth and his wife have been able to accomplish in getting these people together and teaching them so that they understand so well the Church and its doctrines. The saints are also being brought toward economic independence from a condition of great poverty.
>
> All of this is being done with an economy that is surprising. Only the greatest devotion and self-sacrifice on the part of Brother and Sister Booth have made this possible. They are doing as fine a piece of work as I know of being done anywhere; and they have the respect and confidence, not only of the native population, but also of the Europeans and Americans who live in this section.[60]

Taking the Harris report recommendations seriously, the First Presidency began to shift the affairs of the mission into alignment with the proposed direction. On April 10, 1927, President Booth was authorized to travel to Haifa with President Talmage and purchase a home to serve as the new mission headquarters.

In the meantime, President Booth challenged the Saints to read the Book of Mormon in commemoration of the hundredth anniversary of Joseph Smith receiving the gold plates. Such intense study brought new life to the Saints, and one group of thirty-one branch members finished in only nine days.[61] Joseph Booth couldn't have been happier. He also encouraged the production of a two-hour drama depicting the events in Church history during this era.[62] The combined experience of reading the Book of Mormon and re-creating its stories on the stage revitalized the whole branch. President Booth noted that there was "much more union among the saints and . . . a new spirit of hope and peace. We trust it will be permanent."[63]

THE VISIT OF PRESIDENT JAMES E. TALMAGE

Elder Talmage arrived on October 10, 1927—this being his final visit, for Elder John A. Widtsoe had been called as the new president of the European Mission.[64] Joseph Booth was thrilled to have President Talmage in the mission, noting that in his sixteen years of service in the Near East, he had enjoyed the visit of only two presidents of the European Mission, David O. McKay and James E. Talmage. Five other Apostles of the Church had visited the Near East during Joseph Booth's service, bringing the total to seven Apostles as of 1927.[65] The Saints were so anxious to see President Talmage that they traveled a great distance from Aleppo to meet his train at the small station. President Talmage's record of this meeting provides a clear example of how hospitable and kind the Armenian Saints were to visitors at their doors.

Elder James E. Talmage of the Quorum of the Twelve Apostles with his wife, May (sister of Joseph Booth).

As I looked out from the open car window a woman approached and asked in fairly good English "Are you from America?" These were the first English words I had heard since I left Constantinople. On my answering in the affirmative she asked "What is your name?" My reply brought forth an exclamation of joy, and the young woman called and beckoned to others who hurriedly came up. I stepped from the train and was surrounded by an enthusiastic company comprising two brethren, five sisters, with three children. The sister who had first

addressed me handed me a note from President Booth, which
read in part: "These are some of our young people who were
anxious to see you, and have decided to ride out as far as
Mouslimie to meet you. They are carrying a few proofs
[missionary literature such as tracts] with them and will tell you
as best they can how glad they are to see you." . . . One three-
year-old boy was named to me as John Assian who was said to
have been named after our Son John; and a three-months-old girl
named as Merry May Assian, named in honor of [my] wife May.
With this little company I reached Aleppo at 9:30, or there-
abouts, and we were met at the station by President Joseph W.
Booth and a number of the Armenian Saints.[66]

President Talmage visited among the Saints for four days and even
visited the refugee camps on the opposite side of town from the
"Mormon Khan." After witnessing how horrible living conditions
were outside their khan, he described them in his journal as "pitiably
destitute."[67]

The Ninth Dedication

Twenty-five years had passed since Elder Francis M. Lyman had
dedicated the Holy Land. The next dedicatory prayer, number nine,
was offered by Elder James E. Talmage of the Quorum of the Twelve
Apostles. Many political developments had occurred in the region
since Elder Lyman's prayer of dedication. In 1927, the Ottoman
Empire was no longer in existence. It was abolished following World
War I. On July 24, 1923, a treaty was signed at Lausanne, Switzerland,
that preserved the borders of the new Republic of Turkey basically as
they exist today. As deliberations continued regarding the nature of
the new nation, it was determined that the sultanate would be elimi-
nated but that a member of the Ottoman princely line would hold
the office of caliph, which would be limited to religious affairs only.
Soon the position of caliph was abolished altogether. Elections were
held for the Grand National Assembly, and they, in turn, elected
Mustafa Kemal (later known as Kemal Atatürk) to be president of the
new nation. The capital was moved from Constantinople (known as
Istanbul to the Ottoman Turks) to Ankara. All major government

entities were secular in nature. Following World War I, much of the Ottoman Empire was carved up and assigned to the control of the European powers. For our purposes, it is important to reiterate that at this time Syria was placed under a French mandate, while Palestine was placed under a British mandate.

Under these general circumstances, Elder Talmage had received the assignment from the First Presidency to travel to Palestine for the purpose of relocating mission headquarters in the Near East from Aleppo, Syria, to Haifa, Palestine.

When Elder Talmage arrived in Aleppo, President Booth had served among the Armenians for nearly seventeen years.[68] The two men left Aleppo early Friday morning, October 14, and drove by car to Beirut and from there toward Haifa, Palestine. Elder Talmage wrote that "we passed through Sidon and near Tyre. The last part of the journey was along the shore of the Mediterranean, so close that the waves actually reached the wheels of the motor-car. This has been an eventful day, full of sights, scenes, and experiences of interest and profit."[69] They arrived in Haifa on Saturday, October 15, 1927, at 7:00 P.M., taking rooms at the Strand Hotel.

On Monday, October 17, Elder Talmage and President Booth canvassed the city to find prospective quarters for a mission home. After examining several buildings, they came across a house at the southeast corner of Carmel and Allenby Streets (now David Ben Gurion and Allenby Streets). It was undergoing renovations, but the old home was deemed suitable and the rent was lower than they had antici-pated.[70]

With the mission head-quarters located, Elder Talmage now desired to dedicate the land and make further recommendations to the First Presidency regarding the timing and scope of the establishment

The mission home selected by James E. Talmage and Joseph W. Booth, located at 59 Allenby Street (now David Ben Gurion and Allenby Streets).

of a missionary force at Haifa. He had made this a matter of careful thought and prayer. On the morning of Tuesday, October 18, 1927, Elder Talmage invited President Booth to accompany him to the top of Mount Carmel once again. President Booth explained in his journal that they left

> the carriage on the west side of the summit and walked through the trees to the East side, about two rods [eleven yards] in from the road, at a little break in the trees at the end of an old stone wall running along the crest of the hill to the S. E. and there in the grove of young pines we solemnly called upon the Lord in prayer. I was asked to lead in a preliminary petition which was followed by the reading of the following scriptures. Isaiah 35 ch, II Nephi 27—last parts and Doc. & Cov. Sec. 133, last half or nearly. Then with these books opened and spread before us we kneeled together and President James E. Talmage an Apostle of

The promenade leading to Kaiser's Watch atop Mount Carmel, where Elder James E. Talmage dedicated the Holy Land in company with Joseph Wilford Booth. This was the ninth such dedication.

the Lord Jesus Christ, offered a prayer dedicating the city of
Haifa as a place for headquarters for the mission, and rededi-
cating the land of Palestine and Syria to the preaching of the
restored gospel, and for the gathering of the Jews to their
promised land. Special blessings were invoked upon the Saints of
the Armenian Mission, upon the Armenian people who are the
victims of the cruel conditions of these stricken lands, and upon
the children of Judah who are gathering and who will gather to
their latter day inheritance. Intercessions were also made for
Sister Booth and myself, and for all the missions and missionaries
of the Church with all the authorities of the Church and the
Saints of Zion.[71]

The prayer lasted about fifteen minutes, and the Spirit and power
of God attended the meeting. President Booth later declared that the
prayer was the most sublime utterance he had ever heard and yearned
to have a copy of the words then uttered by Apostle Talmage. But
Brother Booth felt "sure that it must be recorded on the delicate
plates of celestial graphophones, to be repeated for multitudes yet
unborn, destined to enjoy the blessings there invoked upon this long
forsaken home of Israel, now soon to be redeemed."[72]

Apparently, Elder Talmage's prayers and supplications regarding
the course of missionary labors in Palestine were answered during the
dedicatory experience. He writes that "immediately after our descent
from the Mount Carmel I sent a cablegram to the First Presidency,
reading: 'Quickmere, Salt Lake City: Recommend six missionaries
Palestine—Talmage.'"[73]

Elder James E. Talmage was the ninth person to dedicate Palestine
for the return of Jews. His sense of history regarding such a sacred privilege was keen. The following Monday, October 24, 1927, Elder
Talmage noted in his journal the eighty-sixth anniversary of the dedication of the land of Palestine by his apostolic predecessor Orson Hyde.

THE MOVE TO HAIFA

President Booth spent the rest of the year organizing the Aleppo
Branch and preparing for the move to Haifa, setting apart Elder
Nazar Bezjian as president of the branch and advancing several men

in the priesthood.[74] With the branch organized, he left for Haifa on January 11, 1928, yet Reba remained for a time to assure that the proper permits arrived at the British consulate which allowed them to take up residency in Palestine.

Within two weeks of President Booth's arrival in Haifa, a school-teacher named Garabed Tashjian inquired after Mormonism at mission headquarters. President Booth talked with him and gave him a series of tracts to read. Two days later, Garabed visited again, and like Johann Georg Grau (the first convert to the Church in Haifa, who was baptized by Jacob Spori), he explained to President Booth that he had dreamed a dream that had convinced him of the truthfulness of the restored gospel and requested baptism at President Booth's hand.[75] Unfortunately, Garabed was not as earnest as Johann Georg Grau was in August 1886. There are occasional entries in President Booth's diary noting that Garabed came to discuss the gospel, but there is no record of his ever being baptized.

President Booth returned to Aleppo on January 29, 1928, to check on affairs in the branch and take his wife, Reba, back to Haifa. On the night of February 7 he had a dream. He explained:

> I thought I was out in a vast field and it appeared that my work was to care for and save a *precious dove* placed in my charge. I wanted to catch it, and if I could not do that, at least I wished to have it keep going toward the West. The dove was set on going eastward. It would not fly far but kept me busy all day in trying to save it from going east. I thought my brother and also Reba my wife advised me to give up the useless struggle, but I kept it up till dusk when the stubborn bird flew away out of sight.[76]

The next day he related this dream to the sisters of the Relief Society in their Wednesday meeting. At priesthood meeting that very evening, the brethren got into an argument which led to criticism of the branch presidency. President Booth felt impressed to share the dream with the brethren. One week later, the Booths moved to Haifa, and the precious dove was left to take care of itself.

GOOD OMENS IN HAIFA

The first baptisms following the move to Haifa took place on Easter Sunday, April 8, 1928. The converts were Sisters Khatun Pilajian and Osanna Polasajian. As the last names suggest, these women were Armenian. Therefore, despite the directive to proselytize among Europeans in Palestine, a natural outgrowth of his work in Syria and Turkey was that many of President Booth's initial contacts in Haifa were made among the Armenian people. These newly baptized members, as well as Garabed Tashjian's inquiries, were the result of such contacts.[77]

With these baptisms and the resultant interest came a wave of anti-Mormon sentiment in the city. President Booth referred to both the increased contacts and the anti-Mormon movements as good omens.[78] The negative sentiments came from a variety of sources, some warning the people of Haifa to stay away from the Mormons,[79] others claiming they'd been told that "anyone who associated with the Mormons were partakers of their sins."[80] Eventually, Booth learned that even his preacher friend from the church next door to the mission home was visiting local investigators and telling them to avoid any contact with the Church.[81] Due to his past experience, President Booth understood that he must be on a good and potentially fruitful errand of the Lord for the adversary to be up in arms over the work he was performing.

In the summer of 1928, Palestine was plagued with pesky locusts. President Booth turned the insect invasion into a brilliant public relations campaign by writing an article entitled "Locusts of Another Land." This article was published in *The Palestine Bulletin* on May 24, 1928. The article compared Utah to Palestine by pointing out many geographic similarities, such as the Dead Sea and the Great Salt Lake. Finally, he described the grasshopper war of 1848 in the Salt Lake Valley, wherein the Saints, newly arrived in the Great Basin of the American West, almost lost their crops to hordes of crickets.

Another very favorable article about the Church appeared in a local Arabic paper, *Aljkdam*. The article included a picture of President Booth and was very complimentary concerning his work. In response to that article, a columnist by the name of Ameen, who published a column claiming that he would not write anything until he had thoroughly investigated it, blasted the editors at *Aljkdam* for publishing such a positive story about the Latter-day Saints. In his article he claimed that Mormonism was false. As it turns out, Ameen had never met a Latter-day Saint. The editors of *Aljkdam* were anxious to print President Booth's brief rebuttal, and the war of words through the press came to a positive end for the Church.[82]

"Heartily Sick"

President Booth spent the month of June in Syria visiting the Saints at Aleppo. On June 18, 1928, he proposed to the members that a small number of families move to Damascus and others to Beirut. The proposal was intended to shore up members in those cities who were isolated from their fellow Saints, bring a greater possibility of financial security to them, and establish two additional branches of the Church in Syria, which would increase missionary activity among the Syrian people. All the plan would require would be the cooperation of a few families in the Aleppo Branch.[83]

The day after the proposal was presented by President Booth, there were arguments, backbiting, and contention regarding the potential of relocation. In the end, a small number of people did move to both Damascus and Beirut. However, the general attitude among the branch members was disgusting to President Booth. He caustically noted in his journal that he was "heartily sick of the quarrels, dissensions and unsaintly acts" among the Armenian members.[84] He left Aleppo on July 3, 1928, "with a sad heart that the members [were] so faithless."[85] As he left the city, one of the sisters handed him four balls of *kyufta* (a blend of cracked wheat and meat), each about the size of an egg. Booth noted that

> I ate only one of them at about 5:30 a.m. That with a drink of water was the last thing that passed my lips till I was in Damascus nearly three [two] hundred miles away, and I sat at 8:30 p.m. in the presence of a family or two of Saints and ate two more of the ounce balls and drank of diluted clabber, as I related to them my sorrow at seeing such unfaithfulness among the members. The hunger and

thirst of that long ride through the burning sands and the hot sun and the torrid winds of Syria were a pleasure compared to the real soul suffering I underwent for the waywardness of the sheep entrusted to my care. If the Lord will accept my little tribute as a sacrifice to His glorious cause I shall be happy to have made it.[86]

On his way back to Haifa, he also stopped in Beirut. The visits to Beirut and Damascus were intended to assist the newly arrived members and to help them settle into their new homes.

Back in Haifa, President Booth's frustrations were only compounded by a letter he received from branch president Garabed Junguzian, explaining that he had decided to leave the Church and join the Armenian Church. According to President Booth, the letter was glaring evidence of a lack of the Spirit in the branch president's life. Brother Junguzian claimed that he had only joined the Church for two reasons: first, to go to America, and second, to get a free education.[87] President Booth remarked in his journal that "it is sad to learn that one so prominent and with such a splendid future to become a great man in the Church would have thrown aside the gifts of God to follow the ambitious desires for the glory of men and the world."[88]

President Booth immediately penned a letter to Garabed, encouraging him to hold on to his faith in the restoration of the gospel. A short time later, the branch president replied, explaining that he had considered his decisions more seriously, had repented of his ill feelings toward the Church, and begged President Booth's forgiveness. He further explained that he was under a great deal of strain and gloom and was pressed upon by the temptations of the adversary to act as he did. Now, however, he was anxious to be numbered again among the faithful. President Booth wrote him an encouraging letter accepting his apology and welcoming him back into the fold.[89]

The months from July to December 1928 were active and productive, with the translation of the Book of Mormon into Arabic progressing[90] and a visit from the world leader of the Baha'i faith, Mohamed Ali Baha'i, whose world headquarters were located in Haifa. After visiting the mission home, he in turn entertained the Booths at his home only two days later.[91]

On September 30, President Booth celebrated the thirtieth anniversary of his arrival as a stranger in Constantinople in 1898. At that time, he had dreamed of one day serving in Haifa, and after three decades the dream had become a reality.[92]

The Passing of Joseph Wilford Booth

In mid-November 1928, President and Sister Booth left Haifa to visit the Saints in Beirut, Damascus, and Aleppo. The purpose of the visit was to help the poor members in Aleppo prepare for the coming winter. They arrived in Aleppo on November 20, 1928, and went about serving their beloved Armenian friends. Following fast and testimony meeting on December 2, 1928, President Booth and Reba visited the grave of Elder Emil J. Huber in Aleppo. Shortly after arriving at his quarters, President Booth became ill. Three days later, President Joseph Wilford Booth died, with Reba by his side. The last entry in his journal was written in Reba's hand. She wrote: "My dear husband Joseph Wilford Booth passed away Dec. 5, 1928, at Aleppo, Syria."[93] The cause of death was determined by the doctor who treated President Booth as angina pectoris. It was later noted that the condition was exacerbated by overexertion and excessive work.[94]

President Booth was laid to rest in the Armenian Evangelical Cemetery in Aleppo on December 8, 1928. The burial site occupies the highest end of the cemetery. In order to appropriately memorialize the great Armenian missionary, Sister Booth and the local Saints erected a headstone in honor of their fallen husband and friend.[95] Five years later, the Church erected and dedicated a large monument at the site of President Booth's grave.

Eulogies and Praise for President Booth

Many were quick to pay tribute to this modern-day Ammon who had served for seventeen years among the Armenian people. President John A. Widtsoe wrote:

> Our hearts are heavy for the departure of our brother and fellow worker, yet gladness comes with the recollection of the valiant service he has rendered the Cause of Truth. Joseph W. Booth has left behind a glorious record. He never faltered, nor did he fail, in

performing the work placed upon him. He spent more than seventeen years, on three different missions, during the thirty years since 1898, in missionary service among the people of Turkey, Armenia, Palestine and neighboring countries. In those lands he was the best known representative that the Latter-day Saints have had; and he was everywhere highly respected. . . . Wherever President Booth went he bore witness of the restoration of the gospel of Jesus Christ. And, his work as an ambassador of the truth of the Lord, always appeared to him as a privilege.[96]

One year prior to Joseph Booth's death, Elder James E. Talmage noted:

With this Mission, whether known as Turkish or Armenian, the name of Elder Joseph Wilford Booth will always be prominently associated, and in the story of the last decade the name of his devoted wife.... President Booth] has served long and faithfully as President of the Armenian Mission, has given nearly seventeen years of his life to work among these people. He has passed through

The grave marker of President Joseph Wilford Booth as it appeared in the early 1930s.

the affliction of black small pox, from which dread disease two of our missionaries lie buried, one at Aintab, Turkey, the other at Haifa Palestine. . . . President Booth has been a true pastor to these members, who verily have come up through great tribulation; he has been a tender and self-sacrificing shepherd to the harassed flock; and he loves his sheep.

In the matter of church training the community is a marvel, and exists as a living monument of praise and honour to the President and his wife. With but a very limited range of literature published in their language, the people have become well versed in a knowledge of doctrine and church organization.[97]

In January 1929, Elder David O. McKay wrote:

No man in the Church could have been truer to his trust; no one less complaining; no one more hopeful; no one more willing to sacrifice personal comforts and convenience to give aid to the poor and unfortunate; no one more ready to give his life for his friends and in the service of his God, than was President Joseph Wilford Booth.[98]

An indication of the respect President and Sister Booth had earned while living in Aleppo is found in the response of the community to Joseph Booth's death. Two men who showed particular sympathies were Lorenzo Y. Manachy, former United States vice-consul in Aleppo (the U.S. consulate in Aleppo had been closed on July 1, 1928, and since that time Manachy had represented the Beirut consulate), and Reverend John E. Merrill, an American missionary and the director of the Aleppo College. At the time of President Booth's death, the funds of the mission were basically depleted. These two men advanced Sister Booth sizable sums of money to assist in the burial and ensure her comfortable passage back to Haifa, after which she was able to reimburse her benefactors.[99]

The Brethren also showed a great deal of concern for Sister Booth. They sent Elder Ralph V. Chisholm, who at the time served as the secretary of the European Mission, to close up the affairs of the mission in preparation for a new president and personally escort Sister Booth back to her home in Alpine, Utah. They departed early in 1929.[100]

A NEW MISSION PRESIDENT—ALMOST

Don Mack Dalton of Salt Lake City, Utah, was called to succeed Joseph Booth as the next president of the Armenian Mission. The call was extended prior to Booth's death. In fact, President and Sister Booth's release was in the mail when Joseph Booth died.[101] It was anticipated that President Dalton and his wife would travel to Haifa in the early days of January 1929. Upon learning of the death of President Booth, the Brethren redirected President Dalton's assignment, and he was called to serve as the president of the South African Mission.[102] Subsequently, the Saints in the Near East were again left to govern their own affairs without the assistance of leaders from Utah. This would be the case for four years.

From 1921 to 1929, members of the Church in the Armenian Mission progressed from near refugee status following World War I to a body of Saints who, despite their struggles, continued to embrace the teachings of Jesus Christ and the latter-day restoration of the gospel. Under the leadership of Joseph Booth, a core of believers continued the legacy of the Church in the Near East that began with Orson Hyde, Jacob Spori, and Ferdinand Hintze. The death of Joseph Booth marked the end of an era. He was the last missionary who had served in the Near East in the nineteenth century and encompassed the general perspectives that grew out of that time period. When the mission reopened in 1933, it would be distinctly different.

NOTES TO CHAPTER 6

1. In general terms, the reasoning behind the name change may be attributed to two fundamental issues. First, the location of mission headquarters was in Aleppo, Syria, and the people who had joined the Church in the Near East were almost exclusively Armenian. At this time it was thought best to retire the title "Turkish Mission" and adopt a mission name that reflected the makeup of the members. Second, the Ottoman Turks had mercilessly driven and murdered the Armenian people during World War I. Hence, the Armenian Mission seemed to be a more fitting and appealing name.

2. Bernard Lewis, *The Emergence of Modern Turkey* (Oxford: Oxford University Press, 2002), 245–60.

3. *Relief Society Magazine,* March 1921, 166–67.

4. For a detailed discussion of the Armenian massacres and deportations to concentration camps that had taken place during the years the mission was closed, please consult Efraim Karsh and Inari Karsh, *Empires of the Sand* (Cambridge, MA: Harvard University Press, 1999), 150–59. Furthermore, Near Eastern historian David C. Montgomery noted that "the entirety of Asia Minor suffered in the fighting of World War I and the half-decade after the war. Approximately 20 percent of its population died—three million people, most of them Muslim Turks—of starvation, disease, exposure, and cruel strife." Interview, by the authors, March 31, 2004.

5. Mission Record, Armenian Mission, June 30, 1925, 64. This entry summarizes events in the mission from the fall of 1921 to the summer of 1925.

6. *Journal History,* October 9, 1920, 7.

7. Journal of Joseph W. Booth, August, 1921, L. Tom Perry Special Collections, Harold B. Lee Library, Brigham Young University, Provo, UT.

8. Journal of Joseph W. Booth, September 14, 1921.

9. Hugh J. Cannon was the son of President George Q. Cannon. Brother Cannon was serving as the president of the Liberty Stake when he was called to serve a special mission with Elder McKay. The two were set apart on December 2, 1920, and their duty was to tour the missions in distant parts of the world and administer relief to the suffering Saints following World War I. See Clare Middlemiss, *Cherished Experiences* (Salt Lake City: Deseret Book, 1955), 79. See also *Millennial Star,* December 15, 1921, 795.

10. Middlemiss, *Cherished Experiences,* 79 (italics added).

11. Ibid. (original italics).

12. Ibid., 80.

13. Ibid., 130–31. It is interesting to note that Elder McKay did not dedicate the Holy Land for the return of Israel. Not all solemn and sacred prayers offered by the Apostles and prophets in the Holy Land are prayers of dedication.

14. Journal of Joseph W. Booth, November 4, 1921.

15. Middlemiss, *Cherished Experiences,* 82–83.

16. David O. McKay, *Millennial Star,* February 28, 1924, 136.

17. Ibid.

18. Ibid.

19. Journal of Joseph W. Booth, November 8–9, 15, 1921.

20. Ibid., December 1, 1921.

21. Ibid., December 7, 1921.

22. Ibid., December 8, 1921.

23. Ibid., December 16, 1921.

24. Joseph W. Booth, *Improvement Era,* vol. 31, 1928, 1050. See also Rao H. Lindsay,

"A History of the Missionary Activity of The Church of Jesus Christ of Latter-day Saints in the Near East, 1884–1929," master's thesis, Brigham Young University, 1958, 158.

25. Journal of Joseph W. Booth, April 6, 1922.

26. Ibid., August 1, 1922.

27. Lindsay, "Missionary Activity in the Near East," 159.

28. Booth, *Millennial Star,* February 23, 1922, 123.

29. Journal of Joseph W. Booth, April 6, 1922.

30. Ibid., April 29, May 13, 25, 27, 1922.

31. Ibid., June 1, 1922.

32. Ibid., June 11, 1922.

33. Ibid., August 1, 1922.

34. Ibid., March 12, 1924.

35. Ibid., October 18, 1922.

36. Heber J. Grant, Letters of President David O. McKay, European Mission President (1922–24), vol. 3, October 30, 1923, LDS Church Archives.

37. Joseph W. Booth, *Millennial Star,* April 12, 1923, 235.

38. Once Elder Snell had finished his report for Elder McKay, he served diligently as a companion to President Booth. His service was invaluable and was only hindered by the aforementioned health concerns.

39. Booth, *Millennial Star,* April 12, 1923, 235.

40. The location of the new mission headquarters was at Jebel Hahar, Azizeya, Aleppo. See Journal of Joseph W. Booth, January 19, 1924.

41. Booth, *Millennial Star,* November 22, 1923, 746.

42. Ibid.

43. Journal of Joseph W. Booth, December 15, 1923.

44. James A. Toronto, "Early Missions to Ottoman Turkey, Syria, and Palestine," in *Out of Obscurity: The LDS Church in the Twentieth Century* (Salt Lake City: Deseret Book, 2000), 357. See also Journal of Joseph W. Booth, January 22, 1924.

45. Grant, Letters of President David O. McKay, European Mission President (1922–24), vol. 3, October 30, 1923.

46. Journal of Joseph W. Booth, January 27–28, 1924.

47. Ibid., August 28–29, September 8–15, 1924.

48. Lindsay, "Missionary Activity in the Near East," 169.

49. Journal of Joseph W. Booth, December 31, 1924.

50. Ibid., January 19, 1925.

51. Ibid., June 28, 1925.

52. Ibid., December 27, 1925.

53. Ibid., June 10, 1925.

54. Ibid., October 27, 1927.

55. Lindsay, "Missionary Activity in the Near East," 170.

56. Journal of Joseph W. Booth, May 11, 1926.

57. Ibid., April 6, 1926.

58. Franklin S. Harris to James E. Talmage, February 11, 1927, L. Tom Perry Special Collections.

59. Franklin S. Harris, "Report Sent to First Presidency by Dr. F. S. Harris," February 10, 1927, L. Tom Perry Special Collections.

60. Harris, *Millennial Star,* July 14, 1927, 444–45.

61. Lindsay, "Missionary Activity in the Near East," 174.

62. Richard L. Jensen, "A Commemoration," *Church News,* September 22, 1979, 16.

63. Journal of Joseph W. Booth, August 31, 1927.

64. Ibid., October 3, 1927.

65. Booth, *Millennial Star,* November 10, 1927, 714.

66. Journal of James E. Talmage, October 10, 1927, LDS Church Archives.

67. Ibid., October 13, 1927.

68. "From Foreign Fields," *Millennial Star,* July 14, 1927, 444. See also James E. Talmage, "The Armenian Mission," *Millennial Star,* December 1, 1927, 760.

69. Journal of James E. Talmage, October 4–November 4, 1927.

70. Ibid. See also Journal of Joseph W. Booth, October 17, 1927.

71. Journal of Joseph W. Booth, October 18, 1927.

72. Booth, "Through Palestine," *Millennial Star,* November 17, 1927, 727.

73. Journal of James E. Talmage, October 4–November 4, 1927.

74. Journal of Joseph W. Booth, October 27, 1927.

75. Ibid., January 23, 25, 1928.

76. Ibid., February 8, 1928 (italics added).

77. Ibid., January 22, 1928.

78. *Millennial Star,* March 22, 1928, 190.

79. Journal of Joseph W. Booth, March 11, 1928.

80. Ibid., April 12, 1928.

81. Ibid.; see also October 11, 1928.

82. Ibid., May 12, 25, June 8, 1928. See also Joseph W. Booth, *Millennial Star,* July 5, 1928, 428–29.

83. Journal of Joseph W. Booth, June 19, 25, 1928.

84. Ibid., June 20, 1928.

85. Ibid.

86. John A. Widtsoe, *Millennial Star,* December 20, 1928, 810–11.

87. Journal of Joseph W. Booth, July 24, 1928.

88. Ibid.

89. Ibid., July 29, 1928.

90. Ibid., August 28, 1928.

91. Ibid., August 19, 1928.

92. Ibid., September 30, November 4, 1928.

93. The last journal entry of President Booth was on December 3, 1928. Following this entry, Reba wrote of the death of her husband. See Journal of Joseph W. Booth, December 3, 1928.

94. In lay terms, President Booth died of a heart attack. The attack was most likely caused by an insufficient supply of blood to the heart due to arterial blockage and/or the damage caused by a mild heart attack President Booth experienced in August 1925. The end result was deterioration of muscle in the heart, which eventually led to a massive hemorrhage, causing death. See Letters of John A. Widtsoe, December 8, 1928, LDS Church Archives. See also Widtsoe, *Millennial Star,* December 20, 1928, 810–11; Richard S. Bennett, *Millennial Star,* August 10, 1933, 525; Mission Record, Armenian Mission, December 1928, 72.

95. *Millennial Star,* August 10, 1933, 521.

96. Widtsoe, *Millennial Star,* December 20, 1928, 810–11.

97. Talmage, *Millennial Star,* December 1, 1927, 760–61.

98. David O. McKay, *Improvement Era,* January 1929, 183.

99. Letters of John A. Widtsoe, December 8, 1928.

100. Bennett, *Millennial Star,* August 10, 1933, 525. See also Lindsay, "Missionary Activity in the Near East," 184.

101. Mission Record, Armenian Mission, January 14, 1928, 72–73. A letter from the Presiding Bishopric acknowledges the honorable release of President Booth and the call of Don Mack Dalton to replace him. The letter is dated November 27, 1928.

102. Mission Record, Armenian Mission, January 14, 1928, 73.

CHAPTER SEVEN

"We'll Find a Place": The Quest for a Latter-day Saint Colony in the Near East

In the collective history of the United States of America, Brigham Young stands as the greatest colonizer the nation has ever had.[1] While Latter-day Saints don't colonize today as they have in the past, in the last decade of the nineteenth century and the first three decades of the twentieth, President Young's pioneering and colonization efforts were still very fresh in the minds of Church leaders, and the viability and success of a well-managed Mormon colony was generally indisputable. Given this context, it should come as no surprise that when a group of Latter-day Saints in the Ottoman Empire in the late nineteenth and early twentieth centuries were struggling spiritually, temporally, and politically, colonization was looked upon as a realistic and advantageous option for relief. In fact, a great deal of thought, time, energy, and resources were devoted to establishing a Mormon colony in the Near East during this time period.

For almost forty years (1889–1928), aspirations for a Mormon colony in the Near East percolated in the minds and hearts of the leaders of the Turkish and Armenian Missions, the highest-ranking leaders of The Church of Jesus Christ of Latter-day Saints in Salt Lake City, and the general membership of the Church in the Near East. However, the dream of a Mormon colony for the often-desperate members of the Church in that region was never realized.

The vision behind the colonization effort was driven by such prominent men as Ferdinand Hintze, Albert Herman, and Joseph Booth. It was seriously considered by the Quorum of the Twelve and was openly endorsed by President Heber J. Grant. With such broad support and enthusiasm extended over so many years, it is surprising that the much-anticipated colony in the Near East never materialized.

This chapter explores in detail the initial motivation for and the events surrounding efforts to establish a Mormon colony in the Near East. Because this movement was so thoroughly laced through and connected with the missionary labors of the Church in the Near East, some aspects of this chapter will, predictably, be redundant. Nevertheless, this overview of the colonization effort should yield a richer understanding of the history of the Church in the Near East.

Why Was There a Pressing Need to Colonize?

It will be remembered that while the Ottoman government allowed religious freedom, there was a millet system in place that required all citizens to deal with the government through a formally recognized religious organization. Practically speaking, this meant that the Ottoman government used the churches to collect taxes, offer education, and even conduct burials. The Protestants had received recognition in 1850. Latter-day Saints, on the other hand, had no governmental recognition. This meant that joining the Church carried additional complexities and considerations because the convert was still under the direct control of his former religious leader.[2] In 1899, Albert Herman, president of the Turkish Mission, summed up the exasperating conditions of the Saints under the millet system.

> The Latter-day Saints here in Turkey are in a precarious condi-
> tion. . . . They have no acknowledged head to represent them at
> the seat of government, no one to legally marry them or perform
> a funeral service, they are absolutely at the mercy of the officials
> to get any formal or legal business done, and in case one should

die without heirs, the priests of the church to which he had formerly belonged may lay claim to the property and get it.[3]

In addition to the disadvantages of the millet system, the predominance of Armenian membership of the Church in Turkey was another source of instability. As mentioned before, the Ottoman government looked upon Armenians with a great deal of suspicion and took every opportunity to keep them in check. These suffocating circumstances led Ferdinand Hintze, the first president of the Turkish Mission, to formulate a plan to alleviate the stifling burden of the empire. His prayerful contemplations led to the first proposal to form a Latter-day Saint colony.

President Hintze's proposal to colonize was presented before Church leaders consistently as he served two terms as president of the Turkish Mission. Colonization also seemed essential to his successors, President Albert Herman and President Joseph Booth. These men pursued this dream for a combined total of forty years.

There were four general premises undergirding the colonization effort. The import and emphasis of each of these premises varied at different times and under different leaders. A colony in the Near East would: (1) facilitate the gathering of the righteous in the Holy Land and also the gathering of the Jews, as pronounced by Elder Hyde and in subsequent apostolic dedications; (2) foster unity among the Saints, given the extreme ostracization from society that followed conversion; (3) protect Armenian Saints, who otherwise might be harmed or even killed to quell nationalistic ambitions; and (4) increase the likelihood of bringing about a spiritual *and* temporal redemption of the people who joined the Church.

PRESIDENT FERDINAND HINTZE (1887—1889, 1899—1900)

The first mention of colonization occurred in a letter from President Hintze to Apostle Franklin D. Richards on May 11, 1889. In that letter, Hintze wrote that it would be "a good plan for us to settle in Palestine and make a colony there."[4]

The colony idea simmered throughout the summer of 1889, and by August, President Hintze was convinced that it would be an enormous boon to the Armenian people he was serving. He wrote to President George Teasdale of the European Mission, explaining that he was much taken up with a colonizing scheme while there [visiting Elder Janne M. Sjodahl in Palestine], and wrote about it to President F. D. Richards. Should it be adopted it would solve our troubles and place us in direct and proper communication with Asia and its people, and also right among the Jews themselves while they gather.[5]

As a result of visiting with President Hintze, Elder Sjodahl also began to consider the colony option very seriously. After close examination of the general proposition, he was prone to conclude that the Latter-day Saints could succeed handily if given the chance to work the land. The bases for his conclusion were twofold: First, the Arab Palestinians possessed outdated equipment, utilized antiquated water management practices, and were very heavily taxed by the Ottoman Empire, and yet they still eked out a living. Second, and more important, the Germans had undertaken to establish several colonies in Palestine, each of which served as a precedent for success, in the mind of Elder Sjodahl. Despite many adverse conditions, the German colonies in Haifa, Jerusalem, and elsewhere were a picture of prosperity. Jews had also successfully colonized in Palestine. Elder Sjodahl thereby concluded that all that was needed was capital and enterprise to make the colony go.[6] As always, enterprise was in good supply among the Latter-day Saint people. However, capital backing for the purchase of land and equipment proved to be a much greater problem.

Despite obvious economic shortfalls in the Church at the time, President Hintze pursued the colony dream with vigor. He even instructed his wife Matilda to take courses in midwifery, as obstetrics were practically unknown to the Armenian people. This suggestion was motivated by the assumption that the First Presidency of the Church would soon send her to Turkey to assist her husband in the work of the mission and the building of the colony. President Hintze expressed his confidence in the progress of the colonization effort in a letter, writing, "I am trying to get a colony started here in Palestine not far from Jerusalem. And I see the Presidency is favorable to the plan. But just when they will make a move I do not know, but I feel certain it will be done."[7]

On September 6, 1889, another piece of the colonization puzzle fell into place. Elder George Q. Cannon published an article in the *Juvenile Instructor* wherein he laid out the views of the Brethren on the subject of colonization in the Near East. President Hintze found the article a boon to his plans. He wrote that President Cannon set forth "the probability of a settlement being made in Palestine. I see it embodies my view as written to the Apostles and that they are thinking seriously of the matter. God speed the day when we may get a settlement started among these people. It will be the day of the salvation of the honest of the oriental nations."[8]

PRESIDENT FREDERICK STAUFFER (1889–1891)

In December 1889, Frederick Stauffer was called to preside over the Turkish Mission. His feelings about colonization were very similar to those of President Hintze. On one occasion, he wrote that "it seems to me that [colonization] is about the only way in which this work can be carried on successfully."[9] On another occasion, President Stauffer recorded the feeling of the Saints in Asia Minor regarding a colony. He explained that they looked to a colony as a partial release from the choke hold of the Ottoman Empire because a colony would probably not be allowed unless the Turkish government granted formal recognition to The Church of Jesus Christ of Latter-day Saints. Furthermore, President Stauffer noted that "they are all anxious to gather to one place, where they can be more fully instructed in the ways of God."[10]

PRESIDENT DONALD MUSSER (1892–1894)

President Don Musser explained that "all in the world this country needs to make it the Eden it formerly was, is a Mormon colony to teach the Arabs how to work, how to be industrious, how to live happily by doing good."[11] Such convictions were made even stronger when, occasionally, others would recognize the industrious spirit of the Latter-day Saints in the Near East and make such comments as the following, made to President Musser: "Although I am not a believer in the Mormon faith, I believe the only redemption for this country will come through your people." The man who said this had investigated the restored gospel and was familiar with Elder

Orson Hyde's dedication of the Holy Land just over fifty years earlier. He explained to President Musser that he had lived in Palestine for forty years, and in that time he had seen steady improvement in the climate and fruitfulness of the land.[12]

President Joseph Wilford Booth (1903–1909, 1921–1928)

As has been mentioned in previous chapters, no one spent more time serving in the Near East as a missionary and mission president than Joseph Wilford Booth. In the mind of President Booth, a Mormon colony in the Near East was almost as important as having the Book of Mormon printed in Turkish and Armenian. In a letter to the First Presidency, President Booth explained that a colony would be worthwhile even if it cost fifty thousand dollars. At the time, this figure was several times the amount of money that was deemed necessary to purchase the land for a colony and thereby illustrates the fervency with which President Booth approached this effort.[13]

This sampling of statements is representative of the long-term homogeneous views toward establishing a Mormon colony in the Near East. In the waning days of 1897, the leading council of The Church of Jesus Christ of Latter-day Saints moved one significant step closer to making the colony a reality.

The Unique Mission of
Anthon H. Lund and Ferdinand Hintze (1897–1898)

On December 29, 1897, Church President Wilford Woodruff and his counselors extended a unique mission call to Elder Anthon H. Lund and former mission president Ferdinand Hintze. The call outlined the First Presidency's expectations for the mission.

> The First Presidency, in Council with the Twelve Apostles, have decided to call you upon a mission to the Eastern Lands, comprising Turkey, Syria, and the Holy Land, for the purpose of visiting the Saints there, learning their true condition, and taking such measures as you may deem necessary to organize them more effectively than they are at present. . . . When you have made yourselves familiar with the conditions which exist in those lands, we desire you to visit such parts of Palestine that you may

think suitable in which to select a place of settlement for the
oriental members of the Church. . . . This is really the great
object to be accomplished by you.[14]

The letter continued by admonishing the missionaries to pay
strict attention to the laws of the land and directing that a full report
should be prepared for the First Presidency before acting. The letter
ended with the following expressions of faith: "We assure you, dear
brethren, that we look upon this as one of the most important
missions which has been assigned to any of our elders since the beginning of the work in the last days."[15]

While he was set apart, Hintze was promised the capacity to work
miracles and the power necessary to work among foreign peoples in
productive ways. He was also blessed with the ability to recognize the
right tract of land for the colony at the time he first laid eyes on it.[16]

Elder Lund and Elder Hintze left Salt Lake City for Palestine on
December 30, 1897, and finally landed at Jaffa on February 17,
1898. While traveling from Jaffa to Haifa, the elders got their first
up-close look at a successful colony when they spent one night at
Hadera, a Jewish colony. Hadera was different from the other colonies
in Palestine, however, because it was operated independent of all
outside funding from wealthy Jews abroad. Instead, the settlers of this
eight-year-old colony were mostly Russian immigrants.

The stop at Hadera was profitable for two reasons: first, the
missionaries witnessed firsthand the success of a well-managed colony;
and second, they learned from some of the failures and drawbacks
that attended the establishment of the Hadera enterprise. For
example, the seven thousand acres of land for the colony were
purchased from a man in Syria for eighteen dollars an acre for a total
cost of $126,000. However, the settlers of Hadera could occupy the
land for only ten months of the year, because, like many large tracts
of farmable land in Palestine, it was also near swampy bogs infested
with malaria-carrying mosquitoes. Hadera was bordered by two
swamps. The health risks were so life-threatening that the people of
Hadera were forced to move away during the months of August and
September until the danger subsided. In order to alleviate the
problem, the people of Hadera paid approximately thirty thousand

dollars to drain one swamp and were waiting to raise the funds to drain the other.

Because these Russian Jews had successfully carried out their colonization efforts and had much in common with Latter-day Saints, the elders' stay in Hadera lifted their spirits. Simply put, these people came from a foreign land, had nothing but hard work to offer beyond their initial investment to purchase the land, and had proven that the land could be profitable. Furthermore, the Russian immigrants knew nothing about farming prior to their arrival in Palestine and had still come off successful.

The people of Hadera had toiled for eight long years to develop the land to the point that Latter-day Saint missionaries could walk through their village and be largely impressed. However, the German and Jewish colonies were not representative of country life in Palestine in 1898. Rather, Hintze's following description provides a more accurate depiction of common country living:

> Really village life in Palestine is so filthy that it cannot well be described with polite language. As a rule the people are poor. . . . Their houses are mere huts, dirty in the extreme on the outside, and smoky and poorly arranged on the inside. The village itself has no streets, it has only narrow crooked lanes with many corners and turns each of which furnish a place for human convenience either male or female. Children and dogs excepted. They enjoy the open street everywhere so that between the animals and humans of a village its narrow, uncomely passages are so filthy that one can only pass by picking his way carefully. . . . Often the filth can be scented a long way off.[17]

Elder Hintze's description of the land may be the best lens through which to view the enormous challenge behind establishing a colony in Palestine. Viewing the land that is described through this lens is a helpful reminder to cautiously consider the missionaries' excitement over a tract of land that seemed "perfect" for the colony undertaking. In reality, almost any land that could be purchased in Palestine in 1898 was deteriorated and severely unhealthy. Only intense commitment and work would change these conditions.

THE LAND IN THE JEZREEL VALLEY

Finally, Elder Lund and Elder Hintze were drawn to a five- to six-thousand-acre tract called El Kireh, located in the west end of the Jezreel Valley (specifically, El Kireh is thirteen miles southeast of Haifa, seven miles northwest of Tel Megiddo, north of and near the village and tel of Yokneam).[18] Given the area that they had considered previously, this land was suitable in just about every way. It had a great

The land near the village of Yokneam, located in the west end of the Jezreel Valley, about thirteen miles southeast of Haifa. Elder Anthon H. Lund of the Quorum of the Twelve Apostles and former mission president Ferdinand F. Hintze selected a five- to six-thousand-acre tract of land in this area as the most suitable site for a Mormon colony in the Near East.

deal of water from springs and streams; in fact, the Kishon River flowed through the property. There were existing huts on the property that, with some work, could be inhabited by initial colonists. Much of the land was exceptionally suited for farming, and at the time, a great deal of the land was put into grain, which was thriving. Most importantly, while there were bogs and swamps near the river, for the most part the tract lacked the terribly damp and marshy bogs that would necessitate draining to avoid mosquitoes.[19] Therefore, success would rest on the Saints' ability to work the property carefully and in a way that would unlock its potential fruitfulness.[20]

Again, compared to what they had seen up to this point, the land appeared to be so good that the missionaries assumed that something had to be wrong with it, or previous Jewish settlers would have purchased this tract long before the arrival of the Latter-day Saints. Nevertheless, the elders felt good about the property. To allay any fears, Elder Anthon H. Lund put the matter into the hands of the Lord, explaining, "He who placed this curse on the land on account of disobedience of the people is able to lift it when His time comes."[21]

El Kireh was owned by an Arab man named Salim Khuri.[22] His asking price was fixed at $120,000, and by May 15, 1898, the decision was made. With the land selection complete, Elder Lund wrote President Woodruff about this plot before departing for Utah, saying, "It is the only place we found that complies with the requirements made in your letter of instructions."[23]

At the departure of Elder Lund, Ferdinand Hintze was appointed pastor of the Turkish Mission and was charged to maintain the general welfare of the Saints in the mission. He was therefore called to stay in the Near East and labor with President Philip Maycock and Elder Andrew Larson, who had been sent to reopen the mission in August 1897.

THE MONEY, THE GOVERNMENT, THE PEOPLE

Elder Lund arrived in Salt Lake City on a Thursday late in June and went straight to the Thursday meeting of the Apostles in the temple. The entire meeting was given over to hear Elder Lund's report. While the colonization effort was viewed favorably, the pressing question the Brethren continually posed was, "Where shall we get the money?"[24]

Two weeks later, after the First Presidency reviewed the formal report, President Cannon said, "I am delighted with the report and I move that we accept it." Elder Lund related that "the brethren were all interested in our description of El Kireh and I believe they thought our selection a good one. The Church at present is very hard up for money."[25] Elder Lund then explained to Pastor Hintze in greater detail the financial crisis the Church was experiencing.

The First Presidency feel very much worked upon by their burden of debt and are determined to make a heroic effort to get the load off their shoulders. I make mention of these things as it will show you that it is at present out of their power to raise means to make purchases of land and meet the other expenses that would be necessary to incur when we start our settlement over there.[26]

However, money was not the only hinderment to colonization. There were two other major concerns: first, the spiritual standing of the Saints; and second, the precarious nature of the Ottoman government and the lack of official recognition of the Church by them.[27] Regarding these concerns, Elder Lund queried of Pastor Hintze:

Has the time come for the establishment of a stake of Zion in the Holy Land? The Presidency thought there must be great change wrought in the government before they dared undertake the work. . . . The question [of the Saints] should be: what can we do to build up the work? And not: How much can the Church give us? Bread and fishes Saints make poor workers and builders.[28]

Given these severe limitations, it was determined not to buy the land in 1898. On November 9, 1898, "President Lorenzo Snow stated that the Church was not prepared to go into [colonization]."[29] This brought the colony dream to a practical close for the moment. At the same time, however, President Snow left the door wide open to future investigation of colony options by encouraging Pastor Hintze to consider tracts of land outside Palestine that were near good roads and close to an American consulate.[30] This Pastor Hintze did by investigating other sites in Palestine and Asia Minor, such as Aleppo and Antioch.

Given this historical context, it comes as no surprise that subsequent leaders of the Turkish and Armenian Mission vigorously pursued the idea of a gathering place for the beleaguered Saints. In this light, Elder Lund summarized the ongoing possibility of a Mormon colony by writing that "when the Lord's time has come, He will open the way to get it."[31]

Joseph Wilford Booth's Arrival

Although Joseph Booth arrived in Turkey on September 30, 1898, by as early as May 1899 his strong feelings in favor of a colony were clearly evident. He wrote, "It seems to me the colonization movement cannot be too rapidly pushed."[32] The motivations behind his passion to establish a colony, however, were somewhat different from Pastor Hintze's, which were centered on ideological or doctrinal ideals. In contrast, Booth's reasons involved spiritual, temporal, and ethnic survival. In regard to spiritual matters, the Ottoman government's intrusiveness made it almost impossible for the Saints to worship. At one point, all the Latter-day Saints living in Marash were imprisoned because Elder and Sister Booth visited the village.[33] Temporally, the Saints suffered serious financial repercussions after joining the Church, frequently losing their jobs or suffering major pay cuts due to their new faith. And ethnically, Booth witnessed first-hand that the Armenian people in Anatolia were in serious danger, being slaughtered in wholesale fashion. It will also be remembered that during World War I, practically the entire membership of the Marash Branch of the Church in Turkey was murdered in the name of "ethnic cleansing." For these reasons, it is obvious why Joseph Booth's pleas for a colony in the Near East went beyond doctrines such as the gathering of Israel; rather, his motivation for colonization was survival.

After Joseph Booth was appointed president of the Turkish Mission in October 1903, he continued to yearn for a colony for the desperate Saints in his care. The perceived potential and stability that could come from an effectively managed colony seemed to haunt President Booth, and he communicated these feelings to the Brethren. On October 5, 1905, the First Presidency discussed his requests during their usual meeting in the Salt Lake Temple and determined at that time to encourage emigration instead of undertaking the work of colonization.[34]

In May 1906, President Booth began to investigate the emigration option in earnest. With the two options before him of Canada or Mexico, he concluded that the Armenians would do better in Mexico. Although the large expense associated with emigration made it very difficult, it was the Turkish government that made it almost impossible.

After three years of battling with these two obstacles, the futility of the endeavor led him to write the First Presidency, suggesting "a colony and recognition if it costs $50,000."[35]

In May 1907, the mayor of Aintab suggested to President Booth that the Saints in his city take up agriculture, since farm implements could be imported free of duty. The recommendation impressed President Booth, and he immediately sought out land to rent in order to begin as soon as the Church granted approval. He found a large piece of land that appeared promising and communicated all of this to the First Presidency in a letter written on July 31, 1907.

Elder Anthon Lund responded to President Booth concerning this request and explained that the proposition to rent 800 to 1,200 acres of farmland had been authorized by the Brethren. They felt that this option would allow them to ascertain exactly how the Armenian Saints would perform in an agriculturally centered economy versus their accustomed industrial pursuits as weavers. But as for Booth's most pressing request, they wrote, "As to the idea of colonizing we particularly desire you to make no promises whatever in this direction to our Armenian brethren and sisters, so that they shall not reap any disappointment whatever in the event of failure on our part to carry out their wishes in this respect."[36]

With this letter in hand, President Booth began the negotiation process, and arrangements were made to ship a series of farm implements to Turkey through the American consulate in order to get the agricultural experiment underway as soon as possible. However, plans were halted when a letter from the First Presidency urged him "to deter negotiations for the present regarding the leasing of a farm, since some changes have taken place recently."[37] President Booth complied, although no specific reasons were provided. This was the last time that the rental of a large tract of land for farming was formally considered in Turkey.

THE COLONIZATION INVESTIGATION OF THOMAS P. PAGE

Elder Thomas P. Page began his first mission to Turkey on March 1, 1890. The fruits of his varied business skills resulted in the identification of alternative markets for the rug-weaving Latter-day Saints in Aintab. Almost twenty years later, the First Presidency called upon Page to travel to the Near East and prepare a report concerning the feasibility of a colony in the region.

President Booth met Brother Page in Adana, Turkey, on March 2, 1909. Still uninformed of the purpose for Page's visit, Booth had great hopes that Page had been sent with the authority from the First Presidency to purchase lands and instigate a colony. He was disappointed to learn that Page was "only to investigate, and report at Salt Lake City."[38] Nevertheless, the two went on to tour the mission, all the while searching for land possibilities. However, events in the Near East were about to change dramatically, thereby altering the realization of this dream.

Not long before Brother Page's arrival, the Young Turks succeeded in restoring constitution-style government. This development had an impact on Page's report to the First Presidency regarding colonization for several reasons. Although the new constitution made travel and emigration more accessible, the recoil of the more traditional Turks was tragic, leading to large-scale massacres among those who supported the Young Turks' movement. This violence took a staggering toll on Armenian Christians—the Latter-day Saints not excluded. One can sense the instability of the situation in his uncertain report to the Brethren. "I am inclined to think the trouble is over now, and though it might be advisable to await developments, it would be fairly safe to purchase land now if it is desired to do so."[39]

Any remaining stability quickly disintegrated shortly after this letter had been written and Page had departed. The Saints were in such great danger that President Booth made a request to the First Presidency that all of the two hundred Armenian members in Turkey be brought to the United States.[40] As it turned out, the mission was closed, the missionaries were withdrawn from the region, and the dreams of a colony in the Near East were dashed—not to be considered again for twelve more years.

Pursuing a Colony in the 1920s

The deprivations suffered by the Latter-day Saints in Turkey during the twelve-year mission closure were exceedingly severe. When Joseph Booth returned to open the Armenian Mission in the fall of 1921, a Mormon colony was a high priority in his mind. In answer to his queries, however, Elder David O. McKay explained that "there is to be no colony until the Authorities indicate what should be done."[41]

During the fall of 1922, direct efforts were made to colonize on the island of Cyprus with the encouragement of the British government. In fact, when President Booth discussed this option with the British consul in Aleppo, James Morgan, he promised to be the diplomatic interface for the Latter-day Saints in the matter. Morgan wrote to the government of Cyprus, and on November 24, 1922, he received an unfavorable reply. He reported three major reasons why the request was rejected: the government had no available land for farming to sell; buying from private owners would be excessively expensive; and an already bourgeoning population of refugees made it impossible for the government to accept more.[42]

1923—A SHIFT IN TONE

Up to this point, Church leaders had consistently supported colonization in the Near East. Generally speaking, its only hindrances had been factors such as finances, internal strife within the Ottoman Empire, war, and so forth. At some point early in the decade, however, the feeling that the colony movement was a realistic option cooled markedly. This shift is evident in correspondence between Booth and Church leaders beginning in 1923.

It will be remembered that Elder Earl B. Snell traveled to the Armenian Mission to make a thorough report for Elder David O. McKay. The full weight of that report would be felt in the fall of 1923, when, upon close investigation, the First Presidency concluded in a letter to Elder David O. McKay that they did "not favor the idea of undertaking to colonize [Armenians] in that country, neither does it appear to us that it would be wisdom to bring them to this country." It would not be inaccurate to describe this letter from the First Presidency as the near ending of all hopes for a Mormon colony in the Near East. However, near the end of the letter they wrote: Brother Snell "thinks we had better rent land or emigrate the people. We think emigration is out of the question and therefore there is nothing to do but rent land."[43]

The suggestion to continue searching for property even to rent was worth pursuing for Booth. An indication of how aggressively he

acted upon this suggestion is seen in a meeting held among the
Armenian Saints some six months later, during which he put several
possible colony locations before the members and had them vote on
their choice.

Two months later, Church President Heber J. Grant again wrote
Booth, reaffirming the Church's stance, which leaned heavily against
colonization of any kind except renting.

> Until conditions have changed very materially we do not wish to
> invest a large amount of money in that country for the benefit of
> a few saints. There are hundreds and hundreds of Saints that
> have lost their property on account of the depression here . . .
> some of whom have been faithful tithe-payers and diligent
> Latter-day Saints for years and years.[44]

Although President Booth recognized the truth of President
Grant's words, with the temporal poverty of the Armenian Saints
looming daily before him, he pursued the one option still available to
him—renting a parcel of land—all the while still hoping that the day
would come when the Church would be able to colonize formally in
the Near East.

The Harris Report

Over the next year, nothing changed markedly. However, in
1925, President Booth made it clear in his personal writings that his
hopes for a colony were still alive.[45] In March 1926, President Grant
wrote Booth again, stating that "the Armenian Mission is being
considered, and the question of a colony for the Saints here has been
talked of. Someone may be sent to see about it."[46] Six months later he
wrote again, explaining that "personally my own feelings have led me
to favor, if we do attempt to establish a colony, to try to establish it in
Palestine."[47] Both communications were obvious confirmations that
the window of opportunity was still open.

On January 28, 1927, president of Brigham Young University
and prominent agriculturalist Dr. Franklin S. Harris was sent by the
First Presidency. He and Booth spent time visiting the members in
Beirut, as well as educators at the American University of Beirut, and

they traveled to Aleppo to continue the investigation.[48] Within six days, he prepared his report for the First Presidency, gave a copy to President Booth, and departed on February 11, 1927.

The Harris report contained eight sections. The first seven sections of the report dealt with issues that would need to be addressed if colonization efforts were to proceed, and the final section of the report contained recommendations relevant only if the First Presidency chose not to colonize. Because an overview of this final section was provided in chapter 6, only sections 1 through 7 will be considered at this point.

Section 1 entailed a description of conditions among the Saints at the time of Harris's visit. He could not have given higher praise to the Booths and their leadership.[49]

Section 2 outlined the fundamental justification for the creation of a Mormon colony in the Near East. Harris explained that because the cultural differences of the Saints in the Near East were so unlike any up to that time in the history of the Church, on many fronts, bringing these people to Utah was not a reasonable expectation.

Section 3 addressed the most favorable locations for a colony. Since the Church had focused consistently on an agricultural settlement, Harris recommended one location in Palestine and another in Syria, as well as delineating the advantages and disadvantages of both.

Section 4 addressed the expense that would be incurred to establish a colony in the Near East. Brother Harris estimated that between $100,000 and $200,000 would be needed to purchase land and then as much as $50,000 more to construct buildings and purchase suitable equipment.

Section 5 was used to describe the Armenian members demographically—the number of Saints, their financial stability, their ages, health, talents, and ability to potentially contribute to an industrial-based colony.

Section 6 suggested that an industrial colony be considered wherein the Saints could operate weaving, needlework, rug-making, and other industrial enterprises that were suited to their interests and talents.

Section 7 provided the alternative that the Saints instead receive assistance from the mission through consulting on marketing strategies, start-up loans for responsible business undertakings, and financial assistance in circumstances of unusual distress. Although this had already been taking place for several years, Brother Harris recommended that this be done more systematically than it had in the past.

It was not a surprise to President Booth when the First Presidency chose not to colonize. The results of the Harris report presented a fairly clear picture against the venture. Despite his disappointment, President Booth was admirably faithful to the Brethren. His dream of nearly thirty years had gasped its final breath, but his loyalty to the Church never wavered.

On October 10, 1927, Elder James E. Talmage was sent to select a new mission home in Haifa, Palestine. Seven days later, President Booth and Elder Talmage began their search and found a home in the German Templer colony. From this location, proselytizing shifted away from Armenians and toward the European communities in Palestine. President Booth still maintained close contact with his beloved Armenian Saints. Fittingly, one year later, when he died while visiting them, President Booth was buried in Aleppo, where so many of his yearnings and hopes had been directed. Subsequent leaders of the mission never again considered colonization as a viable option for the Saints in that region.

Conclusions and Lessons Learned

For all intents and purposes, the Harris report, coupled with the death of President Joseph W. Booth, ended the dream of a Latter-day Saint colony in the Near East. At least four conclusions may be drawn from this historically significant pursuit that may be of value today. First, conversion and baptism into The Church of Jesus Christ of Latter-day Saints does not necessitate deculturalization. Weavers of rugs in Aintab, Turkey, need not become agriculturalists and adopt every mode of living used by members of the Church in the Great Basin of the American West. They can embrace the gospel and maintain their cultural identity.[50] Second, missionary labors in one part of the world may require an entirely different approach from that employed by missionaries in another part of the world. Homogeneity of doctrine from one mission to another is essential. Homogeneity of gospel presentation and implementation of correct principles is not. Third, extending temporal welfare and financial assistance in one culture may be essential and of great benefit, while doing the same in another may be a malediction. Identifying salient cultural nuances in relation to the welfare arm of the Church is essential. Fourth, while a colony may have increased comforts and conveniences for the Armenian people, the colonization movement was not absolutely essential to their spiritual survival. Small branches of Armenian Saints in the Near East suffered abominably through war, corrupt governmental measures, and attempts to massacre their people without the safety of a "Mormon" colony. Simply put, their spiritual convictions, not a colony, would be the means of maintaining faithfulness to the Church. Today it would be difficult to find an Armenian Latter-day Saint in Anatolia. One could, however, find a considerable number of Armenian Saints scattered throughout the valleys of Utah and California. They are the children, grandchildren, and great-grandchildren of those so carefully watched over by Ferdinand Hintze, Philip Maycock, Joseph W. Booth, and others. While their place of refuge was not found in the Jezreel Valley of Palestine, some still found refuge.

NOTES TO CHAPTER 7

1. Susa Y. Gates and Leah D. Widtsoe, *The Life Story of Brigham Young* (New York: Macmillan, 1930), 199–223. See also Hugh Nibley, *Approaching Zion* (Salt Lake City: Deseret Book, 1989), 336.

2. Rao H. Lindsay, "The Dream of a Mormon Colony in the Near East," *Dialogue* 1.4 (winter 1966): 51–52.

3. Papers of Anthon H. Lund, August 10, 1900, LDS Church Archives.

4. Ferdinand F. Hintze, journal; cited in Lindsay, "The Dream of a Mormon Colony in the Near East," 52.

5. Hintze, *Millennial Star,* August 26, 1889, 540.

6. Janne M. Sjodahl, *Deseret Weekly,* April 27, 1889, 574. A group of Americans also established a colony in Palestine at this time. For a compelling description of the struggles and successes of the American colony, consult Bertha Spafford Vester, *Our Jerusalem: An American Family in the Holy City, 1881–1949* (Jerusalem: Ariel Publishing House, 1988).

7. Papers of Anthon H. Lund, September 14, 1889.

8. Mission Record, Turkish Mission, September 6, 1889, 22, LDS Church Archives.

9. Frederick Stauffer, *Millennial Star,* December 1, 1890, 764.

10. Stauffer, *Deseret Weekly,* July 19, 1890, 120.

11. Donald C. Musser, *Deseret Weekly,* May 20, 1893, 693.

12. Ibid.

13. Journal of Joseph W. Booth, February 1, 1908, L. Tom Perry Special Collections, Harold B. Lee Library, Brigham Young University, Provo, UT.

14. Papers of Anthon H. Lund, December 29, 1897.

15. Ibid.

16. Ibid.

17. Hintze, *Deseret Weekly,* July 2, 1898, 82.

18. In the earliest references to this piece of property, Elder Lund and Elder Hintze refer to it as "El Kive." This apparently is a mispronunciation, as they later refer to the property as "El Kireh," which reflects the name used for the shanty-town by locals in the late 1890s.

19. Mission Record, Turkish Mission, April 23, 1898, 41. See also Journal of Andrew L. Larson, April 23, 1898, LDS Church Archives.

20. The Jezreel Valley is the largest and most fertile valley in Israel today.

21. Anthon H. Lund, *Millennial Star,* May 5, 1898, 279.

22. Salim Khuri was a Christian Arab, originally from Syria, who had also lived in Lebanon.

23. Papers of Anthon H. Lund, May 15, 1898.

24. Ibid., June 28, 1898.

25. Ibid., July 14, 1898.

26. Ibid., August 1, 1898.

27. These are the three reasons given by Elder Joseph Booth justifying the First Presidency's decision to halt the purchase of land for a colony in the Near East. See *Millennial Star,* March 24, 1904, 178.

28. Papers of Anthon H. Lund, September 8, 1898.

29. Lindsay, "The Dream of a Mormon Colony in the Near East," 57. It will be remembered that Wilford Woodruff died September 2, 1898, making Lorenzo Snow the presiding officer in the Church.

30. Papers of Anthon H. Lund, November 9, 1898.

31. Ibid., August 19, 1898.

32. Joseph W. Booth, *Millennial Star,* May 25, 1899, 330–31.

33. Booth, *Millennial Star,* July 13, 1905, 433.

34. *Journal History,* October 5, 1905, 8.

35. Journal of Joseph W. Booth, February 1, 1908.

36. Ibid., August 10, 1908.

37. Ibid., September 21, 1908.

38. Ibid., March 3, 1909.

39. Thomas Page to the First Presidency of the Church, May 24, 1909, LDS Church Archives.

40. *Journal History,* June 23, 1909, 7–8.

41. Mission Record, Armenian Mission, September 29, 1922, 46, LDS Church Archives.

42. Ibid., November 22, 1922, 47.

43. Letters of President David O. McKay, European Mission President (1922–1924), vol. 3, October 30, 1923, LDS Church Archives.

44. Ibid., May 28, 1924.

45. Mission Record, Armenian Mission, historical overview, 66.

46. Journal of Joseph W. Booth, March 21, 1926.

47. Mission Record, Armenian Mission, September 30, 1926, 68.

48. Lindsay, "The Dream of a Mormon Colony in the Near East," 64.

49. Franklin S. Harris, "Report Sent to First Presidency by Dr. F. S. Harris," February 10, 1927, L. Tom Perry Special Collections.

50. Lindsay, "The Dream of a Mormon Colony in the Near East," 50.

CHAPTER EIGHT

Public Relations and Proselytizing

1933–1950

T he sudden death of President Joseph Booth in 1928 caused the First Presidency to reconsider the status of the Armenian Mission. The First Presidency deemed it prudent to close the mission and not send another president to replace Booth. This left the local members to carry on the work among themselves. Then, in 1933, the First Presidency moved to reopen a mission in the Near East and call a president to preside over it.

This chapter begins with a brief note about the closure of the mission between 1928 and 1933. The bulk of the chapter will be dedicated to describing the missionary activities of the Church in the Near East from 1933 to 1950. During this time, two men served as president of the mission, and headquarters were moved from Haifa to Beirut, Lebanon. The name of the mission was changed from the Armenian Mission to the Palestine-Syrian Mission. On account of World War II, the mission was closed for eight of the eighteen years of this period. Additionally, the Holy Land was dedicated twice in 1933 by Elder John A. Widtsoe. Finally, new and creative proselytizing techniques were employed in the mission that raised public awareness of The Church of Jesus Christ of Latter-day Saints in the Near East to a new level.

The Interim Period and Subsequent Call of Badwagan Piranian

At the death of Joseph Booth, the Saints in the Near East were left without external priesthood help and direction for four and a half

Badwagan Piranian, president of the Armenian Mission.

Sister Berta Piranian, wife of President Badwagan Piranian.

years. At the end of this period, Apostle John A. Widtsoe visited the people of the mission and declared that "most of them [are] still staunch in the faith"[1] and are "hungry for further instruction in the principles of the gospel."[2]

After careful deliberation, the First Presidency of the Church felt impressed to reopen the missionary effort in the Near East, and on February 10, 1933, Badwagan Piranian was called to be the mission president of the Armenian Mission. Piranian, an Armenian born in Turkey, was forty-two years old and admirably fitted for the job. In his early life, he moved from the Near East to Europe and at the time of his call was a Swiss citizen. He and his family had lived for a time in Utah and thereafter returned to their home in Zurich. The most singular advantage that President Piranian enjoyed at the outset of his missionary service was that he already spoke fluent Armenian. Every other mission president of the Near East missions spent at least two years grappling with the languages.

Arriving April 22, 1933, President Piranian was accompanied to Haifa by his wife, Berta, and daughter, Astchig, and would be joined later by their son, David.[3] He proceeded to reorganize the Haifa Branch. At the time, some considered this reorganization to be the establishment of the first branch of the Church in the Holy Land. However, as we have learned, while the first branch of the Church in the Holy Land in modern times was organized in Haifa, this occurred during the late nineteenth century.[4]

The Near East in the 1930s and 1940s

At the end of World War I, the victorious Allies divided among themselves large portions of what had formerly been the Ottoman Empire. Great Britain was granted a mandate over Palestine, France was granted a mandate over Syria, and Anatolia (the core land of the former empire) became the sovereign nation of Turkey. Furthermore, in 1920, France established a special administration for Lebanon, bringing together the areas of Beirut, Tripoli, Sidon, Tyre, Akkar, and the Bekaa Valley which had a Christian majority. The creation of Lebanon resulted in a local Muslim minority within the region previously known as the district of Mount Lebanon that had been established in 1864 by the Ottoman Empire. This was done at the fervent insistence of European powers to protect and promote the interests of the Christian population of the area. Syrian Muslims saw the creation of the state of Lebanon as an effort by France to fracture Muslim unity in the region. The resulting and ongoing tensions between Syria and Lebanon played a role in missionary labors in the area during this time period.

For most of this time, the French mandate over Syria was still intact. When France fell to Germany in 1940, Great Britain stepped in to assist remaining Free French Forces in the region. Independence was promised to Syrian nationalists, but France did not relinquish control of Syria for several more years. Finally, the French troops withdrew from Syria on May 17, 1946, at which time the Syrian Arab Republic was formed. After three decades of European control, Syrians were anxious to infuse their new government with undiluted influences of Syrian Arab and, frequently, pan-Arab thought. Understandably, Syria was wary of any outside influences (particularly from Europe) that might upset the balance that it was attempting to strike.

Palestine, on the other hand, still had a considerable population of Christian Europeans in 1933. Under the recommendations of the Harris report (February 1927), mission headquarters were once again established in Haifa and proselytizing efforts were to be conducted primarily among these Europeans and not among Armenians in Palestine, many of whom had fled to the British-controlled area to escape conflicts in Turkey.

Moreover, the influx of Jewish immigrants generally rose during this period as a result of the Nazi regime in Germany. This caused tension in the region. By the mid-1930s, strife between Arabs and Jews was approaching the dimensions of a civil war, only carefully kept under control by British forces. Furthermore, Syrian nationalists were opposed to Zionist ambitions because they viewed Palestine as part of the Arab world. Eventually, statehood was proclaimed by the Zionists in 1948 at the closure of the British mandate. This proclamation on the part of the Zionists outraged Syria and the Arab world, resulting in the war of 1948, wherein Israel established its independence. Tens of thousands of Palestinians (both Muslims and Christians) fled to Syria, Lebanon, Jordan, Egypt, and other nations in the Near East. Some sought refuge in the Egyptian-controlled Gaza Strip and the Jordanian-controlled West Bank. The tensions between the Arab world and the new state of Israel concerning the Palestinian refugee problem also played a role in the missionary work conducted during this period.[5]

As can be seen, this was a complicated time in the Near East. As had been the case in previous decades, the prospect of conducting proselytizing efforts in the region was particularly bold.

President Widtsoe's Visit and Dedication of Palestine

One month after the Piranians moved into mission headquarters in Haifa, Apostle John A. Widtsoe, who served as president of the European Mission, and his wife, Leah, arrived in the Holy Land to formally organize the Armenian Mission. The first meeting was held at the mission home at 25 Garden Street on May 21, 1933, and was attended by the missionaries in Haifa—the Piranians and the Widtsoes. After setting Piranian apart as president, President Widtsoe instructed the Piranians to create a new hymnal in the language of the local people, to become acquainted with national leaders, to make friends with newspaper owners and reporters, and to advertise consistently. Finally, Elder Widtsoe instructed that "the time appears to be ripe for proselyting among the Jews. Many of the Jews are tired of the old theological systems. We must move carefully and take our time."[6]

Elder John A. Widtsoe of the Quorum of the Twelve Apostles.

The Armenian Mission Home, located at 25 Garden Street in Haifa, where Elder John A. Widtsoe dedicated the Holy Land for the tenth time.

Testimonies were also shared at this meeting, after which Elder Widtsoe offered a sacred prayer of dedication that the mission "home may be . . . protected against all evil and [also] the whole mission was brought before the Lord . . . [that] His work [move] forward in these lands as never before, that the Spirit of God might find its way throughout the land and touch the hearts of all seekers after truth." Hence, the "land was rededicated, as was also the mission."[7]

Two days after this powerful meeting, eight people were baptized who had been investigating the gospel by correspondence for nearly two years.[8] President Widtsoe wrote that

> the most beautiful picture to us in all Palestine was the baptism
> of eight persons in the Mediterranean, under the shadow of
> Mount Carmel, upon which so many sacred events have
> occurred. . . . The sunlight reflected on the water formed a
> golden bridge from shore to sun. The elder officiating and the
> candidates for baptism standing waist deep in the water, were
> glorified by the halo of the golden way. It was as if a special
> blessing was pronounced upon these ordinances, the first for
> many years in the Holy Land.[9]

On May 31, 1933, Elder Widtsoe, Sister Widtsoe, and President Piranian ascended the Mount of Olives for a second dedicatory prayer. There, looking down on the Holy City and the Garden of Gethsemane, Elder Widtsoe prepared to dedicate the land again. The group gathered under an olive tree, and Elder Widtsoe

> blessed the land for the return of the Jews, that they would come
> home to the land that had been promised them by God. The
> land was blessed that it would be restored to its former fertility
> and productivity, that the returning remnants of Judah would
> build up the land that it would again become a prosperous area
> . . . [and] that their hearts would be softened towards the
> missionaries and they would become receptive to the gospel; that
> they would open their hearts to the restored truth in order that
> they could embrace the gospel. The Jews were promised that if
> they would accept Christ that peace would come to their land

and their persecutions in the world would cease, and this land would be given to them as their inheritance as promised by the Holy Prophets.[10]

These two prayers by Elder Widtsoe at Haifa and Jerusalem constituted the tenth and eleventh dedications of the Holy Land by apostolic authority—the eleventh being the last known dedication by an authorized servant of God.[11] These eleven dedications were given over a period of ninety-one years (October 1841–May 31, 1933), the first and last dedicatory prayers being given on the Mount of Olives.

From Jerusalem, the Piranians and Widtsoes traveled to the principal cities of the mission: Damascus, Beirut, and Aleppo. In each city they held meetings, blessed children, and regulated the affairs of the Church. In Aleppo, the two men walked with the entire congregation after sacrament meeting to the Armenian Evangelical Cemetery, where President Joseph W. Booth had been buried.

At the time of President Booth's death, his family had questioned the feasibility of transporting his remains back to his home for burial in Alpine, Utah.[12] Yet, after much consideration, "the Booth family decided that it would be best to let the soldier lie permanently where he had fallen, among the people and places he had known so long, and where he had spent his life's endeavors."[13] The First Presidency had directed Elder Widtsoe to secure a suitable monument to replace the temporary one that had marked the grave for almost five years. After a great deal of correspondence, President Widtsoe commissioned a granite monument to be made in Liverpool, England. It was then shipped to Alexandretta, Syria, and taken by train to Aleppo, where it was erected by local artisans. With the monument in place, President Widtsoe called a meeting of the Saints at the cemetery to rededicate the grave of President Joseph W. Booth, and the Aleppo Saints gathered accordingly at the gravesite on the afternoon of Sunday, June 18, 1933.[14]

The meeting began with the singing of one of Joseph Booth's favorite hymns, "Come, Listen to a Prophet's Voice." Following the opening prayer, Sister Widtsoe gave a brief address on behalf of President Booth's wife, Reba, and placed on the grave some pressed flowers that Sister Booth had sent from their garden in Alpine, Utah.

Then all the members and friends present came forward with one or two flowers each and placed these on the grave until it was completely covered. President Widtsoe then spoke, after which he dedicated the grave and monument. The service ended at sunset. Elder Widtsoe described the occasion as "a peaceful, happy hour."[15]

DRASTIC CHANGES

Before his departure on June 21, Elder Widtsoe had discussed with President Piranian the prospect of a new name for the mission, but nothing definite was determined. Three weeks later, he notified Piranian that

> the First Presidency answered my letter about the change of the name of the Mission by saying that they would approve whatever we shall decide upon, but that if the word "Palestine" could be included in the name of the mission it would please the people of the Church as well. We have therefore decided upon the name "The Palestine-Syrian Mission", which hereafter use in all of your official correspondence and printing. I trust this meets with your approval.[16]

Early on, President Piranian determined that his work in the Near East could not and should not be consumed by the temporal needs of those he served. He continually taught that the purpose of the Church was to teach the plan of salvation, not to provide for the temporal needs of members and nonmembers of the region.[17] For this reason, a new policy was enacted in the latter part of 1933 that prohibited Church funds from being used to seed business ventures or to generally finance the living expenses of the Saints.

Not surprisingly, many members did not welcome this policy. Their poverty was so acute and their needs so severe that when the Church no longer provided temporal sustenance, they quickly turned away and embraced the tenets of whatever faith or organization was willing to provide for their temporal needs. Subsequently, a purging of the branches became necessary, and fourteen souls were excommunicated for apostasy. After a year in the field, President Piranian was sadly convinced that "*most* of the members had joined the church *only* for financial help and that *very few* have a real testimony of the divinity of the gospel of Jesus Christ."[18]

The pruning came at no small cost. The Beirut Branch was closed in late September, since only two of the thirty-five Saints were active—the branch president and his wife. The other thirty-three members would not attend meetings, even after President Piranian personally visited their homes. By October 1933, it also became necessary to close the Damascus Branch on account of disharmony— exactly half of those excommunicated during this purging were from the Haifa Branch. These seven excommunications in Haifa consti- tuted the entire membership of the branch. Therefore, the only remaining members in Haifa were missionaries.[19]

Gratefully, the Aleppo Branch was prospering and "working in wonderful harmony." In fact, President Piranian was pleased to find that they were following guidelines and directives that branch leaders had received directly from Church headquarters in Salt Lake City. This level of independence was a great comfort to President Piranian.

While this purging of the Church in the Near East was costly, it was not done in vain. President Piranian noted that those members who made every effort to support themselves entirely without assis- tance from the Church experienced a new level of self-sufficiency and attendant joy. As an example, he cited the case of the Hindoian family and explained that

> even Moses Hindoian and his wife, who have been pitying them- selves for years that they could not work and that they are ill, are now cured of their imagination. And the Lord surely blessed them. Sister Hindoian goes out as a laundress, and looks younger and happier than before. Her husband looks ten years younger since he is working.[20]

For over one year, the Piranians labored alone, with only the help of one local elder named Enos Hagopian, who was released on February 28, 1934.[21] However, in the spring of 1934, Elders John C. Dalton and Richard B. Knight were traveling home to America after their missions in South Africa when they paid a visit to Haifa on their return route. It became immediately evident to them that the mission was in desperate need of additional laborers; hence, they did something almost unheard of in mission history—they boldly volunteered to serve for an extra three months. Their selfless offer was conditioned upon obtaining permission from their parents to serve in the Near East. Unfortunately, nine days after their arrival, telegrams arrived from the elders' parents encouraging them to continue their journey homeward. President Piranian's disappointment is evident when he wrote, "It would have been too nice to be true."[22]

About five months later, two missionaries arrived in the Palestine-Syrian Mission to assist in the work—Elder David W. Piranian and his wife, Hildegard K. Piranian, who had been serving in the Swiss-German Mission, joined his parents in Haifa. Then, two weeks later, Elder John B. Fetzer was transferred to join them from the German-Austrian Mission.[23]

The arrival of the missionaries made it necessary to reorganize the Haifa Branch on August 16, 1934, each new missionary receiving heavy assignments of trust, including Elder Fetzer's call as the new branch president.[24] These missionaries relieved much of the Piranians' burden, and while they would not be in the mission long, they were most welcome.

David and Hildegard Piranian were honorably released from their service as missionaries on October 20, 1934. Six months later, Elder John B. Fetzer was honorably released on April 15, 1935. With no full-time missionaries serving under Piranian and excommunications in the mission outnumbering baptisms, President Piranian traveled to a mission presidents' conference in Liège, Belgium. While there, he proposed that mission headquarters be moved to Beirut, Lebanon, which was done at the end of 1935. The mission home was moved to Rue Sioufi, Archafie, Beirut, Lebanon.[25]

For the greater part of the next two years, President Piranian did what he could to maintain a hold on the members in the mission. Unfortunately, it was a time of great apostasy. In the first six months of 1936, there were three baptisms and three advancements in the priesthood. Contrast this with the excommunication of fifty-seven members of the Church. It was a time of great alarm. Most of those who lost their membership were generally disobedient and apostate in spirit. However, two individuals were cut off for their involvement with abortions.[26]

President and Sister Piranian did everything in their power to support and maintain a vibrant body of Saints in the mission. But again and again, evidence of shallow commitments to baptismal covenants based solely on temporal benefits was seen in the behavior of the members. The policies enacted by Piranian as the mission president emphasized *not* carrying the membership's financial and temporal concerns. This stance served to thin out the faithless and rebellious in spirit. While not a pleasant task to oversee, it was essential. After four years of faithful service, the Piranians received their release from the First Presidency and left the Near East in September 1937.

PRESIDENT JOSEPH JACOBS

The First Presidency called Joseph Jacobs to replace Badwagan Piranian as president of the Palestine-Syrian Mission. The call was publicized in Salt Lake City on July 9, 1937. Brother Jacobs was born in Palestine, and his parents were baptized into the Church just a few days before his birth. He had lived in Palestine until he was fifteen, at which time the family had emigrated to Utah. President Jacobs was a veteran of World War I and was an educator by profession. He taught

The Jacobs family, from left to right: Geraldine Jacobs, Sister Maud Jacobs, President Joseph Jacobs, Lamont Jacobs.

at West High School in Salt Lake City. At the time of his call he was pursuing a master's degree at the University of Utah in commerce. His wife was the former Maud Openshaw, and they were the parents of two children. Sister Jacobs and the children did not travel with President Jacobs on his initial journey to the Near East but joined him sometime later.[27]

President Jacobs arrived in Beirut, Lebanon, on August 17, 1937. After a two-day rest, he was taken by President and Sister Piranian on a five-day trip to greet the Saints in Aleppo. Of course, this trip was introductory in nature for Joseph Jacobs but served as a farewell visit for the Piranians, as no news of their release had been made known to the members prior to that time. The Aleppo Saints welcomed President Jacobs with open arms but were saddened by the departure of the Piranians.[28] President Jacobs formally replaced President Badwagan Piranian on September 8, 1937.[29] The Piranians left that day for their home in Switzerland on the SS *Jerusalem.*

In time, President Jacobs would welcome new elders to the mission who would attempt a different approach to the work. On February 8, 1938, Elders Woodrow Washburn and William Clark arrived from Belgium, where they had spent about five months studying French. Part of this lengthy stay in Europe was due to stringent visa and resident requirements imposed by the Lebanese government. It took President Jacobs a good deal of time to prepare the documents necessary for the missionaries to join him in Beirut.

Elders Washburn and Clark went to work immediately on an innovative proselytizing approach that had never been attempted before in the Near East. After considerable effort, the missionaries were able to obtain mailing lists for three Armenian newspapers in Beirut. They also obtained the names and addresses of over eight hundred of the most financially secure residents of the city. With these names in hand, the missionaries procured the appropriate permits from the post office authorizing them to conduct mass mailings of Latter-day Saint literature throughout the mission.

The pamphlet that was mailed to residents was the "Rays of Living Light" series (authored by Elder Charles W. Penrose of the First Presidency), which had been translated into Armenian. The "Rays of Living Light" tract series included twelve different subjects addressed in twelve or thirteen separate tracts. This gave President Jacobs plenty of literature to work with initially. Included with every tract mailed was a request and referral form advising the recipient that the Latter-day Saints would happily provide more information concerning the Church, if desired, through public lectures, additional literature, or personal visits to private residences. President Jacobs wrote, "The mailing out of tracts has paved the way in [a] majority of cases for a warm reception for the missionaries."[30] Six months later he was still enthusiastic, saying:

> It has opened doors to us in many of the cities where otherwise we would have had difficult entrance. Many of the people who are receiving the tracts are following it with interest and are looking forward to the next one. As a result we have had many gospel conversations and invitations to come and explain our religion. . . . It has also caused some bitter comments . . . [from] some of the so called ministers of the gospel. They do not want these tracts . . . telling a lot of truths which expose their errors.[31]

With this increase of interest, it was important that the missionaries spread out to accommodate requests for information. For this and other reasons, President Jacobs took Elders Washburn and Clark to Aleppo and secured a home where they could live and greet callers.[32]

President Jacobs described another approach in an article for the *Deseret News*. He explained how the Word of Wisdom had created many openings for gospel-centered discussions among the people. Because hospitality is taken very seriously in Near Eastern cultures, a visitor would not be sitting long before the hostess would offer cups of rich Turkish coffee, cigarettes, or liquors. Graciously refusing to partake of such culturally embedded delights automatically raised questions that inevitably led to a discussion of the Word of Wisdom and the Prophet Joseph Smith.

To really drive his point home, however, President Jacobs explained that he would then ask his host and hostess a question. The question and subsequent conclusions are taken from President Jacobs's own words:

You being a user of these things for the past 20 years, and I not being a user of them, would you recommend my starting now? Thus far out of the hundreds of questions which I have asked not a single one has answered in the affirmative. NOT A SINGLE ONE. One and all they have answered that they know it is not good, and also know that it is harmful, but they continue because they cannot stop now.

My next question to them is, "Did you like them from the start or did you have difficulty in liking them or getting used to them so that your dislike was smothered under?" Again the answer is in my favor. Their unvarying answer is that they did not like it at first but kept on using them until they got to liking them. And after so many years use they still recognize their harmful effect and advise me against them.

. . . Was Joseph Smith inspired when he gave the Word of Wisdom to the world as coming from God? We can get an answer to this question from the mouths of those who break its injunctions themselves.[33]

This story not only provides an example of a proselytizing technique in the mission but also affords a glimpse at the bold personality of President Joseph Jacobs.

The Reinterment of Elder Emil J. Huber

Elder Emil J. Huber had served under President Joseph W. Booth and died of typhus May 16, 1908, and had been buried in a Protestant cemetery in Aleppo, Syria. In 1938, President Jacobs was notified that this cemetery had been abandoned. Details are sketchy, but it appears that city officials decided to move the cemetery to the outskirts of the city in order to free up land for building development. President Jacobs was then told that Elder Huber's gravestone had already been relocated, and it fell to him to move the actual remains, if he desired.

While visiting Elders Clark and Washburn in Aleppo, Jacobs took them to the cemetery and approached the task reverently. One concern

The gravestones of Joseph W. Booth (left) and Emil J. Huber (right) as they appeared in 1950.

Jonathan E. Jackson standing near the gravestones of Booth and Huber. This picture captures the significant restorative work at the Booth and Huber gravesite directed by Professor James A. Toronto of Brigham Young University between the years 1999 and 2002.

shared by the missionaries dealt with identifying the remains with great confidence. With this in mind, it will be remembered that Elder Huber had felt impressed to carry his temple robes with him into the Turkish Mission. At the time of his death, it seemed obvious that the impression came so that he could be buried in those holy robes. It is interesting that decades later, the only way President Jacobs and his companions were able to absolutely and positively identify the remains of Elder Huber was by seeing pieces of the temple apron with the embroidered design still in place. Soon thereafter, President Jacobs made arrangements with the Armenian Evangelical Cemetery to secure a burial plot immediately adjacent to the grave of Joseph W. Booth.[34] Today there are graves of several other Latter-day Saints in this vicinity at the cemetery. They serve as another indication of the high esteem and respect that the Aleppo Saints had for President Booth and Elder Huber.[35]

The Arrival of Sister Jacobs and Modest Progress

On December 12, 1938, Sister Jacobs arrived at mission headquarters with their two children, Geraldine and Lamont. For close to eighteen months, President Jacobs had eagerly awaited the arrival of his family, writing, "Both myself and the Saints had given up their coming here, so that it was a real surprise and pleasure to welcome them into this strange land."[36] Because the American Community School, where the Jacobs children would attend, was a considerable distance from the mission home, it was decided to move mission headquarters closer. Nevertheless, President Jacobs decided to maintain the old mission home to accommodate new elders who were on the way.

As 1938 came to a close, President Jacobs reported, "We have in the mission field now . . . myself, Elders Clark and Washburn, and sister Jacobs. . . . The mission membership consists of seventy nine souls. Over twelve thousand tracts have been distributed. . . . The people are gradually becoming conscious of our existence and we hope before long our efforts will bear real fruit."[37]

On February 4, 1939, Elders Russell H. Boss and Ellis Dean Orchard arrived, as promised. Soon thereafter, President Jacobs received word from the First Presidency that Bishop W. E. Ryberg was being sent to inspect mission conditions and hold a mission conference.

Jacobs's primary request to Bishop Ryberg was that more missionaries be sent. On the heels of this visit, President Jacobs recorded his own feelings about the condition of the mission. "The progress of the work is very slow. . . . The majority of [the people] are concerned with earning enough to keep body and soul together. And by the time they succeed in doing that they are so worn out that there is not time or energy to think of anything else."[38]

In spite of the challenges, during the month of May there were six baptisms. President Jacobs was jubilant. He wrote that "this makes six baptisms this month, more than during the entire period since my coming here in August 1937."[39]

One month earlier, in April, the first intimations of war were recorded in the mission record. President Jacobs noted that every American citizen had received a letter from the consul general in Beirut explaining that conditions in Europe were not an intense concern at the moment but that each citizen should monitor the news carefully and prepare accordingly. Unfortunately, conditions in Europe grew worse rapidly.

Success from the mass mailing of Latter-day Saint literature insti-gated by President Jacobs took some time to develop. Over the months, however, thousands of people were contacted through this proselytizing medium. Midway through 1939, people throughout the entire mission had received a complete set (twelve in all) of Elder Penrose's "Rays of Living Light," followed by "A Friendly Discussion," which came in a series of four tracts about the restored gospel. That mailing was to be followed by the "Centennial Series," which included a number of sermons from General Authorities of the Church. Hundreds and hundreds of people were reading these tracts, and by late summer 1939, the missionaries were receiving continuous requests from individuals to learn more about the gospel.[40] Unfortunately, at the very moment that a harvest seemed evident, World War II broke out on September 7, 1939.

AN EIGHT-YEAR CLOSURE

President Jacobs was instructed to close the mission, and once again, the Near Eastern Saints were left alone to govern their own affairs. The Palestine-Syrian Mission did not reopen until September 11,

1947. During these years, brother Abraham Hindoian of Aleppo served as acting mission president and presiding elder.[41] The connectedness between leaders in Salt Lake City and the Near East was improved over that of previous closures. Beyond the letters sent to branch leaders from the leadership of the Church, there was also a consistent flow of Church publications sent from Church headquarters. Copies of the *Instructor, Church News,* Sunday School lessons, Relief Society lessons, and the Conference Report were sent to the Near Eastern Saints.

A general picture of Church membership in the Near East during this period can be gleaned from the correspondence between the faithful Saints and Church headquarters. An example of this is found in a letter from Brother Hindoian to Salt Lake City. It arrived after heavy censorship and four months in the mail, dated February 11, 1942.

> I am thanking the Lord that this day, the Church has men to guide the people through these dark times. When I read your letter to the members in the 4 p.m. meeting, all felt that the Holy Spirit had blessed them and that your prayer to the Lord to help us to be good children in His field. We know by prayer that many blessings come to us, and I hope, dear brother, that you will remember us in your prayer. This is a sure cure and remedy under these torn out conditions.[42]

Another letter was written by Brother Joseph Uzanian to Elder Thomas E. McKay, an Assistant to the Quorum of the Twelve who was in charge of the European missions of the Church during this time. Brother Uzanian indicated that by reading the Church publications sent to the Near East

> we understand something about our Church, and especially we received the 112th Semi-annual Conference Report, and we are exceedingly glad for it. Would that we had a chance to attend a conference like that! From it, we are receiving a lot of information and advice to the Saints here in Beirut. The lessons sent by President Amy Brown Lyman were translated and delivered to the sisters. We get a lot of benefit from studying them. . . . We

also were exceedingly glad to read the report of the one
hundredth anniversary of the Society.

> . . . Because of troublous times, the members are closer together.
> I am visiting them regularly and continuously and strengthening
> them in their faith, and I perceive that their troubles are so much
> that it is sufficient; nevertheless, they are firm in the faith and are
> trying to live saintly lives.[43]

Finally, a letter written to President Jacobs in 1943 conveyed the
remarkable news that there were only two individuals in the entire mission
who were receiving financial assistance from the Church. The letter stated
that the Saints were prospering temporally and that spiritually they were
"blossoming as spring roses."[44] These letters convey a picture of relative
stability among the members during the closure of the mission.

REOPENING THE MISSION AGAIN

After President Jacobs had replaced Badwagan Piranian as president of the Palestine-Syrian Mission in 1937, Piranian had returned to
Zurich, Switzerland, where he had remained active in Church affairs
throughout the war. In the summer of 1947, Brother Piranian and his

wife, Berta, were visiting in Salt Lake
City when they were called by the First
Presidency to reopen the Palestine-Syrian
Mission and serve, for the second time, as
its president and matron. Although the
mission had been officially reopened on
September 11, 1947, Brother and Sister
Piranian did not arrive in Beirut until
November 8, 1947. Mission headquarters
were set up in the New Royal Hotel until
a permanent residence could be located.
Because there had not been any meetings
held in Beirut for four years, one of
President Piranian's immediate objectives
was to restore a gospel routine with a full
slate of meetings for the Saints.

Elder Harold G. Connell

From left to right: Elder Stephen L Richards of the Quorum of the Twelve Apostles with his wife, Irene, Berta Piranian, and President Badwagan Piranian.

Elder Carlos E. Asay served as a missionary in the Near East and was later called as a General Authority of the Church.

On November 22, 1947, Elders Carlos Egan Asay from Monroe, Utah, and Harold Gregory Connell from Washington, D.C., arrived in Beirut to begin their service in the Palestine-Syrian Mission. The day after their arrival, November 23, the mission headquarters were moved to a permanent residence on Avenue Clemenceau in Beirut. That day, the first meeting was held at the new location. The four present sat on trunks, since the only pieces of furniture in the home at the time were beds. The first sacrament meeting was held on November 30, and the first Mutual Improvement Association meeting was held just over one week later, on December 9, 1947.[45]

About mid-December, President and Sister Piranian took Elder Connell to Aleppo to view the circumstances and condition of the branch. They planned to return on December 22 but, due to an outbreak of cholera in Syria, were forced to remain through Christmas, not returning to Beirut until December 29. While visiting Aleppo, President Piranian reorganized the branch presidency and generally audited conditions in the branch. Most of the affairs of the branch were in order, and living conditions in Aleppo had improved markedly. However, there was one major problem that had crept into the branch during the war years. It had to do with tithing.

Abraham Hindoian was the president of the branch, and his counselors were Khoren Ouzounian and Kevork Bezjian. The branch presidency paid the expenses associated with running the branch using tithes paid by the members. In all previous years, there had never been an excess of tithing funds. However, financial progress had been made by the members, and their donations had increased; the branch presidency did not know what to do with the surplus. They decided to take the leftover tithing funds and make business loans to themselves and close friends in the branch. All of the loans were kept secret from the other members until Reuben Ouzounian found out and protested. He was told to stay out of Church business that didn't concern him. The problem persisted for four long years.

Needless to say, when fully disclosed, the men's actions caused a serious rift in the branch. When President Piranian learned of this serious problem, he considered excommunicating the men involved but decided that their current circumstances in life were so pathetic that further discipline was unnecessary. Kevork Bezjian, the second counselor in the branch presidency, had emigrated to Russia; although he had sent nothing to repay his loan, he was completely removed from the Saints and the situation. Brother Ouzounian, the first counselor, had died. Brother Hindoian, the branch president, was in no condition to ever repay the loan and could barely provide for his own family.[46]

As President Piranian was smoothing this situation over within the branch through reorganization and the teaching of sound principles, he was approached by Brother Reuben Ouzounian, who carried a parcel in his hands. Reuben handed the parcel to President Piranian and explained that it contained the tithes and offerings of his family

The Reuben Ouzounian family

Dinner at the Ouzounian home following a conference in April 1948. From left to right: President Piranian, Carlos Asay, Sterling Burch, Haratoun Ouzounian, Albert Ouzounian, Mary and Angel Ouzounian (standing), Reuben Ouzounian, Harold Connell (barely visible), Leo Wilcox, and Berta Piranian.

over the past four years. Knowing that the activities of the branch presidency in relation to tithes and offerings were inappropriate, he had saved the donations apart from all his funds in order to deliver them to the first trustworthy priesthood leader of the Church to cross his path who could view the situation objectively.[47]

BASKETBALL AND THE GOSPEL

As leader of the postwar Palestine-Syrian Mission, President Piranian faced challenges that were not present during his first service in office. As mentioned previously, Syria gained its independence in 1946 and was still experimenting with forms of government that would most fully serve Arab interests in the wake of decades of French control. Being foreigners from the West bearing a peculiar Christian message, the Latter-day Saint missionaries in Syria were looked upon with suspicion, their letters were censored, and occasionally they were even jailed. Given these conditions, President Piranian imposed travel restrictions upon his missionaries that basically limited them to work within Lebanon.[48] No missionaries served in Palestine or Transjordan, and only briefly in Syria.[49]

In order to increase public exposure of the Church and bring his missionaries into contact with greater numbers of people, President Piranian encouraged the elders to become involved in as many civic and community affairs as they reasonably could. The medium discovered by the missionaries to heighten awareness of the Church's message in 1947 turned out to be far more unusual than President Joseph Jacobs's mass-mailing campaign undertaken before the war, and in some ways it more favorably impressed the local population.

Elder James McFarlane (left) and Elder Carlos Asay (right) serving in Beirut. They are seen here wearing the clothing they commonly wore as they proselytized among the people of Lebanon.

Elder Carlos Asay was a basketball star. His talent was discovered by the Armenian people with whom the missionaries served. In the latter part of 1947, Elder Asay was invited to play for the Beirut Homenetmen, an Armenian international athletic association that had a basketball league with a team in Beirut. The team traveled throughout the region, playing basketball against other athletic associations. Elder Asay played in games through February 1948, and the exposure was exceptional for the Church. The Armenian population in Beirut was

impressed by the agile and athletic Mormon missionary, and subsequently doors opened and new friendships were fostered.[50]

On March 1, 1948, Elders Asay and Connell were sent to Aleppo to preach the gospel. Elder Connell was appointed to serve as the branch president in Aleppo. While there, Elder Asay was invited to join the Armenian Homenetmen of Aleppo. This team was so happy to have the Latter-day Saint basketball star that they arranged practices around his schedule. This experience opened additional doors, and on March 29, 1948, both elders were invited to participate in the "Annual Easter Celebration of the Homenetmen Organizations of Syria,

Elder Carlos Asay shines his shoes with a neighbor boy on the balcony of the missionaries' Beirut apartment.

Lebanon, Palestine and Cyprus."[51] Elder Asay officiated at the championship basketball games of the men and women's division during this celebration. The missionaries were shown many courtesies, and again they made many new friends.

The transfer of Elder Carlos Asay from Beriut to Aleppo was felt keenly by the Homenetmen basketball coach. He visited President Piranian at the mission home in Beirut, explaining that the "basketball players are homesick for him" and that "Elder Asay was a good example on the young generation." The coach went on to explain that three boys had stopped drinking alcoholic beverages and had given up their heavy smoking habit because of the good example of Elder Asay. The coach had been criticized for having a Mormon on his team, to which he had replied that since "Mormonism produced as fine a fellow as Elder Asay, he wished all the Homenetmen members would be Mormons."[52]

THE ARRIVAL OF NEW ELDERS

On November 29, 1947, the United Nations voted to end the British mandate and to partition Palestine. As proposed by the United Nations General Assembly, this partition would create a Jewish state side by side with a Palestinian state. Given this vote, the British mandate over Palestine would end at 6:00 P.M. on May 15, 1948.

Generally speaking, the Arab world rejected this partition plan and collectively vowed to fight in order to stop the creation of the Jewish state of Israel. From November to May, both sides postured for every strategic advantage they could possibly obtain, knowing that when the British forces withdrew, war would ensue. The Jewish army made every attempt to occupy a series of vital areas of Palestine before the British mandate expired and before the Arab armies converged on the region. For example, on April 18, 1948, they fought for and won the city of Tiberias, on the shore of the Sea of Galilee. Within hours of this victory in Galilee, furious fighting commenced in the port city of Haifa. After about twenty-four hours, the battle was won by the Jewish forces, and Haifa was occupied and controlled by the Jews.[53] It was shortly after this major battle, with tense pockets of fighting still taking place in the port city, that the boat carrying four Latter-day Saint missionaries arrived at Haifa.[54]

President Piranian had sent a telegram warning the Church not to send Elders McFarlane, Shelton, Wilcox, and Burch on a ship to Haifa due to the heavy shooting, bombings, and high number of civilian deaths inflicted during the fighting. Unfortunately, this telegram arrived at Church headquarters after the missionaries had

The Soviet ship Rossia

boarded the MV *Rossia* (a Soviet ship taken from the Germans for reparation following World War II; it was formerly a German luxury liner known as the *Patria*). As it turned out, the elders were sailing on the very vessel that President Piranian had warned against taking. And just as President Piranian had feared, the elders landed in Haifa surrounded by all the dangers of war.

The missionaries had hoped to travel on to Beirut, but all travel from the port had been canceled due to the violent conflict. The missionaries tried to join a convoy of Arabs traveling north, but the Arabs refused to allow the Latter-day Saints to travel with them. Therefore, the elders were stranded in the war-torn city for five days. Appeals were made to the American consulates in both Haifa and Beirut, but each office expressed a complete inability to assist the elders. Fortunately, President Piranian had a friend in Haifa, a Mr. Topalian. Through his generous interventions over five days, the elders were able to secure passage on the Greek ship *Teti*. Even though the port at Haifa was blocked by military vessels not allowing entrance or exit of ships, the captain of the *Teti* ran through the blockade at night and sailed for Beirut. The *Teti* was so overcrowded with anxious travelers hoping to escape with their lives that the missionaries had to find a place on the deck.[55]

After long hours of uncomfortable travel, the missionaries finally arrived in Beirut on April 25, 1948. Of the safe arrival of the

missionaries, President
Piranian wrote:

> Elders arrived safely in
> Beirut. It is a remarkable
> fact that the American
> Consul in both Haifa, and
> Beirut expressed themselves
> that they were absolutely
> powerless to assist the
> missionaries in any way.

It is also remarkable that
the fighting in the city of
Haifa ceased shortly before
the Missionaries' arrival
there, and that Friday
evening a few hours after

*From left to right: Elder James McFarlane, Elder K. E.
Shelton, Elder Carlos Asay, President Badwagan
Piranian, and Elder Leo Wilcox.*

*Missionaries sporting traditional Turkish fez caps. From left to right: Elder Carlos Asay,
Elder Leo Wilcox, Elder Harold Connell, and Elder Sterling Burch.*

*Elder James McFarlane and Adeline Ouzounian (worker in the Aleppo
Branch Primary) hold up the theme of the Primary, which was beauti-
fully embroidered by Armenian members. "The Church of Jesus Christ of
Latter-day Saints" is the overarching phrase (in Armenian). Under the
arch is the phrase "Love and Service," with the year 1948 embroidered at
the bottom of the piece.*

The Syrian city of Aleppo, looking toward the Citadel.

they left, the local newspapers in Beirut loudly proclaimed that fighting had resumed in Haifa on a larger scale than ever before.[56]

Albert K. Ouzounian, president of the Aleppo Branch.

On August 2, 1948, Elder James J. McFarlane was transferred from Beirut to Aleppo, Syria. He found circumstances in the Aleppo Branch to be less than ideal. There was such bitter discord among the Saints of Aleppo that in November, President Piranian sent Elder Harold Connell to gather first-hand information regarding the difficulties and make every possible effort to resolve the problems.[57]

Elder Connell determined that he and Albert K. Ouzounian, the branch president, would visit the home of every member to determine "the spirit present in each family." These visits were fruitful. In every case except one, there was a spirit of repentance and a desire to cooperate and return wholeheartedly to the branch. Then, on Sunday, November 15, 1948, the branch presidency announced during sacrament meeting that there would be a special fast the following day dedicated to reuniting the families of the branch.

That evening the missionaries were notified by the Syrian government that they were all being deported from the country. The underlying cause was traced back to a letter written by Elder James J. McFarlane,

Syrian and Lebanese officials frequently viewed Latter-day Saint missionaries with suspicion. Here the missionaries are seen being escorted by officials following their arrest in Beirut, Lebanon.

intercepted by Syrian government censors, which was somewhat critical of Syrian government practices. The "inflammatory" letter described much of their daily experiences, but it was his description of how they got water from a local well that was considered most troubling. At the time, there was an acute water shortage, and Elder McFarlane's description of both the well and its location was considered a security threat and a clear attempt to share valuable military information.

As ordered, the four elders left Monday, November 16, 1948, for Damascus. Interestingly, the members of the Aleppo Branch strongly believed that the deportation of the missionaries was the direct result of their own unsaintly behavior. They took this action as a warning and a punishment for their disobedience.[58] They were therefore relieved to learn that in Damascus the elders met with the American vice-consul, who secured the return of all the elders except for Elder McFarlane, who ended up finishing his service in the French Mission.[59]

The missionaries of the Palestine-Syrian Mission, 1948. Back row, left to right: Elder Carlos Asay, Elder Harold Connell, Elder James McFarlane, Elder K. E. Shelton. Front row, left to right: Elder Leo Wilcox, Sister Berta Piranian, President Badwagan Piranian, Elder Sterling Burch.

Aleppo Branch Christmas party, 1948.

More Basketball

Basketball continued to play a role in the missionary effort in the Palestine-Syrian Mission. In the spring of 1949, Elder Asay, who had been called to serve as the second counselor to Badwagan Piranian in the mission presidency, was invited to travel with the Lebanese

Elder Albert Perry Ostraff

basketball team and serve as the assistant coach. Of this continuing phenomenon, President Piranian mused: "It seems that we have more success in winning people to be our friends through basketball playing than through distributing tracts."[60]

As time passed, more elders arrived, among them Elder Albert Perry Ostraff. Raised a Jew, Ostraff was converted to the gospel at age eleven while living in Burbank, California; however, at his young age, his parents would not allow him to be baptized. Finally, at age seventeen, Ostraff was permitted to join the Church. During World War II, he was in the United States Navy and was called by Church leaders to serve as a group leader over a small group of Saints. At war's end, he was anxious to serve a full-time mission.[61]

Elder Ostraff made a request to serve in the Palestine-Syrian Mission. The call came about fourteen months after Israel's war for independence, and Arab animosity toward Jews ran high. It was clear in his mind that a Jew entering a predominantly Arab region in the middle of such animosity did so with the possibility of peril. The risks were so real that Elder Ostraff was told to pack his sacred temple robes for burial, although his traveling companion, Elder Scott Beesley, was given no such instruction. Nevertheless, Elder Ostraff felt no concerns for his well-being; in fact, he felt a peaceful conviction that he was supposed to serve in the Near East. President Piranian did

The Latter-day Saint basketball team, made up of missionaries from the Palestine Syrian Mission. Back row, left to right: Elder Harold Connell, Elder Milton Beck, Elder Sterling Burch, Elder Richard Sperry, Elder Carlos Asay, Elder Richard Asay, and Elder P. Otis Rose. Front row, left to right: Elder Albert Ostraff, Elder Dale Marchant, Elder Rao Lindsay, Elder Leo Wilcox, and Elder Reed Seegmiller.

A small billboard in Damascus, Syria, advertising a basketball game to be played October 29, 1950, involving the Mormon missionaries from America.

not share Elder Ostraff's confidence, declaring at his arrival in October, "There must be some mistake, we are afraid that you'll be killed! Don't tell anyone that you're a Jew!" Generally speaking, Elder Ostraff was true to this charge.[62]

With more missionaries now serving under President Piranian, it became possible to organize an all-Mormon basketball team. Elder Ostraff was on this team. Of course, Elder Asay was captain, leader, and coach. On one occasion, the team traveled to Damascus, where they played the Syrian Olympic team. During the half-time break, a musical number was sung by the missionaries. The final score was 38 to 27 in favor of the Syrians.[63] In the words of Elder Ostraff, "We lost the basketball game, but at least 1400 more persons know what Latter-day Saints look like. They gave us a tremendous publicity campaign that will be helpful to the missionaries who will some day be assigned [to Damascus]. . . . Our basketball activity has really helped us to be well known for such a small group."[64]

GATHERING THE SCATTERED

During the first year or so after the mission had reopened, the labors of the missionaries were, in large measure, focused on locating the Saints who had been scattered or lost during World War II. Once located, they were shepherded back to the two major branches in the mission, located in Beirut and Aleppo.[65] After this period of reorganization and stabilization passed, the elders focused their labors on locating interested nonmembers to teach, as had been done

The staircase to the left leads to a missionary apartment in Beirut, Lebanon, in the Palestine-Syrian Mission.

Elder James McFarlane studies in his Beirut apartment, 1948.

in the past. Their efforts did not go unrewarded, and the Sunday School in Aleppo was an example of how active the work could become. President Piranian noted in late 1949 that the enrollment of the Aleppo Sunday School was ninety-three persons, even though there were only fifty-one members of record. "This indicates the enthusiasm with which both members and nonmembers participate in this Sabbath-day activity."[66]

One investigator with whom President Piranian was particularly impressed was Sister Araxie Eskijian. Almost a year before her baptism into the Church, President Piranian wrote:

> Special mention should be given Miss Araxie Eskijian, a friend who has manifested the spirit of a true Latter-Day Saint. A

Beirut Branch Mutual Improvement Association group, 1948.

teacher to Primary, she is also active as an officer in MIA and attends Sunday School regularly. She has shown many kindnesses to the Mission personnel; for example, providing on Thanksgiving Day a dinner which generously served nine and which literally included everything from soup to nuts as well as a very large turkey. Christmas and New Year were made memorable by her generosity, and birthdays of members of the Mission staff were likewise remembered. She has given to the utmost of her time and talent in the Primary and Mutual work, and we feel it only fitting and proper to give special mention to this "near Latter-Day Saint" friend.[67]

Araxie Eskijian's continued involvement with the Church in Beirut eventually led to baptism. On September 19, 1949, she was baptized by Elder Carlos E. Asay and confirmed by Elder Harold G. Connell. In October of that same year, Sister Eskijian left Beirut for Gaza, Palestine, where she worked as a nurse in a United Nations hospital.[68]

NEW MISSIONARIES AND A NEW MISSION NAME

By mid-December 1949, there were fourteen elders laboring in the Palestine-Syrian Mission. They were Elders Connell, Wilcox, Burch, Beck, Daniels, Crosby, Lindsay, Ostraff, Beesley, and Asay, and new arrivals Reed C. Seegmiller, Dean L. Hailstone, Gary L. Love, and James B. Allen Jr. They were all assigned to serve in the Beirut area.[69]

Apparently, President Piranian had made appeals to the First Presidency to change the name of the mission from the Palestine-Syrian Mission to the Near East Mission. Permission was granted to enact this change on January 20, 1950.[70]

During the early months of 1950, there was continued progress in Lebanon. In fact, Elders Ross Crosby and Gary Love were transferred to Tripoli, Lebanon, to open the work in that city. The elders in Syria, however, did not enjoy much stability in their dealings with the Syrian government. Early in February 1950, Elders Daniels and Allen arrived in Beirut after having been deported from Damascus, Syria, for preaching the gospel. The missionaries explained that they were evicted because Syrian officials were working to establish Islam as the state religion, and therefore the Latter-day Saint missionaries were not welcome to remain in the country.[71] One month later, Elders Beck and Beesley were evicted from Aleppo for the same reason. These missionaries described the high level of antagonism that they felt from the Syrian government. They were opposed in all their efforts to proselytize; they were denied the right to distribute written literature; and they were watched closely by the secret police. This being the case, they were reassigned to work in the Beirut area.[72]

Changing of the Guard and Closing of the Mission

The first two missionaries to serve in the newly reopened Palestine-Syrian Mission in 1947, Elders Asay and Connell, were honorably released in April 1950. Elder Asay was released one week early to fly to Istanbul, Turkey, to coach the national Lebanese basketball team in an international tournament. Meanwhile, the other elders continued to spread the gospel message.

Unfortunately, during the year it became painfully obvious that proselytizing efforts were bearing little fruit, with very few seriously investigating the Church. Those few who did desire baptism were frequently denied by President Piranian, because converts were often ostracized from their community and their ability to function in society was jeopardized.[73]

These unfavorable conditions led to the closure of the Near East Mission at the end of 1950.[74] In order to prepare for this, the First Presidency instructed Piranian not to rent the mission home for another year. Accordingly, the Piranians moved into the branch meeting hall, where they established living quarters in one room. They then turned their efforts to gathering all the missionaries back to Beirut and distributing the remaining missionary literature among local members in hopes that with these several tracts, the members could continue to actively share the truths of the gospel message after the missionaries were gone.

Finally, on December 15, 1950, seventeen elders gathered for the last meeting of the Near East Mission. President Piranian recounted the hearty labors of the various missionaries who had served so faithfully during the past three years, then added his own testimony, after which every other missionary present had the opportunity to do so as well.[75] Then, on Christmas Eve, President Piranian reorganized the

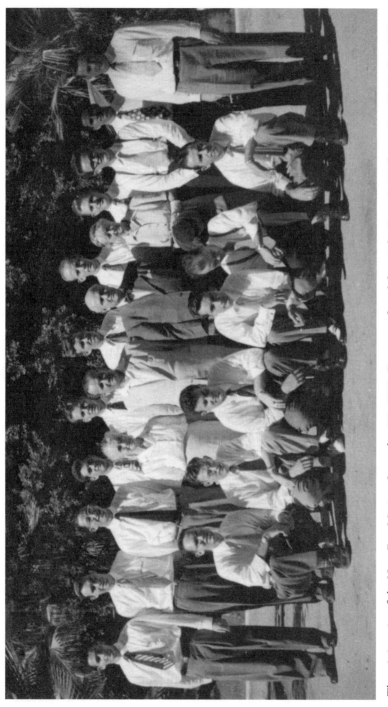

The missionaries of the Near East Mission, September 25, 1950. Front row, from left to right: Dean L. Hailstone, Rao H. Lindsay, Milton Q. Beck, Ross E. Crosby, Howard E. Daniels, Scott L. Beesley. Middle row, left to right: Albert O. Ostraff, Richard A. Asay, Reed H. Kezerian, Berta Piranian, Baduagan Piranian, Apostle Stephen L Richards, Irene Richards, Robert D. Hatch, and Gary L. Love. Back row, left to right: Eldon S. Greaves, Richard D. Sperry, A. Dale Marchant, Reed C. Seegmiller, P. Otis Rose, and James B. Allen.

Beirut Branch presidency. President Milton Q. Beck and his counselors, Joseph Ouzounian and Elder Richard A. Asay, were released. Joseph Ouzounian was sustained as branch president, while Garbis G. Sarafian and Enos Jacobs were sustained as his first and second counselors, respectively. The branch was then in the hands of the local members.

Due to poor mail service during the Christmas season, the transfer orders from the First Presidency still had not arrived by Christmas Day 1950. Knowing that they intended to move the missionaries to other fields of labor as soon as possible, President Piranian booked ship's passage to Marseille, France, for fifteen of his seventeen missionaries; once there, they could easily travel to London and resume their missionary service in the British Mission. However, two elders remained in Beirut. Elder Robert D. Hatch was very ill with yellow jaundice and still too sick to travel, and accordingly, Elder Rao H. Lindsay, who served as President Piranian's assistant, was asked to stay behind with him. They finally left for the British Mission in mid-January. On the other hand, the Piranians received their transfer orders on December 29, 1950, wherein they were transferred to the California Mission to labor among a large population of Armenian immigrants gathered in the San Joaquin Valley. Interestingly, until 1958 this region of California was referred to as the Near East Mission.

From 1951 through the early 1960s, the members of the Church in the Near East were without missionaries from the West again. However, in 1958, the Near East region was placed under the direction of the Swiss-Austrian Mission, and later the Swiss Mission, and missionaries were again sent to proselytize in the Near East. The work of these missionaries was varied and had implications for the development of the Church in the Near East for decades thereafter.

Notes to Chapter 8

1. *Millennial Star,* August 17, 1933, 526.
2. *Journal History,* August 12, 1933, 8.
3. Ibid., 7. See also *Millennial Star,* May 25, 1933, 347.
4. In a letter from John A. Widtsoe to President Rudger Clawson and the entire Quorum of the Twelve Apostles, President Widtsoe explained that Haifa was

the first branch of the Church in the Holy Land. Letters of John A. Widtsoe, June 6, 1933, LDS Church Archives. Furthermore, the entry summarizing the period of activity between December 31, 1896, and July 17, 1897, in Mission Record, Turkish Mission, 37, LDS Church Archives, and more specifically in the Haifa Record, credits Brother Johann Grau for the great assistance he had given to the little branch in Haifa.

5. Efraim Karsh and Inari Karsh, *Empires of the Sand* (Cambridge, MA: Harvard University Press, 1999). See also John F. Devlin, *Syria: Modern State in an Ancient Land* (Boulder, CO: Westview Press, 1983); and Thomas L. Friedman, *From Beirut to Jerusalem* (New York: Anchor Books, 1995).

6. Mission Record, Armenian Mission, May 21, 1933, 76, LDS Church Archives.

7. Ibid., 34.

8. *Millennial Star,* August 10, 1933, 523.

9. John A. Widtsoe, *Journal History,* July 29, 1933, 11.

10. So far as we know, the contents of this prayer were not recorded at the time the prayer was offered. This recollection is taken from an interview with Sister Leah Widtsoe, conducted by Dale Thomas Tingey, and may be found in his master's thesis, "Recent Jewish Movements in Israel in Light of the Teachings of the Latter-day Saint Prophets," Brigham Young University, 1955, 49–50. For additional details regarding this dedication, consult *Journal History,* July 29, 1933, 12. See also *Journal History,* August 12, 1933, 8; and *Millennial Star,* July 6, 1933, 443.

11. *Journal History,* August 12, 1933, 8.

12. Letters of John A. Widtsoe, December 10, 1928.

13. John A. Widtsoe, *In a Sunlit Land: The Autobiography of John A. Widtsoe* (Salt Lake City: Deseret Book, 1952), 204.

14. Ibid.

15. *Millennial Star,* August 10, 1933, 521–22. See also *Journal History,* June 24, 1933, 4; and Mission Record, Palestine-Syrian Mission, June 18, 1933.

16. Mission Record, Palestine-Syrian Mission, July 11, 1933, 75.

17. Letters of John A. Widtsoe, March 13, 1933.

18. Mission Record, Palestine-Syrian Mission, September 14, 1934, 87 (original emphasis).

19. Ibid., August 16, 1934, 86.

20. Ibid., March 26, 1934, 85.

21. Ibid., February 28, 1934, 84.

22. Ibid., March 13, 1934, 85.

23. Ibid., September 1934, 86.

24. Ibid.

25. Ibid., December 31, 1935, 89. See also *Journal History,* February 8, 1936, 6.

26. Mission Record, Palestine-Syrian Mission, March 31, June 30, September 30, December 31, 1936, March 31, June 30, 1937.

27. *Journal History,* July 9, 1937, 3.

28. Ibid., September 30, 1937, 90.

29. Ibid., 89–90.

30. Ibid., June 30, 1938, 91.

31. Ibid., December 1938, 92.

32. Ibid. See also Mission Record, Palestine-Syrian Mission, June 30, 1938, 91.

33. *Journal History,* July 9, 1938, 5 (original emphasis).

34. Mission Record, Palestine-Syrian Mission, December 1938, 93.

35. The Joseph W. Booth and Emil J. Huber gravesite was renovated, cleaned, and beautified under the direction of Professor James A. Toronto of Brigham Young University. For details regarding this project, refer to the Alice B. Reynolds Lecture by James A. Toronto, April 3, 2002, at the Harold B. Lee Library, Brigham Young University, Provo, UT.

36. Mission Record, Palestine-Syrian Mission, December 1938, 93.

37. Ibid.

38. Ibid., March 1939, 94.

39. Ibid.

40. Ibid., June 1939, 95.

41. *Instructor,* December 1949, 700.

42. Ibid., August 1942, 435.

43. *Relief Society Magazine,* November 1942, 792.

44. *Journal History,* September 25, 1943, 16.

45. Mission Record, Palestine-Syrian Mission, November 23, 1947, 95. Carlos E. Asay was later called to serve as a General Authority of the Church.

46. Ibid., April 10, 1948, 97.

47. Ibid.

48. Albert E. Ostraff, *Journal History,* December 21, 1949, 6. See also Steven W. Baldridge, *Grafting In: A History of the Latter-day Saints in the Holy Land* (Murray, UT: Roylance Publishing, 1989).

49. Baldridge, *Grafting In,* 11.

50. Mission Record, Palestine-Syrian Mission, December 31, 1947, 95.

51. Ibid., March 29, 1948, 96.

52. Ibid., 99.

53. Larry Collins and Dominique Lapierre, *O Jerusalem!* (New York: Touchstone, 1972), 336.

54. Mission Record, Palestine-Syrian Mission, March 29, 1948, 99–100.

55. Many of the details regarding this perilous voyage were gleaned from a personal interview conducted by the authors with James J. McFarlane, April 17, 2001. McFarlane shared with us the written memoirs of his mission experience. The manuscript is titled "The Missionary Odyssey of Elder James J. McFarlane While Serving in Palestine-Syria-Lebanon and France as a Missionary for The Church of Jesus Christ of Latter-day Saints during 1947–1948–1949–1950." It was created for family members to ensure that they had a firsthand account of his full-time missionary experiences.

56. Mission Record, Palestine-Syrian Mission, April 30, 1948, 100.

57. Ibid., November 12, 1948, 105.

58. Ibid., November 15, 1948, 105.

59. Ibid., November 12–December 14, 1948, 104–5. See also James J. McFarlane, interview by the authors, April 17, 2001.

60. Mission Record, Palestine-Syrian Mission, March 29, 1948, 99.

61. *Journal History,* December 21, 1949, 6.

62. Albert Ostraff, interview by the authors, February 10, 2004.

63. Mission Record, Palestine-Syrian Mission, October 29, 1949, 110.

64. Albert E. Ostraff, *Journal History,* December 21, 1949, 6.

65. This description of the work from the journal of Elder Carlos E. Asay is found in Baldridge, *Grafting In.*

66. *Instructor,* December 1949, 645.

67. Mission Record, Palestine-Syrian Mission, 106–7.

68. Ibid., September 19, 1949, and October 7, 1949, 109.

69. Ibid., December 18, 1949, 111.

70. *Journal History,* January 25, 1950, 7. See also Mission Record, Near East Mission, January 30, 1950, 112.

71. Mission Record, Near East Mission, February 10, 1950, 113.

72. Ibid., March 6, 1950, 114.

73. Richard Sperry, interview by the authors, October 24, 2000. Brother Sperry served in the Near East Mission in 1950 under President Piranian.

74. In our interview with Richard Sperry, he gave three reasons for the closure of the mission. First, people who joined the Church were severely ostracized;

second, there was limited interest among the people in the region; and third, the intent behind the investigation of the Church was not always pure. For example, many young women "investigated" the Church, but President Piranian would not allow them to be baptized because he was convinced they were more interested in marrying a Mormon elder than joining the Church. This is an important clarification because it has been suggested by others that the mission was closed due to political tensions. Missionaries who were there when the mission was closed have confirmed to us that political tensions did not play a significant role in the closure.

75. Mission Record, Near East Mission, December 15, 1950, 123.

CHAPTER NINE

Unprecedented Growth

1964–1975

After a thirteen-year absence, missionaries returned to the Near East in 1964. As was the case in the days of Ferdinand Hintze, Joseph Booth, and Badwagan Piranian, elders from the Church in Utah added stability and leadership to the small branches in the Near East.

Lacking its own mission headquarters, the Near East was under the direction of the Swiss Mission. The missionaries that were sent to labor in the Near East (primarily Beirut) contributed greatly to the progress and growth of the Church during these years. Some members of the First Presidency and Quorum of the Twelve Apostles had their initial experiences in the Near East during this time period—President Harold B. Lee, Elder N. Eldon Tanner, Elder Ezra Taft Benson, and Elder Thomas S. Monson, to name a few. The importance of their early exposure to the Near East cannot be overstated.

Expatriates also played an important role in the development of the Church in the region. Never before had so many Latter-day Saints from the hub of the Church opted to live permanently or semipermanently in the Near East. Frequently, their move to the area was associated with educational pursuits, such as an assignment at the American University in Beirut; a government position, such as a post at a United States embassy; military assignments; or work in the oil industry. In a few cases, Latter-day Saints were employed by the Church to coordinate emerging BYU Travel Study and Semester Abroad programs in Jerusalem.

As with their predecessors, the missionaries who served in the Near East during this time faced many challenges, ranging from language barriers to acute isolation. They also became deeply attached to the peoples of the Near East, their cultures, and their languages. Upon their return home, some of these missionaries enrolled in universities and furthered their understanding of the Near East. Some became linguists, Arabists, or statesmen. They played a significant role that helped to shift Church focus in the Near East in ways that had not previously occurred. For example, basic Church documents such as Latter-day Saint hymnals, the Gospel Principles handbook, and essential leadership manuals were brought to the people of the Near East in a Near Eastern language and format. The Book of Mormon was translated into Arabic. Also, sensitivities regarding Church perceptions of Islam and other Near Eastern cultural considerations were heightened and refined. Finally, and perhaps most importantly, the temple endowment was translated into Arabic and made available in temples.

With these examples in mind, missionary labors from 1964 to 1975 accomplished at least two significant objectives. First, many people came to the waters of baptism, branches grew, and faith was fostered. Second, a core of men and women were exposed to the Near East through mission experiences or ministries as General Authorities; they went on to facilitate a greater understanding of Near Eastern cultures and values within the Church. This contribution played an important role in the establishment and long-term impact of Brigham Young University's Jerusalem Center for Near Eastern Studies and other ongoing or developing efforts of the Church in the Near East.

Lebanon

Most of the missionary efforts during this time period occurred in or were anchored to happenings in Beirut, Lebanon. Created by France in 1920, Lebanon was home to members of several religions.

Maronite Christians dominated the area of Mount Lebanon. Cities of the Mediterranean coast, including Beirut, Tripoli, Sidon, and Tyre, were predominantly Sunni Muslim, while the southern and eastern regions of Lebanon, including Akkar and the Bekaa Valley, were predominantly Shiite Muslim. Sunnis maintain that the caliph (Muhammad's successor and the highest-ranking spiritual authority in Islam) should be elected by the community of elders, while Shiites maintain that the caliph must be a descendant of the prophet. Maronites, on the other hand, were an Eastern Christian Church established in Syria by a monk named Maron sometime around the fifth century. They acknowledge the Catholic pope but retain their own unique liturgy. Furthermore, since the establishment of the state of Lebanon, there had been a large population of Druze in the Mount Lebanon region. Druze are a splinter group of Islam whose core beliefs and rituals are largely secret.

In the face of this diversity, France fostered the creation of a governmental structure that would ensure Maronite Christian dominance, even though they constituted only fifty-one percent of the entire population in 1932. It will also be remembered that the creation of Lebanon placed a large number of Muslims outside the borders of Muslim-dominant Syria. For Muslims in Lebanon, this arrangement was troubling at best, and they demanded to be joined to Syria. In 1943, when Lebanon became entirely independent of France, the peoples of Lebanon agreed to a "national pact" stipulating that the Maronites would sever relations with France and acknowledge Lebanon to be an Arab nation. In turn, Lebanese Muslims agreed to abandon demands for unification with Syria. With these agreements intact, it was determined that the president of Lebanon would always be a Maronite Christian, parliament would always have a six-to-five ratio of Christians to Muslims, the prime minister would always be a Sunni Muslim, and the speaker of parliament would always be a Shiite. It was hoped that these stipulations would maintain a level of fair representation within the government.

These arrangements functioned rather smoothly until the demographics of Lebanon began to shift. By about 1970, the number of Christians had shrunk to approximately one-third the population of Lebanon. When Muslims demanded political reforms aimed at creating a more representative government, the Maronites bristled and refused. Tensions rose steadily, culminating in civil war that began in 1975.

Couple these circumstances with other considerations—such as the demands of the Druze population in Lebanon for a voice in the government and the rapidly escalating tensions between Palestinian Arabs (many of whom had resettled in Lebanon after having been evicted from Jordan in 1970) and Israelis—and one begins to see the complicated political landscape Latter-day Saint missionaries entered in 1964. As had been the case so many times before, missionary labor in this region was a very bold undertaking.[1]

THE NEAR EAST AND THE SWISS MISSION

In 1967, Rendell N. Mabey, president of the Swiss Mission, explained how the Near East came to be under the jurisdiction of a European mission. An important letter was written, dated March 15, 1955, over the signatures of

President Rendell Noell Mabey

David O. McKay, Stephen L Richards, and J. Reuben Clark, Jr. [the First Presidency], to President Perschon of the [Swiss Mission], stating in part: "We recently received a report from Brother Badwagan Piranian, who, as you may remember, presided over the Near East Mission until the time it was closed about 1951. Brother Piranian advised that there are two branches left in the mission which he recommended be attached to an existing mission for such administration as could consistently be given to them. These two branches are the one in Beirut, Lebanon and the one in Aleppo, Syria. We have decided that these two branches should be included within the jurisdiction of the [Swiss Mission]."[2]

By comparison to later involvement, interaction between the Swiss Mission and the Saints in the Near East was minimal until the spring of 1963, when John Russon, president of the Swiss Mission, and his wife, Mary, flew to Beirut. While there, they became personally acquainted with the work that had been done by local leaders and a small group of expatriate Saints to keep the branch in Beirut functioning.

MAINTAINING THE BEIRUT BRANCH, 1951—1964

When the Near East Mission closed in December 1950, Joseph Ouzounian was called and set apart as the branch president in Beirut. He served in that calling until February 1964. Over the years, the members of the branch, including the Ouzounian, Inglizian, and Takavorian families, met in each other's homes to worship and partake of the sacrament. As membership rose, the YMCA hall was rented by the branch for their meetings. As membership declined, they would return to meeting in the homes of the Saints.

Fluctuation in branch size was partially the result of the arrival and departure of Latter-day Saint expatriates who moved to Lebanon and joined the branch at Beirut. These individuals and families greatly contributed to the stability and activity of the branch. For example, Dr. Clawson Young Cannon and his wife moved to Beirut and diligently sought out less-active members of the branch and encouraged them to return to the fold. Their contribution to the activity of the branch was significant. Also, Darwin and Erma Jepson introduced the family home evening program to the branch members during their stay in Beirut. Expatriates also instituted a home Primary program for the children of the branch. These members brought to Beirut a connection with Church doctrines and policies because of their upbringing in the wards and stakes of Utah and other areas where the Church was established and fully functional and local leaders were well versed in Church government.

The Latter-day Saint expatriate with the longest residency in the Near East during this time period was Maud Pearson of southeastern Idaho. She came to Beirut in 1951 and was present to see the last missionaries of this period leave in 1975, when civil war threatened to tear Lebanon apart. Sister Pearson was described by one Swiss Mission president as "a very dedicated single sister" and "a pillar of strength."[3] She practiced and taught nursing in the hospital at the American University in Beirut for almost three decades. Of her endearing personality, it was written that she "is truly loved by all— she has certainly set a fine example as to how a Latter-day Saint should live."[4] Over the years she served in a variety of callings, and her experience in the gospel was invaluable to the branch.

Not only was Sister Pearson a valuable asset to the Church in the Near East, but her professional skills were acknowledged at the highest levels. For example, she was the recipient of the Order of the Cedars of Lebanon citation. This prestigious award was bestowed upon her by the Lebanese government on account of her valuable and long-term service in the fields of nursing and teaching at the American University. Sister Pearson left Beirut in 1977 to return to her native Idaho. She died in 1997 and was buried in Moore, Idaho.[5]

While they were small in number, the devotion of local and expatriate Saints like Sister Pearson made it possible for the roots of the Church in the Near East to remain healthy. Beginning in 1964, missionaries returned to assist these Saints with the work in Lebanon.

The Return of Missionaries to the Near East

In the spring of 1963, six months after their arrival in Switzerland on September 28, 1962, President and Sister John Milton Russon traveled to Beirut to conduct leadership training and interview five young baptismal candidates to whom Maud Pearson and another expatriate Saint, Mabel Chapman, had taught the gospel.[6] Over the next two days, President Russon held branch leadership training meetings with president Joseph Ouzounian and other branch leaders.[7]

Because of the lasting impression this trip made on President Russon, he returned to the Near East in February 1964 with two full-time missionaries assigned to serve in the Beirut Branch—Elders Lee Amandas Adams and James Tolley. They were the first full-time

Latter-day Saint branch of the Church in Lebanon, 1953. Maud Pearson is in the middle row, two persons to the right of Erma Jepson, who is holding her son Michel.

missionaries to be assigned to the Near East since the departure of Elders Rao H. Lindsay and Robert D. Hatch in January 1951.[8]

Two days after their arrival, President Russon reorganized the branch, calling Elder Adams as the new branch president.[9] Along with the releases and calls among the brethren, the Relief Society presidency was also reorganized, with Sister Maud Pearson called as the new president.[10] After the sustaining vote was given that Sunday, President Russon paid a touching tribute to Brother Joseph Ouzounian for his thirteen years of service as branch president since the closure of the Near East Mission. For the isolated Saints of Beirut, this meeting was spiritual leaven that lifted their souls. They returned to their homes rejoicing.[11]

Under these elders' careful ministry, the Beirut Branch continued to grow in stability. On January 2, 1965, Elder Adams was honorably released and replaced by Elder Hans Michelmann.[12] After the missionaries had been serving in Beirut for one year, President Russon determined to visit the branch again. Elders Tolley and Michelmann escorted President Russon on a visit to the home of every Armenian family in the branch. He was most impressed with the progress that had been made in Beirut and the unity and spirit of love among the members, which was manifested in a well-attended activity they organized.

This unity was also manifested at the branch conference and during their visits to branch members' homes afterwards. By day's end, they had completed their goal to visit every member of the Church in the region, with the exception of those Saints living in Aleppo, Syria. Although the missionaries had traveled to Aleppo a week earlier and attempted to visit these Saints, they were met with a great deal of disinterest and apathy. Given this, as well as the anti-American feeling prevalent there, President Russon forwent a visit to Syria on this occasion.[13]

Before his departure, President Russon gave the elders specific instruction regarding the direction of missionary work in Lebanon. They were to become more aggressive in teaching the gospel, pay particular attention to the part-member families within the branch, and begin teaching English classes as a service to the community.[14] On the whole, the missionaries and President Russon were very encouraged as their time together came to a close.

VISIT TO JERUSALEM

From May 1948 to June 1967, the eastern half of Jerusalem was part of the Hashemite Kingdom of Jordan, while the western half was part of the modern state of Israel. President and Sister Russon traveled to Jerusalem, Jordan, on March 29, 1965. Given the fact that their labors in the Swiss Mission were coming to a close, their visit to the Holy Land was greatly anticipated.

During his short visit to Jordan, President Russon made general inquiries regarding the possibility of Latter-day Saint missionaries being stationed in Jerusalem, Jordan. One YMCA official suggested that while missionary work was greatly needed, he was concerned about the reception Latter-day Saint missionaries would actually receive. The general sentiment conveyed to President Russon regarding his inquiries was not particularly encouraging.[15]

Once the Russons' paperwork was in order, they were allowed to pass into Israel through the Mandelbaum Gate (the entrance for ground passage from Jerusalem, Jordan, on the east, to Jerusalem, Israel, on the west). They traveled to Tel Aviv, Israel, where they were met by Allen Van Potts, one of the few Latter-day Saints in Israel at the time. He worked with Foreign Services in the United States embassy in Tel Aviv.[16] The Russons stayed in his home, and he served as their guide through the Galilee region and other points of interest in northern Israel. On their return trip to Tel Aviv, they stopped at the German Templer Cemetery in Haifa, where they paid their respects at the graves of Elder Adolf Haag and Elder John Clark, who had died while serving in the Turkish Mission in 1892 and 1895, respectively.

Returning to Zurich on April 2, 1965, the Russons were greatly encouraged about prospects for missionary work in the Near East. Their visit had helped them see that a proper foundation had been laid in Lebanon by Elders Adams, Tolley, and Michelmann and that the potential for growth in the Beirut Branch was considerable.

EVALUATION AND PROGRESS

President Rendell N. Mabey and his wife, Rachel, arrived in Zurich on August 12, 1965, to assume leadership over the mission.[17] As the newly called president, one of his first duties was to select a missionary to replace Elder Tolley in Beirut, since he was returning home. President

Mabey decided to send Elder J. Lynn Styler to serve as Elder Hans Michelmann's junior companion.[18]

One month later, President Mabey flew to Beirut to train the elders, survey conditions among the members, and call a new branch president. His initial concern was that although the missionaries were active, involved in the community, and well thought of, no baptisms were forthcoming. To remedy this, President Mabey recommended that the elders focus on preaching the restored gospel instead of merely making friends for the Church. The mission record states:

> At the conclusion of the meeting, President Mabey was of the opinion that the missionaries in Lebanon, in order to accomplish their purpose, must not devote all of their time to teaching classes in English and other subjects to friends of the church. No baptisms apparently have resulted. If feasible, President Mabey wishes the missionaries to tract and use the usual proselyting procedures.[19]

After interviewing the elders there, President Mabey concluded, "There is no question but that the two Elders so far away from mission

Left to right: Robert Milton Odom (branch president), Elder Robert Fowles, Elder Clinton Albano, Elder Terrell Hunt, and local Sammy Farrah on an outing near Beirut.

Left to right: President Rendell Mabey, Elder Terrell Hunt, and Sister Rachel Mabey.

headquarters are under considerable strain."[20] One way to partially relieve this burden was to call a branch president from among the local membership. After his meeting with the elders, President Mabey traveled to the home of Robert Milton Odom, a thirty-one-year-old convert who had found the restored gospel through meeting and marrying a member of the Church from Hawaii. He was faithful and qualified, and he "accepted with humility" the call to serve as the new branch president.[21] At the time, he was serving as the army attaché at the United States embassy in Beirut.

By the summer of 1966, the work in Lebanon had progressed to the point that President Mabey created the Lebanese missionary district. Elders Michelmann and Styler had since been transferred and had been replaced by Elders Robert Burton and Terrell Hunt. Elder Burton was called to be the new district leader. They were joined by Elders Robert Fowles and Clinton Albano, who were transferred from Switzerland to Beirut on June 24, 1966.[22] One month earlier, the missionaries had baptized four people. President Mabey hoped that this recent success, coupled with two sets of missionaries serving in the branch, would markedly accelerate the work in Beirut.

As the missionaries worked, they met Michael Emil Antar. Elder Hunt later told President Mabey that the first time he saw Michael Antar, he knew he had seen him somewhere before. Antar was inter-

Elder Clinton Albano (left) and Elder Terrell Hunt (right) at Sidon, August 1966.

ested in the gospel, and the missionaries began a series of discussions with him. As they came to know one another better, Elder Hunt related to Michael Antar that he was sure he had known him somewhere before. Much to Elder Hunt's surprise, Michael explained that he had felt an uncanny famil-iarity with this American missionary. To be exact, he also felt that this was not the first time they had met. They came to the conclusion that Elder Hunt and his companion had been sent to find Michael Antar and share with him the message of the restored gospel. He was baptized shortly after their meeting.[23]

Elder Robert Burton (left) with Michael Emil Antar at a beach near Beirut, Lebanon.

Lebanon: A "Missionary Paradise"

If baptisms were viewed as a measure of success, the elders in Beirut were leading the mission. Beyond the baptisms, however, was the exciting fact that the people who were joining the Church were, in most cases, actively sharing the gospel with their family and friends. The following entry from the mission record, dated August 25, 1966, describes this trend:

The four Elders working in Beirut advised President Rendell N. Mabey today through their report that the work is progressing there more satisfactorily than expected and in the near future there should be several additional baptisms. The Elders in Beirut state that the newly baptized members in that branch are devoting their talents to the cause of preaching the gospel and are assisting the missionaries greatly through referrals.[24]

First and foremost among these new member-missionaries was a baker in Beirut named Hagop Nerces Danaian. He had been baptized on May 15, 1966, and by the time President Mabey met him at a branch conference in October, he was personally responsible for the baptisms of fourteen additional members of the Beirut Branch. Because of his love of the gospel and his enthusiasm for missionary work, he came to be known as the "Mormon baker."[25]

With such success attending their efforts, it is little surprise that when President Mabey interviewed the missionaries in Lebanon, they each expressed a desire to stay in Beirut for as long as possible. In fact, the progress that was being made in the branch led President Mabey to declare that, at the moment, Lebanon was a "missionary paradise."[26]

As the year came to an end, there had been a total of twenty-eight convert baptisms in Switzerland as compared to twenty-nine baptisms in the Beirut Branch.[27] The frequency of baptisms in Beirut was even evident to Ernst Etter, manager of the Phoenician Hotel, friend to the Church, and long-time business acquaintance of President Mabey. As the heat of summer subsided and winter approached, Etter offered the use of the hotel swimming pool for baptismal services at any time during the cold months ahead. The offer was gratefully accepted during the last week of December 1966. On January 2, 1967, two families were baptized in the heated pool of the hotel.

A WEDDING GIFT FROM JOSEPH W. BOOTH

Occasionally, President Mabey and his missionaries in Lebanon would be reminded that they were not the first to labor and preach the message of the Restoration in the Near East. On one occasion in 1967, President Mabey was in Beirut on the first leg of an extensive tour of the branches and groups in the Near East, including stops in Kuwait,

Iran, Afghanistan, and Iraq. He was enjoying dinner in the home of Abro Hammalian (baptized six months earlier) in company with many Armenian friends. One of the guests was a Mrs. Ouzounian, an aged widow, who held in her hands a copy of the Book of Mormon in Turkish that she and her husband had received as a wedding gift from President Joseph W. Booth decades earlier (most likely in the 1920s). At that time they were both members, but after her husband died she later married a man who was not a member of the Church. She eventually became disaffected and asked that her name be removed from Church records. Her wishes were respected.

Interestingly, she clung to the fundamental teachings of Mormonism and passed those beliefs on to her children. Just prior to President Mabey's visit to Beirut, her children and grandchildren had traveled there from Aleppo in search of the missionaries. They were all taught and baptized. As she conversed with President Mabey, she asked if she could be rebaptized. President Mabey interviewed her and found that her understanding of the gospel was sufficient and that her desires were real. She was rebaptized in the spring of 1967.[28]

"Unlocking One Door after Another"

With the Church's rapid growth in Beirut, President Mabey felt that it was essential to create friendships among people of influence in government, commerce, and education. In March 1967, Mabey traveled to Beirut for a luncheon that the elders had organized at the home of one of their investigators, who knew several influential members of the community. Invitations were sent out informing the guests that they would learn more about the Joseph Smith story in connection with the luncheon. Several people attended, and the missionaries taught the Joseph Smith story and basic beliefs of the gospel for over two hours.

At this luncheon, a very fortunate alliance was struck with one Raymond Edde, a successful attorney in Beirut and member of the Lebanese parliament, whose father was formerly president of Lebanon. During their conversations with Edde, the missionaries explained that the Lebanese police were conducting secret checks on the missionaries regarding their visas in fear that they were really spies for the United States. Edde was quickly convinced that there was no covert element in their missionary labors and suggested that the elders use his name the next time they experienced any difficulties with the police. This proved to be very advantageous.

Also in attendance were one Dr. Moukeibert and Miss Mizna Boustany, both members of parliament. Boustany was also the niece of the president of Lebanon then in office. The Mabeys were astonished by the luncheon's success in allowing them to be acquainted with the highest circles of Lebanese society. These friendships led to additional invitations to future events, where they met many more influential people. Regarding this success, President Mabey commented to Sister Mabey that it was almost as if, after they had decided in which direction they should go, "the Lord started unlocking one door after another."[29]

KUWAIT, IRAN, AFGHANISTAN, IRAQ

In 1967, Kuwait, Iran, Afghanistan, and Iraq all came under the jurisdiction of the Swiss Mission. On March 7, President and Sister Mabey continued their mission tour by flying to Kuwait—beginning their first visits to areas outside of Lebanon and Israel. They were greeted at the airport by Idaho natives Stuart C. Tyler and Jay R. Dobbing, who were working at an oil refinery. They drove the Mabeys to Fahahil, the city where President Mabey would organize a branch of the Church the next day.

The following evening, twenty-one people gathered for the first branch service (according to President Mabey) in Kuwait. Previously, Sister Mabey had discovered that the Saints in Kuwait had no hymnals, so she wrote in longhand several copies of "We Thank Thee, O God, for a Prophet" to be sung as the opening hymn. Following this hymn, Stuart Tyler was sustained as the new branch president. Nine of the people present were not members of the Church, and all were favorably impressed with the Spirit present that evening, which continued throughout the week. In the segment from the mission record below, President Mabey described a sacrament meeting held later in the week which creates a lasting image of this small but faithful group of Saints.

> Eight members and two nonmembers were present at the humble gathering. With no songbooks, no musical instruments, no white tablecloths, and furniture made out of packing boxes, no sacrament cups or trays—testimonies were humbly given. . . . The Spirit was felt and manifest throughout the hour.[30]

Following this Friday-night meeting, the Mabeys flew to Iran, landing in Tehran, where they were met by branch president Gardello C. Nay and his two counselors. The branch in Tehran at that time had seventy baptized members, with fifty-six actively attending. Most of the members were in Iran working with the oil industry.

While visiting the branch in Iran, President Mabey met Francis Burdick Haydock. His wife and children had been baptized recently in the United States, but Haydock had not yet joined the Church, even though he attended meetings regularly. President Mabey felt impressed to frankly challenge him to baptism. Brother Haydock readily agreed, and arrangements were made for a baptismal service. Francis Haydock was baptized by David W. Ream on March 21, 1967. President Mabey noted that according to mission records, this was the first convert baptism ever performed in Iran.[31]

From Iran, the Mabeys flew to Kabul, Afghanistan. In 1967 the Kabul Branch of the Church was four years old. It was organized when Wayne L. Rollins and Robert C. Thompson, both professors of agriculture, arrived in Kabul along with their wives and children. President Mabey arrived in Afghanistan on March 16, 1967, and determined that, up to that time, no general or mission authority had ever visited the country in an official capacity.[32]

Following this brief visit with the Saints in Kabul, President Mabey flew to Baghdad, Iraq, on March 22, 1967. By comparison, Afghanistan was a well-established foothold of the Church. There were two Latter-day Saint families living in Iraq, and they had been meeting with the Christian church in the community for the previous year.[33] The Robert Ray Gibbons and the Robert L. Brown families were in Baghdad to direct the American Institute of Languages, sponsored by the United States embassy. Both the Gibbons family of four and the Brown family of seven had arrived in Iraq on May 2, 1966. One year later, President Mabey organized these Baghdad Saints into a branch of the Church on March 22, 1967, and reported that they were "thrilled at the prospects of now being able to function as . . . other members of the Church."[34]

The visit to Iraq brought the Mabeys' mission tour to a close. On Thursday, March 23, 1967, they returned to mission headquarters in Zurich. Their appreciation for the Saints located in such remote locations in the Near East was greatly heightened.

SIX-DAY WAR

In early 1967, guerilla warfare against Israel was rising sharply. These intrusions were supported financially by Syria and were frequently conducted through Jordanian territory in the West Bank. Israel continued to fortify its military capabilities. At this time, Israel received a good deal of its military weaponry from France. French president Charles de Gaulle was not comfortable with Israel's arms build-up and imposed an arms embargo on Israel. With Syrian, Jordanian, and Egyptian forces posturing for war, Israel launched a preemptive strike in early June 1967. Israel's victory was decisive, driving the opposing armies back. At this time, Israel proceeded to occupy the Sinai Peninsula, the Gaza Strip, the West Bank, and the Golan Heights.

By late May 1967, President Mabey was greatly concerned for the missionaries laboring in Beirut. The previously described signs of war between Arab nations and Israel were increasing. President Mabey contacted his good friend and manager of the Phoenicia Hotel, Ernst Etter, and asked him to take care of the elders should they have pressing needs in the coming weeks. The fact that Beirut Branch president Robert Odom was the army attaché at the United States embassy in Beirut was a great comfort. In conversations with Brother Odom, President Mabey was convinced that the elders were safe at present.

The success of the Beirut Branch was so encouraging that even in the face of war, President Mabey was making every effort to keep the work going. "The work goes well in Lebanon, it will be a shame if it is disrupted through the disagreements of men."[35] As late as the first week of June 1967, President Mabey was "still inclined to work to the purpose of the Church someday establishing a little mission in the Middle East with headquarters in Beirut."[36] Furthermore, President

Mabey notified two more missionaries— Elders Michael Noss and G. Walter Gasser—that they would be transferred to Beirut on June 16, 1967. These plans were interrupted when full-scale war erupted in the Near East on June 5, 1967.

With phone lines in the Near East jammed, President Mabey was unable to make contact with the missionaries or the Saints in Lebanon on June 5. There were no phone or cable lines open for communication out of Beirut, making it impossible for the missionaries to contact the mission office. Under these circumstances, Elder Robert Fowles and his companion were standing in the office of President Odom at the United States embassy when the phone rang. Brother Odom was astonished when he picked up the phone and heard the voice of President Mabey. Brother Odom and the elders were convinced that such a call could not have been connected without the direct intervention of the Lord.[37]

President Odom explained that the situation in Beirut was not good and advised President Mabey to evacuate the missionaries as soon as possible. Unfortunately, there were no available flights out of Lebanon. While the missionaries waited, President Mabey instructed them to wire Apostle Gordon B. Hinckley every two days regarding their location and condition. When the missionaries explained that this would be impossible because all communication lines were blocked, President Mabey instructed them to fly to Ankara, Turkey, or Athens, Greece, or some other safe haven in the region at the earliest possible moment and contact him from there.

Early on the morning of June 8, 1967, eight elders boarded an airplane bound for Rome. They telephoned President Mabey upon their safe arrival in Italy. President Mabey then called Elder Hinckley in Salt Lake City, who promised to notify their families. All were exceedingly grateful to have the missionaries out of harm's way. President and Sister Mabey immediately booked a noon flight to Rome. Upon their arrival, they met the elders at one of the apartments of the Italian missionaries. After brief greetings, President Mabey invited all the missionaries to kneel down in a circle and pray with him. He expressed feelings of deep gratitude for the safe arrival of the missionaries and implored the Lord for guidance and direction in their future decisions regarding missionary work in Lebanon.

Following the prayer, a two-hour meeting was held, wherein decisions were made regarding the missionaries of Lebanon.[38]

President Mabey determined that the Lebanon elders would fly to Zurich and there constitute the Lebanese Zone in the mission, with Elder Terrell Hunt as the zone leader. He would preside over two Lebanese districts, with Elders Fowles and Albano as district leaders. President Mabey's charge to all eight missionaries was to continue their study of the Armenian language so that the moment a return to the Near East became possible, the missionaries could be back in their field of labor with few or no adjustments.

The missionaries remained in Zurich until July 21, 1967, when Elders Hunt and Fowles accompanied President Mabey back to Beirut. Levels of suspicion and tension were still high in the aftermath of the Six-Day War, and it was deemed prudent to take only two elders back to Beirut at first. If all went well, then Elders Albano, Wood, Buck, and Gasser would arrive on July 26, and they would be followed by Elders Bird, Noss, Hood, and Lund on July 28, 1967.[39] This would increase the number of missionaries in Beirut from eight to ten.

The Saints in Beirut were thrilled to have any or all of the missionaries back in their branch. They met President Mabey, Elder Hunt, and Elder Fowles at the airport and drove them to the meetinghouse. Even though it was late at night, the group knelt in a circle and thanked God for allowing the missionaries to return safely. They also expressed gratitude for the providential care extended to the Saints while the missionaries were absent.

During the six-week absence of the missionaries, Beirut Branch president Robert Odom and his family were reassigned to the United States. This made it necessary for President Mabey to reorganize the branch. On Sunday, July 23, the branch met, and Joseph Ouzounian was called to serve as branch president once again. He selected Nerces Inglizian and Antranik Kalaydjian as first and second counselors, respectively.[40]

SUCCESS AMIDST THE "WAR JIDDERS"

On July 26, 1967, four more elders flew to Beirut to join Elders Hunt and Fowles. Shortly thereafter, these six missionaries were joined by four more, bringing the total number of missionaries in Beirut to ten. Success attended their labors. On July 27, 1967, the

Maguerian family of four was baptized, as well as another man the very next day. Then, during the week of August 13, five more souls joined the fold, followed by eight more the week after.[41]

As summer came to a close, attendance at Church services had never been so robust. The elders reported that one Sunday there were 150 people in attendance. They filled the small meeting quarters and then overflowed into the hallways and kitchen. The room was so crowded that they had to open the windows to allow those standing to lean out, making room for others.[42]

This type of success did not continue without opposition. On September 20, 1967, Elder Fowles and Elder Hood were arrested on the streets of Beirut and taken to jail without charge. They spent the night in jail and then were released and sent to their apartment with a message that all Latter-day Saint missionaries had five days to leave the country. Shortly after their return to their apartment, they were contacted and told that they would not be forced to leave the country but that they should refrain from any proselytizing activities. When President Mabey heard of these harassments, he flew to Beirut to investigate and assist.[43]

President Mabey learned that the "whole Middle East has the 'war Jidders' and it is difficult for the police to believe that young Mormon elders of military age have any purpose in Lebanon but to spy."[44] To ease this perception, President Mabey visited the U.S. embassy and met with an official named Wesley Eugene Jorgensen. He was friendly but quite unwilling to do anything to assist. Finally, President Mabey explained that they had to leave in order to keep an engagement with Raymond Edde, the very prominent lawyer the Mabeys had met in March 1967. Upon hearing Edde's name, Wesley Jorgensen immediately became quite concerned for the Latter-day Saint cause. In fact, he volunteered to accompany President Mabey to Edde's office as a sign of the embassy's interest in this case.[45]

Once at the law office, President Mabey and Raymond Edde had a private conversation. Edde revealed that he had already been working behind the scenes in behalf of the missionaries. Two days earlier, he had called the offices of the secret police and personally guaranteed that the missionaries were not a security risk. When President Mabey offered to pay a retainer and subsequent fees for his services, Edde explained that he had acted on behalf of the Latter-day Saints because he had come to admire the Mormons very much and that there would never be a charge for any of his services for the Church. He then suggested that if the Church merely functioned as an organization without proselytizing for a time, these difficulties would eventually dissipate. President Mabey received the same counsel from Mr. D. Porter, United States ambassador to Lebanon. It was determined to follow this course.

During this crisis, four families traveled from Kamishly, Syria (on the Euphrates River near the Iraqi border), to Beirut in search of the missionaries. Twelve members of the families were eight years old or older. They had become acquainted with the gospel in their remote city and wanted to receive further instruction leading to baptism. Furthermore, they had to leave for their homes in Syria in two days.

For security reasons, it was not advisable for the missionaries to conduct a large baptismal service. Therefore, President Mabey instructed a Lebanese Latter-day Saint named Zakar Aroyan to take the four families to the beach at 6:00 A.M. the next morning and perform the twelve baptisms. These ordinances were performed without incident. The newly baptized individuals then congregated in President Mabey's room, where they were confirmed.

To ensure that the new members could function as a branch in Kamishly, Syria, President Mabey ordained Kevork Salkhanian a priest and called him to serve as the branch president. Then he ordained Vahan Norsikian, Hacap Katarkijian, and Mardikes Norsikian deacons in the Aaronic Priesthood. Following their departure to Syria, President Mabey wrote of the group that he "was very impressed with the attitude of the new members and their appearance of sincere desire to serve the Lord and work out their salvations by the commandments."[46]

As Raymond Edde had predicted, problems between the secret police and the elders in Lebanon steadily eased until, by the end of October 1967, proselytizing efforts were back to normal. To further ensure that normalcy, President Mabey transferred two elders with Brazilian passports to replace Elders Hood and Fowles, whose missions were complete. It was hoped that the secret police would be hesitant to accuse Brazilian citizens of being spies for the United States. The new missionaries were Werner Spori and Oswaldo Spat.

As the year came to a close, the missionaries in Beirut were enjoying great success, the mission record confirming that "most of the baptisms have come from Lebanon." Hence, the striking effect that this area had on the mission as a whole cannot be overlooked.[47] Concerning the "marvelous work and wonder" in this area, President Mabey wrote, "There seems to be no end to the present string of baptisms that are possible in Beirut."[48]

A New Year, a New Branch, and a New President

The impressive string of baptisms continued in 1968. On January 27, President Mabey was in Beirut to witness the baptism of the Ganimian and Goulgoulian families, these six individuals bringing the total number of baptisms in Beirut to fourteen in the month of January alone. The Beirut Branch now numbered 243.[49]

The branch was a composite of locals (mostly Armenians) and expatriates (mostly Americans). Because many of the Armenian Saints did not speak English and none of the expatriates spoke Armenian, the branch was divided into two groups to accommodate the language needs. President Mabey had wanted to form a second branch, but until January 1968 the number of Saints in Beirut did not justify it. With the influx of converts, President Mabey felt comfortable organizing the Ras Beirut Branch on Sunday, January 28, 1968. Brother Howard C. Stutz, a visiting professor from Brigham Young University, was called to serve as branch president. The Beirut Branch services were held in Armenian, while the Ras Beirut Branch services were held in English. President Mabey viewed the organization of the Ras Beirut Branch as a benchmark of progress, explaining that he "was well pleased when [he] remembered how far the work of the Lord had progressed in Beirut in the last two and one-half years."[50]

By mid-May 1968, changes were in the air. The First Presidency notified President and Sister Mabey that they would be honorably released from their mission in a few weeks. In addition, Joseph Ouzounian, president of the Beirut Branch, announced that he was moving to America to live with his children. Furthermore, Howard Stutz, president of the Ras Beirut Branch, was returning to his teaching duties at Brigham Young University in Provo, Utah. These changes necessitated one final trip to Beirut during Rendell Mabey's presidency.

On Thursday, June 20, 1968, President Mabey arrived in Beirut and met with his missionaries, whom he described as "dedicated, spiritual, and hard working young men."[51] The following day, he conducted interviews among Beirut Branch members and called Sakag Mikael Mikaelian, a convert of just over one year, as the new branch president. When Mabey extended the call, Brother Mikaelian responded, "My President, I will serve."[52]

President Mabey also reorganized the Ras Beirut Branch, calling Michale Simone Layyous as president. He was twenty-six years old and had been a member of the Church for three years, wholly committed to the gospel ever since his baptism. His fluency in English allowed him to preside over the Ras Beirut Branch; thus, for the first time, both branches were presided over by leaders who were long-term residents of Lebanon.[53]

The mission reached yet another significant milestone during President Mabey's final visit to Beirut when he interviewed Garabed Yeghia Tehakmakjian to serve a mission. Tehakmakjian was a twenty-two-year-old convert who had joined the Church with his family the previous year. Born in Aleppo, he spoke fluent Armenian, English, Arabic, and Turkish. President Mabey noted, "If this young man is called to serve on a mission he will be, so far as [I] know, the first missionary to be called from Lebanon, at least in modern times." It was determined that he would pay ten dollars per month and the East Sharon Stake in Provo would pay the remaining ninety dollars per month to sustain him during his mission.[54]

As President Mabey left Beirut for the last time, he marveled that "during the past two and a half years some two hundred members have been baptized in Lebanon. This with an average of six missionaries in active proselyting."[55]

PRESIDENT M. ELMER CHRISTENSEN

President M. Elmer Christensen and his wife, Mabel, arrived in Zurich on July 4, 1968, to preside over the Swiss Mission. On August 16, they traveled to Beirut for the first time, where they found the elders working hard and enjoying success. Then, on October 24, 1968, they visited Beirut again, this time with Elder Thomas S. Monson of the Quorum of the Twelve Apostles. Elder Monson had

Thomas S. Monson of the Quorum of the Twelve was assigned to the Near East as part of his responsibilities as an Apostle in the late 1960s.

recently been assigned the Near East as part of his responsibilities in the quorum, taking the place of Elder Ezra Taft Benson.[56]

During a mission conference, Elder Monson directed the elders to avoid taking the gospel to the Armenian people at that time. Rather, they were to take their message to the Lebanese middle class. The result of this effort would be the establishment of a population of Lebanese Latter-day Saints who could bring leadership and stability to the branches of the Church because they were not looking to emigrate to America, as the Armenian people so frequently did.[57]

Elder Monson's instruction required a great leap of faith for President Christensen and the elders serving in Beirut. Most of the success in Lebanon had come through contacting and teaching Armenian families. Nevertheless, the president and the missionaries were in full agreement to follow the counsel, and appropriate adjustments were made. By the time President and Sister Christensen visited Lebanon in December 1968, the number of elders had dropped from ten to four, due to transfers and releases.

As the new year commenced, the Church still lacked official recognition from the Lebanese government. From time to time, President Christensen would meet with Raymond Edde, who continued to assist in legal matters when called upon. His counsel was simple and consistent: without official recognition, the missionaries could teach only individuals who inquired about the Church and its beliefs. This restriction, coupled with the directive not to teach Armenians in Beirut, meant the work would come to a veritable standstill, with no apparent solution at hand.

President Christensen flew to Beirut and met with the missionaries. He shared his deep concerns for the work and his desire to follow Elder Monson's counsel. When discussion raised no answers to the problem, President Christensen excused the elders and told them to return in a half hour. When the missionaries returned, President Christensen explained that after they had left he had knelt down and petitioned the Lord for a solution to their problem. He further explained that as he had prayed, very definite impressions rested upon him, and he knew what was to be done. The missionaries would use a religious survey through which they could question the people of Lebanon and gauge their interests, concerns, and beliefs regarding God. The survey would include questions like: What does religion mean to you? What church are you most familiar with? What do you think of the idea of revelation? Does God speak to man? What do you think of a prophet living on the earth today? The missionaries would document responses and field any questions that sprang out of the survey interview. This way the missionaries could interact among the people without directly tracting. At the same time, it gave participants the opportunity to ask questions and initiate gospel discussion if they were so inclined. The missionaries utilized this approach immediately and found success.[58]

THE ARAB BRIGHAM YOUNG

According to Elder Stephen Zwahlen, the most impressive success resulting from this new approach came when he surveyed a twenty-five-year-old single man named Ghassan Bikhazi, whom Elder Zwahlen would later refer to as "the Arab Brigham Young."[59]

Brigham Young, second President of the Church (1847–1877), was quite cautious upon his receipt of the Book of Mormon, pondering the book and its message for eighteen months before he was baptized. He was not necessarily cynical—just very methodical in his approach, giving the Book of Mormon his greatest attention. Once Brigham Young joined the Church, he was fully committed and later became known as the Lion of the Lord.[60] As will be seen, there are enough similarities between his conversion and Ghassan Bikhazi's to justify the comparison.

In the spring of 1969, Elder Zwahlen and his companion, Elder Alan Plowgian, approached an apartment wherein four young adults,

Ghassan Bikhazi

all cousins, were socializing. When the missionaries knocked at the door, Ghassan Bikhazi, a Greek Orthodox Christian, opened it just long enough to hear the missionaries give their introduction and then slammed the door in their faces. This evoked a great deal of laughter from his cousins, and they joked about how their priest had warned them not to let any such missionaries into their homes. Despite all this, Ghassan felt acute discomfort about the way he had treated these young men. He told the group that he was going to find the missionaries and invite them in to talk. He ran out the door, chased after the elders, and brought them back to the apartment.

Once in the apartment, the elders shared the story of Joseph Smith's First Vision. The group listened courteously to the missionaries, but once they were finished, Ghassan jokingly taunted them, saying, "You don't really believe that, do you?" Elder Zwahlen looked him steadily in the eye and firmly said, "Yes, we do." Ghassan sparked back, "No, you're just here trying to avoid the draft." At this point, the entire group joined in the tauntings. Elder Zwahlen handed a copy of the Book of Mormon to one of Ghassan's cousins and challenged them all to read and pray about its truthfulness; his invitation was met by ongoing taunts as they left.

Once the missionaries were gone, Ghassan Bikhazi felt a compelling need to read the Book of Mormon. He borrowed the book from his cousin and took it home. In the next three days, he read the entire book and came to know that it was true. Because the book belonged to his cousin, he became frustrated that he could not mark passages within it, and so he sought out the Latter-day Saints on Sunday morning to request a copy for himself.

He found the missionaries in the middle of a fast and testimony meeting. There were only six people in attendance that day when Ghassan Bikhazi joined the meeting, four of whom were missionaries. When the time was turned over to the congregation to share their testimonies, Bikhazi stood up, pulled his cousin's copy of the Book of Mormon out of his coat pocket, held it up before the small congregation, and said, "I know that this book is true, and I know within it are the answers to the problems that face my people here in this country. It is the stick of Ephraim, and the Bible is the stick of Judah. Together they combine to make up the true Church of Christ." He said nothing more and sat down.

After the meeting, the missionaries made every attempt to teach him more about the Church, but Ghassan was not entirely ready at that time, later confessing, "I ran away from the missionaries and the Church." His father had encouraged him to apply to medical school in Egypt, and this became his "Nineveh," where he hoped to escape his feelings about the gospel. However, as he packed his clothing and personal items for the journey by boat, he could not bring himself to leave behind his Book of Mormon. He read it during the entire voyage to Alexandria.

In Egypt, his attempts to enroll in medical school were unsuccessful, and he quickly returned to Lebanon, again reading the Book of Mormon during the entire voyage home. He marked passages and wrote insights and questions in the margins of the book. By the time the boat docked in Lebanon, he had finished it for the second time and had acquired an even deeper conviction that it was true. He then sought out the missionaries and was taught by them. According to Elder Zwahlen, Ghassan was particularly interested in Lehi's dream.

In fact, he shared insights about that portion of the Book of Mormon that the missionaries had never before considered. After further investigation, Ghassan Bikhazi joined the Church on July 19, 1969.

Shortly after his baptism, Brother Bikhazi was interviewed by President Christensen and invited to receive the Aaronic Priesthood. Brother Bikhazi had such great respect for the priesthood of God that he was hesitant to take that step. He declined, but asked President Christensen to give him some time to think about the opportunity. Shortly thereafter, Ghassan Bikhazi had a dream wherein he was brought into the presence of Heber C. Kimball and Heber J. Grant, both Apostles of the Lord who had died decades earlier. They commended his decision to join the true Church of God but warned him that it was essential that he never turn down an advancement in the priesthood or a calling to serve in the kingdom of God. In his dream, Brother Bikhazi committed that he would never hesitate to answer the call of the Lord again. Shortly thereafter, he had the Aaronic Priesthood conferred upon him and went on to receive the Melchizedek Priesthood and the ordinances of the temple. He served in the Beirut Branch presidency, married in the temple, and has been true to his resolve to this day.[61]

The Organization of the Israel Group

An important event in the history of the Church in Israel occurred on August 28, 1969. Brother Darrel L. Hicken, who was then living in Herzliya, Israel, with his wife, Mildred, and two of their four children, visited President Christensen in Zurich. The Hickens had moved to Israel in 1968, where Brother Hicken worked to build a phosphoric acid plant in the Negev. They had located the few Latter-day Saint families (about twelve people in number) living in Israel and had made efforts to bring them together to worship. At the mission home, President Christensen called Darrel Hicken to serve as group leader of the Saints in Israel. Brother Hicken selected David B. Galbraith to serve as his first counselor.[62] Darrel Hicken was not set apart until President Christensen's next visit to Jerusalem on June 8, 1971. This was done at a meeting that night in the Hicken home in Herzliya. There were twenty-three present.[63]

A PROFILE OF THE LATTER-DAY SAINTS IN LEBANON

In December 1970, an article containing an interview with President Christensen was circulated which greatly affected the Lebanese people in their attitudes toward and understanding of the Latter-day Saints in Lebanon. The article, entitled "Qu'il y a des Mormons libanais?" (Are There Lebanese Mormons?), was published in the French magazine *Magazine,* which enjoyed broad circulation in Lebanon. A general overview of the Church's presence in Lebanon, as well as the history of the Church and basic beliefs, were all included in the article. The branch members in Beirut were all pictured in the layout, as well as the First Presidency.[64] As could be expected, the impact of this article was very positive for the missionaries in Beirut.

In the last months of President Christensen's term as mission president, he was able to travel to most of the branches and groups of the Church in the Near East with visits to Lebanon, Saudi Arabia, Iran, Afghanistan, Turkey, and Israel. President and Sister Christensen were replaced by President Edwin Q. Cannon and his wife, Janath, on July 29, 1971.

PRESIDENT EDWIN Q. CANNON

Prior to his call, President Cannon was serving as bishop of his ward and was the manager of the Salt Lake Stamp Company. He held a master's degree in business administration from Harvard. Sister Cannon was a returned missionary, having served a mission to France and Canada. At the time of her husband's call to serve as president of the Switzerland Mission, she was serving on the Church Adult Correlation Committee. She was formerly a member of the Mormon Tabernacle Choir and was a graduate of Wellesley College.[65]

Six weeks after their arrival in Switzerland, President and Sister Cannon toured the branches and groups under his jurisdiction in the Near East. They were greeted at the airport in Beirut by Elders Cook, Murray, Parkinson, and Lewis on September 17, 1971. President Cannon interviewed the elders, spoke at a fireside, met the members, and regulated the affairs of the branches. From Beirut, the Cannons flew to Iran and then to Kabul, Afghanistan, and visited the Williams and Hoopes families. The Cannons were impressed by the way these families interacted with each other and how they maintained their faithfulness as Latter-day Saints. Specifically, President Cannon noted that "these two fine families are grateful for each other and the gospel in this primitive, often discouraging part of the world."[66]

When the Cannons arrived in Tel Aviv, Israel, on September 22, 1971, they were met at the airport by David Galbraith. The Hicken family had since left Israel, and Brother Galbraith had been called to serve as the Israel Group leader. He was set apart that night. Brother Galbraith took the next two days to guide the Cannons through the Holy Land, from Jerusalem and Jericho in the south to Capernaum and Tiberias in the north.

David and Frieda Galbraith shortly after he was appointed director of BYU's Study Abroad program in Israel.

In the history of the Church in the Near East, the contributions of David Galbraith are on a par with those of Jacob Spori, Ferdinand Hintze, and Joseph Booth. He was born in Raymond, Alberta, Canada, and spent most of his life focusing on the history, issues, events, and cultures of the Near East. In 1961, he moved to Israel to study Hebrew and live on a kibbutz. It was there that he met Frieda

Kruger, a native of the Netherlands, whom he would later marry. Upon completing bachelor's and master's degrees at Brigham Young University, the Galbraiths moved to Israel in 1969 so that David could pursue his doctoral studies in international relations at the Hebrew University of Jerusalem. Specifically, he studied and wrote extensively about conflict resolution in Arab-Israeli relations.

In 1972, Brother Galbraith was appointed resident director of BYU's Study Abroad program in Israel. That year, he was also called to serve as the first branch president of the Church in Jerusalem. He personally managed the Study Abroad experience of thousands of students who came to the Holy Land through BYU. As time passed and the Study Abroad program grew, Brother Galbraith was entrusted by the First Presidency to oversee developments that led to the acquisition of property and the construction of the BYU Jerusalem Center for Near Eastern Studies. In 1987, he was named the first director of the Jerusalem Center.[67] A more detailed description of Brother Galbraith's singular contributions to the establishment of a permanent and physical presence of the Church in Israel may be found in the final chapter.

THE GIFT OF TONGUES

While David Galbraith was laying the foundation for a permanent physical presence of the Church in Israel, a pioneering effort was quietly underway in Beirut. Elder Dilworth Parkinson was transferred to Beirut on November 17, 1970. His companion, Elder Phillip Willis, had been there since August and was suffering from serious allergies requiring him to rest or sleep until ten or eleven each morning. President Christensen had charged Elder Parkinson to learn Armenian while serving in Beirut. This troubled Elder Parkinson on two fronts: first, no Latter-day Saint missionary from the Swiss or Switzerland Mission had ever become fluent in Armenian; second, he had struggled with Spanish in junior high school and was convinced that he lacked ability to learn the simplest of foreign tongues, let alone a language as seemingly complex as Armenian. Nevertheless, he took the time that his companion spent recuperating from his allergies and applied himself each morning to the study of Armenian.

The language came to him with ease, and within a matter of weeks Elder Parkinson was conversant in Armenian. In retrospect, he

Elder Dilworth Parkinson in Beirut, Lebanon.
The unidentified woman in the picture is likely a member of the Church.

attributed this rapid acquisition to the gift of tongues. After a time, he was not only fluent but was mistaken as an Armenian American who had learned the language from his parents during childhood.[68] His language skills astonished the local members of the branch and were a boon to the work, since he could communicate with the Armenians in Beirut as no other elder had during this period.

One of Elder Parkinson's frustrations was that their missionary survey was available only in English. He translated it into Armenian, but it was not available in Arabic. Although Armenian is considered a simple language when compared to Arabic, Elder Parkinson determined that he would learn Arabic. He first had branch member George Djaboury translate the survey into Arabic, and then he memorized the survey verbatim. After several attempts to administer the survey in Arabic, he could recite the words perfectly. People assumed that he was fluent, but unfortunately, Elder Parkinson had no idea what was being said in response to his questions. Again, the Holy Ghost granted Elder Parkinson the gift of tongues, and miraculously, after four months, he was fluent enough to converse in Arabic.[69]

This was a turning point in missionary work in the Near East. Elder Parkinson created a "Missionary Training Center" of sorts in Beirut to help other elders learn the languages. He made audio recordings of the discussions in Arabic and Armenian, allowing the missionaries to memorize and learn the dialogue of the discussions. They would then practice among the locals, who were surprisingly anxious to help these young Americans learn their language.

Speaking the native languages opened many doors that otherwise would have remained shut. Missionaries' attitudes were also changing, since now they could communicate with every person in the country who had an interest in the gospel. As one returned missionary later said, "Parkinson was the father of latter-day missionary work in the Near East" because he pioneered the teaching of six ordered discussions of the gospel in the language of the Near Eastern investigator, whether Arab or Armenian.[70]

It would seem to be more than a coincidence that, as Elder Parkinson was breaking language barriers in the Near East, the same thing was happening in the heart of the Latter-day Saint population in Utah. In 1970, Richard Hatch and Mark Wilcox at Bountiful High School were encouraged by a mutual friend to enroll in the high school's new language program. As fate would have it, Bountiful High was one of a handful, if not the only, secondary school in the United States with an Arabic program. During their junior and senior years, they both studied Arabic, completely unaware of Elder Dilworth Parkinson's efforts half a world away. Nevertheless, in 1972, they were both called to serve in the Switzerland Mission and were sent to Lebanon to serve in Beirut, where they benefited from the labors of Elder Parkinson.[71]

Progress in the Expatriate Branches

As had been the case since the establishment of the state of Israel, the Church had no formally called and set-apart missionaries in Israel

The Orin and Rita Parker family, 1973. Back row, left to right: Orin, Jeff, Tanya, and Jamie. Front row, left to right: David, Rita, and Leslie.

in the 1960s and 1970s. However, some expatriates were occasionally baptized. On January 7, 1972, President Cannon received word from David Galbraith that Susanne Hogan had been baptized.[72] On July 4 of that same year, Marion Jean Hooks was baptized in the Jordan River.[73]

On April 7, 1973, President Cannon traveled to Beirut to reorganize the Ras Beirut Branch. Brother Orin Parker was called to be the president, and he selected Gordon Olsen to serve as first counselor and Ghassan Bikhazi as second counselor.[74] Orin Parker and his wife, Rita, were an expatriate family that added great strength to both branches in Beirut. Brother Parker had been in Lebanon since August 1971 as an overseas vice president of American Friends of the Middle East, an educational foundation that coordinated efforts with Fulbright scholarship recipients and exchange students throughout the Near East. They were a catalyst for social and spiritual growth within the branches, cultivating greater leadership skills and assisting in missionary work whenever they could. Investigators found the doors of the Parker home opened wide to welcome them at any time of the day or night. They had five children attending schools in Beirut and were involved in most facets of Beirut society. They frequently entertained Lebanese government officials and, on these occasions, always invited the missionaries to join them.[75] They fostered a culture of acceptance and love among the Saints and people of Beirut.

The Translation of the Book of Mormon into Hebrew

President Harold B. Lee died on December 26, 1973. One of his hopes that remained unfulfilled at the time of his passing was to see the Book of Mormon translated into Hebrew. He had proposed that a translation be started in the latter months of 1972. Previous efforts to translate the Book of Mormon into Hebrew had been undertaken but had not been published by the Church. For example, Herman Miller, a Latter-day Saint, had translated the Book of Mormon into Hebrew in the 1920s, but it was never published.[76] On January 22, 1973, Irvin Nydegger, of the Church Translation Department, traveled to Jerusalem to meet with Dr. Jonathan Shunary. Nydegger showed Shunary Herman Miller's handwritten translation as they discussed the details of the project. Shunary was favorably impressed with the fifty-year-old manuscript and voiced his interest in the project.

Authorization was granted to begin translating on April 17, 1974, and in 1977 an abridged translation of the Book of Mormon in Hebrew was completed.[77]

However, as construction on the Jerusalem Center advanced in

1984, reprinting ceased, and all Latter-day Saint tracts and literature in Hebrew were removed from the country. This was done to allay fears among some in Israel that the Jerusalem Center would be used as a front for missionary activity. This removal bolstered the confidence of many Israelis regarding the Church's outright commitment to prohibit missionary efforts among the people of Israel.[78]

Jonathan Shunary completed an abridged translation of the Book of Mormon in Hebrew in 1977. Publication of the Hebrew translation ceased in 1984 to allay fears that the Jerusalem Center for Near Eastern Studies would be used as a front for missionary activity.

THE INTERNATIONAL MISSION

On May 6, 1974, Elder Howard W. Hunter arrived at the mission home in Zurich, explaining to President Cannon that while Lebanon and Israel would remain in the Switzerland Mission, jurisdiction over Saudi Arabia, Iraq, Iran, Bahrain, and Kuwait would be transferred to the International Mission, which Elder Hunter oversaw as a member of the Quorum of the Twelve. The International Mission was organized on November 9, 1972, and its first president was Elder Bernard P. Brockbank, an Assistant to the Twelve. The purpose of the mission was to serve the needs of "unattached members worldwide."[79] It was determined that President Cannon would visit the branches in those countries one last time during the month of June, when the affected branches gave their sustaining vote.[80] President Cannon arrived back in Zurich on June 24, which gave him two weeks to prepare for the arrival of President Gary O'Brien, who would replace President Cannon on July 8, 1974.

Beirut Branch, 1974.

PRESIDENT GARY E. O'BRIEN

Gary Edward O'Brien, a native of Provo, Utah, was living in the Salt Lake Valley at the time of his call to preside over the Switzerland Mission. He married Juanita Hansen of Fairview, Utah, on June 18, 1959, in the Salt Lake Temple. They had seven children. All seven accompanied the O'Briens to Switzerland. The oldest at the time was a fourteen-year-old daughter, and the youngest child was a one-year-old daughter.[81]

Three weeks after President O'Brien arrived in Switzerland, he traveled to Beirut for the first time and went tracting with the four elders there, later noting that he was "very impressed with the quality, caliber, dedication, and spirit of the four brethren in Lebanon."[82] Then, in mid-September, he returned to Beirut with Elder Loren C. Dunn of the Seventy. Elder Dunn held a missionary conference wherein he counseled the Beirut elders to "work hard and stay in tune with the Spirit."[83] The elders felt very blessed by his visit.

During a special combined branch meeting held after the missionary conference, President O'Brien encouraged the Saints in Lebanon to focus on three things: paying a full tithe, increasing personal spirituality, and putting forth greater efforts to spread the gospel in Lebanon.

Elder Dunn then stood and endorsed the teachings of President O'Brien and added a significant promise. He expressed his feeling that if the Saints in Lebanon would be diligent, one day their branches would grow to become wards and their wards would eventually grow into stakes.[84] The Saints in Beirut listened earnestly, and their faith and spirits were bolstered and lifted up.

One particular benchmark served to accentuate the good accomplished by missionaries and members in Lebanon—the second full-time missionary was called from the Beirut Branch to serve in the Switzerland Mission. The elder was an Armenian Palestinian named Krikor Chobanian. He arrived in Zurich on April 16, 1975, and the next day Sister O'Brien took him shopping for a new suit, ties, shirts, and other missionary essentials he had been unable to purchase beforehand because of the political unrest escalating in Beirut.[85]

Difficulties in Beirut had become increasingly intense since the early 1970s, when the Palestinian Liberation Organization (PLO) had been ousted from Jordan and had established strongholds in southern Lebanon and the Palestinian refugee districts in Beirut. The primarily Muslim infusion into Lebanon alarmed Lebanese Christians, who wanted the PLO removed from the country. Lebanese Muslims knew that without the PLO's private army, they had no chance for representation in the government. Therefore, Lebanese Muslims generally supported the presence of the PLO and opposed any effort to remove them. Political deadlock resulted, and the Lebanese government and army were paralyzed.

On April 13, 1975, gunmen riding in a speeding car opened fire on a Christian church in east Beirut, killing four men. Later that day, a bus full of Palestinian civilians was ambushed by a Christian militia, and twenty-seven were killed in response to the church shootings. The next morning, there was open fighting in the streets of Beirut. Christians gravitated toward Christian militias, while Muslims gathered to their militia forces. The Lebanese government was basically impotent. Civil war was the result.[86]

These events heightened President O'Brien's concern for the missionaries in Beirut and prompted a trip to Lebanon on May 19, 1975. He spent two days with the missionaries, assessing the situation. He determined that they were safe, but he also noted that their ability to proselytize was greatly hindered because of the unrest. For example, curfews were imposed as the conflict escalated. Eventually, all citizens were to be off the streets by 5:00 P.M. every day.[87] The climate was not conducive to formal missionary activities.

Just over two weeks later, President Parker of the Beirut Branch called President O'Brien and explained that circumstances had worsened—the elders were not safe. President O'Brien immediately transferred Elders Steven Whiting and Joseph Javadi to Switzerland, where they completed their missions, while Elders Bicknell Robbins and John Aswad were transferred to Ankara, Turkey, to serve among the Saints in the Ankara Group.[88] It was anticipated that the situation in Beirut would calm, as it had in the past, and then the elders could return.

On June 25, 1975, President Parker called again to inform President O'Brien that it would be safe for the missionaries to return. President O'Brien did not send any missionaries back to Lebanon, however. That very evening, Elder Thomas S. Monson called to explain that the Brethren had recently determined that the entire Near East was to be withdrawn from the Switzerland Mission and be placed under the jurisdiction of the International Mission.[89] None of the former elders returned to Beirut, because the First Presidency had also determined that all American missionaries were to be withdrawn from Lebanon.[90]

Because Elder Chobanian carried a Palestinian passport, Swiss officials would not allow him to stay in Switzerland. On August 21, 1975, he flew back to Beirut to serve under the direction of the president of the International Mission and the Beirut Branch president. President O'Brien sent with him the records of the Armenian members in Lebanon, many of whom had been disconnected from the Church for many years. He also gave Elder Chobanian a charge to contact these members, inquire after their interest in the gospel, minister to their needs, and invite them to branch services.[91] This series of events brought formal missionary efforts to a close in the Near East during this time period.

SPECIAL REPRESENTATIVES IN ISRAEL

As a postlude to this chapter on missionary work in the Near East, special mention should be made of Church representatives who were called to serve in the Holy Land over a period of about eight years, from November 1976 to February 1985.[92] On October 20, 1976, President David Galbraith wrote a letter to Elder W. Grant Bangerter, then president of the International Mission, requesting that full-time Church representatives be sent to Israel. The purpose of their service would be to make friends for the Church and field the many requests for information about the Church that were consuming Church leaders and BYU Travel Study personnel in Jerusalem. They would also lend stability to the branch through leadership training and service and coordinate public relations efforts on behalf of the Church.

Before Brother Galbraith's letter reached President Bangerter, Ivan and Minnie Barrett had been called to serve as full-time Church representatives in Israel. One month later, they received a letter from President Spencer W. Kimball confirming President Bangerter's call:

> Your appointment brings you the opportunity to serve among the members and friends of The Church and includes the authorization to teach the gospel of Jesus Christ to all who will receive you. It will be your duty to live righteously, to keep the commandments, to honor the Priesthood, to increase your testimony of the gospel, and to be an exemplar in your life of all the Christian virtues.[93]

On January 7, 1977, Ivan and Minnie Barrett arrived in the Holy Land. Just over one week later, the Jerusalem District was organized, and Brother Barrett was called to serve as the president. Daniel Rona was called to serve as the first counselor in the district presidency, and Mark Gomm was called to serve as second counselor. (On June 11, 1977, Daniel Rona was called to take David Galbraith's place as branch president in Jerusalem, while Brother Galbraith was called to serve as first counselor in the district presidency.) In the last week of January, Elder Thomas S. Monson of the Quorum of the Twelve Apostles visited Jerusalem and instructed Brother and Sister Barrett to "walk softly in Israel" when it came to sharing the gospel message.[94] The tenor of instruction to these special representatives was clear—if individuals requested to be taught, proceed slowly, methodically, and in a spirit of love. But overt proselytizing was not an option.

Most of the Barretts' time was spent building friendships between the Latter-day Saints, Israelis, and Palestinians. They hosted dinners in their home, dealt with the media, answered questions from all levels of Israeli society, and followed up on the consistent flow of referrals that came to Jerusalem from points around the globe. They also worked tirelessly with David Galbraith to see that the Church was formally recognized by the government of Israel. This recognition was granted on June 16, 1977.

Brother and Sister Barrett served until July 1978, when William and Margaret Mortimer were called to serve in their place. Over the next few years, about sixty individuals were called to serve as special representatives in Israel (see appendix D). However, as construction on the Jerusalem Center for Near Eastern Studies began in earnest in 1985, the special representatives were reassigned to places outside Israel.[95] Just as the Hebrew translation of the Book of Mormon had been withdrawn from circulation, the representatives were taken out of Israel to allay fears that the Jerusalem Center might be used for missionary activity.

CONCLUSION

The presence of Latter-day Saint missionaries in the Near East commenced on December 31, 1884, when Jacob Spori arrived in Constantinople. The following nine decades constitute a rich history for The Church of Jesus Christ of Latter-day Saints. Jacob Spori, Ferdinand Hintze, Joseph Booth, Badwagan Piranian, John Russon, Dilworth Parkinson, and many others made up a force of latter-day pioneers who helped establish a Latter-day Saint presence in a region of the world that is prophetically significant and holy. We hope that the telling of this history of missionary service will embolden disciples of the Master today, wherever they may be, in their efforts to forge new roads, open new doors, and take the gospel to all the world under the specific direction and guidance of living prophets and Apostles.

NOTES TO CHAPTER 9

1. See Thomas L. Friedman, *From Beirut to Jerusalem* (New York: Anchor Books, 1995), 11–13. See also John F. Devlin, *Syria: Modern State in an Ancient Land* (Boulder, CO: Westview Press, 1983), 105–8.

2. Rendell N. Mabey, *The Reaper*, November 29, 1967, 4. *The Reaper* was a weekly publication of the Swiss Mission; this special edition describes

missionary work in Lebanon. Note that the name of the mission in Switzerland which provided missionaries to the Near East was changed from time to time due to the growth of the Church in Europe and changes in mission boundaries. For example, in the case of this citation, the mission is known as the Swiss-Austrian Mission. Later it would be known as the Swiss Mission, the Swiss Zurich Mission, and the Switzerland Mission. For the purpose of this chapter, the uniform title of Swiss Mission will be employed until the mission name is changed to the Switzerland Mission.

3. Mission Record, Swiss Zurich Mission, March 24, 1966, LDS Church Archives.

4. Ibid., Monday, October 10, 1966.

5. This information regarding Maud Pearson was gleaned from the mission records and from telephone interviews by the authors conducted November 1, 2001, with Jean P. Anderson (Maud Pearson's sister) and Orin Parker (who was a close friend to Sister Pearson and was a fellow branch member in Beirut from 1971 to 1975).

6. Mission Record, Swiss Zurich Mission, April 7, 1963.

7. Ibid., April 7–10, 1963.

8. Ibid., February 21, 1964.

9. Ibid., February 23, 1964.

10. Ibid.

11. Mission Record, Swiss Zurich Mission. Details regarding this branch meeting are found in the mission history quarterly report for the period ending March 31, 1964.

12. Mission Record, Swiss Zurich Mission, January 2, 1965.

13. Ibid., March 28, 1965.

14. Ibid.

15. Ibid., March 30, 1965.

16. Ibid., March 31, 1965; see also July 1, 1965.

17. Ibid., August 14, 1965.

18. Ibid., August 27, 1965.

19. Ibid., September 29, 1965.

20. Ibid., September 30, 1965.

21. Ibid.

22. Ibid., June 23, 1966.

23. Ibid., July 14, 1966.

24. Ibid., August 25, 1966.

25. Ibid., October 9, 1966.

26. Ibid., October 12, 1966.

27. Ibid., December 23, 1966.

28. Ibid., March 2, 1967.

29. Ibid., March 6, 1967.

30. Ibid., March 9, 1967.

31. Ibid., March 21, 1967.

32. Ibid., March 16–18, 1967.

33. Ibid., March 22, 1967.

34. Ibid. Unfortunately, the Baghdad Branch was closed on June 7, 1967, as the result of the war between Arabs and Israelis in Israel. Iraq severed diplomatic ties with the United States, and all American families in Iraq were evacuated.

35. Mission Record, Swiss Zurich Mission, May 25, 1967.

36. Ibid., June 2, 1967.

37. Ibid., June 6, 1967.

38. Ibid., June 8, 1967.

39. Ibid., July 16, 1967.

40. Ibid., July 23, 1967.

41. Ibid., August 18 and 24, 1967.

42. Ibid., August 11, 1967.

43. Ibid., September 22 and 26, 1967.

44. Ibid., September 26, 1967.

45. Ibid., September 28, 1967.

46. Ibid., October 1, 1967.

47. Ibid., December 31, 1967.

48. Ibid., November 24, 1967.

49. Ibid., January 27, 1968.

50. Ibid., January 28, 1968.

51. Ibid., June 21, 1968.

52. Ibid., June 22, 1968.

53. Ibid., June 23, 1968.

54. Ibid.

55. Ibid.

56. Ibid., May 28, 1968.

57. S. Stephen Zwahlen, The James Moyle History Program, interview by John R. Sillito, Salt Lake City, UT, January 3, 1975, LDS Church Archives. Elder Monson referred to this pattern of emigration among the Armenian people as the "Go to America" program. Those who could prove they were part of a religious minority and had suffered persecutions could more easily obtain authorization to emigrate to the United States. Mormons qualified as one such persecuted minority, and some impoverished people were baptized not out of an abiding spiritual conviction but in order to expedite their journey to America—hence the directive from Elder Monson.

58. Ibid., 17.

59. Ibid., 22.

60. See Ronald K. Esplin, "Conversion and Transformation: Brigham Young's New York Roots and the Search for the Bible," in *Regional Studies in Church History: New York* (Provo, UT: Department of Church History and Doctrine, Brigham Young University, 1992), 165–201.

61. S. Stephen Zwahlen interview, 22–24. Details were also drawn from a telephone interview with Ghassan Bikhazi by the authors on October 19, 2001, and telephone and e-mail conversations with Stephen Zwahlen, October 29, 2001.

62. Mission Record, Swiss Zurich Mission, August 28, 1969. See also Steven W. Baldridge, *Grafting In: A History of the Latter-day Saints in the Holy Land* (Murray, UT: Roylance Publishing, 1989), 13.

63. Mission Record, Swiss Zurich Mission, June 8, 1971.

64. Denise Ammoun, "Qu'il y a des Mormons libanais?" *Magazine,* December 10, 1970, 38–43; copy in LDS Church Archives.

65. *Church News,* April 17, 1971, 4.

66. Mission Record, Swiss Zurich Mission, September 19, 1971.

67. "Galbraith Named Director of BYU Jerusalem Center," *BYU Today,* June 1987, 7.

68. Personal communication with Dilworth Parkinson, December 5, 2001.

69. Dilworth Parkinson, interview by the authors, Brigham Young University, Provo, UT, June 19, 2001.

70. Mark Wilcox, interview by the authors, Orem, UT, July 5, 2001.

71. Ibid. Upon his return home, Dilworth Parkinson studied Arabic and was selected as one of the top fifteen Arabic students in America. This led to his study of Arabic in Egypt, where he was a key individual in the beginnings of the Cairo Branch of the Church. At the conclusion of his formal training, he was hired by Brigham Young University in the Department of Asian and Near

Eastern Languages. He was the chief editor for the Arabic translation of the Book of Mormon. In fact, for years, any Arabic translations by the Church came across his desk. Examples of this significant workload include the Doctrine and Covenants, the Pearl of Great Price, the Gospel Principles manual, several handbooks of instruction, a hymnal, and the temple ceremony. Brother Parkinson expressed the feeling that his mission was less about converting people in Lebanon and more about awakening an understanding of the Arabic language and a love for Near Eastern peoples. This, in turn, has led to a significant contribution to the work of the Church among Arabic-speaking people everywhere.

72. Mission Record, Swiss Zurich Mission, January 7, 1972.

73. Ibid., July 4, 1972.

74. Ibid., April 8, 1973.

75. Information gleaned by the authors from telephone interviews with the Parkers, summer/fall 2001.

76. Mission Record, Swiss Zurich Mission, January 22, 1974.

77. David B. Galbraith, D. Kelly Ogden, and Andrew C. Skinner, *Jerusalem, the Eternal City* (Salt Lake City: Deseret Book, 1996), 451, note on 472. See also Baldridge, *Grafting In,* 28.

78. Daniel C. Peterson, *Abraham Divided* (Salt Lake City: Aspen Books, 1995), 342. See also Baldridge, *Grafting In,* 75. Baldridge noted that only one thousand copies of the Book of Mormon in Hebrew were published, and nearly all of these copies were used outside of Israel for purposes of study and evaluation.

79. *1974 Church Almanac* (Salt Lake City: Deseret News, 1974), 187.

80. Mission Record, Swiss Zurich Mission, June 20, 1974.

81. *Church News,* May 4, 1974, 13.

82. Mission Record, Swiss Zurich Mission, August 1, 1974.

83. Ibid., September 16, 1974.

84. Ibid.

85. Ibid., April 16–17, 1975.

86. Friedman, *From Beirut to Jerusalem,* 16–18.

87. Personal history of Orin Parker, 190. Copy in authors' possession.

88. Mission Record, Swiss Zurich Mission, June 4, 1975.

89. Ibid., June 25, 1975. The International Mission was presided over at this time by Elder W. Grant Bangerter, who had recently been called to serve as an Assistant to the Quorum of the Twelve.

90. Mission Record, Swiss Zurich Mission, July 17, 1975.

91. Ibid., August 18, 1975.

92. For additional information regarding the special representatives, please see Baldridge, *Grafting In,* 37–75. See also appendix D of this volume.

93. Ivan J. Barrett, "The Story of the Mormons in the Holy Land," unpublished manuscript, 1977, 101. Copy in authors' possession.

94. Ibid., 104.

95. Ellis and Oda Rasmussen were an exception to these reassignments. They were the last couple to serve in the Holy Land. Brother Rasmussen had been a Study Abroad director in 1982 and had recently retired as the dean of Religious Education at Brigham Young University. He was assigned to help David Galbraith create an academic curriculum for the Jerusalem Center. In 1986, after eighteen months of service, the Rasmussens were released. Ellis Rasmussen, telephone interview, by the authors, November 9, 2001. See also Baldridge, *Grafting In,* 74.

CHAPTER TEN

BYU Travel Study and the Jerusalem Center for Near Eastern Studies

From the moment when Jacob Spori first set foot in Constantinople in 1884, the history of the Church in the Near East has been driven by a single major need: to establish a lasting, visible, physical presence in the region to which Saints can gather for strength and others may come for enlightenment. The first nine chapters of this book have chronicled the numerous attempts of faithful missionaries and Church leaders to find or create such a place. Their efforts came to partial fruition in the latter half of the twentieth century with the dedications of a garden and a magnificent building, both situated on a hallowed hillside overlooking Jerusalem.

The Jerusalem Center for Near Eastern Studies is an architectural masterpiece. It is an eight-story building whose terraces gently cascade down the western slope of the Mount of Olives as if the limestone had been chiseled away to reveal the 117 delicate arches that compose the facade of the building.[1] The intent of the design was to draw in light and capture the ancient city of Jerusalem from a myriad of arched vistas. In fact, from the upper auditorium, visitors to the center will see through the towering glass walls that the entire building is oriented toward the

Old City of Jerusalem. Thus, the modern is linked to the ancient, and light is linked to learning. How did The Church of Jesus Christ of Latter-day Saints come to build such a masterpiece in Jerusalem?

The answer to this question constitutes the final chapter of this book, and it begins with Brigham Young University's Travel Study programs. This chapter will provide a general treatment of how a small and untried Travel Study program ultimately led to the building of Brigham Young University's Jerusalem Center for Near Eastern Studies, a story that shows God's power to accomplish the seemingly impossible.

The Arab Development Society

In 1945, the Arab Development Society received a charter in Jerusalem designating it as a charitable organization with the object of raising the social, economic, and educational standards of the Arab villages of Palestine. The Church, along with other charitable organizations, worked with the society in the 1950s and 1960s to bless the lives of Palestinian boys, many of whom had been orphaned and left homeless by the Arab-Israeli War of 1948. In 1949, the society received permission to develop a ranch for the boys in an area of two thousand acres of wasteland lying between the Jordan River and Jericho. The ranch was located about seven miles north of the Dead Sea and two and a half miles east of Jericho on the road to the Allenby Bridge. Once it was finished, the boys took academic classes there, learned how to work on a farm, and studied agriculture and animal husbandry. It was sometimes called the "Boys' Town" of Jordan.

The Church gave substantial help to the Arab Development Society in 1958. It helped finance a large dairy on the farm at the boys' ranch. Louis B. Bigler and others from Utah helped to purchase Holstein dairy cattle and an expensive Holstein bull. Some on the ranch called them "Mormon cows," since they were paid for by contributions of the Latter-day Saints. In the 1960s, the society had two hundred cows. The Church also purchased equipment for the first modern dairy in Jordan and helped build and operate a milk processing plant, which made some of the most delicious ice cream products in Palestine. Many tourist groups visited the farm to learn more about it and especially to sample the ice cream.

Jerusalem lawyer Musa al-Alami (right) with Bertha Vester of the American colony in Jerusalem.

One of the tourists was Daniel H. Ludlow, who made his first visit to Jordan and Israel in 1963. He stayed several days in Jordan, and part of that time was spent at the Arab Development Society as a guest of its founder and director, Musa al-Alami. Ludlow's hosts were Ned and Nedra Smoot of the Smoot Dairy in Farmington, Utah. Ludlow explained that the Smoots "were there to help develop and install a pasteurization unit for the dairy project at the Arab Development Society, which had largely been developed with funds from the Church."[2]

Unfortunately, the success of the boys' ranch and dairy was short-lived because of the Six-Day War of 1967. Robert C. Taylor, director of Brigham Young University's Travel Study programs, visited the Arab Development Society in the fall of 1967, after the Six-Day War, and recorded in his memoirs that "the boys ranch in Jericho was destroyed and the BYU [dairy] herd decimated."[3] Despite the collapse of the dairy, aid offered by the Church was acknowledged and remembered. This involvement created name recognition for the Church and friendships that helped the first Latter-day Saints who traveled to Israel as representatives and faculty members of Brigham Young University.

Daniel H. Ludlow

Daniel H. Ludlow had been a student at Utah State University and Indiana University and had received his doctorate from Columbia University. He later became dean of the College of Religious Instruction at Brigham Young University and director of Church

Correlation. He was the first director of both the BYU Study Abroad program for students in Israel and the Lands of the Scriptures workshop for BYU religion faculty members, which was held in the Near East. Ludlow was the director of instructional materials for the Church and, along with LaMar Berrett, was the director of the production of TV classes for the study of the Book of Mormon at Brigham Young University. He was one of the leaders in establishing the Church's presence in the Holy Land.

Daniel Ludlow's first opportunity to establish connections with the people in the Near East came in 1963, when he was selected to participate with fifteen other university profes-

Daniel H. Ludlow

sors from the United States in an extensive five-week study and travel program sponsored by the State Department. Since he was on sabbatical from BYU, he was able to travel to the Holy Land several months ahead of the group so he could obtain the necessary background to receive maximum benefit on his first tour of the region.

During Ludlow's first several weeks in Israel, he lived in West Jerusalem. He shared an apartment with a Latter-day Saint student named Charles Stephens, who was doing graduate work in archaeology. Brother Ludlow also spent time on Kibbutz Allonim in the west end of the Jezreel Valley. Between July 23 and August 9, 1963, he toured Israel with other university professors in a program directed by New York University. During their tour of the Negev, Ludlow enjoyed his initial visit with Israel's first prime minister, David Ben Gurion. They met and had dinner at Sde Boker, the kibbutz where Ben Gurion lived in southern Israel.[4] During this tour, Ludlow also became acquainted with many of the religious, educational, and political leaders of Israel.

Daniel Ludlow's second opportunity to build friendships in the Near East was tied to a group of young folk dancers from southern California. They were all Latter-day Saints and came, for the most part, from San Diego, Arcadia, and Pasadena. The youth group had been organized in 1959 largely through the interests and efforts of Mildred Handy and two of her children, David and Lani.[5] They had made friends with Jewish groups in California and were invited to perform in Israel in 1964. They were known as the Yovail dance group.

Robert Taylor, director of BYU's Travel Study Department, asked Daniel Ludlow to direct the three-week tour for the young dancers. Sixty-three young men and women, including chaperones, entertained in cities from Galilee to Beersheba and danced in the National Folk Dance Festival in Tel Aviv. They were so well received in Israel that they were awarded the second-ever Pilgrim's Peace Medal, presented by Abba Eban, the deputy prime minister of Israel. The first Pilgrim's Peace Medal was awarded to Pope Paul VI.[6]

Daniel Ludlow's experience in Israel, studying and teaching the scriptures "on site," heightened his interest in the Holy Land, and the opportunity and accompanying enthusiasm were passed on to many of his colleagues at Brigham Young University. But Ludlow was not the first faculty member to use travel to expand the classroom at BYU. In fact, the roots of Travel Study at BYU reach back into the early decades of the twentieth century. Moreover, the curiosity that led Ludlow to the Holy Land is a reflection of an undergirding philosophy of teaching and learning at the university. Two mottos central to the mission of the school express this philosophy. They are mounted on large and permanent decorative placards on either side of BYU's west entrance. The first motto is "Enter to Learn, Go Forth to Serve." The second is "The World Is Our Campus." Given these institutional imperatives, Travel Study programs offered an ideal educational experience for students and faculty. The early educational trips enjoyed by Ludlow and others eventually evolved into a far-reaching Travel Study program.

Robert C. Taylor

The foremost pioneer in building a Travel Study program in the Near East was Robert C. Taylor. As the director of BYU Travel Study,

Robert C. Taylor

Brother Taylor was heavily involved in creating successful Study Abroad programs in France, Spain, and Austria. Creating a Study Abroad program to Israel was an outgrowth of these successes.

Robert C. Taylor, great-grandson of Church President John Taylor, was appointed director of BYU Travel Study on December 1, 1959. He was captivated by and drawn to the Holy Land, and through his efforts, many members of The Church of Jesus Christ of Latter-day Saints were introduced to the Holy Land and the Near East. The idea to construct a study center in Jerusalem as an extension of the BYU Provo campus was the ongoing passion of his professional life. Therefore, his vision, planning, and execution of Travel Study programs became a major impetus to the realization of his dream to establish a study center in Jerusalem. Brother Taylor was married to Katherine (Kathy) Cook of Salt Lake City. Kathy shared her husband's passion for Jerusalem and helped shape the dreams and plans that eventually resulted in the construction of the Jerusalem Center.

Brother Taylor was a persuasive and likeable person whose personality won him the respect of many during his long tenure at BYU— especially among the Brethren. They listened to his suggestions and supported his desire for educational excellence in foreign lands. This respect assisted Brother Taylor's later efforts to raise money to build the Jerusalem Center. He encouraged wealthy persons to direct large amounts of their money to this cause as well as student aid programs. Brother Taylor's investment of time, energy, and resources was monumental, and when he was finally able to see the beautiful BYU Jerusalem Center for Near Eastern Studies in full operation, he wept openly. To him, the completion of the Jerusalem Center was a latter-day miracle.

When Brother Taylor's health began to fail in 1992, he was hospitalized and sometimes comatose. Over the next three years, Brother Taylor was in and out of the hospital until he passed away in 1995. During one of his hospital stays, he wrote the following in a letter to

President Howard W. Hunter and Elder James E. Faust, with whom he had worked so closely in the development of the Jerusalem Center:

> As I lay in my hospital bed during the past few weeks, I had time to think and ponder about why the Lord had preserved my life. The strongest impressions that came to my mind, with surprising clarity, concerned the finishing of the Jerusalem Center. . . . In retrospect, I see that my life has been filled with a long series of remarkable events that seemed to point me in the direction of Jerusalem, the Holy City, and the development of an impossible dream in that hallowed place. . . . There had not been a day in the last 27 years when my mind had not dwelt on Jerusalem and the Holy Land.[7]

In memory of the many contributions of Robert C. Taylor toward this realization, many friends and family members donated to the Jerusalem Foundation, which planted one thousand trees in the Robert C. Taylor Memorial Gardens on Mount Scopus, not far from the Jerusalem Center. A greater appreciation for the work of Robert Taylor and others may be gained by exploring the early stages of BYU Travel Study in the Holy Land and the eventual realization of the Jerusalem Center dream.

BYU's First Study Abroad Program in Jerusalem

During the early 1960s, Daniel H. Ludlow met several times with BYU administrators about the possibility of having BYU students participate in a Semester Abroad program in the Near East. The proposal was finally approved by the First Presidency with the provision that "half of the program be in Arab territory and half in Israel."[8] The First Presidency's position of neutrality in the region guided the establishment of an educational program.

In the fall of 1966, arrangements were made for half of the program to be conducted at the Ritz Hotel, just north of the Old City in Jerusalem, Jordan, and the other half to be conducted in Israel on kibbutzim and in youth hostels. The 1967 war between Israel and several Arab nations disrupted all arrangements, and it was necessary to put the program on hold for a time. However, in January 1968, the

Study Abroad program began in Jerusalem under the direction of the new dean of the College of Religious Instruction, Daniel H. Ludlow.

It had been difficult recruiting the students because of the Six-Day War, but as final preparations were made, twenty students had enrolled in the program. Robert Taylor felt it was a miracle that they had recruited even twenty. In February 1968, Daniel and his wife, Luene Ludlow, in company with their BYU students, departed for the lands of the Bible. The group visited Paris, Rome, Athens, Egypt, and Jordan (including Petra), with additional stops in Cyprus and Lebanon.

The group did not remain in one place for very long. In fact, their frequent travels throughout the land prompted the Brethren to form a "traveling branch" to accommodate the spiritual and ecclesiastical needs of the group while in the Holy Land. The new branch made it possible for the students to meet independent of the small Latter-day Saint congregation in Jerusalem when travel took them to places such as Galilee and Egypt. Brother Ralph Benson, a student and also a nephew of Ezra Taft Benson of the Quorum of the Twelve Apostles, served as the branch president.[9]

After nearly four months in the Holy Land, the group boarded a plane in Tel Aviv and departed for home on May 31, 1968. This 119-day semester was considered a great success, offering a hands-on experience amidst the sacred places in the life of the Savior.

Daniel Ludlow, with the help of Robert Taylor and others, started a tradition that has blessed the lives of thousands of Study Abroad students in Jerusalem. Fortunately, the positive impact of traveling to the Holy Land was about to be extended to many more Latter-day Saints.

THE LANDS OF THE SCRIPTURES WORKSHOP

On the heels of the success of the student Study Abroad program, Ludlow initiated something similar for the BYU faculty of religion and, eventually, seminary and institute instructors in the Church Educational System (CES), allowing them to have the same hands-on opportunity. The workshop tour came to be known as "Lands of the Scriptures." During the first workshop Ludlow led in 1968, there was some free time while in Istanbul, Turkey. Wanting to fill that time productively, BYU faculty member LaMar Berrett organized a private taxi tour of Istanbul for himself and some colleagues. They saw the original Siloam Inscription taken from the walls of Hezekiah's Tunnel in Jerusalem, the Asian side of Istanbul, and many other places not scheduled for the regular Istanbul city tour.

Seemingly impressed by the organization of this private tour, Ludlow asked a surprised Brother Berrett if he'd like to lead the next Lands of the Scriptures workshop. Although one of the junior members of the religion faculty at BYU, Berrett was formally selected to direct the second workshop in 1971.

Three highlights made this tour noteworthy. First, Yigael Yadin, chief archaeologist of the Masada archaeology dig and author of the books *Masada* and *The Temple Scroll,* gave this group a private slide lecture on the Temple Scroll. Second, the tour itinerary included sites never before visited by the faculty, such as Iraq, with the following significant biblical sites—Nineveh, Ashur, Ur, and Babylon. The third highlight was meeting with the first prime minister of the state of Israel, David Ben Gurion, in his Negev home at Kibbutz Sde Boker.

Many efforts were made by BYU professors to acquaint Israel's leaders with the background of the Latter-day Saints and with the history and standards of Brigham Young University. However, many

LaMar C. Berrett and his daughter Susan with David Ben Gurion, Israel's first prime minister.

of the leaders were already familiar with this background. For example, Daniel Ludlow related:

> The first faculty study tour of the Lands of the Scriptures was in the summer of 1968. As director of the tour I had asked some of the faculty participants to prepare some background information on the Church and on BYU that they could review for the various religious and political leaders as we met with them in Rome, Constantinople, Jerusalem, etc. When we met with David Ben Gurion, the first prime minister of Israel, at the kibbutz where he had retired [Sde Boker], Brother David Yarn and his wife, Marilyn, went with me to meet privately with Ben Gurion while the remainder of the faculty toured the Kibbutz before they came in for their formal visit.
>
> I suggested to Ben Gurion that perhaps Brother Yarn could take a few minutes to provide background on the LDS Church and on BYU, and then he could ask Brother Yarn whatever questions he wanted.
>
> Mr. Ben Gurion responded in his usual blunt direct style, "It seems it would be better if I should tell you what I know about your church and about BYU, then you could add whatever you feel is necessary."
>
> That, of course, is what we did. For about twenty minutes Ben Gurion talked about the Church, quoting quite extensively from the Orson Hyde dedicatory prayer (much of which he had evidently memorized) and from earlier contacts he had with his friend, Ezra Taft Benson, who, as U.S. Secretary of Agriculture, had made a formal state visit to Israel.
>
> Then Ben Gurion graciously turned to Brother Yarn and said, "Now you add anything you want."
>
> And Brother Yarn replied: "I don't know anything important to add."[10]

These experiences illustrate how the Travel Study programs helped establish a credible and trusted presence in the Holy Land. The programs created avenues wherein Latter-day Saints could meet and associate with many notable personalities in the state of Israel, as well as other nations of the Near East. The resulting relationships played a significant role in yet-to-be-undertaken projects of the Church in the region, such as the Orson Hyde Memorial Garden and the Jerusalem Center for Near Eastern Studies.

SECOND STUDY ABROAD IN JERUSALEM

A second Study Abroad for students in Jerusalem was put on hold through 1969, 1970, and 1971 because of lingering regional instability and dangers associated with the Six-Day War. By 1972, however, conditions in the Near East had improved, and the Study Abroad program to Israel was reinstituted. A sampling from this second group's experience illustrates how BYU students in the Near East are acknowledged, respected, and loved by their Near Eastern hosts.

In January 1972, a group of forty students entered Israel by way of Jordan. Led by director LaMar C. Berrett, the group made history as the first tourists since the 1967 war to cross from Jordan into Israel by way of the Allenby Bridge, which spans the Jordan River east of Jericho. Much publicity accompanied this event, including nationwide television coverage in Israel and international coverage that reached the United States.

The Jordanians had given the BYU students the "red-carpet" treatment. The government and Jordan University had assigned two Palestinian students to accompany and host the BYU group of young adults

David Galbraith holds a sign welcoming the first group of BYU Travel Study students to enter Israel following the 1967 Six-Day War.

for seven days. One of these students in particular was a powerful model of the goodness and competence of the Palestinian people. He spoke near-perfect English, dressed very neatly, and treated the group with due respect. Everyone loved Usama Samhuri. After spending a week together visiting the sites, the two student hosts were delivered back to the Jordan University campus. When Brother Berrett got off the bus to say good-bye, Usama said, with tears in his eyes, "If that is the type of students you have at Brigham Young University, that is where I want to go to school."

BYU students crossing the Allenby Bridge, which spans the Jordan River, along Israel's border with Jordan. They were the first tourists to enter Israel following the 1967 Six-Day War. Their entrance received national coverage by Israeli newscasters.

As much as he did not want to admit it, Berrett thought he would never see Usama again, because it was so difficult for Palestinians to get visas to travel to the United States. However, with the help of the caring faculty he had met, Usama was finally accepted at BYU to work on a Ph.D. in microbiology. During his schooling, he fell in love with Cathy Jensen from Barnwell, Canada, and they were married in Cardston, Alberta, Canada. Following the completion of his doctoral work, Usama and Cathy traveled to Irbid, Jordan, where

Usama taught microbiology at Yarmouk University. As time passed, Usama's brothers, Tarak and Moshen, also enrolled at BYU. Moshen and Tarak both graduated from the university, and Moshen also met his wife at the Provo campus. Since this time, many young people from the Near East have studied at Brigham Young University.

THE CITY HOTEL

Students of the second BYU Study Abroad in Jerusalem were fortunate to live in the first facility they could call their own. The facility was the City Hotel in Sheikh Jarrah, north of the Old City of Jerusalem. Additionally, some faculty members were drawn from the local academic community. Aviva Haim was hired to teach Hebrew two hours each day, and prominent Hebrew University archaeologist

The City Hotel, just north of the Old City of Jerusalem.

Yohanan Aharoni taught archaeology. His instruction was built upon by fellow archaeologist Benjamin Mazar, who directed the students' participation in an archaeology dig at the southwest corner of the Holy Mount.

In addition to the City Hotel, most of the students stayed in private Jewish homes during the week of Passover. The students' interactions with members of the community in their schools, and at times in their homes, brought an added dimension of trust to this growing relationship.

As pioneer directors of this early program, LaMar Berrett and his assistant, Keith Meservy, had to invent and reinvent the program, working through its problems and guiding its evolution. Competent friends like David Galbraith, who had considerable knowledge about the region and had developed important sensitivities necessary to interact with the culture, were invaluable.

Frequently, however, the early directors of the program did not have the assistance of anyone. Rather, they were left with the students in a variety of situations that could only be solved by faith, prayers, and determination. For example, when the 1972 group went to the Sinai, Brother Berrett came to realize early in the trip that the bus driver had never been there. In the middle of the Sinai desert, the driver said to LaMar Berrett, "You drive!" Sandy roads branched off in all directions from a barely visible main road. Silent prayers were offered, directions were determined, and at eleven o'clock that night, they arrived at their destination with time to sleep for a few hours before the hike to the summit of Mount Sinai began.

While bus companies and travel agencies made adjustments to become better acquainted with the program's travel destinations, Berrett and Meservy made every effort to bring the fledgling university program to the attention of high-ranking members of the Israeli and Palestinian communities where they lived. For example, the 1972 group visited with the first prime minister of Israel, David Ben Gurion. The group traveled to Tel Aviv to meet with Ben Gurion in his private apartment. Meeting Ben Gurion was a memorable experience for every member of the group. Also, Brother Berrett and Brother Meservy surmised that a very

David Ben Gurion, Israel's first prime minister, surrounded by the 1972 BYU Study Abroad students in his private apartment in Tel Aviv.

positive impression was made on Ben Gurion as he visited with the forty Latter-day Saints. It cannot be overstated how important such meetings were to the establishment of a long-term and trusted presence of the Latter-day Saints and Brigham Young University in the Holy Land.

ELDER N. ELDON TANNER IN THE HOLY LAND

In 1972 a flurry of excitement among the students resulted from the announcement that N. Eldon Tanner, first counselor in the First Presidency, would arrive in April. Up to this time, a member of the First Presidency visiting Jerusalem and Galilee was a rarity. The directors and students immediately made every effort to make his arrival memorable, creating a large banner that stated, "THIS IS THE 'OTHER' PLACE." Berrett took the banner to the Lod Airport and displayed it on the runway when he picked up President Tanner and his wife, Sara. Elder Franklin D. Richards, Assistant to the Quorum of the Twelve, and his wife, Helen, were traveling with the Tanners.

After traveling to Tiberias to meet with the students, they embarked on an eight-day tour of the Holy Land, with LaMar Berrett as their

President N. Eldon Tanner and his wife, Sara, standing beside a banner created to welcome them to the Holy Land.

guide. The tour was very significant, because it was one of the earliest occasions when the idea of building a visitors' center and a memorial to Orson Hyde was mentioned. As it turned out, President Tanner's involvement in both projects was crucial. In fact, as a counselor to President Spencer W. Kimball in 1979, President Tanner would help make the final decision regarding the building site of the Jerusalem Center.

PRESIDENT HAROLD B. LEE IN THE HOLY LAND

In September 1972, Church President Harold B. Lee traveled to the Holy Land. This was the first time a Church President had visited the Holy Land in some two thousand years. According to David B. Galbraith, the visit had five significant repercussions: (1) Sabbath day observance would be moved from Sunday to Saturday; (2) a memorial would be built to honor Orson Hyde; (3) the Book of Mormon would be translated into Hebrew; (4) a building would be constructed to serve as a visitors' center and a permanent place where Latter-day Saint religious services could be held; and (5) the Jerusalem Branch would be organized.[11]

President Harold B. Lee was the first President of The Church of Jesus Christ of Latter-day Saints to visit the Holy Land.

President Lee was traveling with Elder Gordon B. Hinckley of the Quorum of the Twelve Apostles (who, just over two decades later, would become President of the Church) and President Edwin Q. Cannon of the Switzerland Mission. They arrived in Jerusalem from Athens on September 19, 1972, and checked into the Intercontinental Hotel on the Mount of Olives. During their stay in

Jerusalem, President Lee's life was spared because of the power of a priesthood blessing. President Hinckley later recalled:

> On that trip President Lee became quite ill. . . . Late one evening Sister Lee rang our room and asked if I would give her husband a blessing. President Edwin Q. Cannon of the Swiss Mission was traveling with us on this assignment, so I asked him to join me in administering to the President. We did so, and then, with a good deal of concern about President Lee's health, I went to bed.

> Later in the night President Lee began to cough, and it went on for some time. Situated as we were in adjoining hotel rooms, I could hear him. He coughed and coughed and coughed. Finally all of that stopped and I went off to sleep, grateful he had been given some relief.

> Brother Lee said nothing at all of the matter the next day, but on the following day he said to me, "We had to come to the land of miracles to witness a miracle within ourselves!" He then told me how in the most violent coughing, he had coughed up a very large clot of blood. Just a little more than one year later, he died from what was spoken of as a pleural embolism.[12]

SEPTEMBER 20, 1972: A HISTORIC DAY

On September 20, President Lee, Elder Hinckley, and President Cannon visited Jerusalem's mayor, Teddy Kollek.[13] During the meeting, Mayor Kollek said, "You know, we Jews wouldn't be here if it weren't for Mr. Orson Hyde and his prayer on the Mount of Olives." President Lee used this comment as a springboard to inquire of the mayor regarding the possibility of the Latter-day Saints building a combined visitors' center and chapel for Church members in Jerusalem. Mayor Kollek seemed in favor of the idea from its first mention.

That evening, the students and faculty gathered with these leaders for a meeting at the Garden Tomb. During President Lee's talk, he said that he felt impressed that the Garden Tomb was the site where the Savior was buried and resurrected.[14] President Cannon also spoke, mentioning the upcoming arrival of more students to join the

Jerusalem Saints and indicating that he felt impressed to organize them into the Jerusalem Branch. President Lee agreed, and later that day, David B. Galbraith was called and set apart by President Lee as the new branch president. Referring to the events of this meeting, John Tvedtnes wrote, "Our prayers were answered fully—and then some! Mark the date of September 20, 1972, on your calendar as one of the most significant days in the history of the Latter-day Restoration."[15]

This spirit of enthusiasm permeated the branch after President Lee's inspired visit to the Holy Land. Beyond organizing the Jerusalem Branch, President Lee also charged local leaders to search out a parcel of land on the Mount of Olives for the purpose of erecting a memorial to commemorate Orson Hyde's dedicatory prayer of 1841. President Lee also authorized local Church leaders to locate land for the purpose of constructing a building that would serve as a meeting place for the Saints in the Holy Land. This second directive came as a surprise to the Saints in Israel because they were so few in number and, according to Church physical facility policies, did not warrant a building at that time. This search would ultimately lead to the establishment of the Jerusalem Center for Near Eastern Studies. The prophet's vision of future events and future Church needs in the Holy Land greatly exceeded that of the Saints. September 20, 1972, serves as a benchmark in Church history, as many major events and undertakings of the Church in the Holy Land find their beginnings rooted in President Lee's visit.[16]

The Sabbath on Saturday

Jerusalem is home to three major religions: Judaism, Christianity, and Islam. None of the three shares the same day of worship. Islam recognizes Friday as a holy day, Judaism celebrates the Sabbath on Saturday, while Christianity generally adheres to a Sunday day of worship. These differences posed significant challenges in the lives of the Saints living in the Holy Land, and David Galbraith posed questions regarding this matter to President Lee during the prophet's visit to Jerusalem. Following President Lee's visit, branch president David Galbraith wrote a letter to the First Presidency wherein he outlined four major concerns and formally recommended that the day of worship for Latter-day Saints in the Holy Land be changed. The four concerns were as follows: First, for the Jews, public transportation ceases on Saturday, stores and places of entertainment are closed, and in Jerusalem the streets are full of families going to and from their synagogues. Second, Sunday, on the other hand, is a normal working day. Those attending the universities have classes, many of the children have school, and, in fact, everyone except those in the diplomatic corps have other obligations on that day. Third, the members were scattered throughout the country, and the majority relied on public transportation. It would be impossible to hold late afternoon or evening services on Sunday. Fourth, the members of the Church had been holding their meetings on the Jewish Sabbath rather than Sunday for some time with at least the tacit approval of the mission.

Two months after President Harold B. Lee's visit to the Holy Land, he authorized President David Galbraith to conduct worship services in Israel on the Jewish Sabbath (Saturday). This authorization is dated November 20, 1972. This decision in Israel served as a precedent to include Friday observance as a day of worship in countries of primarily Islamic populations, such as Egypt and Jordan.[17]

SINGING, DANCING, AND WAR!

H. Donl Peterson accepted the post of director over the third and fourth BYU Study Abroad programs in Israel, which were conducted in 1973. The first group, composed of forty-three students, arrived in January and stayed through June, while the second group, composed of twenty-seven students, arrived in July and left in December.[18] Brother Peterson selected Richard Openshaw, a student participating in the program, to serve as an assistant director for the first half of 1973, and Russell Rogers, a student from the second group, to serve as an assistant director for the second half of the year. The need for an additional administrator was evident. In 1973, the BYU Department of Travel Study hired David Galbraith to represent and assist the department in its operations in Israel. Galbraith held this position until 1987, when he was appointed to be the first director of the Jerusalem Center for Near Eastern Studies.

Beyond studying the life of the Savior and the prophets of the Old and New Testaments, the most singular experience of the first group of 1973 occurred in the harsh deserts of the Sinai Peninsula. War was brewing in the area, and thousands of Israeli troops had been deployed in the Sinai to discourage the Egyptian army from crossing the Suez Canal to attack Israel. The forty-three participants in the Study Abroad program organized a singing and dancing extravaganza, and the students were invited to tour the Sinai with their show and entertain the thousands of soldiers stationed in the desert. The Israeli army housed, fed, and directed the Sinai tours for the BYU students. The experience of this group as they traveled and performed before thousands of Israeli soldiers in the Sinai was a significant step toward opening hearts and minds of people who would later remember these young Latter-day Saints for their unique qualities of goodness. Not long after their whirlwind tour, the students left Israel for home and were replaced by the July–December Study Abroad students.

Donl Peterson immediately went to work to enhance the academic program and make the new students feel at home in the City Hotel. The semester progressed as planned until the Sabbath of October 6. October 6 was Yom Kippur, or Day of Atonement, the single most important day of the Jewish calendar (see Lev. 16). War erupted on that day in 1973 as surprise attacks were launched against Israel. In the course of the war, Israel was attacked on its northern borders by Syria and its southern borders by Egypt.[19]

To allay fears at home, Donl's wife, Mary Lou Peterson, drafted a letter which was sent to the parents of each student in the program, explaining that everyone was safe and in good spirits. The letter was also sent to BYU president Dallin H. Oaks, who published it in the BYU newspaper, *The Daily Universe.*

While fighting did not break out in Jerusalem, it was deemed prudent to evacuate the Peterson family and all students. They were to spend the remainder of their Study Abroad experience in Europe. Study Abroad students did not return to Israel until January 1974. The combined experiences of these initial Study Abroad groups indicates the progress of the Church's presence in the Holy Land. Their success created a foundation for the decades to follow, including the eventual building of the Jerusalem Center.

The Orson Hyde Memorial Garden
of the Jerusalem National Park

While Jerusalem Study Abroad students came and went, there remained Jerusalem Branch members who were permanent or semipermanent residents of Israel. From the time that President Lee authorized local leaders to search out land for an Orson Hyde memorial, the Saints shared a collective yearning to erect a monument on the Mount of Olives in hopes that it would signify the long-term interests of the Latter-day Saints in the Holy Land.[20]

In retrospect, it seems apparent that two Latter-day Saints made the Orson Hyde Memorial Garden a practical possibility while the project was still in the planning stages. They were Robert Taylor and David Galbraith. Robert Taylor, as has previously been noted, was highly respected by the leaders of the Church. He lived in Provo, Utah (relatively near Church headquarters), interacted with Church leaders on matters dealing with the Near East, and had opportunity to present the idea of an Orson Hyde memorial in Jerusalem. The leaders of the Church looked favorably on the project. Taylor served to keep Church leaders informed and involved. On the other hand, David Galbraith was living in Israel, where he could pursue the project with officials in Jerusalem. This led Galbraith to a significant friendship with the mayor of Jerusalem, Teddy Kollek. Mayor Kollek became a crucial advocate of the Saints as they worked to establish the memorial. In the end, Teddy Kollek's help with the Orson Hyde memorial would serve as an important precursor to the building of the Jerusalem Center.

TEDDY KOLLEK

Teddy Kollek was born in Vienna, Austria. In 1934, he traveled to Palestine and became a member of Kibbutz Ein Gev on the east shore of the Sea of Galilee. As time passed, he was drawn to public service. He was eventually appointed Israel's minister in Washington, D.C., where he served from 1950 to 1952. This post was followed by an appointment to serve as director general of the prime minister's office, beginning in 1952. In this position, Kollek played a key role in building up Israel's tourist industry and in founding the Israel Museum.[21]

In 1965, Teddy Kollek was elected mayor of Jerusalem, and he held that office for twenty-eight years (1965–1993). During his tenure as mayor of Jerusalem, many would agree that Teddy Kollek made special efforts to promote Jewish-Arab cooperation in the city—especially following the 1967 war.

Mayor Kollek was a champion of religious liberty and tolerance. Evidence for this may be found in his treatment of the Latter-day Saints in Jerusalem. His early friendship with David Galbraith grew

into a genuine concern for the Latter-day Saints in the city he governed. Speaking of Teddy Kollek, Robert Taylor wrote that "without his encouragements, even in the face of serious obstacles and political concerns—the BYU Center for Near Eastern Studies would not have become a reality."[22] Teddy Kollek took a personal interest and a leading role in finding a suitable location to build a study center for Brigham Young University, a stance that would bring significant opposition to the mayor and his staff.

Teddy Kollek, mayor of Jerusalem, entering the Jerusalem Center for Near Eastern Studies, May 1988.

Mayor Kollek's friendship with the Saints in Israel, and his contributions to the Church's efforts to establish a monument honoring Orson Hyde and to build the Jerusalem Center for Near Eastern Studies, were recognized in Provo, Utah, in the summer of 1995. At that time, the eighty-four-year-old former mayor was awarded an honorary doctorate by Brigham Young University. This honor suggests that his role in the establishment of the Orson Hyde memorial and the Jerusalem Center was critical and that his character was upstanding and honorable.[23]

A Spiritual Garden

When the subject of a memorial was raised with Mayor Kollek by David Galbraith, it was the mayor's suggestion that the monument should be located in a "spiritual garden" on the Mount of Olives. Mayor Kollek told David Galbraith that parts of the west slope of the Mount of Olives were soon to be declared a national park made up of a series of green and verdant parks intended to encircle and beautify the city of Jerusalem.

Once the mayor's reaction to the proposal was reported to the First Presidency, enthusiasm grew and assignments were made. The First Presidency appointed Elder LeGrand Richards of the Twelve to organize an Orson Hyde Foundation to raise money. This was essential, because research indicated that the Orson Hyde Memorial Garden would necessitate a one-million-dollar donation to the Jerusalem Foundation from the Orson Hyde Foundation. While Elder Richards spearheaded the fundraising, Elder Howard W. Hunter of the Quorum of the Twelve was appointed project manager, with the responsibility to oversee the entire project from planning to construction to dedication. In addition, Orson Hyde's great-grandson Orson Hyde White was appointed chairman of the foundation.

RECOGNITION OF THE CHURCH IN ISRAEL

As David Galbraith worked with Jerusalem officials on this project, as well as searching for property for an educational center, it became increasingly evident that the Church would need to receive official recognition by the government of Israel. Without such recognition, the Church could not formally interface with the Israeli government in certain capacities and could not, among other things, own or lease property in Israel. Therefore, Brother Galbraith made every effort to gain recognition at the earliest possible moment.

In order to be granted official recognition, evidence had to be presented proving that The Church of Jesus Christ of Latter-day Saints had roots in Palestine prior to the establishment of the state of Israel. To assist with this requirement, Brother Galbraith called upon LaMar Berrett for help. At the time, Berrett was teaching in the Department of Church

LaMar C. Berrett (left) with David Galbraith.

History and Doctrine at BYU and had gathered many significant historical documents related to the history of the Church in the Near East.

In a letter to Brother Berrett dated September 23, 1976, David
Galbraith wrote:

> It looks like we are getting closer to buying land [for a center] . . .
> but to do so we must register either the church or the university
> with the government. That will entail some serious problems
> since they are trying to discourage all these new sects and
> denominations from coming into Israel and establishing firm
> roots. If, however, we can demonstrate that we were officially in
> Palestine before the State of Israel was established in May, 1948,
> then we will have no problem.
>
> . . . We need documentary proof that we were here. . . . Getting
> officially registered in Israel will be a big and historic step
> forward for the Church.[24]

Berrett organized the necessary historical documentation which
proved that, while the Church had never owned land in Palestine
before Israel had become a state, there had been a significant, long-
term Latter-day Saint presence in Palestine long before that time.
Some points that were included in Berrett's presentation to Galbraith
were: (1) The Church had established missions (Turkish, Armenian,
and Palestine-Syrian) decades prior to 1948. Each of these missions
established a significant interest and, in some cases, a physical presence in Palestine. (2) The Church had many missionaries who had
labored in the Near East, five of whom were buried in the region,
including two in Haifa.[25] (3) Church branches had been organized in
Haifa and Jaffa and other places in the Near East. (4) The Church
had rented buildings in Palestine, which served as mission homes and
meetinghouses. (5) The Church had operated a school in Aleppo,
Syria, which, while not in Palestine, suggested a long-term interest in
educational pursuits in the region. (6) The Church had strongly
pursued a plan to create a Mormon colony on six thousand acres in
the Jezreel Valley, although the Church's financial position at the time
had made this purchase impossible.[26]

This carefully documented historical information satisfied the requirements of the Israeli government. It was then necessary to present the evidence in a public forum. Therefore, these facts were published in Israeli newspapers every day from April 2 through April 8, 1977. Understanding the importance of receiving recognition, the Saints of the Jerusalem Branch organized a special fast to petition the Lord for success in the undertaking. Their prayers were answered, and on June 16, 1977, the Articles of Association were approved by the Israeli Ministry of the Interior. Article 1 stated:

> The name of the Association is "THE CHURCH OF JESUS CHRIST OF LATTER-DAY SAINTS ASSOCIATION IN ISRAEL", and is hereinafter referred to as "THE ASSOCIATION." The Association is a non-profit, non-commercial organization under the laws of Israel.[27]

Furthermore, article 4 indicated that the association had the right to "acquire, retain and dispose of real and personal property" and "to carry through peaceful means the Church's message throughout Israel sharing its ideals with all interested people."[28]

Although this recognition was not required for the Orson Hyde memorial, it certainly was advisable. However, as plans for a center progressed, it became indispensable.[29]

NINE HUNDRED AND NINETY-NINE YEARS

Plans for the creation of the Orson Hyde Memorial Garden were drafted. At the same time, President David Galbraith worked to secure the desired tract of land on the Mount of Olives. This was a five-and-one-quarter-acre portion of land on the west slope of the Mount of Olives, opposite the Lion Gate of the Old City and just northeast of the Church of All Nations and the traditional site of the Garden of Gethsemane. With the help of many government officials (especially Mayor Kollek), President Galbraith was successful in his efforts to secure property in the desired location. The land was leased by the Jerusalem Foundation to the city of Jerusalem for 999 years, making it possible for the Church to work directly with city officials during the construction and creation of the memorial. It took five years to secure the property, create suitable plans, and raise necessary

The Orson Hyde Memorial Garden occupies a 5.25-acre portion of land on the west slope of the Mount of Olives. This picture of the early construction and landscaping was taken from the Old City of Jerusalem.

The Old City of Jerusalem as seen from the Orson Hyde Memorial Garden.

funds. Landscaping of the garden finally ensued in 1977, with a projected completion date set for the fall of 1979.

After seven years of planning and work, the Orson Hyde Memorial Garden was finished and prepared to be dedicated. The dedication of the memorial garden is a noteworthy day in the history of the Church in the Near East.

OCTOBER 24, 1979

On October 24, 1979, 138 years after Orson Hyde offered his dedicatory prayer, about two thousand people gathered in the memorial garden for the dedicatory services. Most of those in attendance were Latter-day Saints. This was concluded to be the largest number of Saints that had ever assembled on one occasion in the Holy Land in modern times. Many of the Saints came by ship on a BYU Travel Study cruise, including President Spencer W. Kimball, President N. Eldon Tanner, Elder Howard W. Hunter, emeritus Church Patriarch

President Spencer W. Kimball (center) entering the Orson Hyde Memorial Garden for dedicatory services on October 24, 1979. He is being escorted by Israel Lippel, director of the Ministry of Religious Affairs (left) and President Kimball's personal secretary, Arthur Haycock (right). Just ahead of President Kimball is seen Mayor Teddy Kollek, wearing a dark suit and white shirt with open collar.

Eldred G. Smith, and about five hundred others. President Ezra Taft Benson, Elder LeGrand Richards, and Elder Marvin J. Ashton arrived separately. This was by far the largest number of Apostles to gather in Jerusalem since the days of Peter, John, Paul, and other apostolic witnesses of old.[30]

As proceedings were about to start, Israel Lippel, director general of the Ministry of Religious Affairs, escorted Church President Kimball down the winding stone pathway, followed by Sister Camilla Kimball and Mayor Kollek. The stand for dignitaries soon filled, and the dedicatory services began. Speeches and music provided a very spiritual setting and experience for those who attended.

President N. Eldon Tanner of the First Presidency with Kathy Taylor, wife of Robert Taylor, entering the Orson Hyde Memorial Garden for the dedicatory services. Immediately behind them is Ezra Taft Benson (President of the Quorum of the Twelve) and his wife Flora.

Spencer W. Kimball, President and prophet of the Church, gave an address. Some of the comments he gave that day are included here:

President Ezra Taft Benson waves as he enters the Orson Hyde Memorial Garden with his wife, Flora.

My heart leaps and then is subdued as I think of some of the momentous events that have occurred on this historical mount. . . . If a person could have had a vantage seat on this mount down through the ages, what scenes his eyes would have beheld. . . . Jesus Christ traversed this

Elder Howard W. Hunter, flanked by Louis and Mabel Crandall near the podium where the dedicatory prayer was offered.

The stand and podium where President Spencer W. Kimball offered the dedicatory prayer. In this picture, President Ezra Taft Benson is at the podium.

mount on several occasions while traveling between Jerusalem and Bethany. He wept as He looked over Jerusalem and yearned that the people might be gathered in righteousness. On this mount the Savior gave some of the greatest teachings ever recorded in holy writ as He privately taught Peter, James, John and Andrew concerning His future mission. In a garden called Gethsemane, just below us, He fulfilled that part of His atonement which enables us to return to our Heavenly Father if we but repent of our sins and keep His commandments.[31]

Following these words, President Kimball offered the dedicatory prayer. In that prayer he petitioned the Lord to accept the garden "as a special memorial to the prophetic prayer of Orson Hyde."[32] Furthermore, he noted that "the land has become abundantly fruitful again with flocks and orchards and fields. The children of Abraham have returned in great numbers to build up this land as a refuge and the city

From left to right: Mr. and Mrs. Howard Dunn and LaMar C. Berrett. This picture was taken the day the Orson Hyde Memorial Garden was dedicated (October 24, 1979). They are standing in the garden's stone amphitheatre. In the background is a plaque containing selected portions of Orson Hyde's dedicatory prayer.

of Jerusalem has flourished. . . . We pray for Abraham's children. . . . Extend Thy special care to them; draw them unto Thee." (For the complete text of the dedicatory prayer, refer to appendix F.) At the conclusion of the services, there was a feeling of quiet satisfaction that the important mission of Elder Orson Hyde was now appropriately recognized in Jerusalem. The garden is jointly cared for and maintained by the government of Israel and the municipality of Jerusalem.

THE ANNOUNCEMENT OF A CENTER

With the Orson Hyde Memorial Garden project completed, it seemed fitting for President Kimball to authorize the announcement of the Church's plans to construct a center in Jerusalem, which Elder Howard W. Hunter officially did on October 20, 1979.[33] This announcement was a strong indicator that the dreams of so many Near Eastern Saints, as well as the various administrators of the Jerusalem Study Abroad program, would be realized in the relatively near future.

Perhaps the most significant element of the announcement was that the long-anticipated physical presence of the Church in Jerusalem would finally be realized with the construction of a building.[34] In addition, this news came days before President Kimball traveled to the Holy Land for the dedication of the memorial garden, which facilitated his search for a building site the following day. With these two significant events so closely timed and tied together, some even felt that the Orson Hyde Memorial Garden was like an Elias, or forerunner, for the eventual building of the Jerusalem Center. For example, Robert Taylor explained, "The Church members' commitment to Mayor Teddy Kollek and the

Elder Howard W. Hunter served as chairman of the planning committee for the Jerusalem Center.

Jerusalem Foundation for a million dollars to provide a beautiful Garden on the West slopes of the Mount of Olives was the forerunner of evidencing the seriousness the University and the Church had for acquiring property for a building."[35]

This unveiling of plans was not a stunning surprise to the Jerusalem Saints. Serious discussion concerning a center had taken place since President Harold B. Lee's 1972 charge to find property on which to build a center. Prior to the formal announcement, four men had been working diligently on plans for a Jerusalem center in conjunction with their work related to the Orson Hyde Memorial Garden—Elder Howard W. Hunter, Fred Schwendiman, Robert C. Taylor, and David Galbraith. Elder Hunter served as chairman of the planning committee. Brother Schwendiman, who had been responsible for the construction of many buildings on the BYU campus in Provo, Utah, and the acquisition or construction of several Study Abroad facilities throughout the world, was given the task of preparing a plan which would best suit the needs of the Church and the Jerusalem Study Abroad program.[36] Brother Taylor served as a local resource to Elder Hunter on a wide range of issues, given his extensive experience in the Near East. Brother Galbraith lived in Jerusalem and served as resident director of the project. Others were added to this committee as the

From left to right: Robert C. Taylor, Fred Schwendiman, and David Galbraith served with Elder Howard W. Hunter and others on the planning committee for the Jerusalem Center.

Elder James E. Faust of the Quorum
of the Twelve Apostles.

BYU president Jeffrey R. Holland.

project progressed, including Elder James E. Faust of the Quorum of the Twelve and BYU president Jeffrey R. Holland. As early as September 1979, a model of the proposed center was shown to the Jerusalem Saints by Elder Hunter.[37]

LOCATING A SITE: 1979

Brother Galbraith had been investigating potential sites for a Latter-day Saint building in Jerusalem for many years prior to this announcement. He had looked at plots just outside the Jaffa Gate, another plot near the United Nations headquarters, and even existing buildings situated in good locations. However, as October 1979 approached, none of these options proved feasible.

On October 23, 1979, one day before the dedication of the Orson Hyde memorial, President N. Eldon Tanner of the First Presidency went with Robert and Kathy Taylor to view about twenty possible sites for the center, with the intention of choosing seven or eight sites to show President Kimball after the dedicatory services.[38] After viewing all the sites but one, President Tanner had not yet seen a site that deeply impressed him. This changed when the Taylors drove him to the Mount of Olives to see the last site on their list.

Brother Taylor described in his personal writings President Tanner's reaction to the last site. He explained that

> when we arrived on the site, there was obvious disappointment that even though located just above the Old City, the view was obstructed by a ridge to the south. It was further marred by a broken-down building that Bedouin lived in together with their sheep, goats, and donkeys. But Kathy spotted an open area about a hundred yards farther west that she'd had her eye on for some time. Taking President Tanner by the arm, she led him over rocks and through thistles as Sister Tanner and I followed . . . sort of reluctantly picking our way behind. By the time Sister Tanner and I caught up, Kathy and President Tanner had already made the decision. President Tanner said with authority and conviction, "This is where the Jerusalem Center should be built." Of course Kathy had come to that conclusion on a previous trip, but after some investigation, David [Galbraith], Fred [Schwendiman] and I had concluded that it was simply unavailable and a waste of time to pursue further. President Tanner continued by giving

Looking east from the Old City toward the construction site of the Jerusalem Center (center of photo) on the Mount of Olives.

me instructions that when the time came to take the rest of the official party to visit the sites, we should take them to all of the other sites first, and then bring them here.[39]

The view of the Temple Mount and the Dome of the Rock from the upper auditorium of the Jerusalem Center.

The site was low on the list because it was in "greenbelt" land, and Mayor Kollek had said it would be impossible for the Latter-day Saints to build there. Nevertheless, in accordance with President Tanner's instructions, the next day President Kimball was taken to the previous sites before this one on the Mount of Olives. After surveying the lay of the land and its commanding view of Jerusalem, President Kimball shared convictions similar to those of President Tanner's one day earlier and indicated that this was the place where the center should be built.[40]

From this site, the view of the Temple Mount and the Dome of the Rock is breathtaking. Only a few minutes' walk from the Orson Hyde Memorial Garden and the Garden of Gethsemane, it is one of the most impressive and scripturally significant areas of Jerusalem.

SECURING THE ARCHITECT AND SECURING THE LAND

Long before the land on the Mount of Olives was actually secured, Israeli architect David Reznik—in company with a Utah architect, Frank Ferguson—was hired to draw up the building plans, which included a large chapel, classrooms, housing for the Jerusalem Study Abroad students, dining area, library, and visitors' center.[41] Above all, however, the architects had the goal that the center would (1) exhibit BYU's theme, "The Glory of God Is Intelligence" (see D&C 93:36; 88:119); (2) represent Jerusalem and be a reflection of the Near East through design and materials; (3) focus attention on the Old City; (4) give all who enter a feeling of beauty, serenity, peace, and meditation—an oasis on the edge of the Judean desert;

and (5) enhance the extraordinary setting of the Mount of Olives. The result of their work was a strikingly beautiful building of eight stories terraced down the slope of the Mount of Olives.[42]

At the same time, Robert Thorn, former mission president and a Utah building contractor, was assigned by the First Presidency to travel to Jerusalem and secure the desired property. In April 1981, after about one year of searching out numerous sites and working through four different government ministries in Israel, Brother Thorn successfully finished initial negotiations with the Israeli Lands Authority for the Mount of Olives site. The site consisted of twenty dunams of land (about five and a quarter acres) for the Jerusalem Center, plus an additional one and three-quarters acres for gardens.

It is important to note that the land is not owned by the Church—it is leased. While the negotiating phase was completed, the land was not considered completely secure until a five-year development lease was signed on April 2, 1984.[43] A forty-nine-year lease, with an option for an additional forty-nine years, would need to be secured following the expiration of this five-year lease. In retrospect, Robert C. Taylor explained that securing this piece of property was an outright miracle and that the Lord knew where the Jerusalem Center should be constructed all along. He continued: "That's why we failed in our negotiations for other sites. Our vision was simply too limited."[44]

Construction and Opposition

From the time the search for a site began to the time ground-breaking ceremonies took place, about five years had passed (October 1979–August 1984). Construction would take about three years (August 1984–September 1987). On August 21, 1984, bulldozers started making necessary cuts in the mountain for the Jerusalem Center.[45] This was the first visual cue that the Latter-day Saints had acquired one of the finest pieces of property in all Jerusalem.[46] With that visibility, opposition erupted.

Up to this point, the Church had followed every legally essential procedure to the letter. Church leaders and the center's architects had acquired all necessary permits to build, had presented detailed building plans and construction schedules to city and national

On August 18, 1984, Daniel Ben Ogden (son of Jerusalem Study Abroad administrator, D. Kelly Ogden) conducts an informal groundbreaking ceremony.

On August 21, 1984, the first bulldozer began making the necessary cuts in the Mount of Olives to construct the multi-terraced Jerusalem Center.

authorities, had received their written approval to proceed, and had accommodated every requirement for public disclosure. Despite these many efforts, opposition to the project arose quickly and vigorously in the late months of 1984 and escalated in the early months of 1985. The public outcry came primarily from the Jewish orthodox community, who claimed that "a Christian proselyting sect had surreptitiously, if not illegally" obtained the property in Jerusalem for the sole purpose of building a missionary headquarters from which to proselytize Jews.[47]

Opponents of the Jerusalem Center protest outside Mayor Teddy Kollek's office.

In the early months of 1985, more and more articles opposing the center appeared in Israeli newspapers. The most common concern voiced was related to the Church's heavy emphasis on proselytizing throughout the world.[48] Mayor Teddy Kollek took the brunt of the anti-Mormon campaign. His office was often picketed, and as he returned to his home in the evening, he was frequently greeted by angry opponents of the center. Thousands of letters were sent to the mayor urging him to stop its construction. Letters to editors of major newspapers in Israel and abroad were directed at Mayor Kollek, insisting that he bring construction to a halt.

The following statements from newspaper headlines, flyers, bumper stickers, and so forth are a sampling of the many sentiments that were printed and distributed: "Time Bomb on Mount Scopus," "The Religious Right Wishes You Left," "No Mormon Center," "Mormons, Your Place Is Utah," "Stop Converting Our Dead," "Mormons Go Home," and "Teddy for Mayor of Salt Lake City."

In response to these attacks and the many inquiries at his office, Mayor Kollek maintained a steady support for Jerusalem's role as a model of religious tolerance and accommodation. In his rebuttals to the frequent claims against the Latter-day Saints, Mayor Kollek

This picture of two bumper stickers in the window of one Jerusalem car (taken in the fall of 1985) provides two examples of the many slogans created to express opposition to the Jerusalem Center.

consistently made four significant points: (1) missionary activity was practically nonexistent in Jerusalem, with or without the Mormons; (2) the Latter-day Saints had been traveling to and studying in Israel for more than fifteen years, and there had not been a single instance of Jewish conversion due to BYU's Travel Study programs; (3) leaders of The Church of Jesus Christ of Latter-day Saints understood that, given the tragedy of the Holocaust, Israel did not and would not tolerate proselytizing efforts to convert Jews away from their faith; and (4) assurances of the leaders of the Church had been given that the center would not be used as a proselytizing front in any way.[49]

Even with Mayor Kollek's assurances, the opposition raged on. Large rallies were staged, and demonstrations were held in various places in Jerusalem, including Mount Scopus and the Western Wall (sometimes referred to as the Wailing Wall). Thousands of Jews, mainly orthodox, participated. Additionally, a talented and popular group of Jewish vocal artists from New York was retained to compose and record an anti-Mormon song in English. It was titled "Jerusalem Is Not for Sale" and aired on Israeli radio and was sung at a large rally on Mount Scopus. The first lines read:

> *Overnight—a massive construction atop our Jerusalem mountains,*
> *A campus luring innocent souls to drink from the forbidden fountains.*
> *Like many before—they've come here for war.*
> *We're warning them now it won't pay. Jerusalem is not for sale . . .*

The Jerusalem Center was also the center of a national debate within the government of prime minister Shimon Peres and the attorney general's office of the state of Israel. In December 1985, Peres

The Jerusalem Center under construction as it appeared in July 1986. The buildings of Hebrew University may be seen in the background.

established a committee consisting of eight of his cabinet members to investigate the Jerusalem Center and give recommendations as to whether or not the building should be allowed. Four of the eight were generally in favor of the center, and the remaining four were generally against it. Forming this committee was calculated to neutralize the efforts of certain religious parties who were attempting to bring down the Peres government by using the "Mormon Center" as a political wedge and divider. The maneuver was successful, and the Peres government remained intact. At the same time, Israel's attorney general was conducting an inquiry into the Jerusalem Center project. A subcommittee of the Israeli Knesset was also conducting its own investigation.[50]

At the conclusion of their separate inquiries, each investigative team determined that the Church was innocent of wrongdoing and should be permitted to build its center. The attorney general's office issued a statement explaining that there were "no legal grounds for stopping the building of the Center." A similar decision was reached by the Peres cabinet members. While the interior committee of the Knesset came to the same conclusion, they called for an official promise from the leaders of Brigham Young University and the Church that they would not proselytize Jews.[51]

Leaders of The Church of Jesus Christ of Latter-day Saints and Brigham Young University decided to yield to the request of the Knesset committee, despite the fact that the government of Israel was treating the Church as no other Christian denomination had ever been treated in Israel. Nevertheless, in August 1985, BYU president Jeffrey R. Holland presented a formal, signed declaration to the members of the Israeli Knesset, which provided a brief historical background to the building of the Jerusalem Center as an extension of the Provo, Utah, campus. This section was followed by four statements of commitment: First, consistent with past policy, students, faculty, and staff connected with the center would not engage in proselytizing of any kind in Israel. Second, to enforce this policy, the university would continue its established practice of requiring all students, faculty, and staff associated with the center to sign a commitment not to enter into proselytizing activities of any kind in Israel. Any individual in noncompliance with this commitment would be released from the academic program and sent home. Third, as long as it was required by the Israeli Council of Higher Education, no Israeli could be enrolled at BYU's Jerusalem campus for course work which would lead to a degree. And fourth, the center would be open for cultural programs and exhibits designed in keeping with the role of a university but would not design any such program to be used for proselytizing.[52]

Public Relations Campaign

Opposition waned following the submission of these four commitments. Nevertheless, there were still formidable opponents who continued to posture and threaten the Church and university interests in Israel. At this point, the Church went on the offensive. At the request of Mayor Kollek, David Galbraith wrote a statement to the press explaining the motives of the BYU Center and reiterating that it was an extension of Brigham Young University and would not be used for the purpose of proselytizing.[53] Furthermore, in January 1986, the Church and the university mounted a high-profile public relations campaign. Gitam Image Promotion Systems, an Israeli public relations firm, was hired to more carefully and strategically inform the general public concerning the long-term and mutually beneficial presence of the Latter-day Saints in Israel. Interviews were arranged with newspapers wherein university representatives were able to clearly and accurately state Church intentions. Television interviews were also contracted through Gitam that significantly increased positive public awareness for the Church. For example, the David Galbraith family appeared on Israeli television to talk about the Latter-day Saint presence in Israel. At one point during the broadcast, Brother Galbraith played recordings of some of the threatening telephone calls his family had received at their home. One caller said: "This is your last warning: we're bloodthirsty. If you don't leave Israel we're going to kill all of you, one by one."[54] This broadcast had a softening effect on viewers, and an empathy was fostered through this interview that some identify as a turning point in the public relations effort to portray the Latter-day Saints in a positive light.[55] In addition to this, advertisements were purchased in Israeli newspapers and magazines. Finally, one of the most impressive outgrowths of this campaign was a letter signed by 154 members of the United States

Congress supporting the establishment of the center. This letter was delivered to all 120 members of the Israeli Knesset.[56]

This campaign did much to correctly inform the Israeli public and ease tensions. Ultimately, the Church's willingness to enter into formal agreements not to use the center to proselytize Jews, combined with the public relations campaign and the outstanding examples of the Brigham Young University students themselves, represented the beginning of the end of a long and hard-fought battle. Concerning his involvement in this drawn-out drama, Mayor Kollek said:

> Of all the struggles during my 25 years as mayor of Jerusalem, the one concerning Brigham Young University—Mount Scopus Campus—was perhaps the most difficult and certainly among the most important. This was not a struggle for the Mormons, but rather it was a struggle for tolerance in a city that should set an example to the world. A city in which everyone may pray to his God in his way without restriction.[57]

"WE WILL NEVER SAY NEVER"

As opposition to the building subsided and construction on the center neared completion, opponents to the center orchestrated one final attempt to thwart the project. In February 1987, Church and university leaders were approached by Israeli government officials with a demand to sign an affidavit wherein The Church of Jesus Christ of Latter-day Saints would agree not to proselytize among the Jews in Israel—*ever.* Up to this point, a distinction had been made, through legal dialogue, between the *Church, Brigham Young University,* and the *Jerusalem Center.* Formal statements had already been signed by Brigham Young University and the Jerusalem Center wherein firm commitments were made to refrain from proselytizing in *any* way in Israel. Now, under pressure from "a powerful yet vocal minority of orthodox activists," the government of Israel demanded that the *Church* sign a similar document with the added stipulation of committing *never* to proselytize in Israel under any circumstances.[58]

Given all the Church had done to comply with the law and accommodate real and perceived sensitivities among the Jewish people of Israel, this final request was particularly troubling. It crossed a fundamental line of Christianity—the charge from the Savior to take the gospel to all the world. During Elder James E. Faust's January 1987 visit to Jerusalem, he addressed this latest request by saying, "We will never say never."[59]

Of this exchange, BYU professor Daniel C. Peterson wrote:

> This most recent demand touched on a matter of fundamental importance, a matter beside which even the expensive and long-dreamed-of building on Mount Scopus was relatively unimportant. Latter-day Saints obey the law. This is a matter of principle and religious belief, enshrined in their Articles of Faith. They are willing to limit their missionary efforts when the law demands it. But they make no secret of another principle of their faith, namely that it is their ultimate goal and duty to take the gospel to all nations of the earth, including the Jews. They cannot renounce this principle and certainly will not do so merely to satisfy the excessive demands of any human government.[60]

The Church remained firm and resolute on this position, and the opposition withdrew their demands. Eventually, another document was signed by Elder Howard W. Hunter on behalf of the Church. The "forever" clause was removed, and the commitment was that neither the Church nor any of its members would proselytize until such time as the government of Israel allows.[61] This document was signed on May 18, 1988. (The text of this agreement may be found in appendix G.)

Seven Years and Four Months

After seven years and four months of what Jeffrey R. Holland would later refer to as time filled with "blood, sweat, and tears," the building was finished enough for occupation on March 4, 1987.[62] A new landmark had arisen in the city of Jerusalem. The Jerusalem Center featured 117 Roman arches as part of its graceful façade and could be seen from points throughout the city. The building size was 11,500 square meters (approximately 125,000 square feet); it could house 162 students and 26 personnel.[63] In an additional description of the building, Steven Baldridge wrote that it features an entrance on the lowest level; four levels of housing space; . . . the cafeteria, gymnasium/weight room and four classrooms on level six; [and] the main office, a 44-car parking garage and the main entrance to the 338-seat lower auditorium . . . on level seven. Level eight has the main building entrance, two seminar rooms, office space, the library (with a capacity of 15,000 volumes), the learning resource center, restrooms, a security office and the entrance to the 300-seat upper auditorium. . . . Everywhere is seen the use of teakwood from Burma and marble from Italy. . . . Just outside the outer gate an 800-year-old olive tree commands the grounds of grass and flowers, set around the great stone boulders.[64]

By way of review, prior to 1972, the Saints had met in private domiciles and, when students were present, in the Ritz Hotel. Beginning in 1972, BYU officials had arranged to rent the City Hotel

The Jerusalem Center for Near Eastern Studies

The first four presidents of the Jerusalem Branch standing in front of the "Mormon House." They are shown here in order of service, from right to left: David B. Galbraith, Daniel Rona, D. Kelly Ogden, and Garland Dennett.

to house both the Study Abroad program and the Jerusalem Branch. By 1977, the Jerusalem Study Abroad program had outgrown the facilities at the City Hotel and moved to the Vienna Hotel. At the same time, the branch had rented space in the basement of the Swedish consulate, which came to be known as "Mormon House."[65] As the Study Abroad program expanded in numbers, it became necessary to move once again, this time to Ramat Rahel, a kibbutz on the southern edge of Jerusalem, on April 18, 1978. The Diplomat Hotel just north of the kibbutz and the now-distant Mormon House were used for Sabbath meetings and other activities (like Scouts) until worship services were finally moved to the Jerusalem Center in August 1987.

Moving In and Finishing Touches

Although it was not entirely completed, on March 8, 1987, students and faculty moved into the Jerusalem Center.[66] Amazingly, the dream of a Church-owned center in Jerusalem had become a reality. Latter-day Saints had a permanent home in Jerusalem. Three months later, Jerusalem Center administrator and teacher D. Kelly Ogden, speaking to a Church Educational System tour group in the unfinished upper auditorium of the center, stated:

> The Lord preserved the site for the very structure we [are] sitting in. I watched the bulldozers during the weeks of preparing the infrastructure and foundations for our Center. There was no evidence of a cemetery or any building on our site in all of history. That is utterly amazing to contemplate—a unique panoramic view out over one of history's most coveted pieces of real estate, and there was no building on the site through all those centuries. I believe the Lord knew millennia ago that in the latter days this great Center would be erected on this location, and He preserved it, kept it unoccupied and unmolested by a host of potential detractors and complicators.[67]

As weeks and months passed, the building became more and more complete. By the end of the year, the cafeteria, known as the Oasis, was finished, making it no longer necessary to eat meals at the Commodore Hotel, across the street to the south. The first Jerusalem Branch meetings were held in the center on September 5, 1987, in the lower auditorium (also known as the Forum), and in mid-December, services were moved to the newly finished upper auditorium.[68] Some Latter-day Saints claim that this room commands the most striking view of any Church building on earth. The side and front walls of this large auditorium are made up of huge plates of glass framed by teakwood. Nothing stands between this room and its view of the Old City of Jerusalem.

Possibly the most impressive final touch to the building was the acquisition of a half-million-dollar Danish Marcussen organ. One of the finest instruments in all of Israel, the organ, with its dramatic series of pipes, many of which are trumpet-shaped and project out horizontally from the rest of the vertical pipes, was installed on the back wall of the upper auditorium. Several world-renowned organists have performed recitals in the Jerusalem Center. In addition to the

The Danish Marcussen organ, located in the upper auditorium of the Jerusalem Center.

organ, biblical gardens, fountains, furnishings, and learning resources (including computer labs and re-creations of historical artifacts, such as a variety of ancient olive and grape presses) were added to enhance the beauty and utility of the already stunning building.

Forty-nine Years plus Forty-nine Years

It will be remembered that Robert Thorn negotiated a five-year development lease for the property on which the center was built and that another long-term lease would be essential in order to secure the future of the building itself after construction was completed. The prime minister's cabinet approved the measure to issue the lease on May 8, 1988. Ten days later, on May 18, 1988, the President of the Quorum of the Twelve Apostles, Howard W. Hunter, was in Jerusalem and signed the lease. The lease on the property was for forty-nine years with rights secured to BYU to renew at that time for an additional forty-nine years. According to the terms of the lease, the first forty-nine years began with the signing of the five-year development lease on

While in Jerusalem to sign a forty-nine-year lease, Howard W. Hunter took time out to visit the Garden Tomb. From left to right: Mary Holland, Ruth Faust, Howard W. Hunter, John Hunter, James E. Faust, Patricia Holland, and Jeffrey R. Holland.

March 4, 1984.[69] The contract was signed by President Hunter, representing The Church of Jesus Christ of Latter-day Saints by assignment of Ezra Taft Benson, Church President. Signing for the state of Israel was Yehuda Ziv, district administrator of the Lands Authority.[70] The Latter-day Saint presence in Israel was now an established fact.

DEDICATION OF THE JERUSALEM CENTER

The efforts to build the Jerusalem Center for Near Eastern Studies stand as a valuable case study in the exercise of faith. It was faith that gave Latter-day Saints in Israel the power to endure intense opposition and persecution in one of the most politically sensitive regions of the world, with absolutely no guarantees that the venture would succeed. Mayor Teddy Kollek exhibited faith in God's love for all peoples when he rose up fearlessly to defend the right of Latter-day Saints to establish an educational campus and, by special provision, a religious meeting center in Jerusalem. Certainly, the leaders of the Church exercised great faith when they followed impressions to build a multi-million-dollar facility on land over which the Church had no long-term control. With the long-term lease signed on May 18, 1988, one year later, almost to the day, on May 16, 1989, a small group of Latter-day Saints gathered to dedicate the building. After thanking God for being born in the dispensation of the fullness of times and for the Savior's atoning sacrifice, Elder Howard W. Hunter prayed:

> We thank Thee, Father, for the establishment of Brigham Young University as a subsidiary institution of the Church of Thy Son where many of Thy sons and daughters may receive learning coupled with spirituality and knowledge of Thee. Bless, we pray Thee, its officers, its faculty and the students who attend with a knowledge of Thy ways and a desire to follow. This building wherein we are seated has been constructed for the housing of those who would love Thee and seek to learn of Thee and follow in the footsteps of Thy Son, our Savior and Redeemer. It is beautiful in every respect, complying with all the beauty it represents. Oh Father, we thank Thee for the privilege of building this house to those who will come here and be here for the benefit and learning of Thy sons and daughters. We pray, Father, that Thou wilt bless this house in every way. Bless the land on which it rests and the beautiful grounds. Bless its foundations. Bless the walls and roof and all its details. We pray that it will be kept from damage or destruction from the hands of man or the ravages of nature and will remain beautiful and representative of that which is sacred and that which pertains to Thee. We, Thy children, therefore dedicate to Thee, Father, that which has been built in our hands in love, this beautiful building, the Jerusalem Center for Near Eastern Studies, and all of its appurtenances, praying that it will be acceptable in every respect to Thee. May all who enter therein to teach, to learn, or for whatever purpose be blessed of Thee and feel Thy Spirit. This is our prayer and our dedication to Thee in the name of Jesus Christ, amen.[71]

Six of the many key figures in bringing about the Jerusalem Center enjoy a moment together in the beautiful upper level of the center. From left to right: D. Kelly Ogden, James E. Faust, David B. Galbraith, Dann W. Hone, Howard W. Hunter, and Robert C. Taylor.

President Thomas S. Monson of the First Presidency conducted the dedicatory service. Toward the end of the meeting, he said, "It is a miracle that this building stands complete with every facet attended to with tender, loving care. . . . Everyone who comes to this center will leave a better person for having been here."[72]

At the conclusion of the few days involving the signing of the long-term land lease, BYU president Jeffrey R. Holland spoke in a faculty meeting at the center. He borrowed the words of Sir Winston Churchill to describe his feelings. He said that the dedication and signing of the lease "is not the end of the end, not the beginning of the end, but maybe the end of the beginning."[73] And so it was.

A Final Thought

The Jerusalem Center for Near Eastern Studies stands at the end of the beginning of a remarkable journey. One century earlier, missionaries such as Ferdinand F. Hintze and Joseph W. Booth envisioned a colony of Latter-day Saints in the Holy Land who would strive to fulfill their covenants and bless the people of the land with their spirit of industry and anxious concern for the community. While that dream never came to fruition in their lifetimes, it is reasonable to conclude that they would be particularly pleased that the dream of a Jerusalem Center for Near Eastern Studies became a reality.[74] The future of the Jerusalem Center and the Church's presence in the Holy Land is unknown. However, if events commencing with President Harold B. Lee's visit in 1972 are any indication of future happenings, we may expect God to work mighty miracles in the decades, and even centuries, to come in the lands made holy by faith and sacrifice.

Notes to Chapter 10

1. Today the Jerusalem Center is commonly referred to as being on Mount Scopus. However, in the earliest Jerusalem Center literature, it is described as being on the Mount of Olives. Both are acceptable designations. Mount Scopus is the name of the north end of the Mount of Olives range. "*Skopeo* is Greek and means 'to watch.'" LaMar C. Berrett and D. Kelly Ogden, *Discovering the World of the Bible* (Provo, UT: Grandin Book, 1996), 38. With this important explanation in mind, we will refer to the location of the Jerusalem Center as the Mount of Olives.

View from the Jewish Quarter of the Old City of Jerusalem. The Western Wall (sometimes known as the Wailing Wall) is in the foreground. The Dome of the Rock rises behind the wall to the left, and the white limestone arches of the finished Jerusalem Center for Near Eastern Studies on the Mount of Olives are on the right.

2. Journal of Daniel H. Ludlow; copy in authors' possession. See also LaMar C. Berrett, *Discovering the World of the Bible* (Provo, UT: Brigham Young University Press, 1973), 308–9; *Church News,* November 3, 1979, 7, and July 15, 1984, 14.

3. Robert C. Taylor, "A Modern Miracle in Jerusalem, the Holy City," unpublished manuscript, no page numbers. Copy in authors' possession.

4. Journal of Daniel H. Ludlow. See also Berrett, *Discovering the World of the Bible* (1973), 420–21.

5. Lani Handy went on to marry Arnold Green, professor of history at BYU. Professor Green served as director of the Jerusalem Center for Near Eastern Studies from 2000 to 2002.

6. This information comes from a telephone interview of David Handy conducted by LaMar C. Berrett on June 13, 2001. Additional details were given to the authors by Daniel H. Ludlow in personal correspondence.

7. Taylor, "A Modern Miracle in Jerusalem."

8. Ernest L. Wilkinson and Leonard J. Arrington, *Brigham Young University: The First One Hundred Years,* 3 vols. (Provo, UT: Brigham Young University Press, 1976), 3:723. See also Dann W. Hone, *General Survey and Orientation to the Peoples and Cultures of the Holy Land for Applicants to the BYU Jerusalem Center Programs—Near Eastern Studies 100* (Provo, UT: Department of Independent Study at Brigham Young University and The Jerusalem Center for Near Eastern Studies, 2001), 25. See also Howard W. Hunter, "All Alike unto God," *Ensign,* June 1979, 72–74.

9. Daniel H. Ludlow, interview by LaMar C. Berrett, Provo, UT, April 23, 2001.

10. Ludlow, personal correspondence to authors, December 9, 2003.

11. This information was taken from a talk given by David B. Galbraith on July 30, 1983. Notes taken by and acquired from Haws Marble.

12. Jeffrey R. Holland, "President Gordon B. Hinckley: Stalwart and Brave He Stands," *Ensign,* June 1995, 12. The Swiss Mission Record notes that this blessing was given on the evening of September 20, 1972.

13. Mission Record, Swiss Zurich Mission, September 20, 1972, LDS Church Archives.

14. Ibid.

15. Letter written from Jerusalem by John A. Tvedtnes to D. Kelly Ogden, September 25, 1972. Today John Tvedtnes is a senior resident scholar at the Foundation for Ancient Research and Mormon Studies (FARMS), Brigham Young University. At the time the Jerusalem Branch was organized in 1972, he was a Hebrew University postgraduate student and served as the Jerusalem Group historian. Steven W. Baldridge, *Grafting In: A History of the Latter-day Saints in the Holy Land* (Murray, UT: Roylance Publishing, 1989), 14.

16. David B. Galbraith, D. Kelly Ogden, and Andrew C. Skinner, *Jerusalem, the Eternal City* (Salt Lake City: Deseret Book, 1996), 452–56.

17. Baldridge, *Grafting In,* 139. Point number three requires further clarification. In an interview conducted by the authors on January 17, 2004, David B. Galbraith provided a helpful explanation: "Point number three, as originally written, can only be understood in the context of trying to make Sunday work for us. We had just been told by President Lee that there was no precedent for such a request (to hold meetings on Saturday) and that Sunday was established by revelation as the Lord's day of rest. Some members felt we could hold services after work, or after university classes had finished late Sunday afternoon or evening. But even though buses were running, many could not make it back home that night in time for work or school on Monday. In other words, point three was made to help the Brethren understand the almost impossibility of meeting on Sunday for many of the members."

18. Dann W. Hone was a student in this first group led by H. Donl Peterson. Brother Hone went on to work in the BYU Travel Study office as an administrator and later was appointed to be the first academic coordinator of the Jerusalem Center. Brother Hone lived in Jerusalem for eight years in conjunction with this post and played a key role in the development of academic programs for the Jerusalem Center for Near Eastern Studies.

19. For a brief but insightful overview of the Yom Kippur War, see Paul Johnson, *A History of the Jews* (New York: Harper Perennial, 1987), 535.

20. H. Donl Peterson, "All the Jews Don't Live in New York City," unpublished manuscript, 1993, 79–94. Copy in authors' possession.

21. Cecil B. Roth and Geoffrey D. Wigoder, eds., *The New Standard Jewish Encyclopedia* (Jerusalem—Ramat Gan: Masada Publishing, 1970), 38–39.

22. Taylor, "A Modern Miracle in Jerusalem."

23. See *Daily Herald,* Provo, UT, August 18, 1995.

24. David B. Galbraith to LaMar C. Berrett, September 23, 1976, personal files of LaMar C. Berrett.

25. Some well-intentioned guides, professors, and other students of the history of the Church in the Near East have claimed that the missionary graves of Elders Haag and Clark (located in the Templer Cemetery in Haifa) were *the* key factor in the Church's acquisition of official recognition. We would point out that the graves were significant but not essential to the successful presentation of facts to the government of Israel. While it is not necessary to organize these facts in order of import, LaMar C. Berrett suggests that the single most important factor that led to proving the Church's presence in Palestine prior to 1948 was the establishment of mission homes in Haifa.

26. Evidence used to prove that the Church was an entity in Israel before 1948, as

well as a notarized copy of the Articles of Association, are located in the personal files of LaMar C. Berrett.

27. There are twelve articles in the official copy of the association, and the original notarized copy is kept at the office of the District Commissioner of Jerusalem in file number 11/2780. Copy in authors' possession.

28. Ibid.

29. The Articles of Association gave the Church official status from 1977 to about 1987, when they were not renewed by the Church. The renewal process would have brought the Church under further public scrutiny, and this was deemed unnecessary. During this time, some visas granted to university employees were clergy-status visas. Travel Study administrator Dann Hone was the last individual to hold one of these visas. It lapsed in 1989 when he was placed on B-2 status. Personal communication between Dann Hone and the authors, January 25, 2002.

30. Daniel C. Peterson, *Abraham Divided,* rev. ed. (Salt Lake City: Aspen Books, 1995), 340–41.

31. Dell Van Orden, "Orson Hyde Garden Is on Vantage Seat of Biblical History," *Church News,* November 3, 1979, 3.

32. Ibid.

33. Hone, *General Survey,* 27. According to David B. Galbraith, "This first official announcement was made aboard the cruise ship, enroute to the Holy Land for the Orson Hyde Memorial Garden dedication. It is true that Elder Hunter made the announcement, but President Spencer W. Kimball stood by his side. It was at that moment a model of the proposed center was unveiled." Personal correspondence with the authors, January 21, 2004.

34. Galbraith, Ogden, and Skinner, *Jerusalem, the Eternal City,* 452–56.

35. Taylor, "A Modern Miracle in Jerusalem."

36. Galbraith, Ogden, and Skinner, *Jerusalem, the Eternal City,* 452–56.

37. Ibid.

38. Taylor, "A Modern Miracle in Jerusalem."

39. Ibid.

40. Ibid.

41. Baldridge, *Grafting In,* 53.

42. For a complete listing of nine major design goals, see Hone, *General Survey,* 33.

43. Baldridge, *Grafting In,* 53–54.

44. Taylor, "A Modern Miracle in Jerusalem."

45. Hone, *General Survey,* 27. See also Daniel C. Peterson, *Abraham Divided,* 342.

46. Galbraith, Ogden, and Skinner, *Jerusalem, the Eternal City,* 458.

47. Ibid. Not all Israelis were alarmed by the idea that Latter-day Saints would convert Jews throughout Israel. For example, Aharon Nahmias, a member of the Israeli Knesset, made an effort "to soften the hyper-suspicious attitude of religious members of the Knesset to Mormon activities in Israel" by saying: "Don't be so anxious. They're not allowed to drink tea or coffee, not to mention any kind of alcohol, and the faithful have to give a tithe to the church. How many Israeli Jews would convert under such terms?" (*Jerusalem Post,* June 14, 1985, 5).

48. For a sample of statements expressing opposition to the Jerusalem Center that appeared in a variety of publications, see Galbraith, Ogden, and Skinner, *Jerusalem, the Eternal City,* 458–59. See also Alan Casper, "Opposition to the Construction of the Brigham Young University Jerusalem Center," master's thesis, Brigham Young University, 2003.

49. Galbraith, Ogden, and Skinner, *Jerusalem, the Eternal City,* 460.

50. Ibid., 462. See also Baldridge, *Grafting In,* 86–87.

51. Galbraith, Ogden, and Skinner, *Jerusalem, the Eternal City,* 462. See also Baldridge, *Grafting In,* 86–87.

52. Galbraith, Ogden, and Skinner, *Jerusalem, the Eternal City,* 463–64.

53. Daniel C. Peterson, *Abraham Divided,* 346.

54. Ibid., 345.

55. Ibid.

56. Galbraith, Ogden, and Skinner, *Jerusalem, the Eternal City,* 465–66.

57. D. Kelly Ogden, *Pioneering the East* (n.p., 2002), 293, entry for February 22, 1992. This book is a private publication but is available in the Harold B. Lee Library at Brigham Young University, Provo, UT.

58. Ibid., 280–82, entry for February 13, 1987.

59. Baldridge, *Grafting In,* 86–87. See also Ogden, *Pioneering the East*, 282, entry for February 13, 1987.

60. Daniel C. Peterson, *Abraham Divided,* 346.

61. Baldridge, *Grafting In,* 86–87, 141. See also Ogden, *Pioneering the East,* 280–82, entry for February 13, 1987.

62. This quotation is taken from a videotaped presentation of Jeffrey R. Holland at a Jerusalem Center orientation meeting held January 5, 1988. Even with the assistance of the Jerusalem Center staff and video archivists at BYU, we were unable to locate the videotape; thus, the quotation is the recollection of Blair G. Van Dyke, who was in attendance.

63. Ogden, *Pioneering the East,* 283, entry of March 8, 1987. Approximately seven years later, several apartments were added on the lower level of the Jerusalem Center, making it possible to accommodate 185 students. Dann Hone, Jerusalem Center administrator, interview, by the authors, February 12, 2004.

64. Baldridge, *Grafting In,* 91–92.

65. Ibid., 41.

66. Daniel Peterson and Baldridge both note that the cost of the Jerusalem Center was approximately twenty million dollars. See Daniel C. Peterson, *Abraham Divided,* 346. See also Baldridge, *Grafting In,* 87.

67. Ogden, *Pioneering the East,* 284–85, entry for mid-June 1987.

68. Baldridge, *Grafting In,* 89.

69. Ibid., 94. See also D. Kelly Ogden, "Excerpts from the Journal of D. Kelly Ogden, etc.," May 19, 1988, n.p. Copy in the authors' possession.

70. Baldridge, *Grafting In,* 141.

71. Hone, *General Survey,* 29. Dann W. Hone served as scribe for the dedication ceremonies of the Jerusalem Center for Near Eastern Studies.

72. Ibid., 28.

73. Quoted in Ogden, *Pioneering the East,* 290, entry for May 19, 1988.

74. To review similar conclusions drawn in this regard, refer to Daniel C. Peterson, *Abraham Divided,* 349.

Missions and Mission Presidents:
Turkish, Armenian, Palestine-Syrian, and Near East Missions

1887–1975

Turkish Mission (1887–1909)

1. President Ferdinand Friis Hintze	September 1, 1887–December 12, 1889
2. President Frederick Stauffer	December 13, 1889–November 6, 1891
3. President Joseph F. Schoenfeld	November 7, 1891–February 29, 1892
4. President Donald C. Musser	February 29, 1892–May 5, 1894
5. President Edward W. Robinson	May 6, 1894–January 29, 1896

Mission Closed: February 1896–September 1897

6. President Philip S. Maycock	September 8, 1897–June 24, 1899
7. President Ferdinand Friis Hintze	June 25, 1899–February 1900
8. President Albert Herman	July 1900–October 1903
9. President Joseph Wilford Booth	October 1903–September 30, 1909

Mission Closed: October 1, 1909–September 14, 1921

Armenian Mission (1921–1928)

10. President Joseph Wilford Booth   September 14, 1921–December 5, 1928

............................*Mission Closed: December 1928–February 1933* ....

Palestine-Syrian Mission (1933–1939)

11. President Badwagan Piranian   February 10, 1933–September 7, 1937

12. President Joseph Jacobs   September 8, 1937–September 7, 1939

.... *Mission Closed: September 7, 1939–September 11, 1947* ....

13. President Badwagan Piranian   September 11, 1947–January 19, 1950

Near East Mission (1950)

14. President Badwagan Piranian   January 20, 1950–December 24, 1950

............................*Mission Closed: December 24, 1950–Summer 1960* ....

Swiss/Switzerland Mission (1960–1975)

15. President William S. Erekson   Summer 1960–September 28, 1962

16. President John Milton Russon   September 28, 1962–August 12, 1965

17. President Rendell Noell Mabey   August 12, 1965–July 4, 1968

18. President Martin Elmer Christensen July 4, 1968–July 29, 1971

19. President Edwin Q. Cannon Jr.   July 29, 1971–July 8, 1974

20. President Gary E. O'Brien   July 8, 1974–August 18, 1975
                                        (missionaries withdrawn from Lebanon)

Latter-day Saint Burial Sites
in the Near East

MISSIONARIES FROM AMERICA

Name	Birth Date	Death Date	Cause of Death	Grave Location
Edgar D. Simmons	Apr. 25, 1863	Feb. 4, 1890	Smallpox	Northwest edge of the Protestant Armenian Cemetery at Aintab, Turkey
Adolf Haag	Feb. 19, 1865	Oct. 3, 1892	Typhoid	German Templer Cemetery, Haifa; row 5, grave 2, on the right
John A. Clark	Feb. 28, 1871	Feb. 8, 1895	Smallpox	German Templer Cemetery, Haifa; row 4, grave 4, on the right
Emil J. Huber	Mar. 7, 1885	May 16, 1908	Typhus	Armenian Evangelical Cemetery northwest of Aleppo, Syria
Joseph W. Booth	Aug. 14, 1866	Dec. 5, 1928	Heart Failure	Armenian Evangelical Cemetery northwest of Aleppo, Syria

LOCAL MEMBERS

Name	Location of Grave
Johann Georg Grau	German Templer Cemetery, Haifa; northwest corner of cemetery, in the last row of graves (row 10), grave 15 on the left from the center aisle
Magdalene Frey Grau	German Templer Cemetery, Haifa; under an olive tree in the center of the cemetery, row 7, grave 7 to the right from the center (Note the bas-relief of the angel Moroni carrying the Book of Mormon with the inscription of Revelation 14:6.)
Fred August Kegel	German Templer Cemetery, Haifa; row 6, grave 10 to the right from the center
Christiane Sahra Kegel	German Templer Cemetery, Haifa; row 6, grave 9 to the right from the center
Heinrich Voukenroth	Templer Cemetery, Jerusalem, near the railroad station
Garabed Kamajian	Armenian Cemetery, Mount Zion, Jerusalem (Kamajian [1914–1981] was baptized at age eight in Aintab, Turkey. He moved to Jerusalem in 1931 and died in 1981. His white marble tomb, with a black stone slab in the center, is located about forty feet east of the west wall of the cemetery and about eighty feet south of the north wall of the cemetery, which is just outside the southwest corner of the walls around the Old City. Garabed Kamajian is the only known baptized Latter-day Saint to be buried within the walls of Jerusalem that once enclosed Mt. Zion.)

The specific locations of all these Latter-day Saint graves in Israel were determined by LaMar C. Berrett. The descriptions of these graves and their locations are taken from LaMar C. Berrett and D. Kelly Ogden, *Discovering the World of the Bible* (Provo, UT: Grandin Book, 1996), 56–57, 156–57.

Missionaries Who Served in the Near East:
European, Turkish, Armenian, Palestine-Syrian, Near East, Swiss, and International Missions

1885–1975

Indicates service as mission president   † *Indicates death while on mission*

Name	Mission	Date of Call or Initial Service in Near East
1. Jacob Spori	European	Dec. 31, 1884
2. Joseph M. Tanner	European	Dec. 4, 1885
3. Ferdinand F. Hintze*	European/Turkish	Jan. 16, 1887
4. George Clove	Turkish	Last quarter 1887
5. Janne M. Sjodahl	Turkish	Jan. 23, 1889
6. Charles U. Locander	Turkish	Jan./Feb. 1889
7. Johann Georg Grau	Turkish	Jan. 25, 1889
8. Friederich Dieterle	Turkish	Mar. 22, 1889
9. Frederick Stauffer*	Turkish	June 6, 1889
10. Edgar D. Simmons†	Turkish	June 6, 1889
11. William H. Smart	Turkish	June 6, 1889

Name	Mission	Date of Call or Initial Service in Near East
12. Nishan Sherinian	Turkish	Apr. 1890
13. Joseph F. Schoenfeld*	Turkish	Oct. 6, 1891
14. Albert Herman	Turkish	Oct. 6, 1891
15. Donald C. Musser*	Turkish	Feb. 29, 1892
16. Adolf Haag†	Turkish	Summer 1892
17. Frederick A. Huish	Turkish	May 21, 1893
18. John A. Clark†	Turkish	Early 1894
19. Edward W. Robinson*	Turkish	Early 1894
20. Neils G. Christiansen	Turkish	May 18, 1895

·································· *Mission Closed January 1896–August 1897* ··································

21. Philip S. Maycock*	Turkish	Sept. 8, 1897
22. Andrew L. Larson	Turkish	Sept. 8, 1897
23. Ferdinand F. Hintze	Turkish; Colony investigation	Dec. 29, 1897
24. Anthon H. Lund	Colony investigation; Dedicate Holy Land	Dec. 29, 1897
25. Joseph W. Booth	Turkish	Sept. 30, 1898
26. J. Alma Holdaway	Turkish	Sept. 24, 1899
27. Thomas P. Page	Turkish	Jan. 1900
28. Albert Herman*	Turkish	Spring 1900
29. Willis Lester Mangum	Turkish	Fall 1900
30. Francis M. Lyman	Dedicate Holy Land	Feb. 26, 1902
31. Sylvester Q. Cannon	Dedicate Holy Land	Feb. 26, 1902
32. Charles Teuscher	Turkish	Apr. 1902
33. Henry Teuscher	Turkish	Apr. 1902
34. Joseph W. Booth*	Turkish	July 1903
35. Reno W. Vance	Turkish	Aug. 1903

Name	Mission	Date of Call or Initial Service in Near East
36. Mischa Markow	Turkish	Early 1904
37. Reba Booth	Turkish	Spring 1904
38. Stephen B. Newman	Turkish	Oct. 1905
39. John T. Woodbury	Turkish	Oct. 1905
40. Joseph T. Thorup	Turkish	Feb. 1906
41. Bertrand W. Clayton	Turkish	Spring 1906
42. Joseph O. Phelps	Turkish	Summer 1906
43. John D. Stevenson	Turkish	July 6, 1907
44. Joseph Shepherd	Turkish	Aug. 1, 1907
45. Emil J. Huber†	Turkish	Aug. 10, 1907
46. Loy Woods	Turkish	Jan. 3, 1908
47. Loren R. Dunkley	Turkish	Oct. 24, 1908
48. Ira Owen Horsfall	Turkish	Oct. 24, 1908
49. William A. Budge	Turkish	Oct. 24, 1908
50. Charles C. McAllister	Turkish	1909
51. Don C. Loveland	Turkish	1909
52. Thomas P. Page	Investigate colony options for First Presidency	Feb. 17, 1909

Mission Closed October 1, 1909–September 1921

53. Joseph W. Booth*†	Armenian	Sept. 14, 1921
54. David O. McKay	Relief mission to Armenia	Nov. 1921
55. Hugh J. Cannon	Relief mission to Armenia	Nov. 1921
56. Wilford Owen Woodruff	Extended visit from Swiss and German Mission	May 27, 1922
57. Earl B. Snell	Investigate and report to the First Presidency	Mar. 26, 1923
58. Reba Booth	Armenian	Nov. 19, 1923

Name	Mission	Date of Call or Initial Service in Near East
59. Franklin S. Harris	Report on colony options to First Presidency	Jan. 1927
60. James E. Talmage	Move mission to Haifa; Dedicate Holy Land	Oct. 1927

················· Mission Closed December 1928–February 1933 ·················

61. Badwagan Piranian*	Palestine-Syrian	Feb. 10, 1933
62. Berta Piranian	Palestine-Syrian	Feb. 10, 1933
63. Astchig Piranian	Palestine-Syrian	May 21, 1933
64. John A. Widtsoe	Organize mission; Dedicate Holy Land	May 1933
65. David W. Piranian	Palestine-Syrian	July 26, 1934
66. Hildegard K. Piranian	Palestine-Syrian	July 26, 1934
67. John B. Fetzer	Palestine-Syrian	Aug. 1934
68. Joseph Jacobs*	Palestine-Syrian	July 9, 1937
69. Woodrow Washburn	Palestine-Syrian	Feb. 8, 1938
70. William Clark	Palestine-Syrian	Feb. 8, 1938
71. Maud Jacobs	Palestine-Syrian	Dec. 12, 1938
72. Russell H. Boss	Palestine-Syrian	Feb. 4, 1939
73. Ellis Dean Orchard	Palestine-Syrian	Feb. 4, 1939

················· Mission Closed September 7, 1939–September 11, 1947 ·················

74. Badwagan Piranian*	Palestine-Syrian	Sept. 11, 1947
75. Berta Piranian	Palestine-Syrian	Sept. 11, 1947
76. Carlos E. Asay	Palestine-Syrian	Nov. 22, 1947
77. Harold G. Connell	Palestine-Syrian	Nov. 22, 1947
78. James J. McFarlane	Palestine-Syrian	Apr. 1948
79. K. E. Shelton	Palestine-Syrian	Apr. 1948
80. Sterling L. Burch	Palestine-Syrian	Apr. 1948

Name	Mission	Date of Call or Initial Service in Near East
81. Leo C. Wilcox	Palestine-Syrian	Apr. 1948
82. Ross E. Crosby	Palestine-Syrian	Aug. 1949
83. Milton Q. Beck	Palestine-Syrian	Aug. 1949
84. Howard E. Daniels	Palestine-Syrian	Aug. 1949
85. Rao H. Lindsay	Palestine-Syrian	Aug. 1949
86. Scott L. Beesley	Palestine-Syrian	Oct. 1949
87. Albert P. Ostraff	Palestine-Syrian	Oct. 1949
88. Reed C. Seegmiller	Palestine-Syrian	Dec. 18, 1949
89. Dean L. Hailstone	Palestine-Syrian	Dec. 18, 1949
90. Gary L. Love	Palestine-Syrian	Dec. 18, 1949
91. James B. Allen Jr.	Palestine-Syrian	Dec. 18, 1949
92. Richard A. Asay	Near East	Feb. 12, 1950
93. Alan D. Marant	Near East	Feb. 12, 1950
94. Richard P. Sperry	Near East	Feb. 12, 1950
95. P. Otis Rose	Near East	Feb. 12, 1950
96. Robert D. Hatch	Near East	Aug. 27, 1950
97. Eldon S. Greaves	Near East	Aug. 27, 1950
98. Reed H. Kezerian	Near East	Aug. 27, 1950

················ *Mission Closed December 29, 1950–Summer 1960* ················

99. John M. Russon*	Swiss	Feb. 21, 1964
100. Mary Russon	Swiss	Feb. 21, 1964
101. Lee Amandus Adams	Swiss	Feb. 21, 1964
102. James Tolley	Swiss	Feb. 21, 1964
103. Hans Michelmann	Swiss	Jan. 2, 1965
104. J. Lynn Styler	Swiss	Apr. 27, 1965
105. Rendell N. Mabey*	Swiss	Aug. 12, 1965
106. Rachel W. Mabey	Swiss	Aug. 12, 1965

Name	Mission	Date of Call or Initial Service in Near East
107. Robert Preece Burton	Swiss	Dec. 10, 1965
108. Terrell Evan Hunt	Swiss	Mar. 4, 1966
109. Robert Earl Fowles	Swiss	June 24, 1966
110. Clinton J. Albano	Swiss	June 24, 1966
111. Howard E. Bird	Swiss	Nov. 18, 1966
112. Lawrence Ernest Hood	Swiss	May 12, 1967
113. Douglas Mark Wood	Swiss	May 12, 1967
114. Gary Blair Lund	Swiss	May 12, 1967
115. Roger Glen Buck	Swiss	May 12, 1967
116. G. Walter Gasser	Swiss	July 26, 1967
117. Michael Noss	Swiss	July 28, 1967
118. Kimball A. Faragher	Swiss	Sept. 8, 1967
119. Oswaldo Walter Spat	Swiss	Nov. 24, 1967
120. Werner Spori	Swiss	Nov. 24, 1967
121. Ingo Schmidt	Swiss	Dec. 22, 1967
122. Royce B. Lee	Swiss	May 17, 1968
123. S. Steven Zwahlen	Swiss	June 14, 1968
124. W. Don Gubler	Swiss	June 14, 1968
125. Elmer Christensen*	Swiss	July 4, 1968
126. Mabel Christensen	Swiss	July 4, 1968
127. Jerrold J. Schriever	Swiss	Fall 1968
128. Geoffrey K. Leigh	Swiss	Nov. 28, 1968
129. Alan Griggs Plowgian	Swiss	June 4, 1969
130. David James Hill	Swiss	June 4, 1969
131. Larry Jess Ellis	Swiss	Dec. 12, 1969
132. Steven L. Christensen	Swiss	Mar. 13, 1970

···*Mission Name Changed June 10, 1970* ·································

Name	Mission	Date of Call or Initial Service in Near East
133. Phillip Willis	Switzerland	June 26, 1970
134. Donald Cook	Switzerland	Aug. 10, 1970
135. Dilworth Parkinson	Switzerland	Nov. 17, 1970
136. Phillip Lewis	Switzerland	Jan. 19, 1971
137. Steve Alley	Switzerland	Mar. 22, 1971
138. Edwin Q. Cannon*	Switzerland	July 29, 1971
139. Janath R. Cannon	Switzerland	July 29, 1971
140. Kevin Murray	Switzerland	Aug. 10, 1971
141. Ronald Bert Malouf	Switzerland	Dec. 31, 1971
142. Richard Hatch	Switzerland	Jan. 25, 1972
143. Robert Wilde	Switzerland	Feb. 1, 1972
144. Richard Ward	Switzerland	Aug. 16, 1972
145. Mark Wilcox	Switzerland	Dec. 21, 1972
146. Scott Woolley	Switzerland	Jan. 5, 1973
147. Frederick Axelgard	Switzerland	Sept. 2, 1973
148. Bicknell Robbins	Switzerland	Sept. 13, 1974
149. Joseph or Youssef Javadi	Switzerland	Sept. 13, 1974
150. Steve Whiting	Switzerland	Jan. 9, 1975
151. John Aswad	Switzerland	Jan. 9, 1975
152. Gary E. O'Brien*	Switzerland	July 8, 1975
153. Juanita O'Brien	Switzerland	July 8, 1975
154. Krikor Chobanian	International	Aug. 18, 1975

Special Representatives of The Church of Jesus Christ of Latter-day Saints in Israel

1977–1986

* No date of release available; calculated on usual period of eighteen months
† Date of reassignment

Name of Representatives	Called	Released	Area
1. Ivan J. & Minnie Barrett	Jan. 15, 1977	July 14, 1978	Jerusalem
2. Wayne & Leona Hansen	Feb. 4, 1978	Aug. 4, 1978	Herzliya
3. William E. & Margaret Mortimer	Feb. 25, 1978	Aug. 25, 1979	Herzliya
4. Chester & Mary Zollinger	Mar. 1978	*Sept. 1979	Haifa
5. George & Ellen Everton	July 1979	*Jan. 1981	Jerusalem
6. LeRoy I. & Merle Jorgensen	Aug. 17, 1979	Feb. 17, 1981	Jerusalem
7. David E. & Helen Wright	Aug. 29, 1979	Feb. 17, 1981	Haifa
8. Wendell & Arlene Christenson	Sept. 20, 1979	Mar. 31, 1981	Herzliya
9. Llewellyn & Margaret Leigh	Oct. 18, 1979	Sept. 4, 1980	Tel Aviv
10. Donworth & Harriet Gubler	Aug. 7, 1980	Dec. 1, 1981	Jerusalem
11. Wayne & LuRee Ottley	Aug. 7, 1980	Feb. 7, 1982	Tiberias
12. David & Maxine Thompson	Oct. 16, 1980	Apr. 1, 1982	Haifa
13. John & Cora Van Drimmelen	Mar. 11, 1981	Aug. 31, 1982	Haifa

Name of Representatives	Called	Released	Area
14. John & Mary Cook	May 6, 1981	Oct. 15, 1982	Haifa
15. Frank & June Swallow	May 20, 1981	Nov. 18, 1982	Jerusalem
16. Rex & Knell Skidmore	June 1, 1981	Sept. 23, 1982	Jerusalem
17. Melvin & Alice Ludlow	June 17, 1981	Nov. 30, 1982	Herzliya
18. Harold & Vellis Salway	Oct. 27, 1981	Dec. 1, 1982	Jerusalem
19. Thomas & Nathel Steele	Jan. 7, 1982	June 21, 1983	Tiberias
20. John & Nancy Poulton	Sept. 1, 1982	Mar. 2, 1984	Jerusalem
21. Nolan & Lois Oswald	Oct. 6, 1982	Apr. 3, 1984	Herzliya
22. William H. & Louise Dalebout	Jan. 19, 1983	July 26, 1984	Jerusalem
23. Vernon & Carol Cooley	Apr. 6, 1983	*Oct. 1984	Tel Aviv
24. LeRoy & Eva Hill	June 1, 1983	*Dec. 1984	Tiberias
25. Gordon & June Holt	Feb. 8, 1984	†Feb. 3, 1985	Jerusalem
26. James & Margaret Huber	Mar. 24, 1984	†Feb. 3, 1985	Tiberias
27. Keith & Carol Oakes	July 23, 1984	†Feb. 3, 1985	Jerusalem
28. Victor & Marva Jex	Nov. 27, 1984	†Feb. 3, 1985	Herzliya
29. Ellis & Oda Rasmussen	Aug. 1984	Mar. 1986	Jerusalem

Dedications of the Holy Land:
Ten by Apostles and One by Ferdinand Hintze,
Pastor of the Turkish Mission

Apostle	Date	Location	Page
1. Orson Hyde	Oct. 24, 1841	Mount of Olives	19–25

Land become fruitful; Gather Jews and soften their hearts; a plea for acceptance of covenants among Jews; constitute them a distinct nation and people; raise up Jerusalem as Jews' capital and Christ as their king

2. Albert Carrington	Mar. 2, 1873	Mount of Olives	27–33

Bless and dedicate land generally; no further details available

3. Lorenzo Snow	Mar. 2, 1873	Mount of Olives	27–33

Bless and dedicate land generally; no further details available

4. George A. Smith	Mar. 2, 1873	Mount of Olives	27–33

Fruitfulness of land; confounding of enemies; gathering of Jews to Holy Land

5. Ferdinand Hintze, under direction of Elder Anthon H. Lund	May 8, 1898	Mount of Olives	134 35

Return of Judah and gathering of Israel

Apostle	Date	Location	Page
6. Francis M. Lyman	Mar. 2, 1902	Casa Nova Hospice, Old City Jerusalem	172–73

Fruitfulness of land; prosperity of people; gathering of Jews to Holy Land

| 7. Francis M. Lyman | Mar. 4, 1902 | Mount of Olives | 173–74 |

Jews gather to Jerusalem to fulfill prophecy; land become fruitful; rebuild Jerusalem and temple

| 8. Francis M. Lyman | Mar. 16, 1902 | Kaiser's Watch, Mt. Carmel | 174–76 |

Fruitfulness of land; soften hearts of people of Holy Land

| 9. James E. Talmage | Oct. 18, 1927 | Kaiser's Watch, Mt. Carmel | 226–29 |

Gathering of Jews; redemption of land

| 10. John A. Widtsoe | May 21, 1933 | Haifa, Mission Home | 268–70 |

Prophecies of old to be fulfilled; bring about new period of enlightenment; thirst for truth among people

| 11. John A. Widtsoe | May 31, 1933 | Mount of Olives | 270–71 |

Jews gather to Jerusalem and their hearts softened; land become fertile; peace to region based on acceptance of Christ

Dedicatory Prayer Offered
by President Spencer W. Kimball,
Orson Hyde Memorial Garden

October 24, 1979

Our Heavenly Father, who art also the Almighty and the Everlasting God of Abraham, we gratefully and humbly approach Thee in prayer. We pray Thee, O God, to give ear in the heavens to the petition of Thy servant and the servants of today; that we might all be blessed and edified thereby. We are grateful, O Lord, for the privilege of assembling on this Mount of Olives, which has known the footsteps of many of Thine ancient prophets and which was made more holy by the presence of Thy divine Son. We reverently sense that we are on sacred ground, O God, our Eternal Father.

We acknowledge Thy rule in the heavens and on the earth and seek to do Thy will. We incline our hearts unto Thee in humble supplication. We pray that Thou wilt accept of this beautiful garden as a special memorial to the prophetic prayer of Thy servant, Orson Hyde, in which, we understand, by inspiration he dedicated and consecrated this land.

We acknowledge, Father, that through this power, much that Thou hast spoken in Thy name is already come to pass. The land has become bountifully fruitful, with flocks and herds, with orchards and fields. Thy scattered children of Abraham have turned in great numbers to the ability to preserve this land as a refuge. The city of Jerusalem has flourished, and we know that in Thine own due time, other things will also be prospered and come to bring peace and joy to this land.

We pray for Abraham's children, both those of blood and those by their faithfulness through adoption, also; we would have Thee bless them all. Extend Thy special care to them, draw them in unto Thee, and put into their hearts that which is needed by them to fulfill in righteousness. In this sacred land which Thy Beloved Son so much loved, and overlooking the beautiful city of Jerusalem, we call down Thy blessings upon all Thy children everywhere. Let them find room in their hearts for the gospel of peace. We pray that this tranquil peace may symbolize to them the inner calm that comes from the knowledge they now have and the comfort they receive from Thee. We can rely upon this divine concern for each man's eternal destiny.

Father, we ask for an endowment of Thy power and Spirit in proclaiming the good news of salvation which comes to us through Jesus Christ, that His words may prove a blessing to all the world. Help us to embrace strangers with love and draw them to us and to Thee. Help us to realize in our lives the special responsibility of a chosen people, quick to do Thy will. Remember the leaders of all nations and the people of every nation, kindred, tongue, and people, that they might seek after Thee and ever turn toward Thee in righteousness.

We pray for Thy blessings upon those through whose generosity this memorial has come to be. Let their storehouses abound with plenty and their hearts turn with gladness to Thee in having helped to bring to pass so great a work.

O Thou, Master Gardener, who in the creation of this earth did create a garden to give our first parents and their companions, to till this earth and bring it into production, we ask Thee to accept our humble efforts in helping to create this garden in memory of Orson Hyde. We dedicate and consecrate this Orson Hyde Memorial Garden unto Thee and to Thy people and [ask Thee] to bless it every way possible for righteous purposes.

Bless the soil of this garden, that it may produce abundantly and help fulfill that promise to Ezekiel that the desolate would become like a Garden of Eden. Father, bless these grounds, these walks, these structures, the flowers, shrubs, and trees, that they may radiate with loveliness and give pleasure to those who visit Thee here. Protect this garden from the ravages of war, and storm, and depravation of every kind. Let it be a haven where all may meditate upon the glory Thou hast shed upon Jerusalem in ages past and the greater glory yet to be.

Let those who come here feel of Thy Spirit and influence and the spirit of the holy prophets who have traversed this beautiful land. Accept of this gift, our Father, as an expression of our faith in Thy goodness and mercy and power. As we dedicate this garden to Thee and to Thy glory, so also we dedicate our lives individually and in group to Thee and Thy servants.

We lovingly dedicate this to the Author, the Giver, and Sustainer of life and every good gift. We thank Thee for Thy bounteous blessings and [pray] for Thee to continue them in our lives. By the power of the holy Melchizedek Priesthood, we dedicate this Orson Hyde Memorial Garden unto Thee, our Holy Father, and this we do humbly and gratefully in the name of Thy beloved Son, Jesus Christ. Amen.

(Orson Hyde Memorial Garden Dedication Service, Jerusalem, October 24, 1979, BYU Eastern Mediterranean Peace Cruise, Western Advertising Agency: Provo, UT, tape no. 24)

Agreement

TO: THE GOVERNMENT OF ISRAEL
        JERUSALEM, ISRAEL

Dear Sirs:

We the undersigned, The Church of Jesus Christ of Latter-day Saints, hereinafter "the Church", undertake that the Church will not engage in any missionary activity within the borders of Israel, as long as such activity is not allowed by the government of Israel. For this purpose, "missionary activity" means organized activity to induce or persuade a person not a member of the community of that Church to become a member of the community of that Church, by preaching or teaching the tenets of the Church or otherwise. This obligation applies to our Church and each of its branches and departments and to every institution under its control.

[Dated] this 18th day of May 1988

THE CHURCH OF JESUS CHRIST OF LATTER-DAY SAINTS

by: [Signed by Howard W. Hunter]
Howard W. Hunter
Authorized Representative

(Steven W. Baldridge, *Grafting In* (Murray, UT: Roylance, 1989), 141)

PHOTO CREDITS

Endsheet Map
  Courtesy of Brandon Plewe, David Nixon, and Sterling Quinn.

Introduction
  3   Portrait of Joseph Smith Jr.: Courtesy of the Church Archives, The Church of Jesus Christ of Latter-day Saints.
  5   Kirtland Temple: Courtesy of LaMar C. Berrett Archives.

Chapter 1
  13   Orson Hyde: Courtesy of LaMar C. Berrett Archives.
  19   Old City of Jerusalem: Courtesy of LaMar C. Berrett Archives.
  20   Mount of Olives: Courtesy of LaMar C. Berrett Archives.
  25   Pile of stones: Courtesy of LaMar C. Berrett Archives.
  27   George A. Smith: Courtesy of LaMar C. Berrett Archives.
  28   (top left) Albert Carrington: Courtesy of LaMar C. Berrett Archives.
  28   (top right) Eliza R. Snow: Courtesy of LaMar C. Berrett Archives.
  28   (bottom left) Feramorz Little: Courtesy of LaMar C. Berrett Archives.
  28   (bottom right) Clara Little: Courtesy of LaMar C. Berrett Archives.
  29   Lorenzo Snow: Courtesy of LaMar C. Berrett Archives.
  31   Looking east atop Mount of Olives: Courtesy of LaMar C. Berrett Archives.

Chapter 2
  40   Spori wedding day: Courtesy of LaMar C. Berrett Archives.
  41   Jacob Spori: Courtesy of the Church Archives, The Church of Jesus Christ of Latter-day Saints.
  47   Joseph M. Tanner: Courtesy of the Church Archives, The Church of Jesus Christ of Latter-day Saints.
  52   Mischa Markow: Courtesy of the Church Archives, The Church of Jesus Christ of Latter-day Saints.
  55   Ferdinand Friis Hintze: Courtesy of LaMar C. Berrett Archives.
  61   Janne M. Sjodahl: Courtesy of the Church Archives, The Church of Jesus Christ of Latter-day Saints.
  76   Edgar D. Simmons: Public Domain.
  77   Edgar D. Simmons gravestone: Public Domain.

Chapter 3
  100   Adolf Haag: Public Domain.
  101   Adolf Haag gravestone: Courtesy of LaMar C. Berrett Archives.
  105   City of Aleppo from Citadel: Courtesy of Kent P. Jackson.
  106   John A. Clark: Courtesy of the Church Archives, The Church of Jesus Christ of Latter-day Saints.
  109   Gravestones of Clark and Haag: Courtesy of LaMar C. Berrett Archives.

INDEX

Page numbers in bold indicate images.